£45

Auditing Contracts

Auditing Contracts

ANDREW CHAMBERS

Professor of Audit & Control, Hull University
Emeritus Professor, City University and Dean of City
University Business School from 1985–91

GRAHAM RAND

Technical Director, Management Audit Ltd

FINANCIAL TIMES

PITMAN PUBLISHING

PITMAN PUBLISHING
128 Long Acre, London WC2E 9AN

A Division of Longman Group UK Limited

© Andrew Chambers and Graham Rand 1994

First published in Great Britain 1994

British Library Cataloguing in Publication Data
A CIP catalogue record for this book can be obtained from the British Library.

ISBN 0 273 03767 6

Phototypeset in Linotron Times Roman by PanTek Arts, Maidstone, Kent.
Printed and bound in Great Britain by Biddles Ltd., Guildford and King's Lynn

The Publishers' policy is to use paper manufactured from sustainable forests.

To Amy and Florence

CONTENTS

PREFACE

The reader will see from a glance at the Bibliography (Appendix 4) that there is much written material on contracts and a certain amount on contract auditing more specifically. In writing this book we set out to fill a significant gap in what has been available to date. Now, the subject of contract auditing is in book form and with a treatment which, we trust, takes the art a few stages further than before.

In the past most of the focus in contract auditing has been upon construction projects and from the perspective of the employer of the contractor (that is, from the perspective of the enterprise which is letting the contract). It has usually been assumed that the employer is a public authority or public utility. It is not surprising that this orientation has been taken as it is vitally important for public enterprises to control their capital projects and an essential aspect of control is the *review* of control by means of audit. So there is much in this book which deals with construction contracts from the perspective of the employer of the contractor. We have, however, endeavoured to give the book a wider appeal by including, especially in Part I but also more generally throughout the book, other types of contract (such as service contract and Information Techonology contracts) and also by addressing the control and audit interests of the contractor as well.

Contract auditors have long seen their audit universe as a cake which is capable of being cut in two ways. First, there are the contracts themselves which are being entered into, executed or reviewed. Then there are the sub-systems of contracting – such as tendering procedures, and controlling price fluctuations to name but two. Both the contracts themselves and the sub-systems of contracting will benefit from audit review. We divide the system of contracting into three major sub-systems each of which we divide further into more detailed sub-systems which are the subjects of the chapters in Part II, Management Environment and Pre-contract Processes, Part III During the Currency of the Contract and Part IV Upon and After Contract Completion of this book.

Each of the chapters in these three parts concludes with a carefully designed control matrix for the contract sub-system covered by the chapter. Chapter 5 on Information Technology (IT) contracts also contains a *risk analysis* control matrix. We believe these control matrices represent a completely fresh approach which has not, so far as we know, been applied to contract auditing before. Readers can use the book at two levels. First they can consider and apply the subject-matter covered in the text of the chapters – which we believe holds together coherently without any reference to the control matrices. Second they can go further and adopt the control matrix methodology of evaluating risk. Chapter 32 explains the method in detail and readers will be able to apply the technique to other areas besides contract auditing.

Determining which contracting sub-systems and which contracts warrant audit attention, and then allocating appropriate amounts of audit resource on a timely basis to each, are important challenges facing the audit manager. Chapter 33 explains a successful *risk analysis* method for doing this.

The risk analysis methods explained and applied in this book may be applied readily by readers using spreadsheet software. Alternatively we would be pleased to let you know about **Organis.IT MIDPLAN** and **Control.IT MIN-PLAN** software, which is already available for this purpose. Readers may also find useful our companion books in this series: *Effective Internal Audits – How to Plan and Implement* (1992) and *Auditing the IT Environment* (1994).

Andrew Chambers
Graham Rand

Management Audit Limited
The Water-mill, Moat Lane, Old Bolingbroke,
Spilsby, Lincolnshire, England PE23 4EU
Tel: (44) (0)790 763350; Fax: (44) (0)790 763253

ACKNOWLEDGEMENTS

In producing this book we are very aware of the dedicated development work which has been carried out by so many professional people. They have generously shared their wisdom and we hope we have acknowledged them all here and in the Bibliography (Appendix 4) to this book.

In the world of contract auditing no acknowledgement would be complete without a tribute to The Chartered Institute of Public Finance and Accountancy (CIPFA) for their pioneering work on contract auditing over many years – especially through the members of their Audit Panel. We learnt much of what we know from CIPFA people and feel sure that many others would acknowledge a similar debt to CIPFA. We are grateful for permission to reprint their *Statement on Contract Auditing* (Appendix 5)

With inspiration on risk analysis approaches to auditing, many have helped us on our way, but none more so than David Lewington who brought together, and in several respects developed, many of the ideas which underpin the control matrix risk analysis approach we have used in this book.[1]

Preparing the manuscript, using our software to print out all the tables in this book, and searching for bibliographic material have been some of the major tasks for which we have relied upon Jackie Badley who has completed them superbly well.

Our thanks to everyone who has assisted us.

NOTE[1] *vide*: Lewington, D., A. D. Chambers, et al, *Risk Analysis for Internal Auditing* (Research Report No. 19. The Institute of Internal Auditors – UK). 1986.

Part I

BASIC PRINCIPLES AND CONTRACTING SITUATIONS

1

LEGAL CONSIDERATIONS

Scope

This chapter aims to provide the reader with basic descriptions of the nature and form of contracts, and simple definitions of the principles involved. The text includes very basic guidelines to some of the legal terminology and matters relevant to the use of contracts, that are referred to elsewhere in this book. The contents are not intended to be either definitive or comprehensive. Readers requiring more specific information should refer to the bibliography in Appendix 4.

Other relevant matters such as European and international implications, Scottish legal differences, etc., are also briefly reviewed. The selection of the appropriate form of contract is more fully discussed in Chapter 17.

DEFINITIONS

Noted below are simple definitions of aspects of contracts and selected legal elements as relevant to the law in England and Wales. Readers are advised to seek further guidance, and Appendix 4 includes appropriate sources.

Contracts

A contract defines a relationship between parties. The relevant arrangement may relate to the supply of goods or the provision of service by one party to another. A contract is a legally binding agreement, that is one which the law will either enforce or recognise in some way. In order for the contract agreement to be legally binding, the parties to it must 'intend' that the agreement will be duly carried out. The making of an 'offer' should be followed by the 'acceptance' of same. The obligations placed on the parties to contracts are defined in the 'terms' or 'conditions'.

Contract documentation

The actual documents that form and support the contract will vary between contract and project types. For example, in a construction scenario the contract documents are those which define the contractor's obligations, and normally include some or all of the following:

- Articles of Agreement
- Conditions of Contract (i.e. the clauses)
- Appendix (contains factors which vary between contract, such as the completion date and the value of any liquidated damages)
- Drawings and/or Specifications (these may be supported by schedules of dimensions and quantities of frequently used items)
- Bills of Quantity.

More details of the above noted document types are provided in Chapter 15.

Of course, other forms of contract should incorporate adequate and legally appropriate documents to support the activity which is the subject of the contract.

Offer

In contract terms, the offer has to take a particular form to be valid. For example, a relative quotation submitted by a prospective supplier does form an offer, whereas an estimate does not, and is regarded as an invitation to treat. To be valid an offer should be capable of becoming a contract when it is appropriately accepted. In this latter context a tender is a form of offer.

Acceptance

Assuming that the form of offer is appropriate (*see* definition of 'offer'), complete acceptance of all the requirements will form a contract. If any of the defined requirements are not accepted, no contract is formed. This underlines the need to ensure that tenders submitted by contractors fully comply with the requirements and the conditions referred to in the form of contract. For example, if a supplier submits a number of quotations costed on different bases, the employer must ensure that the acceptance is specific in order to identify the chosen form.

Breach

A breach of contract occurs when one party fails to meet his obligations under the terms of the contract. The normal remedy in such situations is the award of damages, the nature and limit of which may be defined in the contract. In the first place it should be possible for the parties to agree damages relevant to contract conditions between themselves. If this is either not the case or damages are sought outwith the contracted terms, the matter is referred to the courts for judgement.

Damages

Generally, and in simplistic terms, the award of damages should place the plaintiff (i.e. the claimant) in the same financial position he would have enjoyed had the contract terms been fully and correctly performed. Of course in actual situations the determination of damages is somewhat more complex, especially if the value is to be determined via the courts. In order to remove some of the uncertainty about the level of damages in cases of breach of contract, etc., the parties can agree a predetermined estimate of damages for defined situations for inclusion into the contract. Such values are known either as liquidated damages or liquidated and ascertained damages (*see* Chapter 19 for further details).

Arbitration

When a contract is established between two parties and there is a dispute which cannot be settled either within the conditions of the relevant contract or by mutual agreement between the parties, it may be possible to refer the matter to a form of arbitration. This is a process, which operates outwith the court system, where the dispute is reviewed and decided by persons who may be nominated by the two parties. In some situations independent arbitrators are involved. The standard forms of construction and engineering contract can incorporate arbitration processes.

Frustration

A contract can be taken as frustrated when an external event, which is not caused by the fault of either the employer or contractor, is not provided for in the contract. In such cases, which are rare as forms of contract are becoming more comprehensive in nature, the contract can be duly terminated. The key issue is the determination, by the appropriate court, that no existing contract condition relates to the particular situation.

Terms of Contract

A contract imposes obligations upon the parties to it, and these are defined in the terms. There a three types of terms that could apply, and these are defined as follows:

- *Express Terms* These are contained in the main contract document, although they may also be in the form of an oral statement.
- *Terms Incorporated by Reference* These terms can be contained in documents to which the main contract refers, such as those supporting the design aspects.

- *Implied Terms* Implication in this context is relevant to either the law or matters of fact. For example, unless the contract in question was extremely well defined, it may be implied that the products supplied in fulfilment of the contract would also be subject to the terms of the *Supply of Goods and Services Act 1982*. This would be an implication in law.

Tort

A tort is a breach of legal duty owed by one person to another. This operates outwith any other contractual liability, and can therefore include claims from persons who are outside the contract, such as passers-by or subsequent users of the building. Settlement of tort claims is normally by the recovery of damages. An example would be the payment of damages by the contractor for a workmanship fault which caused injury to a person visiting or using the building. This is referred to as a tort of negligence.

Tort claims have an advantage in that the period in which claims can be made is markedly longer than would apply under breach of contractual obligations. However, there is some debate as to whether contracted parties can take advantage of this situation where it offers wider scope than the conditions of contract. On the distaff side, claims in tort are subject to court proceedings and in the case of claims brought by contracted parties this could be both costly and time-consuming. Therefore it may be preferable to settle any disputes within the provisions of the prevailing form of contract.

CONTRACTS – GENERAL POINTS

Contract clauses are mechanisms for allocating or transferring risk(s) associated with the relevant activity. Where the allocation of such a risk is unreasonable, it may be possible to defray some or all of the likely effects by increasing the bid accordingly. Alternatively a degree of balance may be achieved by a compensating clause allocated to the other party to the contract. When reviewing contract clauses, both parties will have to judge whether, on balance, they are subject to any undue net risk, and this may require negotiation to resolve. Placing or transferring excessive levels of risk upon the other party, assuming that they will readily accept it, may lead to their eventual demise, in which case neither party gains.

Generally speaking there are three basic types of contract:

- Works (relative to building or civil engineering schemes and activities)
- Service (affecting the provision of a service)
- Supply (where materials, components or goods are being provided).

The factors affecting these three classifications are explored in detail in Chapters 2, 3 and 4 respectively. Contract issues in the realm of Information Technology (IT) are specifically reviewed in Chapter 5.

Appendix 2 provides brief details of a number of commonly used standard forms of contracts used in the building, civil engineering, electrical and mechanical engineering fields. Some of these contracts are very functionally specific and take into account the required method of payment, the scale of the works in value and nature terms, whether or not sub-contractors are involved, and whether the employer is from the public or private sector. This diversity of standard forms when viewed in conjunction with the very complex conditions that can apply in each case, make it impossible for us to comprehensively review all the merits and disadvantages of each form. However, guidance notes and commentaries are available for the majority of such contracts, and some of these are featured, for your information, in the bibliography (Appendix 4).

The use of standard forms of contract should generally provide a balance of risk allocation, based upon collective previous experience. It should be noted that clauses, even those in standard forms of contract, can be struck out upon mutual agreement. One-off contracts should be subject to close scrutiny by all parties, and the appropriate balance of risks derived.

The issues surrounding the selection of the most suitable form of contract are explored in Chapter 17, and the administration affecting contract documentation is discussed in Chapter 15. Explicit features of contract conditions and the relevant key issues, for example regarding price fluctuations, interim payments, contractual claims, etc. are examined in detail in separate chapters.

In order to cater for the variations under Scottish law, either suitable versions of standard contracts or Scottish law supplements will need to be utilised. Appendix 2 mentions, where applicable, the availability of such amendments in relation to the more common standard forms of contract.

Different forms of contract relevant to specific sectors, tend to refer to the parties in varying terms. For example the organisation seeking a contractor can be called the employer, the client or the purchaser. For the sake of consistency we have standardised throughout the text on employer and contractor. Additionally there can be various terms to describe the person effectively in charge of the project or representing the employer. For example the terms 'Architect' or 'Engineer' are common in construction projects, the broader term 'Contract Administrator' is also used, and finally in government contracts this key role is performed by the 'Superintending Officer' (SO).

RELEVANT UK STATUTES

It is possible that in establishing or enforcing a contract, there could be interplay with matters of the general law. Noted below are some of existing statutes that may have a bearing on various contractual matters:

- *Arbitration Acts of 1950, 1975 and 1979*
- *Building Act 1984*
- *Civil Liability (Contributions) Act 1978*
- *Consumer Protection Act 1987*

- *Contracts (Applicable Law) Act 1990*
- *Health and Safety at Work Act 1984*
- *Latent Damage Act 1986*
- *Law Reform (Frustrated Contracts) Act 1943*
- *Limitation Act 1990*
- *Misrepresentation Act 1967*
- *Sale of Goods Act 1979*
- *Supply of Goods and Services Act 1982*
- *Unfair Contract Terms Act 1977*

EUROPEAN AND INTERNATIONAL IMPLICATIONS

It is now more common for projects and contracts to cross international borders, both physically and legally. Obviously great care needs to be applied to the establishment of such international arrangements, especially in the selection of the most appropriate legal environment.

Within the European Community (EC) there has been much effort expended in the development of a single market environment, and although the underlying Articles allow for the approximation of the laws of member States to the extent required for the proper functioning of the Common Market, much remains to be done. Although certain EC laws may become part of the relevant national law without further steps being necessary, the United Kingdom (and others) will normally only integrate such laws by the passing of a statute. Where differences exist between national and community law, the question arises of which law takes precedence. In a number of cases considered by the European Court of Justice, where this issue has arisen, the general view was that EC law should prevail over the national law of the affected State. In practice, the issues are potentially extremely complex and consequently beyond the scope of this book.

The underlying Articles of the EC include aspects, some of which are the subject of supporting legislation, which may have a bearing on selected forms of contract. For example, such principles as the rules relating to competition, free movement of goods, freedom to provide services, etc.

Before leaving the realms of the EC, a brief comment upon Directives. A Directive does not become binding in a member State until that State transforms it into a national law. The form of the law is left to the judgement of the national State concerned, but obviously it must comply with the agreed requirements of the Directive. There are, for example, a number of EC Directives which relate to the awarding of supply, works and service contracts in the public and utilities sectors. These Directives are listed in the bibliography under HMSO within Appendix 4.

In a contract with international dimensions, the key question must be 'which national law should apply?' This matter should in practice be the subject of necessary research taking into account the nature of project or goods to be supplied, currency considerations, the form of law offering the best control of risk, previous case law, communication problems, and so on. This process, supported by relevant legal advice, could result in the parties electing to use a particular nation's law as the basis of the contract.

From the English Law viewpoint, in the case of a dispute over a contract with a foreign element, it is necessary for the court to ascertain the 'proper law of the contract' so that the case can be judged in the appropriate legal context. This process is obviously very straightforward where the parties have clearly chosen a suitable national legal framework, in which case it is termed 'the Express Choice of the law'. In the absence of such clear cut arrangements, the court will apply a body of rules known as the 'Conflict of Laws' which should determine the relevant national system of law. The Rome Convention defined a uniform method for deciding the law governing (worldwide) international contracts, and this was embodied into the UK Statute called *Contracts (Applicable Law) Act 1990* which came into force on 1 April 1990.

Selected professional bodies have been active in attempts to develop a broader form of contract for international usage. For example the International Federation of Consulting Engineers (FIDIC) in consultation with the European International Federation of Construction (FEIC) have issued the FIDIC Conditions of Contract in various forms. Additionally, the Association of Consulting Engineers (ACE) have produced the New Engineering Contract (NEC), which although based upon the Institution of Civil Engineers (ICE) Conditions of Contract relative to civil engineering schemes, reflects a more flexible and internationally acceptable approach (*see* Appendix 2 for further details).

Where an organisation is contemplating international involvement, it is prudent to ensure that the appropriate specialist legal advice is sought and duly acted upon prior to formalising any contractual relationships.

2

CONSTRUCTION PROJECTS

Scope

Although we intend to provide guidance which can be applied to all manner of matters relating to contracts, irrespective of the sector or type, this chapter concentrates specifically upon both construction projects and the construction phase. Many of the issues discussed in this chapter are deliberately examined in summary form only. However, they are expanded upon in other separate chapters and appropriate cross-references to these are provided.

For the purposes of this text the term 'construction' is intended to incorporate building and civil engineering projects and the related sub-contracted activities. The authors acknowledge that there are differing requirements and contractual subtleties between these elements, some of which are highlighted in subsequent chapters.

Contracted relationships play a high-profile and critical role in the construction industry. The web of contractual relationships established between the employer, main contractor, sub-contractors, consultants, engineers, architects and suppliers is often very complex and unique to the project in question. Considerable amounts of work have been undertaken by the relevant professional bodies in the development of appropriate forms of contracts and best practice in the construction industry. This development is an ongoing process and further refinements will continue to be applied to available forms of contract. Some of this revision is applied as a result of case law and the changing business and legal environments.

In relation to contract auditing, most of the currently available material is concentrated upon construction and civil engineering projects, with a bias towards the public sector. In particular CIPFA has been prominent in the development of current contract auditing techniques and training in the UK. However, auditors working in other fields outwith the public sector can acquire many useful pointers concerning the key issues in any contract scenario by drawing upon the material developed by CIPFA.

In the project lifecycle, construction is the phase where the theory becomes reality, where the plans are transformed into the physical structure. Beyond these obvious manifestations, there is a complex web of responsibilities, relationships and formalities, which, when successfully combined, hopefully result in the achievement of the project within the required cost and time constraints and to the appropriate standards. In the real world, there are of course many potential obstacles to attaining the desired goals, some of them are technical and some related to human factors. Whenever you drive past a major construction site and view the apparent state of chaos, it is worth remembering that all the actions on that site are dictated by a combination of contract conditions, skill and professional practice, although not necessarily in that order.

Managing the project will require the timely flow of accurate information on progress, problems, etc. Such information has to be obtained from reliable sources and based upon good practices and professional protocols.

During the course of a construction project one of the greatest enemies is change. Changing the design or having to change the application of the available technology in order to cope with local conditions. Such changes create costs, perhaps partly borne out of implied delays. However, in the case of projects running over long time periods, there can be legitimate reasons for considering changes that would not have been apparent at the commencement of the project. For example, the availability of a newly developed and potentially cheaper material. Additionally, the employing organisation is not a static entity, and the need for change may be a reflection of its changing requirements.

The issues of management information and managing change, although noted in this chapter, are discussed in more detail together with the other discrete aspects of construction projects, in separate chapters. The use of standard forms of contract reinforce some of the requirements and specify the methods to be applied in certain areas.

ROLES, RESPONSIBILITIES AND RELATIONSHIPS

Client or Employer

The employer should appoint a project manager or a specific individual with responsibility for the project. This can be a suitably qualified architect or engineer either in the client's direct employ or separately contracted as a consultant. He or she should maintain liaison with the relevant professionals, act as a linkage between those involved on the project and the client management, represent the client management at team or site meetings and have a devolved (but clearly defined) responsibility to act on their behalf when appropriate (*see* also Architect, Engineer or Consultant below).

Contractor

The contractor should obviously operate within the defined limits of the contract design and required technical standards. It is his responsibility to plan, in the most effective way, the application of resources to achieve the various defined objectives and time deadlines. In attaining these objectives the contractor will also have an eye to optimising his own profit, and this will involve avoiding wastage, controlling costs and ensuring that any required variations, extensions of time, etc. are adequately supported and approved. Prompt settlement of claims and payments for completed work will also be significant in maintaining cash flow.

Architect, Engineer or Consultant

In the public sector this role may be performed by a member of the technical staff of a local authority or public body. Alternatively, the client, whether in the public sector or not, can elect to use the services of a suitably qualified external consultant. This latter relationship is formalised in a further contract. (The issues relevant to engaging external consultants are explored in Chapter 10.) The architect will normally be responsible for designing the building, etc. and for co-ordinating the project team. Additionally, the architect or engineer will have responsibility for administering and supervising the project, and ensuring that the contractor conducts the required work in accordance with the design and prevailing contract conditions. Please note that the actual responsibilities of each professional do vary in accordance with the form of contract in use. Within the confines of the contract, he will also assess, when required, the need for variations from the design and issue the appropriate instructions to the contractor. Where payment for the work is to be staged, the architect or engineer will have to issue the appropriate certificates authorising the relevant payments to be made (*see* Chapter 22 for full details).

The role performed by architects or engineers is a critical one and is subject to best practices established and promoted by the relevant professional bodies. They are obliged to act in an impartial way and thereby demonstrate an independence in their decision making, otherwise they may be in breach of their duties and therefore the target of legal action.

Clerk of Works

The clerk is responsible for both supervising the site and ensuring suitable collaboration with the architect or engineer (or their site representatives). It is also the clerk's responsibility to ensure that all the required records are accurately maintained and are up to date. The quality of his various records will ensure that payments, claims and disputes can be readily and appropriately supported with facts and accurate details of past events. The data held may also form the basis for the compilation of management information.The administrative records will include data on site labour, details of relevant incidents, details of site plant and equipment, deliveries and stock of materials, persons visiting the site, etc.

Quantity Surveyor

This professional is primarily responsible for ensuring that all measurements of work and material usage are accurate and in accord with the contractual and design requirements. The quantity surveyor will also play a critical role in assessing the cost implications in relation to valuations for interim and final payments, any associated claims by the contractor or for insurance purposes, matters relative to running costs, etc. As part of this quantity and cost duality, the quantity surveyor will also have a considerable input to accounting and financial aspects of the project, such as projecting cash flows, determining costs against original and adjusted budgets and so on.

The auditor should undertake site visits as part of his review of control processes and should not be afraid to get muddy boots during this phase of the project. There is much to consider during such visits and the opportunity exists to positively contribute to the project and the control environment. Chapter 6 examines the methods to be employed by auditors to ensure that their site visits are effective whilst maintaining good working relationships with the technical staff and professionals.

Auditors may be concerned about approaching construction contracts for the first time. They can be seen as overtly technical areas which are the natural domain of the relevant professionals. Auditors should obviously be concerned about their credibility in such situations, and they should temper their approach by adopting attitudes which avoid antagonising technical staff. For the public sector, CIPFA and the related professional bodies have issued a number of joint statements which aim to define or clarify the roles and responsibilities:

- Joint Statement by CIPFA/RICS on the Roles of the Quantity Surveyor and Auditor in Building Contracts for Public Authorities
- Tripartite Statement and Practical Guide by CIPFA/RICS/SCALA on the Control of Building Projects. The role of professional officers in local government
- Joint Statement by CIPFA/ICE Defining the Respective Functions of the Engineer and the Auditor.

One must not lose sight of the formal interrelationships between the parties to the contract, which are defined by a combination of the form of contract, established professional practices, specific procedures and regulations applied by the employer, and other proven methods. Invoking the contract places certain obligations on participants, for example the independence and impartiality of the architect.

DOCUMENTATION AND MANAGEMENT INFORMATION
(*see also* Chapter 18)

The development, over time, of recognised site practices and standard forms of contract has also created standardised forms of site documentation (for example, the Royal Institute of British Architects [RIBA] publishes various standard forms for use by architects and surveyors relative to the administration of standard contracts, such as JCT80 and IFC84 – *see* glossary in Appendix 1). These forms combined with traditionally accepted site records should provide the basis for the flow of subsequent management information.

The nature of site- and project-level records can be summarised under the following types of events:

Event	*Nature / characteristic of record*
Progress	Daywork records Minutes of site meetings Contractors programme Reports to employers
Valuations	Certificates issued by the architect or engineer Bills of Quantity Variation costings (*see also* Variations below) Documents issued by the quantity surveyor Nominated suppliers and sub-contractors invoices Details of materials held on site
Quality Control	Evidence of inspections conducted by the engineer or architect
Delays	Records of time lost due to technical problems, bad weather, disputes,shortages of materials, labour shortfalls, etc.
Extensions of Time	Approved forms of documentation issued by the architect or engineer Correspondence and recognised submissions from the contractor
Variations	Variation orders (from architect/engineer)
Contractors Claims	Appropriate forms of claim documentation, supported by the requisite calculations and schedules
Materials	Stock, delivery and usage records Official orders Suppliers' delivery notes
Labour	Time sheets Sub-contractors timesheets/invoices
Price Fluctuations	Correspondence between contractor and contract administrator Supporting financial and factual data Calculations generated by the application of the approved fluctuation formulae

Event	*Nature/characteristic of record*
Plant and Equipment	Registers Hiring agreement copies and record of periods of hire
Financial	Phased budgets and comparisons to actual costs to date Projected cash flows and costs Projected obligations for sub-contractors and suppliers
General	Correspondence, accident records, register of visitors, etc.

Some of the above records will be completed by the contractor, others by the supervising architect or engineer.

In order that the employer or his agent can assess progress, reliability of data, etc. there should be a formal arrangement whereby either the contractor or consultant is obliged to afford suitable access to documents and records. Such an arrangement should encompass that required by the employer's auditors. In order to allow for the smooth application of rights of access, and to avoid any unnecessary disruption or souring of relationships, there should be a protocol for making prior requests for site visits through the appropriate channels.

Regular reports should be forwarded to the employer including details of the progress of the project, financial data, effects of identified variations, etc. The nature and extent of the project and its significance to the employer will, among other things, determine the optimum frequency and form of such reports.

INTERIM VALUATIONS
(*see also* Chapter 22)

As the work progresses it is usual for interim payments to be made. The frequency and nature of these are determined primarily by the form of contract employed for the project. It is normal practice for either the architect, engineer or relevant consultant to officially certify the payments due based upon the measurements and assessments of the quantity surveyor and the available documentary evidence.

The certificates produced by the appropriate professional will normally reflect the cumulative valuation of work completed to date based upon a recognised form of measurement, less the effects of previous payments. Additional factors such as the contract-defined percentage of retention, and the net effect of any price fluctuation allowances will also be adjusted against the total due, so as to arrive at a net value due. Full supporting documentation, including bills of quantity, dayworks records, invoices, etc., should be available.

VARIATIONS TO THE WORK SPECIFIED IN THE CONTRACT/DESIGN
(see also Chapter 24)

In the course of the construction phase it may be necessary to amend or augment the design in some way in order to cater for unforeseen eventualities or a change in requirements, etc. The usual standard forms of contract make provision for such variations and permit the employer to apply changes within defined procedures.

The prime requirement is that variations must be at the order of the responsible architect, engineer or supervising consultant. Such orders must be suitably documented, costed, and advised to the contractor. Establishing the appropriate rate for the additional work is dependent upon whether it is of a similar nature to that being performed under the terms of the contract, in which case the rates agreed in the appropriate bill of quantity will be applied; otherwise an acceptable rate will need to be agreed.

This is a very significant area for the auditor when he is considering the current control environment. On major projects it is possible that many changes will prove to be necessary and it is incumbent upon the relevant professional supervisors to ensure that the additional or amended work is justifiable. There are, of course, potential interrelated implications on both the cost of the project and the completion of same within the required time limits.

Chapter 24 contains further details of this subject including references to the appropriate clauses in the commonly used standard forms of construction contract.

CLAIMS
(see also Chapter 26)

Claims in this context relates to certain specified categories of additional costs borne initially by contractors which are due to circumstances beyond their control. Forms of contract contain clauses defining the general eligibility of claims against the employer for the recovery of such costs.

All claims should be subject to effective scrutiny by either the architect, engineer or other supervising professional. Some claims have a direct relationship with action prescribed or taken by the architect, for example an amendment to the design. Other claims are more difficult to pin down, such as encountering unexpected changes in site ground conditions.

PRICE FLUCTUATIONS
(see also Chapter 23)

Where contracts span long periods (for example in excess of twelve months), it is usual practice to apply some form of price fluctuation calculation based upon a recognised formula in order to take account of the inevitable macro- and microeconomic factors, etc. There are established bases for calculating the effect of such fluctuations for most types of standard contracts: the specific clauses and formula options are examined more fully in Chapter 23. When applicable, the effects of applying such fluctuation formulae are incorporated into the interim and final account payments prepared by the supervising professional.

LIQUIDATED DAMAGES
(*see also* Chapter 19)

This is a closely defined element in most contracts, and represents a value which can be claimed from the contractor if there is an unauthorised delay in completing the contract. The value is calculated in accordance with both specific contractual requirements, and guidelines and formulae established by the professional bodies. The calculated value is reflected in the tender/contract documentation and this becomes the amount of any subsequent application of the option irrespective of whether the actual loss to the employer is greater or less than the defined amount.

In reality, the contractor may elect (where applicable) to make a claim under the terms of contract which counteracts the effects of any liquidated damages claimed by the employer. An understanding may be reached between the parties concerned to the effect that no claim for liquidated damages will be made if the contractor refrains from pursuing the counter claim(s).

CONTRACTOR LIQUIDATION AND BANKRUPTCY
(*see also* Chapter 27)

In recessionary times, company liquidations are everyday news. The construction industry is not immune to the effects of the general economy and has suffered particularly badly in recent times with a great contraction of scale due in part to reductions in public spending and the general reluctance of the private sector to invest in new development while completed projects stand unoccupied. When taking decisions about the selection of a contractor, the employing organisation should extensively review the financial stability of the contractor and/or the holding company. While this is no guarantee against the eventual financial failure of the contractor it can serve to avoid the engagement of the more vulnerable companies.

In the event of a contractor going into liquidation, the standard forms of contract make clear provision for the actions to be taken. However, the matter may take many years to settle and there are normally urgent matters to be addressed, such as the cost of completing the project. Even if the employer had arranged for performance bonding, obtaining payment from the surety company may also take a long time.

There is the possibility of complex relationships being created between any monies owed to the contractor by the employer and the financial impact upon the employer created by the liquidation. Any payments to the liquidators will need to be strictly controlled in light of the prevailing legal and financial situation.

The employer should take appropriate professional and legal advice and carefully appraise the available options, before selecting the route to take. The existence of adequate and accurate project-related records will assist considerably in the recovery process.

POINTS TO CONSIDER UPON COMPLETION OF THE PROJECT
(*see also* Chapter 31)

Upon completion of the construction, it will be necessary to ensure that it is appropriately commissioned for use. The project planning and management procedures should take adequate account of the need to ensure that all manner of related issues are effectively addressed, including the following:

- allocating responsibilities for maintaining the building and its systems
- establishing the required forms of insurance cover
- ensuring that all health and safety matters are addressed
- dealing with security, fire precaution and detection issues
- providing safe custody for all the relevant building and system plans
- providing a method to identify, record and resolve defects, especially where the contractor is still liable for rectifying same
- ensuring that the required furnishings and fittings are supplied in accordance with the original specifications and budgets
- establishing suitable setting and monitoring of operating and running cost budgets.

Beyond the need to ensure that the above noted factors are addressed at the completion of a building project, there should of course already be mechanisms in place to provide such services on an ongoing basis. Auditors may wish to review the effectiveness of such mechanisms in relation to a specific project or generally as determined by priorities, scales of risks, and so on.

POST COMPLETION OF THE PROJECT AND ITS FINANCIAL OUT-TURN
(*see also* Chapter 30)

All projects should be subject to a comprehensive form of review following the completion stage. This is partly to ensure that all the identified benefits which justified the initial project are in fact realised, but also to ensure that any lessons learned about the conduct of the project can be appropriately incorporated into future administrative arrangements.

3

SERVICE CONTRACTS

Scope

This chapter addresses issues relating to contracts where there is a service being provided, for example office cleaning. Service contracts in the information technology context are featured separately in Chapter 5.

Readers who have not already done so, may also wish to read Chapter 1 on the general legal aspects of contracts. Matters relating to employment contracts are purposely excluded. However, matters relevant to the engagement of consultants or other specialists are explored in Chapter 10.

Large organisations are likely to require a myriad of different services in support of their operations and general administration. Even activities which historically have been handled in-house, are increasingly being outsourced for a variety of reasons including cost reduction, release of staff to concentrate upon the critical business processes, avoidance of having to maintain specialist skills, and so on. In the public sector moves to contract out services are being swept along by a prevailing government idealogy.

The basic point of decision about the efficacy of seeking external sources to handle selected activities is whether the nature or scope of the particular process is crucial to the organisation and best handled in-house in a relatively controlled way. Organisations will be aware of these key operations and activities, and the amount of specialised knowledge required to apply them. The interruption or disruption of such activities is likely to generate an impact upon the organisation, whether it be financial, operational or relevant to the reputation or image of the organisation. Therefore the first logical step is to assess, in risk and impact terms, the criticality of the process targeted for possible outsourcing, in order that a rational decision can be applied. Understandably, there may be situations where although the activity may represent a high degree of risk, there are more economic ways of conducting it.

Before actively seeking possible solutions it is necessary to clearly establish the nature of the requirements and the motivation for researching alternative ways of achieving them. A recurrent theme throughout this book is the imperative of clearly defining, and subsequently communicating, the requirements for a contracted service, product or project. Time expended on this process is well spent, and the production of a precise and unambiguous statement of requirements or specification will ensure that the latter stages of the process have a better chance of success.

The organisation should be equally clear about why they are seeking alternative solutions or processes. For example, the main drive may be cost reduction or speed of service. If the activity is a significant one, it is possible that seeking alternative high-quality or more economic ways of fulfilling the need is a requirement of top-level strategic business planning. Internal procedures and policies may further determine whether justification on cost and other grounds is required in a particular case.

The precise functional requirements should be determined, time related considerations such as response time will also need to be established. All the requirements, perhaps in the form of a specification, should be documented for use in subsequent contact with potential suppliers or contractors. The subsequent reflection of all requirements, critical timings, etc. in the contract documentation will have to be ensured.

The nature of the service being sought and the relative market conditions will naturally shape the methods to be used in approaching potential contractors. The requirements may be very specialised with a limited number of providers who can apply a premium charge. Alternatively the requirements may be of a very common nature, such as office cleaning, with strong competitive angles influencing prices. These factors should be borne in mind when considering the best approach, and whether for example it is economic to seek tenders for the contract. The overall costs of the procurement process should always be taken into account, and where the organisation is regularly involved in contracting activities, the establishment of a procurement policy may be justified.

The optimum time period for a service contract arrangement will vary between service types and the nature of the relative market. Organisations should avoid becoming tied into long-term arrangements with a contractor especially in a competitive market for either straightforward or commonplace services. One must also be aware of the fluidity of the relevant target market, for example, where the nature of the service is subject to progressive technological changes which may have a direct bearing upon the optimum contract period so as to avoid being locked into outdated equipment or techniques. Time factors also have a role to play in terms of the operations of the organisation seeking the service, in that their own market may require periodic realignment.

Whether or not tendering is a viable and appropriate process to apply will be dependent upon many factors, not least the associated administrative costs. Tendering procedures are fully described in Chapter 14.

The proficiency and financial stability of prospective contractors should be established prior to entering into any formal relationship. Assessing the quality of their work or service may be aided by contacting existing customers where protocol permits. Even though a contractor may have been accredited under BS5750, there is still no concrete guarantee that your requirements will be satisfied. Further matters relevant to the assessment of contractors, are examined in Chapter 12.

Management authority or sanction may be required before proceeding with the contracting arrangements. This is especially valid for activities with a profound relevance to the business operations of the organisation, particularly where a new business venture may be at stake.

Assuming that the appropriate contract arrangements have been formalised, the provision of the related services will need to be either regularly or progressively monitored by the organisation in order to ensure that quality and time requirements are being satisfactorily addressed. All manner of factors should be monitored, not least of which will be the accounts submitted by the contractor to ensure that the charges are in accord with the contract definitions. Additionally, matters of service levels, quality of service, rectification of problems, ease of relationships, etc. should be encompassed in the monitoring responsibilities.

Ideally a member of the organisation's staff should be made responsible for monitoring performance of the contract and acting as main point of contact for the contractor. Any apparent problems should be promptly communicated, the impact assessed and relevant corrective action taken. Serious problems will need to be reported to senior management so that the relative authority can be obtained to support necessary actions. The nominated person should be conversant with the contract provisions and ensure that all actions, by either party, are in accord with the conditions.

It is in the nature of some services and operations that requirements may change over time and in relationship to business levels and all manner of other parameters. Where this type of eventuality is probable, the employing organisation should ensure that the contract conditions enable subsequent revision of service levels, etc. Without this safeguard and the appropriate determination of an optimum contract period, the organisation may find itself locked into either a long-term arrangement or an inappropriate service level. Of course, market conditions may dictate that the relative service level should be reduced, although there is less likelihood that the contractor will be willing to incorporate the option to reduce service provisions into the contract conditions without some form of compensating financial penalty arrangements.

Serious breaches of contract will need to be pursued within the scope of any enabling contract clauses. Settlement of problems within the contract mechanisms is obviously preferable to taking any relevant matters before the courts. All actions should be relevant to and in proportion with the nature of the service being provided and the cost of same. However, it is possible that a relatively low-key service may have disproportionately significant impacts upon the organisation. Where this is the case prior legal advice should be sought so that the contract can incorporate appropriate clauses entitling the employer to compensation for losses incurred due to the failure of the contractor to provide the required service(s).

When service-related contracts are approaching the point of renewal, it is in the organisation's interest to review their current requirements in relation to the performance of the existing contractor, the market conditions, the degree of contractor competition, etc. before finalising their approach. There may be cogent financial reasons for either continuing the relationship with the current contractor or researching alternative solutions. In either case the performance of the contractor to date should be reviewed. This requirement supports the need for ongoing performance monitoring throughout the contract lifetime, which may reveal specific points for incorporation into any new arrangements.

As previously stated, any decision to either re-establish or extend contract relationships with current contractors, will need to be considered against the background of performance to date and the current financial conditions. Authority to proceed may be required from management, following the presentation of the available options supported by all the associated costs and possibly a recommended course of action.

4

PURCHASING AND PROCUREMENT

Scope

This chapter addresses two subjects which may be interrelated in a particular organisational setting. Purchasing processes are generally examined with a bias towards the audit perspective, although we do not venture into all the issues surrounding the interfaces with stock control and accounting. The broader subject of procurement, which may include the purchase of goods, is examined in the context of an organisation's strategic approach to sourcing goods and services. In this latter respect there is some intentional overlap with the contents of the previous chapter.

PURCHASING

The levels of purchasing activity will be conditional upon the nature of the organisation, the services it provides, the required flow of materials, and so on. Some companies, for example those engaged in manufacturing, will require a steady flow of components in order to maintain their production as a means of satisfying their own customers. Where such critical factors apply, it is obviously important to ensure that the supplies of the appropriate items arrive in a useable condition, at the right site, at the right time, and at the most competitive price.

We do not intend to examine all the possible scenarios, but aim to provide general guidance to the key issues which could be applied to the purchase of either raw materials, components or finished goods in situations where contracts can be established with the suppliers. This perspective suggests that the related purchasing is of either a critical mass, a specialist nature, or beyond the scope of a one-off requirement. These and other factors may well apply in your situation, but before considering adopting a more formal contracted arrangement with a supplier, such matters will need to be identified and reviewed in connection with the benefits of contracted relationships beyond the normal purchase-order-based methods.

By means of an example, the price of a component may be critical for a motor manufacturer over a predetermined period. Additionally, quality and reliability may be equally important, as will the need to respond promptly to supply demands. The selection of the supplier in these circumstances will therefore represent a critical element in the business operation, and the employer will need to be fully satisfied that the supplier is stable, reliable and capable of meeting all the potential demands made upon him.

Whether the employing organisation is either approaching the requirement to purchase for the first time, renewing a previous arrangement, or researching alternative sources of supply, it is imperative that the market is fully explored. This will involve acknowledging the key market factors such as degree of specialisation, flexibility on pricing, and so on.

In considering all the required stages of purchasing, the key stage is the accurate definition of the requirements. This may involve the development of a technical specification supported by drawings and computer design data. The requirements, however they are documented, will form the basis for all that follows, therefore accuracy and completeness are of paramount importance.

In this context requirements will also incorporate matters of quantity and call-off. These factors may have a profound effect upon production flow and market timings such as seasonal peaks. Such demands must be accurately predetermined and communicated to the prospective suppliers at the appropriate stage. More frequently call-off arrangements form part of the Just in Time approach and employers should be fully satisfied that prospective contractors can cope with the additional demands of these techniques. Where the quantification of requirements is more difficult to assess in advance, the contract conditions should facilitate a mechanism to cater for changes to requirements within an agreed operational timetable.

Pricing is yet another key element especially where the company or authority has to achieve defined cost targets for the eventual product or service. Tendering may be a viable option where the administration costs can be justified against the significance of the requirements. Tendering processes are noted in Chapter 14. The factors to be considered when selecting a contractor as a source of supply are reviewed in Chapter 12 and are therefore not expanded upon here.

From the contractor's point of view it is equally critical to apply a full assessment of the client's requirements so that capacity, flexibility, etc. can be appropriately accommodated. Where the supply flow is subject to variable demand from the client, the contract should provide for adequate periods of notice so that the contractor can plan his reaction accordingly. The contractor should seek to clarify any unclear aspects of the client's requirements before the contract is finalised. Internal procedures should ensure that all the probable demands can be successfully accommodated.

Conditions of contract which have a bearing upon the price, quantity and call-off arrangements also have a dual relevance to the time period to be covered by the contract. Patently the actual periods will depend on the nature of the business and the requirements, but should be balanced so that the foreseeable demands are satisfied whilst avoiding becoming locked into uneconomic relationships.

Where policy permits, a particular supplier may be nominated to fulfil the order. This decision, which should ideally be sanctioned by senior management, may be sustained on the ground of quality requirements, previous reliability, cost or other grounds.

All the above factors and considerations should, as appropriate, be incorporated into the contract. Where the form of contract is normally determined by the supplier, this should be fully reviewed, by a legal representative where this is warranted, so as to ensure that the operational interests of the employing organisation are adequately protected by the conditions. Senior management approval of the terms should be evidenced prior to the letting of the contract.

During the active lifetime of the contract compliance with all the key requirements should be ensured by ongoing monitoring. All the contractor's obligations, such as delivering the correct quantities at the right time, should be confirmed and any transgressions reacted to accordingly.

Matters of either material or performance quality should be confirmed upon receipt of the goods and any unsuitable items promptly returned. Controls should be in place to ensure that only suitable items are paid for in accordance with the pricing terms specified in the contract. This requirement presupposes that mechanisms are in place to ensure that supplier's invoices are checked to either orders, call-offs or contracts in relation to price, etc. Additionally, the person taking custody of the items for the organisation should confirm the relevant quantity and quality details prior to payment being made. Any variations or rejections should be correctly reflected in the purchase ledger and stock accounts. As with all other forms of contractual relationship, the performance of the contractor should be monitored partly as a determinant in the future engagement of his services.

PROCUREMENT

Procurement in certain organisations can be a major contributing factor to their success. For example, in the private sector, obtaining the right products at the right price and at the right time will be crucial for a consumer electronics retailer. Alternatively, health authorities under the aegis of the National Health Service, will need to actively demonstrate the achievement of value for money in the procurement of medical supplies.

Differing optimum methods of procurement can be applied to a number of situations, for example:

- obtaining goods, materials, components, etc.
- obtaining services, (such as office cleaning or machine maintenance)
- developing software applications
- building, construction or civil engineering, etc.

Private and public sector activities can be broken down into discrete operational or functional areas, and each of these will have very specific characteristics, such as:

- price sensitivity
- reputation or obligation for service provision
- market strengths and weaknesses
- financing considerations or limitations
- statutory or regulatory compliance obligations.

Additionally there are externally influenced factors which should also be borne in mind. For example interest rates or the rate of inflation.

It follows that where the organisation is regularly involved in the purchase or procurement of goods or services, a consistent approach, which optimises the associated benefits and addresses any specific characteristics, should be developed and adopted. Given the enormous potential range of variations represented by combinations of all these factors, the basis for any regular procurement approach will vary accordingly for each scenario. Therefore the determination of the most apposite procurement strategy or policy for any one organisation should aim to appropriately address all the aspects of the procurement process. These include, the type and form of contract, the pricing basis for the contracts, the necessity to invite tenders as a means of obtaining value for money, and so on.

Following the necessary research, a formal and authorised procurement strategy or policy should be documented and put in place as part of the procedural framework. The underlying objectives of such procedures should be to control and minimise exposures to risk, protect the organisation's interests and obtain value for money.

Formalised procurement procedures are, not surprisingly, quite developed in Government departments. For example the body responsible for information systems (the Central Computer and Telecommunications Agency [CCTA]), currently utilises a procedure based upon a method called TAP (Total Acquisition Process). The CCTA publishes a very informative guide to the process – please refer to Appendix 3 for details of the contact address. The procurement procedures should enable the conduct of effective management monitoring to ensure that the optimum approach is consistently applied.

All activities are subject to change, both generated from within an organisation and triggered by external events. Therefore it follows that the administrative policies and procedures should be subject to ongoing review in order that they can keep pace with all changes and developments. Any such amendments should be authorised by senior management and communicated clearly to the appropriate personnel.

The overall aim should be to achieve the most cost-effective, secure and appropriate approach.

5

INFORMATION TECHNOLOGY

Scope

In this chapter we discuss the general attributes of information technology, and the key issues to address in related contractual activities. Many of the constituent factors to be considered are also discussed, in full detail, in other chapters.

In the context of this chapter the term 'information technology'(IT) is used to mean both hardware and software. In practice the successful use of IT, in both businesses and the public sector, is heavily dependent on all manner of factors, including prevailing security measures, operating disciplines and data backup. It is not our intention to provide in this work a comprehensive guide to the assessment of all such IT factors, but to concentrate upon those issues and measures relevant to contract negotiations and administration. However, the broader issues are fully discussed in our companion volume Auditing the IT Environment *(1994). The purchase of computer consumables and the arrangement of bureaux services, such as data preparation, are not specifically addressed in this chapter.*

CONTRACTS IN THE IT CONTEXT

For small scale purchases of standard products it is unlikely there will be a need for formal contract arrangements, other than perhaps for maintenance purposes. The more complex or extensive the arrangements are, the greater the justification for a contract to provide a clear understanding of the precise nature of the required deliverables.

It is most probable that the suppliers of IT goods and services will have standard contracts in place. The client should ensure that such contracts are reviewed, as part of the overall acquisition process, prior to entering into any relationship. Suitable legal advice should be sought and any suggested amendments negotiated with the supplier, as it is likely that the standard form of contract will be biased towards the supplier.

Management should be aware of the relative importance of the IT project in relation to the corporate business objectives. Therefore, they should ensure that the optimum protection is provided in the contractual conditions. In the real world, the driving objectives of client management may openly conflict with the contractor's own targets and aims, and a form of balanced compromise will have to be struck. Clients will do well to avoid timid acceptance of 'standard contract terms' and aim to ensure that their best interests are protected. Legal advice should be sought on such matters before entering into any binding arrangements.

It is vital that all the employer's requirements are provided for in the contract and supporting documentation. The importance of accurately determining all the requirements cannot be overstressed, as the basis for all that follows. Short cuts or limitations applied at this stage will be likely to result in failure to achieve the organisation's objectives, after considerable expenditure and effort has been incurred.

The contract should also include accurate descriptions and definitions of the following, where necessary:

- the principal computer hardware, including technical details such as processor type, memory size and performance criteria
- any modifications to the standard hardware, cross-referred to supporting specifications
- any peripheral equipment, such as printers, tape backup
- any required infrastructure, such as network cabling
- operating software by type and version
- standard software packages by name, type and version
- reference to the supporting specifications of either software requirements or modifications (discussed elsewhere in this chapter)
- the precise nature and extent of the service to be provided
- the timescale of the service provision, and the performance criteria applicable to that service
- details of any support services such as equipment commissioning, training, on-line support, ongoing maintenance
- warranty arrangements (taking note of relative periods and any exclusions)
- maintenance obligations where this is not the subject of a separate contract
- procedures for dealing with changes in requirements identified during the currency of the contract, for example the required authorisations
- the terms and basis for determining the acceptance of the goods and services
- regular charges (for example the renewal of annual software licences)
- any retention values to be held over until the employer is satisfied with, for example, the hardware or bespoke software
- the determined costs for the supply of the relevant goods and service
- the terms of settlement for the sum(s) due including any staged payments due progressively throughout the life of the project
- the frequency of payments for services provided
- conditions for amending the charges for long-term service provision (such as data preparation)
- definition of ownership of software, including copyright and marketing rights
- definition of required system or equipment documentation

- protection for the client's business interests, data, etc. where the contractor's staff will have access to the client's operations.

Procurement of IT-related services in government departments is currently normally undertaken using a formal procedure called TAP (Total Acquisition Process). A suitably tailored version of the process for use in the IT context, has been developed by the CCTA. This is a very structured approach aimed at achieving value for money and the realisation of benefits. TAP incorporates procedural variations for different scales of systems, and although not every aspect will be relevant to the private sector, the guidelines stress the key issues which should be common to all information technology procurement activities. Appendix 3 contains a contact address for the CCTA.

INFORMATION TECHNOLOGY CHARACTERISTICS

Information technology can present tremendous opportunities for businesses and service providers, but it can also be associated with unexpected cost, delay and disruption. There have recently been a number of spectacular system development failures, perhaps the most notable being the Taurus project. The accounting and computing specialist press is littered with articles describing, in profit-shrinking detail, problems associated with failed system developments, inadequate hardware performances, crippling delays, and uneconomic facilities management deals. Indeed, implementing and integrating IT can be difficult to get right.

The information technology marketplace is affected by a number of factors, some of them specific to the industry, for example:

- rapid development of new technologies
- generally reducing costs in relation to performance
- a bewildering choice of hardware platforms and software products
- a large number of potential suppliers and developers, representing an equally wide range of qualities
- products which are platform or environment specific, with little opportunity to move between suppliers
- considerable up-front development and hardware costs
- the explosion of end-user computing.

Given the crucial role played by information in an organisation, it is vital to ensure that whatever processes and equipment are used to gather, hold, manipulate, and present it, they should be reliable, economic, functionally appropriate, and secure.

In periods of rapid and exciting change, it is very easy to become enraptured by the technology, and as a result be disproportionately driven by it. This, in turn, can generate a 'leading edge' mentality which, without a justifiable need, can lead to inappropriate and costly solutions being adopted. It is vital that all IT acquisition and change is directly geared to the strategic and practical needs of the business or activity, and not dominated by the technology itself. In this regard, organisations should ideally establish and document an information technology strategic plan which defines the acquisition and use of IT (in all its forms) in direct relationship to the established business objectives. This method of applying IT should hopefully ensure that IT activities are justified, cost-effective, appropriate, reliable, secure and serve the business.

A feature of the strategic plan may be the establishment of a deliberate procurement policy in favour of a standard type of hardware or even a particular supplier. Management may consider this necessary because of either the level of previous investment in selected product types or as a result of a positive and strong relationship with an existing supplier. Cases for this form of restricted commitment need to be well-reasoned and fully explored so as to ensure that the requisite degrees of business and operational flexibility can be incorporated.

Establishing an IT strategy is not, in itself, the complete answer. There also needs to be an IT culture within the organisation which is sustained by positive user involvement in, and contribution to, IT-related activities. This form of approach further ensures that systems are based upon identified user requirements and not solutions created in technological isolation.

The other key issue in the application of IT in business is flexibility. Businesses and public sector activities are not static entities. In order to remain competitive and cost-effective, an organisation has to be able to apply necessary changes to operations and activities. Therefore it is crucial to ensure that the IT facilities in use will facilitate any required changes, for example in relation to capacity, scale of operation, and performance. Applying an inappropriate hardware platform or software product could lead to further development of the business being constricted, unless costly upgrades or new solutions are applied. Management should ensure that any chosen hardware and software is capable of being upgraded and supported into the future.

The underlying danger in the IT industry is that events will overtake the benefits and cost-effectiveness of upgrading on the same product path, by the inevitable subsequent availability of faster, more powerful new products. The pace of IT change can be alarming in the context of a major investment, as the product you install today may be obsolete tomorrow. The organisation should be seeking assurances from suppliers that they will continue to support a particular product line, and that subsequent development routes will be natural extensions of the current range. The IT development road is littered with abandoned products, cast off by virtue of a combination of unceasing technological change and a built-in obsolescence mentality.

The rate of technological change can also be a major factor in determining the optimum financing route for IT-related projects. New technologies normally carry a premium until both fully proven and established at a level where production economies can be passed on to the end-user. The relatively high cost of large-scale or mainframe equipment also deters most users from purchasing such machines outright. The determination of whether to either purchase or lease such equipment is partly dependent on these and other business driven factors. Leasing and rental arrangements each have their advantages, but management will need to be mindful of the future needs for flexibility and requirement levels when fixing the most apt periods in such arrangements.

The organisation will need to assess project costs against prevailing financial policies governing, *inter alia*, depreciation policy, expected returns on invested capital, etc. Agreeing the optimum financing arrangements should be the subject of considerable analysis, and this process should also take into account all the ancillary requirements and costs. For example, the provision of suitable environmental conditions such as air conditioning and fire protection devices. Providing all the required services and facilities may require the letting of a number of separate, but simultaneous, contracts.

Before we turn our attention to the details of acquiring IT facilities, it may be useful to summarise some examples of the types of IT-related products and services that could be subject to contractual processes:

- acquisition, hire, or leasing of hardware (from personal computers to mainframe system)
- upgrading or expanding hardware installations
- maintenance arrangements for hardware
- purchase of peripheral computing hardware (i.e. printers, scanners, etc.)
- purchase of standard software packages (i.e. accounting systems)
- development of bespoke software solutions
- modification or update of existing software
- re-engineering of business processes and systems
- facilities management services, or selective outsourcing of specific IT services or functions (such as development)
- specialist IT-related consultancy (for example network planning, expert systems or Electronic Data Interchange (EDI).

In recent times there has been an upsurge in outsourcing IT-related activities. This is especially true of the public sector, where computer operations and system development projects have been put in the hands of external private concerns. In some cases 'privatisation' of public IT facilities has also taken place including management buyouts. This has led to public organisations subsequently establishing contracts with former employees to provide (or should it be continue to provide) IT facilities. There can, of course, be great advantages in passing over responsibilities for such activities. For example, outsourcing software development, can free the organisation of all the relevant staff recruitment and skill training matters. By outsourcing IT facilities, the organisation should obviously aim for achieving value for money and reduced costs, but also to at least make the changes transparent to the end-user.

The key issue in relation to all outsourcing, is whether the arrangement still enables the organisation to exercise sufficient control and flexibility, and thereby protect their business and operational interests. If badly handled the outsourced tail can start to wag the organisational dog. For example, long-term facilities management arrangements could severely restrict the potential for change and development of the business, unless the contract includes provisions to cater for periodic reviews of both hardware and software requirements.

Time periods defined in IT contract arrangements are another fundamental issue, bearing in mind the pace of change and development in the industry as a whole. Being 'tied in' to hardware suppliers for long periods can be unhealthy, especially in business markets where change and development are necessary for continued survival. Mainframe computers, for example, are often only capable of running generic systems provided by a limited number of suppliers, although there has been some co-operation between manufacturers in developing systems which can run on a number of hardware platforms. Changes in the market or new business opportunities, may generate a need for new IT solutions outwith the current hardware scenario. Implementing the required business changes, could in IT terms, be excessively expensive if previous inflexible long-term arrangements had to be abandoned and new deals struck.

The scale of the organisation and the extent of any in-house IT facilities should also be borne in mind when alternative solutions are being considered. A company may, for example, have a systems development department in place at a time when it is considering the replacement of major operational computer systems. In order to successfully develop the new applications, the existing staff may require training in the use of current methods and new software tools. The company is therefore faced with a basic choice, either to commit additional expenditure to providing the necessary training or to reduce in-house development staff and have an external software house undertake the new development. The cost reductions achieved by the staff rationalisation may be on a different timescale to the development expenditure. This is a simplistic example, but underlines the attractions of passing over IT activities to external concerns, where the organisation can relinquish the responsibilities for maintaining the necessary skill base in return for known IT costs over a future period. Additionally, by shedding direct responsibility for specialist activities, the organisation can get on with the important matter of running and developing the business.

It is likely that most organisations depend to a great extent on IT as the basis of their operations, accounting, planning, etc. Given the way in which IT has inveigled itself into everyday business and public sector life, any disruption or loss of IT facilities will have an impact on the ability to continue normal operations. In some areas, such as the financial services sector, maintaining a sufficient service in the absence of the various principal systems would be unthinkable. In light of this critical dependence upon computers, software and a mass of business data, any arrangements made with external concerns to provide and manage such services will need to reflect high levels of service, resilience, and security.

GENERAL POINTS TO CONSIDER

There are a number of recurrent general themes that can be applied to the acquisition of most IT-related products and services. The majority of these points for consideration have a natural affinity with the inherent mechanisms of the IT industry, and generally reflect the uncertainties engendered by rapid change taken against the user's basic requirement for stability and assurance.

In considering the contents of this section, we have assumed that the organisation will be following a conventional project lifecycle route, including the feasibility, justification and approval of the project. Subsequent chapters address, in detail, the specific stages of progressing a contracted project through a complete cycle of control, including the prior assessment and approval of project proposals. To avoid duplication of text, these fundamental and critical processes are not discussed in detail in this chapter, but their application is implied.

The impact of significant IT-related change should not be underestimated. Procedures, policies and a range of measures need to be in place in order to determine, plan for, and counteract such implications. What appears, on the surface, to be a quite straightforward situation can, when related to information technology, become complex and more critical. Events in the IT world can rarely be viewed in isolation, as they have the potential for impacting upon such factors as staffing, training, operational procedures, technical compatibility, communication protocols, and so on. Therefore any review of a possible IT project should be broadly based and aim to capture details of all the implications, including all the contingent costs.

If an organisation is seeking to involve external concerns in the provision, development, supply or maintenance of IT-related services and products, there are some consistent golden rules that should be applied:

- Identify all the related key business objectives and ensure that subsequent solutions adequately address them.
- Select suppliers with a proven and reliable track record, contact previous users and undertake an assessment of stability and competence of intended suppliers.
- Ensure that all your requirements are thoroughly researched, identified and communicated, this should aim to avoid incorporating subsequent changes at an unknown cost.
- Ensure that all requirements are driven by justified business or operational needs.
- Ensure that possible solutions address all the identified needs.
- Assess and establish the necessary budgetary limits.
- Ensure that there are demonstrable upgrade routes available as a progression from your chosen point of entry.
- Opt for industry standard products linked to an accepted and proven technology or method.
- Avoid acting as the 'guinea pig' users of new products, you could end up being the test bed and there is no guarantee that the solution will work.

- Ensure that matters of technical compatibility are addressed.
- Ensure that offered solutions are geared to the appropriate timescale.
- Ensure that the arrangement offers suitable flexibility for future business and operational needs. Project your likely future needs and match these with the inherent capability of the product or service.
- Ensure that all the costs are identified, including future operational and maintenance costs based upon expected levels of growth.
- Ensure that the supplier or contractor can provide the required level of service.
- Ensure that security and resilience matters are appropriately addressed.
- Ensure that arrangements for future support and maintenance are formalised and the costs identified in advance.

Perhaps the most critical of the above points is the accurate identification of your requirements. This process lays the foundations for all that follows, and therefore should be approached and undertaken with great care. Involve representatives of all the interested parties in the determination of the requirements from both the functional and performance viewpoints. Do not lose sight of the key business-related scenario and try to express specific features and requirements in this driving context. Document all aspects of the requirements in the form of a user, functional and/or performance specification. This document can then be used as the basis for both testing the IT market and establishing the subsequent contract. Operational factors, such as either the ease of use or additional security features, may be relevant, and these should be appropriately incorporated into the requirements specification.

The following sections aim to address some of the significant issues with regard to discrete IT services. Where necessary, the conditions of contract and supporting documentation should aim to incorporate the points noted.

HARDWARE

References to hardware in this section are intended to encompass all manner of computers (personal to mainframe), peripheral equipment and any other physical devices, such as networks or communication facilities.

Users and those seeking IT-based solutions face an enormous and bewildering potential choice of equipment. There are many ways to crack the IT nut, but only a few which are likely to be correct and appropriate in terms of scale, performance and cost. We do not intend to explore the relative merits and disadvantages of all the various hardware platforms as the basis for providing solutions, this book is not the natural rostrum for such complex considerations. It is clearly the responsibility of management, perhaps with the assistance of suitably skilled consultants, to accurately determine the most appropriate methods of providing the required computing facilities. In some cases, the choices will be clear-cut, in others the alternatives need to be weighed in respect of the state of the art, the overall costs, the required functionality and reliability, and so on.

The provision of hardware may be driven by an established IT purchasing policy shaped by the existence of an IT strategic plan. In situations where either successful long-term associations, the use of particular industry standard devices, or the pursuance of a technical upgrade path are relevant, such a plan has a part to play. However, outwith such constraints the user is presented with a myriad of choice, and the added potential dimension of technical incompatibility.

With the expansion of opportunities offered by, among other things, networked personal computers, organisations are moving away from large, central mainframe-driven operations. This trend also provides greater choice of suppliers if items incorporating generally available technologies are chosen. It is possible to mix and match hardware components so long as technical compatibility is proven.

No one solution is logically correct for all situations and there are benefits in being associated with one hardware platform and supplier. This form of 'tie-in' does however need to be carefully considered in connection with the objectives of the organisation, and the state of development they have reached in IT terms. There need to be very strong justifications for continuing such a relationship, and the stability of the supplier is a crucial element to consider. The large mainframe suppliers that have survived the savage contraction of the industry are no longer immune from danger and inviolate.

Assessing the requirements is the first step, and these should include the following considerations:

- types of applications to be run
- the scale of operation expressed in terms of data volumes, transactions, etc.
- the performance criteria, including response times, machine loadings, etc.
- the current and future loading and facility requirements
- the location of all the users (this data can be used to determine the best method for providing the necessary communication and networking facilities).

All the requirements should be formally documented as the basis for all subsequent assessments. Care should be taken to ensure that all the relevant factors are recorded in the specification, as this will avoid subsequent piecemeal amendment of the points noted in light of supplier reactions, etc. Furthermore, where tendering is a viable and economic option, the requirements specification can be circulated to all candidate contractors. The specification should incorporate such factors as performance criteria, future expansion options, and required industry standards.

Organisations may wish to call upon the services of a suitable consultant to advise on the technical specification of hardware, so that the selected equipment is capable of supporting the achievement of the related business plans and aspirations. Technical compatibility with existing systems may be a crucial element, or alternatively radical changes may prove to be necessary to address new business opportunities. Although investing in new technologies, perhaps with unfamiliar suppliers, presents the potential for increased exposure to risk, such moves may be unavoidable if the business is to remain competitive in either its chosen market or a new venture. The application of suitable measures can assist in counteracting the relevant risks and the application of balanced contractual terms, approached in a controlled way, will hopefully limit the implications.

Predicting the performance of hardware is not a precise process, and can only be regarded as an indicator. Users should be cautious when assessing the processing abilities of hardware, unless suitable and realistic tests can be applied. In any case, the projected loading data should contain a hefty contingency, and also take account of likely future needs based upon anticipated business and transaction growth. Future upgrade options and routes should also take note of future business developments.

The stability and reliability of equipment suppliers are important considerations. Chapter 12 examines the mechanisms for assessing contractors and so we will not expand upon the requirements in this section. The provision of maintenance is discussed in one of the following sections, although it would be necessary to consider such implications concurrently with the purchase of the relevant hardware.

SOFTWARE

In the context of business or function-related software applications, the purchaser has a basic choice between standard off-the-shelf packages and bespoke developments based upon the user's specific requirements. In order to fulfil particular user requirements, the standard packages may also be subject to some degree of customising. In choosing between these two fundamental routes, it is necessary to consider the nature of the problem the user is aiming to solve by the use of the software. Although it is possible that some portion of the development work could be handled by in-house analysts and programmers, we have deliberately chosen to disregard this possibility in this text. Most of the points discussed in this chapter can be related to either package or bespoke software situations.

A structured approach to the selection of a suitable software developer should be adopted, which should include the following actions:

- identifying all requirements and performance criteria
- researching the market for potential products and suppliers
- ensuring that earmarked suppliers have the required skills and competence
- matching requirements to facilities available
- attending relative demonstrations and assessing the ease of use, etc.
- satisfying security and resilience requirements
- ensuring compatibility with hardware and technical constraints
- assessing supplier in terms of performance, track record, financial stability, reputation, etc.
- contacting existing users and obtaining their views of service, etc.
- obtaining full details of all costs.

If the system requirements relate to a commonplace activity, such as accounting or word processing, an existing standard package should suffice, and it would be somewhat pointless to 'reinvent the wheel' by developing your own version of such a basic system type. Alternatively, you may have a very specific or specialised need to address, for example providing an internal auditing expert system for training audit staff, and in this case the system is likely to be a bespoke development. In either case the starting point is the same, namely the determination of an accurate and comprehensive specification of requirements. This document should include not only the functional aspects of the required system, but also the required level of performance, perhaps expressed in terms of data capacity or minimum system response times. The need for reports and data interrogation facilities should not be forgotten, and assurances sought that the system is capable of providing accurate information in the appropriate form at the correct time.

In order that the eventual design can be matched to the operating requirements, realistic estimates of the required workload will need to be assessed. Data and transaction volumes will be required as the basis for determining the processing, storage and hardware capacity requirements. Where the development of the system also entails the acquisition of the necessary hardware, it follows that such capacity and size factors need to be very accurately determined and need to allow for the planned growth of the business.

The specification should be the cornerstone of subsequent dialogue with the supplier or software house. Prior to entering into any relationship, the supplier should confirm that he is able to address all the needs expressed in the specification or suggest viable and acceptable alternatives, which should then be incorporated into an agreed base document. Matters of performance should also be duly incorporated into the contract documentation.

The introduction of the related system may be time critical and realistic timetables should be agreed. There should be some allowance made for contingency. The timing requirements and key dates will also need to be specifically defined in the resultant contract.

The use of a software product, especially standard packages, is normally subject to standard licensing conditions. These conditions will need to be examined in order to ensure that they allow the intended use of the software taking into account the location and number of sites where it is to be installed. Violation of the licensing conditions may invalidate other aspects of the relationship with the supplier, such as continued upgrades and maintenance. In the case of bespoke software developments, the eventual ownership of the software should be clearly established, as this may affect the employer's ability to extend its use or have subsequent amendments applied by a third party. The developers will often wish to retain control over ownership, marketing rights and copyright. The employer should confirm that ownership and licensing conditions are appropriate for both the current and potential uses of the software. When necessary, the parties should negotiate agreed terms and have these incorporated into the relevant contractual arrangements.

Adequate project resources should be made available, including the nomination of key members of the employing organisation to represent the corporate and user viewpoints. External developers should be able to confirm that they can provide suitable numbers of appropriately skilled staff throughout the lifetime of the project. Adequate communication channels should be established and the flow of project information predetermined and formalised. External software developers should have a proven ability in relation to both the functional and technical aspects of the project.

Selecting a suitable software developer may include a full assessment of their business and relative products. Assessing the viability and competence of contractors is fully discussed in Chapter 12. In addition to the cost of acquiring or developing the software, there should be an awareness of other related costs such as the involvement of user staff in the project, computer resources for testing and data conversion, training, and so on.

The progress of the project should be subject to a formal project management method, with appropriate levels of resource planning and progress reporting. Discrete project stages should be incorporated for designing, programming, testing, implementing, etc. (*see also* Chapter 8).

In common with most project types, dealing with subsequent changes to the design requirements in a software project, can generate considerable cost and delay. This underlines the need for a thorough approach to the initial specification. However, the need for some changes can be inevitable, and their assessment and incorporation should be subject to objective review and approval, especially where additional costs are incurred. The contract should make clear the liability for the costs associated with subsequent change, and the conditions under which it should be considered. Account should be taken of the effects of change on the project timetable and therefore the contracted completion date. Once again the conditions of contract should clearly delineate between changes caused by the employer and those generated by some action on the part of the contractor. An example of the latter would be where a change in the structure of the underlying database is proved necessary to achieve the defined system response times, where the contractor previously determined the optimum database structure and form. All changes should be assessed for cost implications and suitably approved by the employer prior to commitment being given.

The contract should be clear in respect of the treatment of delays which affect the defined completion date. In practice there may be severe consequences for failing to introduce the operational system by a specific date, therefore the contract conditions relevant to delay will need to reflect this significance.

A pivotal point in any software development is when the programming is complete and the software is ready for testing. Obviously in order to ensure that the software achieves all the required performance and functional requirements, as defined in the initial specification, it should be subject to thorough testing. Such testing should ideally be conducted in accordance with a documented test plan, and all results recorded and assessed. Changes necessitated by the test results should be agreed, incorporated and themselves tested until all requirements are met. This stage is crucial as it will determine whether the obligations established for the developer have, in fact, been discharged. Great debates can ensue about failures to match requirements, unless those requirements are clearly and unambiguously determined at the outset. Additionally, the effect of changes incorporated during the project may have a confusing influence upon apportioning blame for failure to achieve the target. This undesirable end can be averted by firmly setting the base requirement, monitoring progress throughout, and agreeing and adequately controlling all stages, changes and implications.

There comes a time when employers may need to sign off the system(s) as acceptable, this should only be done when they are fully satisfied with the system, all approved changes have been incorporated, and the testing results support all the critical requirements. User involvement throughout the project should have enabled the resolution of problems and the confirmation that all the key requirements have been successfully addressed.

The implementation of the system will need to be planned, and this may form part of the contractor's responsibilities. Although outwith the scope of this chapter adequate attention should be given to preparing and training staff to use the new system. Sign off and final payments may only be applied when the system has been proven to operate as intended in a live situation. The contractor/developer should have the responsibility for correcting any problems encountered during live use, although such problems should have been previously flushed out during the testing phase of the project.

One of the keys to the successful implementation of new systems is the provision of comprehensive, clear and user-friendly documentation. This should encompass user manuals, and where appropriate, program documentation to readily support the future maintenance of the application. In the case of strategically significant systems, it may be desirable to have a systems maintenance contract with the developer so that required changes and modifications can be incorporated in step with changing business needs, and so on.

FACILITIES MANAGEMENT

This has become one of the growth areas of the 1990s, as an increasing number of private and public sector concerns unburden themselves from the responsibilities of operating part or all of their IT facilities. The media headlines tend to concentrate upon the IT jobs lost in the employing organisation and play down the real business benefits. The available services are provided by a variety of concerns including, subsidiaries of consultancy firms, financial institutions, an airline, and former public sector employees who have staged management buyouts.

There are a range of services that can be described as falling under the generic facilities management (FM) umbrella, including:

- operating existing systems such as mainframe-based applications
- taking over responsibility for operating the complete data centre, including preparation, processing, security, etc.
- providing development support for existing systems
- developing new application systems.

The basis upon which such arrangements are made will vary. For example, ownership of the associated hardware may remain with the original organisation, or be transferred to the FM company. Similarly, the operations can be conducted either on hardware which remains at its original site, hardware which has been moved to the FM operator's site, or on the FM operator's own equipment.

The transfer of responsibilities may be selective. For example, an organisation facing the need to develop new applications may offload the operation of all their current systems to an FM contractor, so that they can concentrate upon the development of new systems for future business requirements, using their skilled development workforce.

The choice of the most apt and optimum solution will depend upon the condition of the company, their market position, the need to address other priorities, the explicit financial situation and the need to rationalise the high costs normally associated with maintaining an IT infrastructure. In a constantly changing environment, continued investment in IT and related developments can be a notable drain on corporate resources, and a large proportion of the outlay is relative to providing the necessary staff and expertise. By opting to use FM, an organisation will free itself from the concerns of keeping pace with changes in technology and having to maintain a suitably skilled IT team. The costs associated with the aspects passed across to the FM supplier should, within limits, be known for some time ahead.

Before we become over-excited about the benefits of FM as a means of ensuring the continued ability for a concern to be competitive and contain costs, there are, naturally, some risks and concerns associated with the process which need to be addressed. The following points should be borne in mind when considering the possibility of entering into a contract with a FM provider:

- The organisation needs to be assured that the relevant service will be reliable and enable the accurate processing and presentation of data at the appropriate time.
- Mechanisms should exist which enable the operation to cope with disruption or loss of service, and to promptly recover from disasters.
- The user's data should be adequately protected from loss, corruption and unauthorised leakage.
- Defined service levels and performance criteria should be established and maintained in support of business activities and requirements.

With these and other factors in mind, suitable research should be undertaken to appraise the feasibility of the available options and to specify the precise operational requirements. It is possible that this approach will be determined by the needs of a strategic-level decision to assess alternative methods of addressing the organisation's IT requirements, for example, as a means of streamlining the organisation to concentrate upon the critical operational and marketing aspects of the business. All the requirements will need to be registered and documented in the form of a requirements specification, which could form the basis of subsequent supplier tendering and contracting.

Obviously the choice of a reliable contractor is crucial to the success of the move to outsourcing IT facilities. Potential candidates will need to be assessed for their suitability and stability prior to being invited to submit a quote for providing the required services. Chapter 12 concentrates upon the assessment of contractors, and Chapter 14 examines the ideals of a tendering procedure.

Once again the matter of flexibility will need to be considered, especially in relation to the period to be covered by the FM arrangement. Agreeing long-term arrangements, perhaps at favourable terms, may be negated by a lack of flexibility with regard to the likely need for future changes, expansion, etc. It is very difficult to accurately assess future information technology trends, with or without the implications for the business. Contract arrangements should cater for both reassessment of requirements and the need to incorporate changes with respect to workload, methods, equipment, and so on.

The organisation should allow sufficient time near the end of an FM contract for the full and realistic consideration of alternatives, required changes, developments, and so on. Planning for change should be a continuous process in line with business needs, economic and market trends, technological developments, and the condition of the FM market.

The contract should also be clear about relevant responsibilities, rights, and liabilities on a day-to-day basis. Particular attention should be given to the adequacy of planning surrounding the implementation of the FM service, which may incorporate the physical movement of hardware, the transfer and loading of relevant systems and data, and the re-routeing of communication facilities. This exercise will need to be carefully planned and specific responsibilities allocated.

We have included an example matrix for the subject of facilities management as Table 5 and full details are noted in the section headed 'Control matrix examples' below.

IT CONSULTANCY

The engagement of external IT consultants may be necessary for a number of reasons, including the following:

- to aid in the determination of an IT strategic plan
- to either assess the need for or introduce new techniques or technologies
- to examine the effectiveness of existing IT security arrangements
- to explore alternative hardware and software solutions
- to recover systems and data following virus infection
- to support the re-engineering of processes in order to maximise benefits from IT investments.

The market place for consultancy is basically polarised between the consultancy arms of large firms such as accountants on the one hand, and small independent concerns on the other. Although some hardware and software suppliers appear to offer consultancy services, this is normally linked, perhaps not unnaturally, to their own product ranges. The employer should be ideally aiming to receive an independent view of the relevant situation.

As with any other form of specialist advice, the employer should be assured that the advisers are suitably experienced and qualified. This fundamental requirement presents certain difficulties in the IT environment, in that although there are recognised qualifications for selected specialist areas, there are no generally determined standards for assessing the competency of 'consultants'. The question of engaging consultants is more fully addressed in Chapter 10, but given that few reliable benchmarks exist, it is possible that the employer may either have to react to recommendations or investigate a consultant's performance by contacting previous clients to obtain their views.

MAINTENANCE

In the context of this chapter the term 'maintenance' covers both hardware and software. Additionally, the provision of maintenance services can be construed as either by the original supplier or by a third party. The provision of maintenance cover for equipment on either lease or rental is assumed to have been arranged via the source contractor.

In the case of hardware items, the cost-effectiveness of extended maintenance agreements should be viewed in the light of generally increased device reliability and the 'serviceability' of the equipment. The latter term is meant to express the relationship between the construction techniques used and the methods employed in servicing the equipment. For example, with the proliferation of highly integrated circuits contained in single devices or panels, the ability to apply repairs is reduced, if not removed altogether. This often results in complete assemblies being automatically replaced, without the need to specifically trace the offending device or retain the original for subsequent repair and reuse. Beyond the initial warranty period, the costs of replacing these highly complex units can be very expensive, but this consideration should be viewed against the generally improving reliability of same.

In the case of computer hardware maintenance, it is usual for the original manufacturer or supplier to offer maintenance arrangements as part of an overall package, albeit that the actual service company may be a third party. Indeed, it may be a condition of the purchase or lease that the equipment has to be maintained by the supplier or a nominated sub-contractor. Any deviation from this arrangement may invalidate any warranty provisions. Clients and users should be aware of the nature and terms of the maintenance arrangements and ensure that all the conditions are met in the interests of securing the required response when a problem occurs.

When reviewing the ongoing warranty, service and maintenance conditions, the organisation should initially take a view of their dependence upon the relevant hardware or software and extrapolate the potential risks. All the relevant terms should then be correlated against the risks as a means of assessing their effectiveness. The objective should be to provide adequate coverage to address the operational and business needs of the organisation. For example, the choice between 'same day' and '24 hour' call-out services may be critical in operational terms for a company engaged in providing an on-line service for its customers. Warranty periods for equipment and possibly selected components should be determined. Whether or not labour and parts cover is applicable in every situation may also have significant cost implications. All these aspects should be clearly defined in the contract. There are likely to be defined exclusions in relation to service and maintenance arrangements. For example, either operating the equipment in inappropriate environmental conditions or the unauthorised fitting of non-approved components, may invalidate the arrangement and make the client liable to pay the costs associated with rectifying any resultant problems. The renewal or extension of maintenance arrangements should be viewed in relation to the general reliability and age of the equipment, and the importance of its continued operation to the organisation.

The direct engagement of third party maintenance companies may prove to be more economic following a suitable assessment of the terms and conditions. However, care should be taken to ensure that the original supplier or manufacturer will permit such a course of action. There may be restrictions applied to the concerns that are permitted to undertake subsequent work, for example on the basis of authorised dealers who are obliged to use approved parts. Beyond the defined warranty period, the choice of maintenance arrangements may be unrestricted if so defined in the relevant contract, and the user will be free to either seek alternative arrangements or re-engage the services of the original supplier.

In the case of software the maintenance and support arrangements will be partially dependent upon whether the software was a standard package or a bespoke development. Support for a standard application is normally restricted to a limited period, and the licensing arrangements may exclude a direct liability to address bugs and other problems. In this and other respects the licensing arrangements normally favour the developers. Standard software, such as spreadsheets and word processors, are also subject to constant upgrades. These upgrades may provide new or revised facilities, and also address problems apparent in earlier versions. If a user consciously chooses not to apply all the upgrades, for which a charge is normally made, he could find that the software developer no longer guarantees and supports the older versions of his product. If a user wishes to maintain support arrangements over time, he should allow for the cost of upgrades in his project costings.

Determining the ground rules for the maintenance and upgrading of bespoke software is potentially more complex, in that it may be dependent upon a number of the following considerations:

- the ownership of the relevant software
- determining whether a problem is due either to an inherent 'bug' or a subsequent change to the specifications
- contract conditions permitting or excluding a period of maintenance
- establishing clearly whether subsequent maintenance is the responsibility of either the developer or the user
- user access to the source code
- whether or not a periodic maintenance fee is charged
- the ability of in-house staff to apply subsequent modifications
- the extent of the changes required
- whether the operating environment has been changed by the user.

Where the significance of the system dictates, it may be possible to negotiate an arrangement for ongoing software maintenance and protect against the effects of a major failure due to the software. In any event, the modification or amendment of software should always be followed by adequate testing. No amended software should be brought into live use until it has been proved to operate satisfactorily.

Control matrix example

Table 5 is provided to illustrate a number of IT-related factors. The method applied to the construction of this matrix is described in Chapter 32 .

The subject of facilities management is featured in this table, which is *Objectives*-oriented. This matrix is not exclusively linked to contracting processes, but aims to explore the broader issues associated with the subject in relation to the achievement of a range of objectives, including the abilities of the supplier. *Scale* 30 has been used to reflect a situation which suggests a high degree of dependence upon FM facilities, and details of *Scale* 30 can be found in Appendix 7.

Table 5 Facilities Management Contract – Objectives

Overall Inherent Risk (Size) Score [5 is worst risk; 1 is best] = 3.16

A Ensure accurate assessment of current & future requirements
B Ensure that IT-related costs are reduced/contained
C Ensure the comprehensive research of options for change
D Ensure that selected FM contractor is reputable & reliable
E Ensure contractor option will provide necessary flexibility
F Ensure that required service levels will be achieved
G Establish effective & protective contracts/agreements
H Ensure allocation of responsibilities, rights & liabilities
I Ensure adequate security is exercised over company data
J Ensure that company data is accurate and reliable
K Establish the ownership of programs and applications
L Ensure disruption/loss of service is effectively addressed
M Ensure company auditors can assess adequacy of operation
N Ensure that any new systems or amendments are agreed/tested
O Ensure that transaction trailing is adequate
P Ensure costs & performance are monitored against targets
Q Ensure FM contractor applied effective standards & methods
R Ensure migration to contractor is adequately planned, etc.
S Ensure that user staff are supported to achieve objectives

Scale 30 (abridged)

6 = Strategically vital to the business or organisation
5 = Makes a contribution to business operations
4 = Contributes to reliability of data, records and information
(Contract auditing Objectives-orientated scale)

3 = Avoids disruption/meets regulatory & accountability needs
2 = Leads to administrative/operational economies/efficiencies
1 = Generates administrative economies

	Facilities Management Contract		OBJECTIVES	A	B	C	D	E	F	G	H	I	J	K	L	M	N	O	P	Q	R	S
	Calculated Risk Score:	Risk		4	3	3	3	3	4	3	3	3	4	2	4	2	3	2	3	2	3	3
	Scale 30 (6 is most serious)	Type		6	6	5	6	6	6	6	4	6	6	3	6	3	4	3	5	4	3	3
	Size (3 is maximum)	Size		3	2	2	2	2	3	2	3	2	3	2	3	2	2	2	2	3	2	3
	MEASURES																					
1	Output of Strategic Planning exercise provided basis for future IT requirements	Best		5				4														
		Test		?	?			?														
		Both																				
2	Current & proposed alternatives are subject to cost/benefit analysis and comparison	Best		4	4	4																
		Test		?	?	?	?															
		Both																				
3	Formal evaluation & feasibility methods were used to assess FM contractor options	Best			4	5	3	4												3		
		Test		?		?	?	?	?											?		
		Both																				
4	Quality, service & operational criteria established for assessment of relevant suppliers	Best							4	3	4											
		Test		?					?	?	?											
		Both																				
5	Current users contacted and subject to standard interview, re performance, quality, etc.	Best							3	3												
		Test		?					?	?												
		Both																				
6	Contract defines required minimum service levels and critical operational timetables	Best								5	4											
		Test		?						?	?											
		Both																				
7	Service level performance is subject to ongoing monitoring and feedback	Best								4									4			
		Test		?						?									?			
		Both																				
8	Comprehensive contract has been established; defines rights, responsibilities and liabilities	Best								5	5											
		Test		?						?	?											
		Both																				
9	All liability in the event of disruption or loss of service > X hours, lies with suppliers	Best								4												
		Test		?						?												
		Both																				

Table 5 continued

			Risk	A	B	C	D	E	F	G	H	I	J	K	L	M	N	O	P	Q	R	S
				=	=	=	=	=	=	=	=	=	=	=	=	=	=	=	=	=	=	=
	Calculated Risk Score:		Risk	4	3	3	3	3	4	3	3	3	4	2	4	2	3	2	3	3	2	3
				–	–	–	–	–	–	–	–	–	–	–	–	–	–	–	–	–	–	–
10	Data preparation, input, reporting & reconciliation procedures defined	Best									4	3										
		Test	?								?	?										
		Both																				
				–	–	–	–	–	–	–	–	–	–	–	–	–	–	–	–	–	–	–
11	Company auditor undertook review of supplier's controls prior to relationship	Best									4	4										
		Test	?								?	?										
		Both																				
				–	–	–	–	–	–	–	–	–	–	–	–	–	–	–	–	–	–	–
12	Pilot exercise undertaken to assess live conditions- results were satisfactory	Best									4	4										
		Test	?								?	?										
		Both																				
				–	–	–	–	–	–	–	–	–	–	–	–	–	–	–	–	–	–	–
13	Processed data is reconciled	Best									3		4									
		Test	?								?		?									
		Both																				
				–	–	–	–	–	–	–	–	–	–	–	–	–	–	–	–	–	–	–
14	Programs developed for the company remain the property of the company – per contract	Best												5								
		Test	?											?								
		Both																				
				–	–	–	–	–	–	–	–	–	–	–	–	–	–	–	–	–	–	–
15	Contingency plan is in place (reviewed prior to contract) and tested for effectiveness	Best													5							
		Test	?												?							
		Both																				
				–	–	–	–	–	–	–	–	–	–	–	–	–	–	–	–	–	–	–
16	Contract specifies conditions of access for company auditors to obtain assurance re controls	Best													5							
		Test	?												?							
		Both																				
				–	–	–	–	–	–	–	–	–	–	–	–	–	–	–	–	–	–	–
17	All amendments to existing programs are specified, developed, tested & signed off	Best															4		3			
		Test	?														?		?			
		Both																				
				–	–	–	–	–	–	–	–	–	–	–	–	–	–	–	–	–	–	–
18	New programs are developed using an effective development methodology and framework	Best															4		3			
		Test	?														?		?			
		Both																				
				–	–	–	–	–	–	–	–	–	–	–	–	–	–	–	–	–	–	–
19	Full audit trail is available	Best																4				
		Test	?															?				
		Both																				
				–	–	–	–	–	–	–	–	–	–	–	–	–	–	–	–	–	–	–
20	All relative costs are monitored against budget and variances are investigated	Best																4				
		Test	?															?				
		Both																				
				–	–	–	–	–	–	–	–	–	–	–	–	–	–	–	–	–	–	–
21	Satisfactory operating procedures are in place – site is accredited with BS5750	Best																		5		
		Test	?																	?		
		Both																				
				–	–	–	–	–	–	–	–	–	–	–	–	–	–	–	–	–	–	–
22	Initial transfer process subject ot agreed implementation plan – with milestones/targets	Best																			4	
		Test	?																		?	
		Both																				
				–	–	–	–	–	–	–	–	–	–	–	–	–	–	–	–	–	–	–
23	Training and new documentation provided as per contract	Best																				
		Test	?																		4	
		Both																			?	
				–	–	–	–	–	–	–	–	–	–	–	–	–	–	–	–	–	–	–

A Ensure accurate assessment of current & future requirements
B Ensure that IT-related costs are reduced/contained
C Ensure the comprehensive research of options for change
D Ensure that selected FM contractor is reputable & reliable
E Ensure contractor option will provide necessary flexibility
F Ensure that required service levels will be achieved
G Establish effective & protective contracts/agreements
H Ensure allocation of responsibilities, rights & liabilities
I Ensure adequate security is exercised over company data
J Ensure that company data is accurate and reliable
K Establish the ownership of programs and applications

L Ensure disruption/loss of service is effectively addressed
M Ensure company auditors can assess adequacy of operation
N Ensure that any new systems or amendments are agreed/tested
O Ensure that transaction trailing is adequate
P Ensure costs & performance are monitored against targets
Q Ensure FM contractor applied effective standards & methods
R Ensure migration to contractor is adequately planned, etc.
S Ensure that user staff are supported to achieve objectives

Scale 30 (abridged)

6 = Strategically vital to the business or organisation
5 = Makes a contribution to business operations
4 = Contributes to reliability of data, records and information
(Contract auditing Objectives-orienated scale)

3 = Avoids disruption/meets regulatory & accountability needs
2 = Leads to administrative/operational economies/efficiencies
1 = Generates administrative economies

6

AUDIT SITE VISITS

Scope

Patently not every project will have a 'site' where any major construction, fabrication, development or administrative activity will be taking place. However, outwith the obvious building and civil engineering examples, there may be some relevance to large scale mechanical or electrical engineering projects such as shipbuilding, chemical plant equipment and specialised defence projects.

This chapter differs from others in the book, in that it deliberately offers more direct advice to auditors in order that they can achieve the maximum benefit from site visits and foster good working relationships with technical or professional staff. Most of the existing material about audit visits to contractor's sites is geared to the public sector, with an understandable bias towards civil engineering and building projects. Whereas some of the issues we discuss in this chapter are only specifically relevant to these selfsame situations, our aim was also to provide some general points which could be applied in other circumstances.

The larger construction companies will probably have formal site operation standards which may be reinforced by staff who undertake site visits to confirm compliance. In the course of either systems evaluation or subsequent compliance activities, auditors in certain sectors are likely to have to undertake the required work on site. In the case of construction projects there are a number of discrete systems (e.g. contractor's claims) which will have a relevance to site-level records. These discrete systems are examined in detail in other chapters in this book, and the appropriate comments in this chapter are therefore intentionally restricted.

JUSTIFICATION FOR SITE VISITS

What is the motivation for undertaking a site visit during the course of a project? Despite the degree to which auditors can become enraptured by the processes of administration and the application of effective management control during system audits, there are likely to be very fundamental aspects of project control which are focused at the site of most of the activity. It is at the construction or factory site where opportunities for waste, inefficiency or delay can exist. Additionally it is at 'the sharp end' where the foundations of the key information flows are initially established. Very often all the prime documents are retained at the site or factory. If the creation of data is affected by poor control and inaccuracy, then all that follows will be correspondingly tainted. Finally, it is at the site where the true performance of the contractor is usually at its most visible.

We are not suggesting that the auditor should in any way, supplant the relevant management responsibilities for monitoring the site activities. However, in the course of his review of the effectiveness of administration and control systems, the auditor can achieve a great deal by the taking the time to conduct a well-planned site visit.

As we shall see later in this chapter, the extent of the role played by the auditor during site visits may be understandably restricted by a combination of the etiquette of relationships with other professionals, limitation of his jurisdiction per the terms of the relevant contract, the extent of administrative activities devolved to the site, and other specific practical considerations. The auditor will need to take careful account of the environment in which he operates and the established protocols that apply.

The list below features all manner of motivations for auditors to undertake site visits. Not all will apply in every case, and in some instances they would be openly discouraged on the grounds of proficiency, jurisdiction, etc. Readers will have to be selective in order to extract those elements which are both permitted and practical in their particular sphere of operations.

- assessment of financial control systems at the site level
- assessment of the accuracy, reliability, integrity, timeliness and completeness of information emanating from the site as the basis for subsequent actions and decisions by the contractor and employer alike
- assessment of controls over standards applied to work and other site activities
- verification of key assets and material stocks
- assessment of physical security arrangements exercised over materials, goods and relevant documentation
- assessment of the channels of communication between all parties and the resolution of queries, problems, etc.
- assessment of the effectiveness of all relevant procedures
- assessment of the control exercised over such key elements as contractor's claims, variation orders, extensions of time, and the performance of contractors, sub-contractors and suppliers
- assessment of safety matters and general conduct of staff.

In addition to the points noted above, a visit to the site can be a very informative process for the auditor, although it should not be regarded as a day out from the audit office. There are opportunities to meet with the key players in the project at the scene of the crucial activity, and this can be extremely useful in the development of good working relationships. The visit can add shades of grey (or even colour) to the picture of the project held by the auditor, in that he or she can get a flavour of the practical considerations that may naturally pre-occupy the technical staff.

SCOPE AND FREQUENCY OF SITE VISITS

These factors will vary in respect of some or all of the following considerations:

- the significance of the project in financial, strategic or timescale terms
- the extent and significance of site based project activities
- the allocation of administrative responsibilities and the proportion of same which are site based
- the amount of audit resource available and the allocation of that resource to the project as a whole
- the determination of risk represented by the project and in particular of the site based activities and administration
- the strength (or otherwise) of the project and management control systems in place, based upon earlier audit coverage
- indications of potential project control problems.

THE PITFALLS OF AUDIT SITE VISITS

The last thing auditors want for either the sake of their own or their department's credibility is to make nuisances of themselves or waste time. Therefore they should openly demonstrate consideration and courtesy when arranging and participating in site visits. Auditors should be remembered by the site staff for being interested, contributive and constructive, and not being aggressive, combative and putting themselves (and perhaps others) in danger by disregarding the appropriate safety requirements.

There is, of course, a first time for everyone and confidence in another professional's arena usually develops with time and experience. For the most part, and if approached in the right way, most professional or technical staff are only too happy to conduct someone around their normal habitat and explain what is going on. This may be a sensible way to start for an inexperienced auditor, although it may not always be practical in light of pressures that may apply in a live project situation.

ACTIONS REQUIRED BY THE AUDITOR BEFORE A SITE VISIT

Plan the nature and content of your visit beforehand so that you can both maximise your time on site and make best use of other people's time. Be clear about what you want to examine and the supporting reasons. Note down any specific questions you may have and try to identify the staff you will want to speak to, either by name or their job title.

Confirm the protocol that applies in your sector, organisation and audit department, and ensure that you adhere to the advice provided. In the public sector, much work has been done by CIPFA to promote mutual understanding between auditors and the various construction and engineering professionals. A number of joint statements have been developed by CIPFA and the professional bodies which clearly define the roles of the parties concerned, these include the following:

- The Institution of Civil Engineers (ICE)
- The Royal Institution of Chartered Surveyors (RICS)
- The Society of Chief Architects of Local Authorities (SCALA)
- Society of Chief Quantity Surveyors in Local Government (SCQSLG)

Confirm the access rights granted to members of employer's staff under the terms of the relevant contract. You will need to ensure that your subsequent visit is effective, so avoid treading on people's toes.

It is more than a courtesy to make a prior appointment with the key contractor's employee well before your visit, it also ensures that all the people you wish to see will be available on the chosen day. When making the appointment be as honest as you can about the purpose of your visit and any particular records you wish to inspect. In the normal course of events, it is not acceptable to turn up unannounced at a site.

Major construction sites can be dangerous places, especially if the most hazardous activity the auditor normally engages in is collecting hot coffee from a vending machine. Your employer should provide adequate insurance cover in respect of both personal injury and consequent third party liability. Before the visit make sure you are fully aware of the prevailing site health and safety requirements and that you make arrangements beforehand to obtain the required protective clothing such as a hard hat, appropriate footwear, safety goggles, etc. Finally, it may be necessary for you to carry some form of official identity noting who you are, your specific responsibilities, and the purpose of your visit. If physical security at the site is a key issue, hopefully you will be asked to prove that you are who you claim to be.

GENERAL CONDUCT DURING THE VISIT

When visiting sites the auditor will be entering someone else's domain. The contractor is responsible for activities on the site and is obliged to conform to all manner of health and safety requirements. Therefore, the auditor should follow the direction of the contractor and others on the site, and not wander about or disregard the obvious dangers of plant, machinery, and physical hazards.

The auditor should ideally have a prior understanding of the formal roles and relationships that apply to the type of site he is to visit. This will not only ensure that he directs his questions to the appropriate person, but also avoid generally wasting other people's time. If the auditor detects any problems or shortcomings during the site visit, he or she should take care in determining who to discuss them with at the time. Some of the matters revealed may be out-with the responsibility of those at the site. If the maintenance of site visitor records is a recognised administrative requirement, ensure that details of your visit are duly recorded.

COMMON CONCERNS ABOUT VISITS

From an auditor's point of view, there can be real concern that their level of knowledge and understanding will be sufficient to cope with the site visit without the possibility of being misled by the professionals or technicians involved. Personal credibility is a two-way phenomenon, and the auditors may also be understandably concerned about the image they project and the way in which their contribution is viewed. Where the audit work involves the examination of specialist areas, it is obviously critical that the auditor's observations and conclusions are accurate and in context.

Adequate and appropriate preparation can partly address some of these concerns. In certain situations the absence of specialist knowledge can be viewed as an advantage, as the auditor will be likely to ask the sort of fundamental questions that would not ordinarily occur to others who are well versed in the subject. This type of inquisitive approach can demonstrate a basic interest in the subject and a commitment to gaining a suitable, and accurate degree of understanding.

The option to employ audit staff with the requisite backgrounds is not always economic or practical. Although such staff will be able to exhibit the necessary knowledge and be able to interact confidently with auditees, they are likely to be few and far between if their main interest is a career in the relevant discipline rather than in auditing. An employer would also have to weigh the advantages of specific knowledge against the level of relative activity in the organisation and the associated recruitment and employment costs.

From the professional's point of view, the concerns about audit visits are more likely related to the effectiveness of the audit coverage and degree of understanding. A great deal depends on the general views held about audit involvement. The joint statements issued by CIPFA and the construction-related professional bodies define a basis for the appropriate interactions, but outside of the public sector such mutual recognition is not generally formalised. In the interests of mutual respect and understanding, it may be relevant for the auditor (or his manager) to take the time to explain the context of the audit involvement in the project to the affected parties. This approach may serve to clarify the areas of concern for all parties and also to establish a foundation for a positive and constructive relationship.

AREAS TO REVIEW

The following subjects represent the areas that may be relevant for auditors to review during site visits. Not all the aspects noted will be relevant in every situation and/or contract, and readers can select the factors that are germane to their own environment. There is an intentional bias towards comments which are specific to the construction site scenario. In order to avoid duplicated content, where other chapters address the details of a particular subject a suitable cross-reference is provided, otherwise brief guidance on the subject is noted. A recurring requirement, which is not explicitly mentioned in every case, is the need for comprehensive site-level documentation supporting the key issues. This is especially true where judgements or decisions are concerned, as the full details and rationale need to be recorded in support of actions taken so that subsequent review can be effective.

Site and project management
(*see also* Chapter 8)

The allocation of responsibilities and the issue of clearly defined operational mandates will contribute to the success of a project. This is especially true when the relationships are outwith the organisation, and there may be a degree of unfamiliarity. Combinations of contractual conditions and recognised professional protocols may further assist in the clear definition and division of responsibilities.

Communication is a key issue, and appropriate lines of communication will need to be established, and further supported by defined requirements for reporting and meetings. Matters of communication and information flow apply with equal importance to those within the project team and more generally to contractor and employer management. It will be necessary to define the required information flows for the employer.

Formal methods of project management may be in place with identified milestones and dependencies. The use of such methods requires the allocation of overall co-ordination to a specific individual such as the project manager, usually representing the employer.

General and accounting information
(*see also* Chapter 18)

This section is intended to include all management information relevant to the project which should reflect the progress being achieved against that planned and the financial status of the project. All such information should be accurate, complete, up to date, relevant, and enable all parties to plan and take actions to ensure the completion of project on time and within budget.

The explicit types of records will differ between project types, contract requirements and the professional environment. Additionally not all the forms of reporting will be generated at the site, but may be based upon source data gleaned from site records. General progress reporting may be based upon project management programmes which plot activities against a required time base or on simple progress charts. The activities of employees, tradesmen and subcontractors may be recorded on various time-related records. In reviewing management information systems, auditors should ensure that arrangements for distributing all manner of documents are adequate.

General adequacy and security of records

As stated in the previous section, all manner of records may be necessary to ensure that the project is adequately documented and accurately supported. Responsibilities for completing and maintaining all the relevant records should be clearly allocated, and supported by documented procedures, instructions or requirements. The nature and form of administrative requirements may be supported in some part by the contract conditions. However, the overall form of administration should be agreed and documented between employer and contractor prior to the contract period.

Other sections in this chapter feature specific forms of documentation and records, some of which are either required by certain forms of contract or are required and promoted by the relevant professional bodies. All such forms should be appropriately and accurately completed and maintained in accordance with defined requirements.

The project information contained in site-level records will be crucial to the smooth running of the contract for all parties. Therefore due consideration will need to be given to matters of filing and security of documents. Physical security and access arrangements should aim to prevent the loss, damage, destruction and leakage of documents and records. The off-site storage of copies will provide added assurance. Records and information may also be held on computer systems, and additional precautions will be necessary in order to ensure that data is backed up, subject to access controls and generally protected from loss, corruption or misuse.

Where records or information are either confidential or commercially sensitive, additional measures should be in place to ensure that the copying, distribution and filing arrangements are secure. Consider what the fall-back arrangements are in the event of a problem, such as a fire in the site office which destroys all or part of the relevant records.

Measurement and valuation of work
(*see also* Chapter 22)

In the construction context, monthly valuations based upon specified systems of measurement are normally submitted by the contractor. These valuations should be examined and certified as correct by either the architect, engineer or other supervising professional.

A contract-defined timetable is normally established for submitting, reviewing, amending, certifying, and forwarding interim valuations to employers for payment. Examination of interim monthly valuations has traditionally been an audit preoccupation. The valuation will normally include all work completed to date, and the amount claimed will be that after deduction of previous payments made by the employer.

All such interim valuations should be supported by the appropriate certificate, summaries and bills of quantity, details of any variations, claims, price fluctuation calculations, invoices from suppliers and nominated sub-contractors, and details of materials held on site, where these elements are relevant. Lower-level supporting documentation, such as daywork records, should be appropriately organised and referenced to the relevant valuation. The valuation should have been subject to arithmetic examination and confirmation of the prices and rates applied before submission to the employer for payment. Account should be taken, where appropriate, of retention calculations.

Labour-related records

The contractor may be obliged to maintain accurate and detailed records of his various employees who are engaged in the project. These are especially important if they are to form the basis of subsequent charges to the contract client for areas of work on the project or development. Examples are tasks to be charged as dayworks or to support the subsequent invoices submitted by sub-contractors. In a non-construction context an example of such records may relate to service staff undertaking field calls on behalf of the client, where the auditor may wish to verify the contractor's records against the organisation's own activity details.

The type and level of detail to be recorded will vary, but may include cross-references to specific tasks, the number of hours worked, details of any idle time perhaps occasioned by inclement weather, the standard or nationally agreed rate of pay, etc. The auditor will seek reassurance that the details are relevant and correct, and that the records are up to date.

The auditor will be interested in who compiles the records, and whether they are either authorised or checked for accuracy. Responsibilities for compiling records should be clearly allocated, and appropriate precautions taken to prevent the records from tampering or loss. The records may form the basis for subsequent analysis before being converted into invoices and accounts. The accuracy and completeness of the source and target records may have to be confirmed.

Where the contractor submits a contractual claim (if this permitted in the conditions of contract), he is usually obliged to maintain detailed supporting records which substantiate his claim. For example, he may have to prove that an event beyond his control resulted in additional workload, therefore he should be able to support his case with appropriate records.

Materials and goods
(*see also* Chapter 21)

The ordering, receipt, usage, movement, storage and security of all materials and goods should be subject to effective controls. One aim should be to procure only those items authorised as required for the project at the appropriate price and at the appropriate time. Additionally, the technical specification and quality of materials should be subject to checking before they are accepted.

Records of all movements and holdings of stock should be accurately maintained and subject to frequent verification. Stocks should be protected from damage, theft, deterioration and pilferage. Charges for materials and goods used in the project will need to be authorised and checked for correct calculation, and so on.

Variations to the contract
(*see also* Chapter 24)

Instructions to the contractor to undertake work which is either outwith the contract or necessary due to the conditions encountered, should only be given by the engineer, architect or their representatives. The site records should include all such variation orders, including confirmations of those initially given verbally.

In issuing instructions, it is important to ensure that the method of valuation should be clearly specified so that subsequent contractor's accounts can be verified. A record of the financial implications of all the active variation orders should be available, and the details reported to the employer.

The auditor will be interested in confirming that all variation orders are accounted for, properly completed, in accord with the relevant conditions of contract, and issued by an authorised person. The actual work conducted on variations should be suitably identified on the appropriate records, for example the dayworks or plant usage records.

Extensions of time
(*see also* Chapter 25)

Contracts may specify that extensions of time can be granted as the result of either an initial claim made by the contractor or at the determination of the engineer or architect. In either event, the need for such extensions should be fully reasoned, supported by evidence of the necessity for the extension and sanctioned by the supervising professional. Extensions of time relate to the reassessment of the defined completion date. However, not all extensions automatically equate to additional cost claims being allowed.

Contractual claims
(*see also* Chapter 26)

The principal concerns for the auditor will include ensuring that claims conform to the appropriate contractual conditions, the required notification, acknowledgement and documentation processes have been followed, the claims have been examined and validated by the engineer or architect, and that all relevant records are maintained. The architect or engineer is required to examine the claim and decide whether it is valid or not, both under the terms of the contract and in light of the evidence available. The contractor should supply full supporting details to enable the claim to be effectively appraised; this is especially important with respect to the calculation of the value of the claim.

Records should ideally indicate the status of each claim and the details of relevant accounts submitted and payments made to date. The employer should be kept informed of all claims on a regular basis.

Contract price fluctuations
(*see also* Chapter 23)

The formulae for calculating price fluctuations will vary between sectors. Standard forms of contract will often incorporate the appropriate industry form of calculation. The auditor will want to confirm that the correct formula has been accurately used in accordance with the contract conditions.

Responsibility should be allocated for applying and verifying the calculations. Where the formula is applied using nationally published factors and indices, use of the appropriate data should be confirmed. Full supporting documentation should be available.

Site equipment and plant
(*see also* Chapter 21)

The principal concerns here are that all the relevant equipment is recorded, capable of identification, and that charges for hire and use can be substantiated.

Sub-contracting considerations
(*see also* Chapter 20)

The contractor will need to maintain records reflecting the activities undertaken by sub-contractors. This is especially important where the relevant costs are to be passed on to the employer.

Part II

MANAGEMENT ENVIRONMENT AND PRE-CONTRACT PROCESSES

7

CONTRACT MANAGEMENT ENVIRONMENT

Scope

The need for a co-ordinated approach to contract management is argued in this chapter. In addition to exploring a number of possible procedural requirements, the role of internal audit is also examined.

In approaching any system where there are significant inherent risks, there is a natural propensity to view the mechanism negatively in terms of what can go wrong. This is of course the traditional orientation of the auditor. In the application of a contracted solution, the employer may be seeking a certain and secure solution to a particular problem or requirement. In selecting the contractor and the form of contract, the employer may be aiming to reduce or remove the relative uncertainties. In practice the processes and dependencies can be so complex as to make the complete neutralisation of risk an impossibility, and all parties should be aware of this truth. However, there are methods that can either reduce the chances of problems occurring or contain their effects.

Where an organisation is regularly or progressively involved in activities requiring contracts to be established, some form of co-ordinated administrative and procedural structure may need to be in place. This can serve the best interests of the organisation and ensure that all projects are well controlled and are completed on time, within budget, and to the necessary standard.

Where organisations are only occasionally involved in contracting matters, the establishment of a formal structure may be neither cost-effective nor justified. However, some control measures should be considered in such situations if all the benefits of the contracted activity are to be realised and all the pitfalls avoided.

In the public sector, where regular contract activity is generally more common, the establishment of a reliable relevant management framework may be subject to the regulatory requirements. For example, the Local Government Act (1972) obliges local authorities to put in place standing orders regarding contract procedures. As with any form of procedure, they need to be relevant, unambiguous, up to date, and effective, this latter condition being verified by adequate monitoring and review processes.

In any case it should be management's responsibility to establish a suitable and effective control environment, thus ensuring that projects are adequately controlled during their lifecycle. A key feature of this type of approach is a clearly defined process for formally approving the key stages of a project, supported with adequate documentary trails for monitoring purposes.

In this chapter we are less concerned with the explicit details of procedures, as these are dealt with in other specific chapters. Cross-references to the relevant chapters are noted. Our general emphasis is deliberately strategic in tone and relates more to the provision of an appropriate administrative and management framework which is capable of effectively handling the conduct of all contract-related activities. We shall identify the essential elements of such a framework and the associated requirements for adequate management involvement and commitment.

The degree to which internal procedures are formalised will partially depend upon the culture of the organisation, the nature of its prime activities, the general economic conditions and the management style. The scale and range of procedural arrangements will always need to be in proportion to the relative risks and the administrative overhead generated by the procedures and controls. The issues that we explore in this chapter may not all be relevant in every situation. Readers should appraise their own circumstances in relation to these matters and concentrate upon those with particular relevance. Auditors should always exercise a realistic sense of scale when considering recommendations for enhancing or updating procedures. The auditor will be concentrating upon the effectiveness of established measures and controls. These can be formally represented by official policies, written procedures, allocated responsibilities in job descriptions, and so on.

Before considering the elements which form the overall framework, we should consider the objectives of establishing a framework. Objectives will vary between operational sectors, but may include some or all of the following points, which are not listed in any priority:

- Ensure the standardisation of approach in all operating divisions/departments.
- Provide effective financial controls.
- Obtain the best value for money.
- Ensure that all payments to contractors are valid and authorised.
- Ensure that responsibilities are clearly defined and allocated.
- Ensure that only financially stable and competent contractors are engaged.
- Exercise technical quality control.
- Demonstrate accountability.
- Ensure that all the requirements are identified and documented.
- Ensure that the design stage cost-effectively addresses all the requirements.
- Provide a fair and equitable basis for selecting contractors.
- Ensure that the organisation is adequately protected in the event of the contractor defaulting.
- Ensure that the most appropriate form of contract is utilised.

- Ensure that all contractual claims are assessed and relevant damages are obtained.
- Ensure that all regulatory and statutory obligations are correctly addressed.
- Ensure that the optimum solution is selected.
- Ensure that all assets, plant and materials are protected and accounted for.
- Ensure that management information is accurate, relevant, complete and timely.
- Ensure that solutions satisfactorily address all the requirements.
- Ensure that the most cost-effective solution is adopted.
- Ensure that the strategic objectives of the organisation are appropriately met.
- Ensure that all projects are fully assessed for viability, etc.
- Ensure that all projects are justified and duly authorised.
- Promote appropriate best practice.
- Ensure that any delays or extensions of time are controlled.
- Ensure that the risks of fraud and malpractice are minimised.
- Ensure that projects are suitably staffed and resourced.
- Ensure that projects are well controlled and delivered on time to the required standard.
- Ensure that all subsequent changes and modifications are controlled and justified.
- Ensure that all stages are adequately and appropriately documented.
- Ensure that appropriate action is taken in cases of liquidation or bankruptcy.
- Ensure that projects are subject to post-completion review as a means to identify improvements for the future.

In taking account of the above objectives various forms of procedures and policies will be required. Noted below are some suggested elements which range from those concerned with the strategic direction of the organisation to lower-level mechanisms. However, in practice the form that they should take and the degree of detail required will be driven by specific circumstances. Accordingly not all the items listed will apply in every instance:

- The development and application of a corporate strategic plan, which should be used to trigger and justify projects in line with the requirements driving business development or the fulfilment of required service provisions. This form of plan should take a long-term view and aim to address those issues which are vital to the continued success of the organisation (irrespective of how this may be measured). Such planning should aim to maximise advantages, prioritise action plans, permit planning for change, enable resource planning, and so on.
- Establish clear statements or policies defining organisational responsibilities, spheres of influence, etc. These can be reinforced by suitably detailed job descriptions or personnel policies such as resource planning, and addressing training needs.
- Formulate a range of financial procedures (or regulations) which address the needs of justifying and authorising financial transactions. Additionally they should specify areas of responsibility for such authorities, the provision of

accurate and timely financial data, the provision of specialised assessment of the financial implications of various alternatives, checking the accuracy of accounts submitted and obtaining authority to pay, etc.

- Create procedures governing the identification, assessment and appraisal of potential projects, including determining all the requirements, examining all the possible options, and the identification of the optimum solution.
- Establish mechanisms for senior management review of the recommended solution and authorising the continuation of the project.
- Set in place procedures controlling the design process, ensuring that the identified requirements are correctly and cost-effectively addressed. (*see also* Chapter 11).
- Consider the use of formal project management processes with accountability, reporting requirements, monitoring of key stages and dependencies, and so on. It is crucial to ensure that all the requirements are addressed on time and within budget. The procedures should incorporate performance monitoring responsibilities. In the case of construction projects such procedures should incorporate provisions for dealing with valuing work for interim accounts, controlling claims, controlling variations to contracted requirements, etc. (Most of the discrete construction project elements mentioned here are separate chapters, however general project management is explored in Chapter 8.)
- Procedures for selecting the most suitable contractor, incorporating tendering procedures when applicable. (*See* Chapters 12, 13 and 14 which examine assessing contractors, maintaining approved lists of contractors, and tendering procedures respectively.)
- Procedures covering the review of the legal, insurance and bonding implications of contracts, such as selecting the most appropriate form, documentation requirements, etc. (*see also* Chapters 15, 16 and 17).
- Procedures relating to management information incorporating requirements to ensure that data is accurate, complete and timely (*see* Chapter 18).
- Security and safety procedures.

Whatever the procedural requirements are, they should include arrangements for adequate monitoring so that compliance can be confirmed. Additionally, they should not be allowed to stagnate, or there may be a danger that they will be regarded by staff and others as superfluous. Regular reviews of procedures will need to be undertaken if they are to remain relevant and in tune with both the organisation and the prevailing conditions.

Large or complex projects often suffer from the lack of clearly allocated responsibilities. The absence of a recognised responsibility structure can lead to confusion, wasted resources and costly delay. However, allocating responsibility is but one aspect of attempting to avoid such problems, for example there also needs to be devolved authority otherwise matters for agreement will continue to be referred upwards irrespective of their significance. Appointing a key representative or manager for a project is the usual solution and there are a number of established role examples in specific sectors, for instance the superintending officer in government contracts or the architect and engineer in the construction sector.

AUDIT ROLE AND RELATIONSHIPS

The role of the internal auditor has been seen to develop and expand in recent years, and this process is continuing. Greater degrees of professionalism are now apparent due, in part, to the work of the Institute of Internal Auditors, CIPFA and the various academic bodies who have developed higher education and degree level courses in auditing. It has been traditional to suggest that auditors comment upon compliance with existing management controls, and other procedures and policies. However, there is an underlying need to assess the basic appropriateness of those controls, procedures and policies in the prevailing commercial or service provision climate, and where necessary recommend appropriate and cost-effective improvements. In order to satisfactorily address this broader type of requirement, auditors need to ensure that they have a firm understanding of the underlying aspects of their relevant business or service sector.

In order to foster the development of constructive relationships, there is a need to ensure that staff, and particularly key management auditees, are aware of the role and objectives of auditors. In the public sector, CIPFA has consulted the relative professional bodies and developed a number of joint statements about the role of auditors and professionals involved in the contract management process, and these are as follows:

- joint statement by CIPFA/RICS on the roles of the quantity surveyor and auditor in building contracts for public authorities
- tripartite statement and practical guide by CIPFA/RICS/SCALA on the control of building projects. The role of professional officers in local government
- joint statement by CIPFA and ICE defining the respective functions of the engineer and the auditor
- joint statement by CIPFA and SCQSLG on performance bonding and the financial vetting of contractors
- joint statement of CIPFA and the NJCC for building retentions.

Additionally, the CIPFA statement on contract audit, which has been the subject of a recent review and is due for reissue in 1994, outlines the objectives for auditors involved in this area. This statement is reproduced (with the kind permission of CIPFA) as Appendix 5.

It is of paramount importance that the auditor does nothing which either impinges upon or prejudices the defined roles of professionals. The contractual and professional relationships are defined, and it is usual for engineers in particular to act in an impartial way between the contractor and the employer with responsibilities to both parties. For example the contractor will normally only take instructions on contractual matters from the engineer or his representative. The auditor should therefore route his findings to the organisation's management in the first instance, so that the proven and established communication processes can be applied without damaging the integrity of the fundamental contractual relationships.

With the possible exception of specific investigations into potential fraud or malpractice, it is beneficial to engender a fairly open and constructive audit approach. This not only establishes a rapport with the affected staff or officers, but creates a positive audit image which will hopefully optimise the communication process with auditees. However, it is paramount that an auditor's independence and objectivity are maintained when reviewing systems and contracts.Therefore it is necessary that he or she does not become an active part of any management control mechanism, or is viewed as a 'longstop' by management who otherwise may abdicate their own responsibilities for control matters.

The requirements for public sector audit services are documented in existing regulations, but the private sector is more open to localised interpretation, although the influence of the Institute of Internal Auditors in the development of suitable standards is acknowledged. Audit staff operating in the private sector, especially where they are either viewed as 'expendable' in times of crisis or very tightly provisioned, may have to operate in a more fluid procedural environment. The promotion of good public sector audit practices is championed in the UK by CIPFA, but local arrangements are potentially affected by the establishment of financial regulations and policies.

Corporate held attitudes towards audit credibility (whether they are justified or not), actions taken on audit recommendations and the general reaction to audit plans are all barometers of the position held by audit in the great scheme of things. Of course there are many things auditors can do to improve their image, but the way in which the organisation views the audit function can often affect the motivation and professionalism of individual auditors. In the private sector, auditors have become more proactive and are abandoning their purely compliance-related role to become more directed by the prevailing and significant corporate objectives as a means of raising their profile in a constructive light. Accordingly it will be necessary for the auditor to maintain an awareness of the broader company strategic objectives and the direction supported by contract activities. A reliable channel of communication will also need to be established so as to ensure that all contract activity is identified at an early stage. An initial form of audit evaluation of the key issues associated with project proposals will also aid the identification of those representing greater risks where further audit work will be necessary.

Despite some of the difficulties concerned with the effective practice of internal audit, it is our view that auditors should be involved in assessing and reviewing the systems at all stages of contracts, from the initial feasibility stage through to the post-completion review. This statement suggests that formal procedures already exist in the auditor's organisation, whereas this may not be case in practice. Furthermore, relative risks at the various stages will dictate the amount of audit attention that it is prudent to apply. If auditors undertake the relevant investigations and can contribute credible, objective and positive points to management, then hopefully a suitable and cost-effective control environment can be subsequently developed.

Control matrix example

An example of an *Objective*-oriented matrix is provided as Table 7. Readers should refer to Chapter 32 for an explanation of the technique used to generate the matrix. The table uses *Scale* 30 which is described in Appendix 7. The situation represented by Table 7 relates to a large organisation, regularly involved in contracting activities and where accountability plays a significant procedural role.

Table 7 Contract Management Environment – Objectives

Overall Inherent Risk (Size) Score [5 is worst risk; 1 is best] = 2.80

A Ensure key business/service objectives cost-effectively met
B Ensure selection & approval of optimum and quality solution
C Identify & address all legal implications to limit exposure
D Ensure requirements are identified, justified & addressed
E Engage only financially stable & competent contractors
F Ensure risks are assessed & the most suitable contract used
G Ensure contracts are to time, within budget & to standard
H Define, allocate and monitor responsibilities & obligations
I Minimise the financial, operational & liability exposure
J Ensure adequate & skilled resources are made available
K Management data is accurate, appropriate, complete & timely

L Ensure regulatory & statutory requirements are correctly met
M Ensure subsequent design changes are costed & authorised
N Ensure delays & extensions of time are reported & minimised
O Ensure all contractual claims are controlled and resolved
P Leads to contract obligations are correctly & accordingly met
Q Ensure only correct & authorised contractor's a/cs are paid
R Ensure that all claims for damages due are pursued and paid
S Ensure that the risks of fraud & malpractice are minimised
T Ensure procedures are valid, effective, justified & current

Scale 30 (abridged)

6 = Strategically vital to the business or organisation
5 = Makes a contribution to business operations
4 = Contributes to reliability of data, records and information
(Contract auditing Objectives-orientated scale)

3 = Avoids disruption/meets regulatory & accountability needs
2 = Leads to administrative/operational economies/efficiencies
1 = Generates administrative economies

Contract Management Environment		OBJECTIVES																			
		A	B	C	D	E	F	G	H	I	J	K	L	M	N	O	P	Q	R	S	T
Calculated Risk Score:	Risk	4	3	3	3	4	3	4	3	3	3	3	3	3	3	2	3	3	2	2	3
Scale 30 (6 is most serious)	Type	6	6	4	6	5	5	6	5	4	5	5	3	4	5	3	5	4	4	4	5
Size (3 is maximum)	Size	3	2	2	3	2	3	2	3	2	2	2	2	3	2	2	2	2	1	1	2
MEASURES																						
1 Strategic Plan identifies key objectives and the approved means of achieving same	Best		3	3																		
	Test	?	?	?																		
	Both																					
2 All projects/contracts are subject to full assessment and appraisal processes	Best		4	4	2	2																
	Test	?	?	?	?	?																
	Both																					
3 All projects are subject to management approval per Board Minutes, etc.	Best		4																			
	Test	?	?																			
	Both																					
4 Design and evaluation processes examine all potential options & generate recommendation	Best		4	3																		
	Test	?	?	?																		
	Both																					
5 Contract Management Procedures are documented & in place. Training is provided as required.	Best		3	3	2	3	3	3	3	3		2	2	3	3							3
	Test	?	?	?	?	?	?	?	?	?		?	?	?	?							?
	Both																					
6 Legal Dept./Advisers undertake full review and issue report for management approval	Best			5			4			3			3									
	Test	?		?			?			?			?									
	Both																					
7 Negotiation/Tendering documents contain any relevant clause modifications or additions	Best			3			3			3												
	Test	?		?			?			?												
	Both																					
8 A formal process is applied to identify & justify all requirements and functionality	Best				5																	
	Test	?			?																	
	Both																					
9 Requirements specification is produced and agreed as the basis for contract	Best				5																	
	Test	?			?																	
	Both																					

Table 7 continued

#	Description		A	B	C	D	E	F	G	H	I	J	K	L	M	N	O	P	Q	R	S	T
			=	=	=	=	=	=	=	=	=	=	=	=	=	=	=	=	=	=	=	=
	Calculated Risk Score:	Risk	4	3	3	3	4	3	4	3	3	3	3	3	3	3	2	3	3	2	2	3
10	Formal selective tendering process is applied per documented procedures	Best					4															
		Test	?				?															
		Both																				
11	List of Approved Contractors is maintained and used for tendering	Best					4															
		Test	?				?															
		Both																				
12	Entry on to the Approved List is supported by financial and technical evaluations	Best					4															
		Test	?				?															
		Both																				
13	Insurance & bonding arrangements are systematically applied to counter risks and liabilities	Best								4												
		Test	?							?												
		Both																				
14	Risk Analysis exercise is conducted and measures in place are assessed/upgraded	Best						4		3												
		Test	?					?		?												
		Both																				
15	Only recognised Standard forms of Contract are utilised	Best		4				4	4						2	2						
		Test	?	?				?	?						?	?						
		Both																				
16	Project Management techniques are applied during life of the contract	Best				3			3	4												
		Test	?			?			?	?												
		Both																				
17	Financial data is provided throughout the project & monitored by appointed staff	Best							3		3		3		2							
		Test	?						?		?		?		?							
		Both																				
18	Delays or disruptions are identified and appropriately managed	Best							3							3						
		Test	?						?							?						
		Both																				
19	Quality control is applied by suitably qualified staff – noted faults are corrected	Best							4													
		Test	?						?													
		Both																				
20	Procedures & contract conditions define specific responsibilities and obligations	Best							4										3			
		Test	?						?										?			
		Both																				
21	Monthly management reports are generated, circulated and discussed at progress meetings	Best							2	3			3		3							
		Test	?						?	?			?		?							
		Both																				
22	All additional costs are authorised by the Contract Administrator and management	Best							3		3											
		Test	?						?		?											
		Both																				
23	Skill requirements are assessed prior to contract. Consultants are engaged as required.	Best							2				3									
		Test	?						?				?									
		Both																				

Table 7 continued

#	Item		A	B	C	D	E	F	G	H	I	J	K	L	M	N	O	P	Q	R	S	T
			=	=	=	=	=	=	=	=	=	=	=	=	=	=	=	=	=	=	=	=
	Calculated Risk Score:	Risk	4	3	3	3	4	3	4	3	3	3	3	3	3	2	3	3	3	2	2	3
24	Contractor's experience and resources are evaluated prior to the award of contract	Best					3				4											
		Test	?				?				?											
		Both																				
25	All management information is from reliable sources and reconciled before release	Best									3											
		Test	?								?											
		Both																				
26	Management information requirements are established prior to contract/project	Best									3											
		Test	?								?											
		Both																				
27	Management Information timetable circulated, agreed and monitored for performance	Best									3											
		Test	?								?											
		Both																				
28	Procedures cater for all prevailing regulatory and EC requirements	Best							3				3									
		Test	?						?				?									
		Both																				
29	Compliance with requirements is confirmed by the Legal Department on ongoing basis	Best											4				3					
		Test	?										?				?					
		Both																				
30	All subsequent changes are subject to review by Contract Administrator & approved	Best												4								
		Test	?											?								
		Both																				
31	All additional costs are thoroughly assessed and authorised by management	Best												3	2	3		3				
		Test	?											?	?	?		?				
		Both																				
32	Extensions of Time are agreed as necessary by the Contract Administrator	Best														4						
		Test	?													?						
		Both																				
33	All claims are fully reviewed and either rejected or approved for settlement	Best															4					
		Test	?														?					
		Both																				
34	All accounts are subject to review against Tender, contract or official work records	Best																	4			
		Test	?																?			
		Both																				
35	Accounts are authorised for payment per established mandate procedure	Best																	4			
		Test	?																?			
		Both																				
36	Accounts are adjusted if in error	Best																	3			
		Test	?																?			
		Both																				
37	All contract details are recorded as regards status and payments made, etc.	Best																	3			
		Test	?																?			
		Both																				

Table 7 continued

			A	B	C	D	E	F	G	H	I	J	K	L	M	N	O	P	Q	R	S	T
			=	=	=	=	=	=	=	=	=	=	=	=	=	=	=	=	=	=	=	=
	Calculated Risk Score:	Risk	4	3	3	3	4	3	4	3	3	3	3	3	3	3	2	3	3	2	2	3
			–	–	–	–	–	–	–	–	–	–	–	–	–	–	–	–	–	–	–	–
38	Damages are recorded, assessed and pursued by the Legal Dept.	Best																		4		
		Test																		?		
		Both																				
			–	–	–	–	–	–	–	–	–	–	–	–	–	–	–	–	–	–	–	–
39	All key duties are subject to strict segregation and defined authority limits	Best																			5	
		Test																			?	
		Both																				
			–	–	–	–	–	–	–	–	–	–	–	–	–	–	–	–	–	–	–	–
40	All procedures are regularly reviewed & amended if necessary	Best																				4
		Test																				?
		Both																				
			–																				

A Ensure key business/service objectives cost-effectively met
B Ensure selection & approval of optimum and quality solution
C Identify & address all legal implications to limit exposure
D Ensure requirements are identified, justified & addressed
E Engage only financially stable & competent contractors
F Ensure risks are assessed & the most suitable contract used
G Ensure contracts are to time, within budget & to standard
H Define, allocate and monitor responsibilities & obligations
I Minimise the financial, operational & liability exposure
J Ensure adequate & skilled resources are made available
K Management data is accurate, appropriate, complete & timely

L Ensure regulatory & statutory requirements are correctly met
M Ensure subsequent design changes are costed & authorised
N Ensure delays & extensions of time are reported & minimised
O Ensure all contractual claims are controlled and resolved
P Ensure contract obligations are correctly & accordingly met
Q Ensure only correct & authorised contractor's a/cs are paid
R Ensure that all claims for damages due are pursued and paid
S Ensure that the risks of fraud & malpractice are minimised
T Ensure procedures are valid, effective, justified & current

Scale 30 (abridged)

6 = Strategically vital to the business or organisation
5 = Makes a contribution to business operations
4 = Contributes to reliability of data, records and information
(Contract auditing Objectives-orientated scale)

3 = Avoids disruption/meets regulatory & accountability needs
2 = Leads to administrative/operational economies/efficiencies
1 = Generates administrative economies

8

PROJECT MANAGEMENT FRAMEWORK

Scope

As a means of ensuring that projects, whether contract related or not, achieve their objectives, some form of management and/or administrative framework will need to be in place. The previous chapter examined the broader environmental considerations, and the following comments aim to more precisely focus upon the project-level management issues.

The principal aim of the project management approach should be to ensure that the project is completed on time, within budget and to the required standard. This somewhat simple statement disguises a considerable challenge when it is interfaced with the real world, with all the variables and unpredictable events that could apply.

Prior to the commencement of any significant project, either the Board or appropriate management committee should ensure that the appropriate administrative framework and resources are provided. This should include the establishment of adequate policies and procedures which should aim to contribute to the controlled and efficient conduct of the project.

OBJECTIVES OF PROJECT MANAGEMENT

Project management techniques should aim to ensure that:

- strategically significant factors, objectives and requirements are established and clearly communicated to the project team
- the nature of problem to be solved or the situation to be created is accurately determined and documented
- the project team is effectively managed by a nominated individual
- roles and responsibilities are clearly defined and allocated, so as to avoid duplication of effort and unnecessary wastage
- all the required functionality, design constraints, and user requirements are identified and provided on a cost-effective basis
- all possible solutions are considered and reviewed, and that the optimum solution is selected and applied
- all key stages, including proceeding with the recommended solution, are

appropriately authorised by management
- realistic and attainable targets are established, and matched to the resources made available
- the most appropriate form of contract is utilised, which both balances the risks and addresses the best interests of the organisation
- only suitable, financially stable, and technically competent contractors are engaged
- appropriate and sufficient resources are made available to the project, at the appropriate time
- the whole project is subject to staged planning and management
- all objectives are achieved
- risk is minimised or contained
- the contractor's performance is monitored in relation to his contractual obligations
- monitoring of progress, costs, problems, etc. is adequate and accurate
- management are kept suitably advised of project costs, progress, etc.
- project documentation is accurate, timely and complete;
- all the required channels of communication and interfaces are established and effective
- key events, milestones and all dependencies are identified and catered for (critical path analysis techniques may be applied to achieve these objectives)
- all timing issues are considered and planned for
- progress is monitored and managed in accord within both the required timetable, budgets, and technical constraints
- changes are minimised, and authorised where either proven necessary or unavoidable
- all disputes and contractual claims are fully investigated, authorised and resolved
- all accounts submitted by the contractor and any other suppliers are accurate, valid, within budget and authorised for payment
- all contract and other legal issues are reviewed, authorised and resolved in the context of the contract conditions.

A number of the above elements are addressed in greater detail in subsequent chapters as discrete subjects, but their treatment should form part of an integrated project-based method.

Although the contents of the above list are more naturally aligned to the employer's point of view, a number of the points could also apply to the contractor's involvement in a project. He too will need to be sure that his part in the project is suitably controlled and managed, especially if the required profit margins are to materialise. The contractor may also appoint a project manager to represent his interests and ensure that his contractual obligations are discharged with the minimum of dispute. There may be opportunities for further work with this employer and the smooth, professional and trouble-free conduct of the project may have an influence on the placing of such additional work.

All significant projects (whether in the private or public sector) should have a sponsor or client/user department. A senior member of the initiating department should be given the responsibility for representing their views, ensuring that the necessary functionality and requirements are appropriately identified and reflected in the specifications, and possibly even acting as the project manager.

It is not uncommon for projects to be brought to life under the pressure of time, especially where there may be either pressing business considerations or time limits, for example related to obtaining tax or other financial advantages. Initiating and proceeding too rapidly with projects has attendant dangers. This is particularly true of the earlier stages, such as identifying the specification and design, which are crucial and can, if inappropriately determined, generate subsequent problems with increased costs and delays. The old adage about the costs of rectifying problems increasing disproportionately the further the project progresses is true. All the preparations and assessments should be thoroughly, accurately, and proficiently undertaken so as to minimise the potential for future problems. The aim should be to improve the accuracy and precision of the cost estimates, and reduce the tolerance for errors, as the project progresses.

All relevant matters should be reviewed, considered and planned for. For example, projects with international implications should take prior account of language considerations, local business practices, necessary permits and regulations, and so on. In the international project context, the selection of a suitable contractor is even more critical, as the lines of communication may be longer or indirect, and the local requirements and conditions generally unfamiliar.

THE PROJECT MANAGER AND HIS TEAM

The client should appoint a suitably experienced and skilled member of staff as the project manager, and empower him or her with the relevant responsibilities for co-ordinating the project, ensuring that the cost and time targets are achieved, and that the required functionality and quality factors are correctly addressed. Overall project briefs should be issued. Where necessary the requirements of any relevant legislation and policy should also be taken into account.

The project manager will ideally be totally integrated with the organisation's objectives, and it is preferable that this appointment is made at the earliest opportunity so that he or she can effectively contribute to the direction and strategy of the project, and not just inherit a truncated view of the requirements. Additionally the project manager, and other key members of the project team, should also be appointed for the duration of the project as changes of personnel can be disruptive. The project manager will need to be well versed in the organisation's procedures and the conditions, scope and constraints represented by the contract, and if the project is to be effectively and efficiently managed in accordance with the contract, the appointee must be capable of interpreting its meaning in the context of everyday situations.

The success (or otherwise) of a project is normally directly linked to the calibre of the project team. In selecting team members, due consideration should be given to matters of experience and skill. Where necessary suitable training should be provided in good time.

The physical location or normal operating base of the project manager should be carefully considered during the project. For example there is little merit in a permanent location at the London head office, if all the action is taking place on a site three hundred miles away. The nature of the project will to some extent dictate the optimum location for the project manager and the project team. This is compounded by the level of active contribution and input that is required by the employer's representative. Face-to-face involvement or representation at project meetings can be the most effective way of ensuring results in the appropriate circumstances.

HUMAN FACTORS

Where projects necessarily involve or implicate a number of departments or functions, there is a greater probability of procrastination, inappropriate decision making, and so on. Lines of communication can become unworkable and complex, and may have an influence on the overall project timetable and the achievement of the established deadlines. All interactions need to be co-ordinated, concise and accurate. Meetings, in particular, can be become unwieldy affairs and need strong chairmanship if they are to be effective organs of direction, decision and action. Effective and constructive communication between the affected parties throughout the course of the project is essential. In order to be effective, meetings should be planned in advance with a clear agenda. Regular or recurring topics such as the financial performance of the project should be supported by accurate and consistent data.

Senior management should clearly demonstrate their commitment for projects, and generate the required motivation. Matters of management style may also have a bearing upon the morale of any affected staff, especially where the project is linked to change. The successful achievement of corporate objectives can be directly affected by management's inherent attitudes to change.

The effectiveness of any contribution to the project can be adversely affected if the project manager or any other members of the team, continue to have significant responsibilities outwith the project. This situation obviously depends on the scale of the project and the nature of the role normally performed by the individual, but where the project has a notable significance for the organisation, timing or availability conflicts can have a dramatic impact upon progress and effectiveness. The initial setting of unrealistic performance targets or expectations can, in addition to leading to disappointment when they are not achieved, affect team morale when goals are either significantly or continually missed. All the team spirit can evaporate when initial optimism turns into pessimism.

In the public sector, the role of suitably skilled and experienced technical staff is often crucial. Matters of quality, technical ability, and professionalism are usually paramount if the desired goals are to be attained. It is often necessary for such specialist staff to be aware of their wider responsibilities for controlling the destiny of projects, and in this context the appropriate professional bodies are active in promoting the required levels of awareness and best practice.

Control matrix example

Table 8 reflects a mid-range significance contract situation in a relatively well-organised and control-conscious company. The matrix is *Objectives*-oriented and uses *Scale* 30, which is described in Appendix 7. Chapter 32 provides full details of the theory underlying the matrix approach.

Table 8 Project Management Framework – Objectives

Overall Inherent Risk (Size) Score [5 is worst risk; 1 is best] = 2.35

A Ensure corporate objectives are communicated & addressed
B Ensure project is on time, within budget & to standard
C Ensure requirements & targets are identified and addressed
D Ensure roles and responsibilities are defined and allocated
E Ensure that appropriate & adequate resources are provided
F Ensure progress, costs & problems are monitored & reacted to
G Ensure that exposure to risk is controlled and minimised
H Ensure that all the contractor's obligations are met
I Provide effective means of communication with all parties

J Provide accurate & reliable management information
K Ensure problems, disputes & delays are promptly resolved
L Control and contain the extent of additional costs
M Exercise control over extensions of time & design changes
N Ensure the correct interpretation & application of contract
O Control and minimise the extent of contractual claims
P Ensure all regulatory & statutory requirements are observed
Q Ensure that quality standards are monitored and achieved
R Ensure accuracy of all accounts prior to authorised payment
S Ensure that established policies and procedures are applied
T Ensure project activity is accurately documented & trailed

Scale 30 (abridged)

6 = Strategically vital to the business or organisation
5 = Makes a contribution to business operations
4 = Contributes to reliability of data, records and information
(Contract auditing Objectives-oriented scale)

3 = Avoids disruption/meets regulatory & accountability needs
2 = Leads to administrative/operational economies/efficiencies
1 = Generates administrative economies

Project Management Framework		A	B	C	D	E	F	G	H	I	J	K	L	M	N	O	P	Q	R	S	T
		=	=	=	=	=	=	=	=	=	=	=	=	=	=	=	=	=	=	=	=
Calculated Risk Score:	Risk	3	3	3	3	3	3	3	3	2	3	3	2	3	2	2	2	2	3	2	2
Scale 30 (6 is most serious)	Type	6	6	5	5	5	5	5	4	5	5	5	4	4	4	5	3	3	6	4	5
Size (3 is maximum)	Size	2	2	2	2	2	2	2	2	1	2	2	1	2	1	2	2	1	2	1	2
MEASURES																					
1. Strategic issues and factors are documented and provided to the project team as a brief	Best		5		3																
	Test	?	?		?																
	Both																				
2. Formal Project management methods are applied per documented procedures	Best		3	4	3	2		2				2									
	Test	?	?	?	?	?		?				?									
	Both																				
3. Time targets, Cost budgets established for project as output of appraisal & design	Best		2	4	4			2													
	Test	?	?	?	?			?													
	Both																				
4. All elements are planned against defined and realistic deadlines & dependencies	Best			4	4			3				3		2							
	Test	?		?	?			?				?		?							
	Both																				
5. Tender and contract documents contain the key factors and requirements	Best		2		3				4												
	Test	?	?		?				?												
	Both																				
6. PC-based system records progress on identified stages & reports shortfalls, etc.	Best			4	3		2	3			3	3									
	Test	?		?	?		?	?			?	?									
	Both																				
7. Quality of work is inspected and signed off by a nominated individual	Best			3				3										4			
	Test	?		?				?										?			
	Both																				
8. Project Manager responsible for monitoring progress and responding to problems & delays	Best			3	3	2	2	4		2		2			2						
	Test	?		?	?	?	?	?		?		?			?						
	Both																				
9. Project Team formed. All responsibilities defined in writing and allocated to team	Best				4			2													
	Test	?			?			?													
	Both																				

Table 8 continued

			A	B	C	D	E	F	G	H	I	J	K	L	M	N	O	P	Q	R	S	T
			=	=	=	=	=	=	=	=	=	=	=	=	=	=	=	=	=	=	=	=
Calculated Risk Score:	Risk		3	3	3	3	3	3	3	3	2	3	3	2	3	2	2	2	2	3	2	2
10 Weekly Team meetings (including Contractor) to review progress, budgets, solutions, etc.	Best						3																
	Test	?					?																
	Both																						
11 Prior assessment of skill and resource requirements – Staff identified and provided	Best			4	2		3			3													
	Test	?		?	?		?			?													
	Both																						
12 Training needs addressed prior to contract. Specialist advice obtained for known areas	Best			3			2			2													
	Test	?		?			?			?													
	Both																						
13 Resource planning controlled by Deputy Project Manager using PO-based system	Best						3			3	2												
	Test	?					?			?	?												
	Both																						
14 Costs in excess of budget are reported from Financial Accounts system on monthly basis	Best								4							3							
	Test	?							?							?							
	Both																						
15 All potential additional costs are approved by management	Best								4														
	Test	?							?														
	Both																						
16 Management kept informed of progress, costs, problems, etc. via weekly summary reports	Best			3	3					3					3		3						
	Test	?		?	?					?					?		?						
	Both																						
17 Contract conditions reviewed and progress, costs, problems, etc. via weekly summary reports	Best			2						3			2		2	3		2					
	Test	?		?						?			?		?	?		?					
	Both																						
18 Relevant insurance cover in place. Performance Bonds obtained for main contractor	Best								2	3													
	Test	?							?	?													
	Both																						
19 Each defined stage of work is examined and signed off against specification & contract	Best								2	3													
	Test	?							?	?													
	Both																						
20 Shortcomings, etc. are documented and referred to contractor for rectification per contract	Best									2	4												
	Test	?								?	?												
	Both																						
21 Either Liquidated damages or other recompense sought in the event of contractor default	Best						3					3	3	3		3							
	Test	?					?					?	?	?		?							
	Both																						
22 Ongoing communication between project manager, Contractor, Users & technical staff	Best														3								
	Test	?													?								
	Both																						
23 All management data checked for accuracy and reconciled before release	Best														3								
	Test	?													?								
	Both																						

Table 8 continued

		A	B	C	D	E	F	G	H	I	J	K	L	M	N	O	P	Q	R	S	T
		=	=	=	=	=	=	=	=	=	=	=	=	=	=	=	=	=	=	=	=
Calculated Risk Score:	Risk	3	3	3	3	3	3	3	3	2	3	3	2	3	2	2	2	2	3	2	2
24 All delays, claims, extensions of time are analysed for cost implications & reported	Best						3					3	3	3		3					
	Test	?					?					?	?	?		?					
	Both																				
25 Extensions of Time only granted after investigation & approval by management	Best												3								
	Test	?											?								
	Both																				
26 Any required design changes are sanctioned by the relevant technical officer	Best												3								
	Test	?											?								
	Both																				
27 Initial design process is comprehensive so as to minimise the need for subsequent changes	Best												3								
	Test	?											?								
	Both																				
28 Legal Dept. opinion sought if required to interpret or resolve contract conditions	Best							2							4	3					
	Test	?						?							?	?					
	Both																				
29 Project manager is responsible for ensuring & signifying satisfaction of conditions	Best														3						
	Test	?													?						
	Both																				
30 Aim to amicably settle claims after assessment and approval	Best															3					
	Test	?														?					
	Both																				
31 Contractor is responsible for Health & Safety matters	Best															3					
	Test	?														?					
	Both																				
32 Legal Dept. monitors any legal implications and refers matters to relevant manager for action	Best															3					
	Test	?														?					
	Both																				
33 Any faults/shortcomings in workmanship or materials are noted & referred to contractor	Best																5				
	Test	?															?				
	Both																				

A Ensure corporate objectives are communicated & addressed
B Ensure project is on time, within budget & to standard
C Ensure requirements & targets are identified and addressed
D Ensure roles and responsibilities are defined and allocated
E Ensure that appropriate & adequate resources are provided
F Ensure progress, costs & problems are monitored & reacted to
G Ensure that exposure to risk is controlled and minimised
H Ensure that all the contractor's obligations are met
I Provide effective means of communication with all parties

J Provide accurate & reliable management information
K Ensure problems, disputes & delays are promptly resolved
L Control and contain the extent of additional costs
M Exercise control over extensions of time & design changes
N Ensure the correct interpretation & application of contract
O Control and minimise the extent of contractual claims
P Ensure all regulatory & statutory requirements are observed
Q Ensure that quality standards are monitored and achieved
R Ensure accuracy of all accounts prior to authorised payment
S Ensure that established policies and procedures are applied
T Ensure project activity is accurately documented & trailed

Scale 30 (abridged)

6 = Strategically vital to the business or organisation
5 = Makes a contribution to business operations
4 = Contributes to reliability of data, records and information
(Contract auditing Objectives-oriented scale)

3 = Avoids disruption/meets regulatory & accountability needs
2 = Leads to administrative/operational economies/efficiencies
1 = Generates administrative economies

Table 8 continued

				A	B	C	D	E	F	G	H	I	J	K	L	M	N	O	P	Q	R	S	T
				=	=	=	=	=	=	=	=	=	=	=	=	=	=	=	=	=	=	=	=
	Calculated Risk Score:	Risk		3	3	3	3	3	3	3	3	2	3	3	2	3	2	2	2	2	3	2	2
			−	−	−	−	−	−	−	−	−	−	−	−	−	−	−	−	−	−	−	−	−
34	All account and invoices are examined for relevance and accuracy prior to authorisation	Best																			4		
		Test	?																		?		
		Both																					
			−	−	−	−	−	−	−	−	−	−	−	−	−	−	−	−	−	−	−	−	−
35	Accounts are checked to defined rates and terms in Contract prior to payment	Best																			4		
		Test	?																		?		
		Both																					
			−	−	−	−	−	−	−	−	−	−	−	−	−	−	−	−	−	−	−	−	−
36	Corporate policies & procedures are in place. Compliance is monitored by Project Manager	Best																				5	
		Test	?																			?	
		Both																					
			−	−	−	−	−	−	−	−	−	−	−	−	−	−	−	−	−	−	−	−	−
37	Existing procedures & contract define the documentary requirements for main activities	Best																					4
		Test	?																				?
		Both																					
			−	−	−	−	−	−	−	−	−	−	−	−	−	−	−	−	−	−	−	−	−
38	Document and information trail is in place	Best																					4
		Test	?																				?
		Both																					
			−																				

A Ensure corporate objectives are communicated & addressed
B Ensure project is on time, within budget & to standard
C Ensure requirements & targets are identified and addressed
D Ensure roles and responsibilities are defined and allocated
E Ensure that appropriate & adequate resources are provided
F Ensure progress, costs & problems are monitored & reacted to
G Ensure that exposure to risk is controlled and minimised
H Ensure that all the contractor's obligations are met
I Provide effective means of communication with all parties

J Provide accurate & reliable management information
K Ensure problems, disputes & delays are promptly resolved
L Control and contain the extent of additional costs
M Exercise control over extensions of time & design changes
N Ensure the correct interpretation & application of contract
O Control and minimise the extent of contractual claims
P Ensure all regulatory & statutory requirements are observed
Q Ensure that quality standards are monitored and achieved
R Ensure accuracy of all accounts prior to authorised payment
S Ensure that established policies and procedures are applied
T Ensure project activity is accurately documented & trailed

Scale 30 (abridged)

6 = Strategically vital to the business or organisation
5 = Makes a contribution to business operations
4 = Contributes to reliability of data, records and information
(Contract auditing Objectives-oriented scale)

3 = Avoids disruption/meets regulatory & accountability needs
2 = Leads to administrative/operational economies/efficiencies
1 = Generates administrative economies

9

PROJECT ASSESSMENT AND APPROVAL

Scope

This chapter examines the issues surrounding the appraisal of potential projects incorporating the justification for a project, comprehensive examination of the possible methods of addressing the identified needs, and the approved selection of the optimum solution. In the context of this book the term project is intended to relate to a broad range of activities and not just those relative to construction activities.

The project assessment or appraisal processes set the scene for all that follows. The principal objectives are to ensure that the project is justified (in commercial, operational and financial terms) and that the most suitable option is selected. Choosing an inappropriate solution can be costly, disruptive, lead to poor staff morale, directly affect customers or clients, and potentially damage the image and reputation of the organisation.

The need for a project or development may arise for a variety of reasons, for example:

- to exploit new business opportunities
- to improve business performance or maintain market position
- to conform with government or legislative requirements
- to fulfil service provision obligations
- as a means to improve efficiency or make savings.

It is necessary to set all projects in the context of the organisation and relative to its identified objectives and goals. In practice these events should be driven by an established strategic plan that specifies the critical elements for the business or service for several years into the future. Such plans should consider the likely internal and external forces that have a bearing on the operations, finances and legal framework, etc. of the organisation. Establishing a formal and documented strategic plan is an essential ingredient in ensuring the appropriate development of an organisation so that it can either meet its service obligations, remain competitive or successfully exploit new business opportunities.

It is vital that all significant projects are in accord with the aims and targets set by the strategic plan, and senior management should be assured that all project activity is justified in the context of the plan. This presupposes that there is a formal method of project appraisal and approval in place and that senior management are required to authorise all project activity.

In order to remain in touch with the direction of the organisation, the auditor should have access (directly or indirectly) to the top-level management process, and thereby be alerted to forthcoming project assessments, etc. A form of awareness is necessary if the audit department programme of work is to appropriately reflect the important aspects of the organisation and the associated systems and issues.

When triggering a project appraisal process, senior management should consider the merits of issuing a briefing document to the appraisal team. This should define the key objectives linked to the driving strategy or policy, and also set out the ground rules, procedures, timescales, cost and operational constraints, etc. for the project assessment team.

A formalised project assessment process is preferable as this should incorporate mechanisms for each logical stage, documenting and reporting standards, guidelines on representation, specific responsibilities, quality control considerations, and so on. However, the level of project (and related contract) activities within an organisation will normally drive whether or not a formal method is either justified or established. Such policies are more likely to exist on a formal basis in the public sector and may form part of any required standing orders or financial regulations. In any event, in actual situations such procedures may operate at two levels, the theory reflected in the documented procedures and as applied in practice where the dimension of human interpretation may be applicable. Simple management review responsibilities should be featured in the process so that compliance can be monitored and confirmed.

All activities in business, the public sector and indeed life can be said to have associated risks. There may be strong arguments for formally identifying and assessing the risks related to a project, not only in terms of it (or any other proposal) proceeding but also of failing to offer any form of solution. Some of the associated risks will be fixed in nature (i.e. the counteraction of physical limitations such as building on land subject to subsidence), others will be less tangible such as unforeseen changes in government policy and requirements which may be politically (and therefore potentially ethereally) motivated.

Considering the demands placed upon both the private and public sectors, it is likely that resources (both financial and physical) will always be outstripped by identified requirements, therefore it is probable that requirements will have to be prioritised in some way. This is especially true of the public sector where there may be strong pressure applied from central government to either reduce and contain expenditure in certain areas or to proceed with specific projects such as road improvements or other infrastructure development schemes.

An important consideration when deciding whether to proceed with a project may be the availability of grants or subsidies from local or central government. Such incentives may be available for either public or private sector activities, ranging from improving the local infrastructure to the encouragement of suitable developments in enterprise zones. All the required eligibility factors will have to be taken into account and there may be an administrative overhead associated with ensuring compliance with all the requirements and the maintenance of the required records. Procedures should be established to ensure compliance and that the organisation remains eligible for the relevant payment. Appropriate financial assessments will have to be undertaken, and eligibility for the scheme incorporating the amount payable confirmed in writing before proceeding with the project (*see also* Chapter 28 regarding taking account of grant and subsidy receipts during subsequent accounting processes).

The organisation may have established and developed internal policies which reflect the requirements of their strategies. Therefore, projects may have to satisfy the requirements of such policies in order to remain within the direction set by the long-term strategy.

In order to ensure that all projects are suitably examined, the organisation would ideally need to establish a formal project appraisal process which is subject to formal and documented procedures. This process should address the following elements, which are explored more fully in subsequent sections:

- Confirm the necessity of the project in commercial or service provision terms.
- Identify the objectives of the project.
- Identify the requirements and specification of the project.
- Ensure that all affected parties are involved and consulted.
- Identify all possible ways of achieving the objectives and requirements.
- Fully appraise all the implications (financial, operational, demographic, legal, etc.).
- Examine the identified options and select the optimum solution.
- Report upon the selected option and provide supporting data for this decision.
- Ensure that the project is authorised to proceed at senior level.

As stated above the need for a particular project should ideally flow from the direction established by the strategic plan, which for example may take the form of a five-year corporate plan. The need for a project may stem from the existence of a problem which requires to be solved or a new venture which has to be built up from scratch. In any event it is essential to accurately define the nature of the requirements and to quantify the various elements. This process should incorporate assessment of all the driving factors, such as demographic data, market analysis, legislation, statutory obligations, any relevant historical factors, etc. These constituent factors will, of course, vary considerably between sectors, organisations and indeed project types.

Authority to proceed with project appraisal should be formally given, perhaps by a senior management group, committee or board. Decisions to proceed to the appraisal stage should ideally be documented, perhaps in the form of meeting, committee or board minutes. The appraisal process will incur costs which will need to be identified and approval to proceed given in the context of the cost constraints relative to this stage of the process.

The nature of the problem or need should be fully documented as the basis for setting the context of offered solutions. If there is an existing system or facility which relates to the scenario, this will also need to be assessed and any strengths and weaknesses noted. There may be obvious time constraints relative to the scenario, and certain aspects may be time critical if the driving objectives are to be met. A recent public sector example is the development of operational Council Tax systems to replace the Community Charge. All time critical elements must be identified and examined in relation to the offered solutions and accurately carried forward into subsequent stages of the project. All the possible ways of addressing the problem should be examined and their advantages and disadvantages honestly considered. The implications of doing nothing should be included in this process.

In order to ensure that any subsequent project is progressed on a stable basis, it is critical that all the requirements are accurately identified. The nature of requirements will be dependent on the type of project, for example:

- functional (as for a building or IT system)
- physical (as for construction)
- operational
- performance (technical and time-measured)
- social
- environmental
- legal or other compliance aspects.

There may be design and quality standard aspects to take into account, especially in the construction and engineering environments. In order to ensure that all the relevant requirements are established, it will be necessary to involve representatives from all related departments and disciplines in the appraisal process. Most projects will have a natural sponsoring department or function and therefore it is essential that a senior representative is nominated from that area and is held responsible for ensuring that the appropriate functionality, etc. is clearly established. This can avoid any subsequent abdication of responsibility if the initial appraisal process was artificially or deliberately restricted.

In physical projects, such as building or civil engineering schemes, there will be design factors to establish and document, although at this stage they may be only outline in nature and require more detailed expansion at later stages. Additionally, legal aspects and land ownership matters may have to be identified, considered and fully assessed, thus involving specific areas of expertise.

Forming project appraisal teams can be a delicate balancing act in practice between ensuring that the needs are adequately and efficiently addressed, and avoiding overburdening the process with too many viewpoints or an excess of data with the result that the timescale is elongated and related costs are excessive. Representation in all project stages should take into account skill and knowledge requirements, and particular attention should be paid to the relevant seniority of representatives to reduce the undue necessity to refer decisions out-with the project management group whilst maintaining accountability. We do not intend to suggest an ideal mix as this would vary between organisational and project types; however representation of the user (or sponsoring) department and of the finance (or accounting) function is taken to be essential.

In fairly assessing projects the question of independence should be considered. In some commercial organisations a degree of independence is provided by the involvement of non-executive directors on review committees. A balance may have to be achieved between those with direct interest in the project and those who represent external viewpoints. The common principles of segregation of duties can be brought to bear on the formation of review committees if there needs to be a positive demonstration of objectivity and accountability.

All potential solutions should be examined in relation to the identified operational, physical, financial and other criteria. The effects and consequences of each option should be documented, including those applicable if nothing was done and the status quo applied. A number of key measures or critical factors are likely to arise and these can be useful when subsequently comparing the merits of competing solutions.

In the real world it is most likely that proposed projects will not be isolated from other activities and therefore have impacts on existing systems, operations and perhaps other ongoing projects or schemes. The effects of such impacts will need to be recognised and accurately assessed in a variety of contexts as part of the appraisal process, for example timing implications, affect on corporate cash flow, maintenance of service levels, operational disruption, and so on. Having identified the impacts, any offered solutions should include the measures and methods necessary to counteract or minimise the relevant implications.

Interproject implications can be of significant concern, especially where limited resources can be further stretched by the concurrent progression of related projects. Severe disruption and delay can occur unless adequate resources exist and are made available. Financial resources will undoubtedly play a fundamental role in any significant project. It is essential that senior members of the finance or accounting functions are actively involved in the project processes. In both the private and public sectors there are normally a number of financing options which could be applied to a project scenario, and given the often substantial sums involved, selecting an inappropriate method can be costly. Furthermore operational or government restrictions, for example over the application of capital receipts, may further limit the options available in specific instances. Assessment of the viable financial options should be undertaken by the appropriate professionals and their recommendations presented for authorisation. Deciding between internally or externally funding capital projects, and whether the necessary reserves or credit lines are available are all factors which will need to be addressed.

Assessing the cost-effectiveness of possible solutions will also be necessary including the comparison of all solutions on a common measurement basis. Project solutions should offer value for money. This is particular relevant in the public sector where both government emphasis and public watchfulness can influence decisions. Assessing the potential costs of a project, such as a building development, should be based not only on the up-front capital cost, but also incorporate ongoing running and maintenance costs. Specification limitations designed to reduce initial building costs may result in either increased operating costs or the need for more frequent maintenance.

As a means of assuring the integrity and reliability of the project appraisal process, it is necessary to ensure that all the base data, assumptions and analysis are accurate. Sources of such ingredients should be proven and reliable, especially when obtained externally (i.e. as for demographic data). All sources should be recorded and adequately trailed. Financial and statistical data which may have been subject to analysis and summarisation, should be suitably reconciled to source. Wide-ranging assumptions may have to be agreed by senior management before being applied in the appraisal context. The need for a reliable and effective documented trail for all project appraisal elements is self evident as it may be necessary to revisit working papers at later stages of the project.

Assumptions used throughout the appraisal process may represent significant issues, therefore it may prove necessary to seek the approval of senior management as to their accuracy before applying same. This may be especially true where the assumptions reflect measures of business effectiveness, etc. established as part of a strategic planning exercise. In the case of construction projects (and particularly in the public sector) it will be necessary to address various matters relevant to land, including ownership, acquisition, classification of use, planning permissions, clearance and preparation.

Certain categories of project (for example information technology or major constructions) will naturally generate the need for expert knowledge or advice. Adequate levels of related expertise may either already exist within the organisation or will need to be addressed externally. For example, a local authority may have access to in-house staff with the requisite experience to handle a building project, or may decide to engage specialist consultants if their own resources are either already fully committed or lack specific knowledge. The appraisal process should take account of all specialist requirements and review how they should be effectively and economically addressed. This latter process should identify the costs associated with acquiring the appropriate levels of expertise including those for providing any in-house training.

Where a project is likely to require the engagement of consultants, the project brief and requirements should provide all the essential details to enable them to discharge their responsibilities. However, the brief should also avoid situations where the consultant has too much leeway which could result in additional costs being incurred.

Projects may draw considerably upon the human resources of an organisation and therefore the likely needs should be identified (an example would be the involvement of the Direct Labour Organisation in a local authority construction project). Existing and proposed staffing levels should be taken into account together with existing workloads and demands which may impinge upon the proposed project in terms of timescale and the achievement of critical deadlines. It may prove necessary to involve the Personnel or Human Resource Departments so that the wider implications of either manpower or succession planning and their financial ramifications can be assessed.

Given the scope or significance of a proposed project a full feasibility study may prove to be necessary as either a precursor to the approval stages or as a product of their recommendations. As with project appraisal processes objectivity is a vital ingredient, and in order to reinforce this aspect the organisation may prefer to engage external consultants with the appropriate expertise to carry out the study. The engagement of consultants is addressed in more detail elsewhere (*see* Chapter 10), however is it important to ensure that they are issued with a sufficiently detailed brief and that cost, performance and timing criteria are clearly established for the study.

If the organisation is actively involved in projects or contracting, any relevant feedback gleaned from the review of previous projects should also be incorporated into the appraisal process as means of improving effectiveness. The activity of the appraisal team should be suitably and comprehensively documented throughout the process, partly to appropriately support their final decisions and partly to provide a trial for either new team members or management.

It is usual for a report to be issued by the appraisal team, this should incorporate the following elements:

- a summary of the problem or objective
- key requirements and specification
- key impacts, timing implications and other environmental factors
- brief details of all the options examined
- financial data for all the options
- a recommended option supported by an appropriately detailed rationale. *

The report is normally addressed to the relevant senior management group, board or committee for consideration. It not obligatory for them to accept the recommended solution and indeed they may request further details or research before making their decision. However, if they decide not to opt for the recommended option, they should justify and support their decision in writing.

Throughout the appraisal process, from the top level or strategic initiation through to the final report, there should be adequate and sufficiently detailed documentary trailing so that the auditor can be satisfied as to the effectiveness of the system in place. As a consequence of the system review, the auditor may be recommending procedural changes or improvements; these should be realistic, cost-effective, and relative to the potential risks or exposures.

---

* In some organisations it is the established role of senior management to select the option.

Control matrix example

The example matrix provided as Table 9 illustrates the key objectives for an organisation considering a project with medium-level significance. The points noted suggest a high level of control awareness with the intention of revealing an optimum project solution. Please note that although the relevant project may involve external contractors, matters relevant to their selection are not addressed in this example, as these aspects are covered in Chapters 12 to 14. However, it has been assumed that the feasibility study phase would incorporate a general review of the likely market for contract activity.

Chapter 32 describes how a matrix is constructed. Table 9, which is *Objectives*-oriented, utilises *Scale* 30, details of which are provided in Appendix 7.

Table 9 Project Assessment and Approval – Objectives
Overall Inherent Risk (Size) Score [5 is worst risk; 1 is best] = 2.38

A Ensure that strategic objectives & goals are addressed
B Ensure that business objective/service obligations are met
C Ensure all requirements, factors & limits are considered
D Ensure that the project is justified and feasible
E Ensure all the objectives are identified and communicated
F Ensure that all risks are analysed and planned for
G Ensure adequate user representation in assessment process
H Ensure that all options/solutions are fully examined
I Ensure all implications and impacts are taken into account

J Ensure all legal and regulatory requirements are addressed
K Ensure that the optimum solution is selected
L Ensure that funding requirements are accurately established
M Ensure all initial & ongoing costs are identified/assessed
N Ensure that project is appropriately authorised to proceed
O Ensure all factors are documented for subsequent action
P Ensure project resources are adequate & suitably skilled

Scale 30 (abridged)

6 = Strategically vital to the business or organisation
5 = Makes a contribution to business operations
4 = Contributes to reliability of data, records and information
(Contract auditing Objectives-oriented scale)

3 = Avoids disruption/meets regulatory & accountability needs
2 = Leads to administrative/operational economies/efficiencies
1 = Generates administrative economies

OBJECTIVES (columns A–P)

#	Project Assessment & Approval		=	A	B	C	D	E	F	G	H	I	J	K	L	M	N	O	P
				=	=	=	=	=	=	=	=	=	=	=	=	=	=	=	=
	Calculated Risk Score:	Risk		3	3	3	3	3	2	2	2	2	2	2	3	3	3	2	3
			–	–	–	–	–	–	–	–	–	–	–	–	–	–	–	–	–
	Scale 30 (6 is most serious)	Type		6	6	5	6	5	5	5	4	5	3	6	4	5	5	4	5
	Size (3 is maximum)	Size		2	2	2	2	2	1	1	1	1	2	1	2	2	2	1	2
	MEASURES	—	–	–	–	–	–	–	–	–	–	–	–	–	–	–	–	–	–
1	Strategic Plan used as the basis for all project initiation	Best		4	4														
		Test	?	?	?														
		Both																	
			–	–	–	–	–	–	–	–	–	–	–	–	–	–	–	–	–
2	Briefing document provided by the Board which identifies the key objectives	Best		4	4	3		4											
		Test	?	?	?	?		?											
		Both																	
			–	–	–	–	–	–	–	–	–	–	–	–	–	–	–	–	–
3	Financial limits, etc. are provided per document in Measure 2 above	Best				3													
		Test	?			?													
		Both																	
			–	–	–	–	–	–	–	–	–	–	–	–	–	–	–	–	–
4	Full requirements specification created and agreed at the outset	Best				4													
		Test	?			?													
		Both																	
			–	–	–	–	–	–	–	–	–	–	–	–	–	–	–	–	–
5	Feasibility study conducted and approved	Best					5												
		Test	?				?												
		Both																	
			–	–	–	–	–	–	–	–	–	–	–	–	–	–	–	–	–
6	All appropriate demographic, market and other data is obtained and analysed	Best						3											
		Test	?					?											
		Both																	
			–	–	–	–	–	–	–	–	–	–	–	–	–	–	–	–	–
7	Formal risk analysis of likely solutions is undertaken. Results included in final report	Best							4										
		Test	?						?										
		Both																	
			–	–	–	–	–	–	–	–	–	–	–	–	–	–	–	–	–
8	Key user representatives involved in all project stages	Best								5									
		Test	?							?									
		Both																	
			–	–	–	–	–	–	–	–	–	–	–	–	–	–	–	–	–
9	Research reveals all possible options. Each is fully examined and costed	Best									4								
		Test	?								?								
		Both																	
			–																	

Table 9 continued

			A	B	C	D	E	F	G	H	I	J	K	L	M	N	O	P
			=	=	=	=	=	=	=	=	=	=	=	=	=	=	=	=
	Calculated Risk Score:	Risk	3	3	3	3	3	2	2	2	2	2	2	3	3	3	2	3
10	All business & financial impacts and all related project dependencies are identified	Best						3		4								
		Test	?					?		?								
		Both																
11	Legal Dept. is responsible for assessing & reporting upon all statutory/regulatory matters	Best										5						
		Test	?									?						
		Both																
12	A consistent approach is applied to all possible solutions	Best								4	4		4					
		Test	?							?	?		?					
		Both																
13	A recommended solution is highlighted per Measure 12 above	Best											4					
		Test	?										?					
		Both																
14	A report is issued to management outlining the key factors and the recommended solution	Best											4					
		Test	?										?					
		Both																
15	Finance Dept. prepare a comprehensive analysis of all financial factors for reporting	Best												5				
		Test	?											?				
		Both																
16	Financial assessment includes all ongoing operating and maintenance costs	Best													5			
		Test	?												?			
		Both																
17	Recommendation is reviewed and authorised by the Board. Noted in Board minutes	Best														5		
		Test	?													?		
		Both																
18	All relevant data for selected option is documented for the subsequent project stages	Best															4	
		Test	?														?	
		Both																
19	Resource planning is undertaken as part of the appraisal process	Best																4
		Test	?															?
		Both																
20	Training requirements are identified and addressed	Best																4
		Test	?															?
		Both																

A Ensure that strategic objectives & goals are addressed
B Ensure that business objective/service obligations are met
C Ensure all requirements, factors & limits are considered
D Ensure that the project is justified and feasible
E Ensure all the objectives are identified and communicated
F Ensure that all risks are analysed and planned for
G Ensure adequate user representation in assessment process
H Ensure that all options/solutions are fully examined
I Ensure all implications and impacts are taken into account
J Ensure all legal and regulatory requirements are addressed
K Ensure that the optimum solution is selected
L Ensure that funding requirements are accurately established
M Ensure all initial & ongoing costs are identified/assessed
N Ensure that project is appropriately authorised to proceed
O Ensure all factors are documented for subsequent action
P Ensure project resources are adequate & suitably skilled

Scale 30 (abridged)

6 = Strategically vital to the business or organisation
5 = Makes a contribution to business operations
4 = Contributes to reliability of data, records and information
(Contract auditing Objectives-oriented scale)

3 = Avoids disruption/meets regulatory & accountability needs
2 = Leads to administrative/operational economies/efficiencies
1 = Generates administrative economies

10

ENGAGING,MONITORING AND PAYING CONSULTANTS

Scope

A requirement for a specialised skill may generate the need to engage a suitable consultant. Whether the consultant is playing either a transitory or ongoing and key role in a project, the employer will wish to ensure that competent advice is being obtained at the right price. This chapter suggests methods for selecting and engaging consultants with these objectives in mind.

In the context of this chapter, the term 'consultant' is also intended to encompass any form of expert or specialist with the appropriate skills required to address the requirements of any given project. Readers from the construction sector will already be aware of the usual type of professional advisers and contract administrators involved in their projects, but the following comments are aimed at factors common to all consultants and operational sectors.

In order to achieve the controlled completion of a project it may prove necessary to engage the service of consultants, experts or specialists. This very act of engagement may generate the need for a suitable form of contract to be established and in such instances it is possible that other subjects addressed in his book will become relevant (e.g. tendering processes or maintaining an approved list).

In recent times the term 'consultant' has become somewhat broad in meaning and is used very loosely throughout the business world to cover a variety of services. Apart from the major professions there have been some limited attempts to establish degrees of standardisation and recognition for certain sectors of the consultancy market. Anyone can be called a consultant and there are, as yet, very few reliable or accredited yardsticks to measure proficiency and competence. The limited number of representative groups that do exist are generally more associated with the networking of opportunities rather than the promotion of consistency and high standards. Outside of the large and established consultancy practices and outwith the auspices of the professional regulatory bodies who generally exercise tight control over the provision of relevant services, the principal of *caveat emptor* still applies.

An organisation may seek the services of consultants for a range of reasons, including:

- very specialist subject areas with limited expertise available
- limited need to address a short term skill requirement

- absence of in-house knowledge or practical experience
- shortage of requisite staff
- inability to recruit suitable staff in the required timescale
- time or economic constraints which prevent the suitable training of existing staff
- existing workload pressures which prevent the release of existing skilled employees
- the desire to avoid the high and long-term costs of employing or training own staff
- where external forces are dictating the timescales and employing external resources is only viable option
- the project is a one-off and the required skills are therefore transient
- to provide an objective and unbiased view of a situation
- to concur with prevailing policy on staffing given the projected long-term workload
- to avoid internal conflicts of interest.

As can be seen from the above list it is possible that the need to engage external consultants may stem from internal staffing policy issues. In practice these are likely to differ considerably between sectors and commercial environments, and in any event they will be generally affected by the predominant macroeconomic factors. In the current economic climate it is likely that organisations will wish to be 'lean and mean' and there may be a longer-term trend towards outsourcing particular skills rather than maintaining a costly in-house establishment. It is possible that, in certain scenarios, consultants can be used to strategic advantage.

Despite the apparent ease with which the employment of consultants can be justified on practical grounds, we must not lose sight of the considerable costs that can be associated with this approach. The need to employ specialists, perhaps at significant cost, should remain proportional to the significance and scale of the related project, and the clear indication of a proven need. Therefore before opting to engage consultants, it is necessary to assess all the relative factors and obtain the authority of senior management to proceed with the most suitable option.

Where a consultant is also a member of a professional body, his charges may be regulated by the application of scales of fees promoted by that body. Alternatively, some professionals are now permitted to operate a 'free market' approach to fees, and can quote on a competitive basis.

Where either the scale of operation dictates or the associated costs and risks are significant, there should be a properly structured method for dealing with consultants. This type of considered approach will need to co-incidently protect the best interests of the organisation and clearly establish the operational circumstances for the consultant concerned. Established professional best practice and standard forms of contract may already be available for selected occupations. As with other aspects of seeking optimum solutions, there are many factors affecting the engagement of consultants which can vary considerably between organisations and therefore we will accordingly refrain from prescribing a universal panacea.

SELECTION

In organisations where large projects are commonplace it may be prudent to maintain a list of approved consultants with proven abilities and reliable track records. In the public sector the use of such a standing list can openly illustrate the requirement for accountability so long as inclusion on the list is a matter of independent scrutiny without the direct involvement of those with the responsibility to allocate commissions.

In the appropriate organisation, for example a large public authority, the list of approved consultants should be 'organic' rather than static. Additional entries should be encouraged, after suitable vetting processes have been applied, and the entries for those consultants who either repeatedly decline offers of work or appear to fall short of current trend requirements should be removed, although they should be free to reapply for inclusion at a later date. In any event the list should be subject to detailed scrutiny periodically in order that it remains pertinent and so that the data is confirmed as correct.

A demonstrable independence should be applied to the maintenance of the approved list and all entries, amendments and deletions should be supported by suitably detailed documentation and subject to ratification (or at least scrutiny) by senior management. In the public sector the use and maintenance of such a list should be the subject of specific standing orders or financial regulations in accordance with any prevailing statutory requirements. Exercise of sensible controls should prevent irregularity and malpractice.

New entries to the list should only be made after the most careful examination of the financial stability, technical competence and track record of the relevant applicant. This type of vetting process should also be applied to prospective consultants in instances where a list is not maintained or where the project activity level does not justify the existence of same.

The list of approved consultants will need to reflect the relevant areas of expertise for each entry and an indication of any constraints (financial or otherwise) which should apply to project allocation. The relative values of any parameters may be subject to change following satisfactory completion of a commission. Where the consultant is a major player in the organisation's project, perhaps with concurrent involvement in a number of discrete projects, data reflecting the degree of the consultant's resource commitment should also be held so as to avoid establishing unrealistic workloads and any associated potential erosion of service.

It is possible that a particular consultant will be recommended by a previous client. Great caution needs to be exercised in such scenarios and the proper assessment of the consultant should still be applied so that the relevant hard factors are evaluated.

If a consultant has performed well in a previous project, there may be natural tendency to engage him again, given that he would have become familiar with the organisation and its specific administrative requirements. On the other hand, the engagement of specialists for the first time may inject much needed objectivity and at a lower cost.

As part of the process of assessing whether consultants would be best placed in addressing a particular need, account should also be taken of whether the task will appeal to the likely target contractors. Difficulty may be experienced in securing services if the scale of the requirements is too small or the timescales are unrealistically demanding. There are further dimensions to attempting to seek solutions to such unsuitable tasks in that consultants may either deliberately overstate their tender to counter what they perceive as nuisance value or reluctantly take on tasks which subsequently overrun time and cost constraints.

The market for consultants, including the recognised professions, is now very open and on a competitive basis, and this presents the organisation or client with a further dimension for consideration. Broad economic factors will influence the current meridian level of fees and the level of market activity will further influence them. However, the matter of choice should not be restricted to cost considerations alone, quality and reliability of services will need to be taken into account as part of the vetting and selection processes. There is no point in automatically opting for the lowest tender only to discover subsequent problems with competence and ability to achieve deadlines.

The selection of a consultant (with or without an approved list) should be a controlled process where personal bias, favouritism, etc. are prevented. There are two main avenues of approach to the selection process, with and without the prior receipt of tenders. The former situation does offer the potential for increased cost competition. Either of the two options can be associated with the use of approved lists which should further support the equally important quality and reliability factors.

The direct selection of the successful consultant from an approved list should be undertaken with further safeguards including the formation of an objective and independent selection committee or group, where this is justified by the significance of either the project or expenditure. Membership of such a group should be balanced and represent the appropriate level of authority. Alternatively a similar selection group may short-list a number of potential candidates who will be subsequently invited to submit their tenders based upon the documented requirements of the project and their appropriate responsibilities.

In instances where a consultant is directly selected without prior tendering, the eventual fees will have to be carefully and economically negotiated. The adoption of this method of selection may have been necessary because of a limited availability in the required field of expertise, and this constraint may result in the fees being subject to a premium.

In the public sector where conspicuous accountability is an everyday necessity, opting not to seek competitive tenders may be justifiable on the grounds of providing a higher quality service or as a means of avoiding the additional administrative costs or delays associated with the tendering process. This is precarious ground, dealing as it does with some intangible factors. Generally speaking, the necessity for accountability and an impartial approach to project set up has been well addressed in the public sector, but does not automatically prevent either significant projects from failing or instances where consultants are inappropriate, ineffective or negligent.

Where the tender option is applied measures should be in place to ensure that all the invited parties are approached and handled in the same impartial way, without favour or bias (*see also* Chapter 14 for more details). The scale of the project and the frequency of project involvement are but two factors which may influence the organisation's decision to opt for the tender approach to consultant engagement. It should be borne in mind that handling tendering processes adequately can involve significant additional costs for the organisation and therefore the use of the method may have to be justified in proportion to the costs incurred and relative to the nature and scale of the target project.

The tender documentation should incorporate sufficient and appropriate details to enable the consultant to prepare all aspects of his quotation, including the critical matter of the basis for remuneration. Setting the appropriate level of detail will hopefully avoid the generation of subsequent questions or requests for further information and clarification. In order to ensure equality of treatment for the parties invited to tender, any information provided subsequent to the initial invitations (perhaps in response to an isolated enquiry) should be distributed to all such parties.

The early stages of the project (i.e. project appraisal or design) should flush out and accurately document the technical requirements which should support the selection of consultants. It is possible that these earlier stages themselves require the services of specialists and therefore it is crucial that the driving requirements and constraints are also effectively documented so as to provide a firm foundation for seeking and engaging the necessary specialists. Such documentation should clearly define any technical data and/or descriptions of the required standards; any areas of potential ambiguity should be avoided. There may be very specific aspects of the overall contract or project which will be the responsibility of the consultant, and these will also have to be clearly defined in the relevant contract.

As is discussed in Chapter 14, in order to ensure fair play any tendering procedures should incorporate the controlled receipt, opening, recording, and storage of submissions prior to full examination and evaluation of same. The selection of the most appropriate submission will depend on a range of factors, some of which have been explored in earlier sections. Where a project is time critical, it will be necessary to ensure that any consultant being considered for a key role can commit the required amount of resource to comply with the defined timetable.

APPOINTMENT AND SUBSEQUENT MONITORING

In the public sector and particularly in relation to construction projects there are well-established operational guidelines in place which support the application of a controlled and balanced approach to the appointment of consultants. This is especially true where the consultants may have key or high-level responsibilities for the project, for example the role of the architect in public building developments. The relevant professional bodies provide further guidance to their members on matters of best practice and appropriate procedures. We do not intend to explore these prevailing measures in any detail, and readers requiring more discipline-specific information are advised to contact the appropriate professional body for details of available publications (*see* Appendix 3 for a selection of useful addresses). The Local Authority Association advises its members on a wide range of matters including those relative to conditions of engagement, some of which are generated by central government. The specific issues in this field are quite complex, with some conditions being relevant to very specific scenarios, it is therefore necessary for responsible officers or managers to be appropriately conversant with the relevant requirements. In order to gain the appropriate level of awareness of these (and indeed other general) factors, it may be necessary to seek the opinions of legal advisers.

Whether in the private or public sector, the organisation should ensure that the appointment of consultants is based upon clearly defined written terms of engagement incorporating the nature and standard of the required services. The objectives should be *inter alia* to prevent misunderstanding, avoid disputes, establish the relevant responsibilities, and define the methods for supporting payments. Specific forms and conditions of engagement are produced by some professional bodies and institutions. Copies of these are normally available for purchase and client organisations may wish to examine the relevant contents before finalising the assessment and selection processes. Alternatively the appointment may be documented in the form of a letter of appointment or an official procurement order.

The precise contents of letters of appointment will, of course, vary with regard to the nature of the project, etc. The Audit Inspectorate has provided guidance on the recommended contents of such a letter for use in the public sector, which may also have a selective relevance to the private sector. Among the recommended elements are:

- the appropriate basis for the calculation and charging of fees
- the scope of the commission
- definition of cost limits
- responsibilities for variations from the design
- the basis for liaison and other forms of collaboration with the client and other consultants
- access to and custody of records relevant to the contract or project
- professional indemnity insurance cover arrangements.

Other details such as an overall project timetable and the procedures for controlling variations from the timetable may also be relevant. The ownership (and where relevant the copyright) of project elements may also have to be defined in the terms of engagement. In certain sensitive project situations there may be justification for specifying confidentiality clauses over and above any which may already exist in guidelines issued by a professional body.

Lines of communication should be established both within the project and beyond into the realms of general management. A named individual should be appointed as the project manager or co-ordinator, and all project team members, including any consultants, should be required to report to this person. The method and frequency of formal reporting requirements should be defined in writing, especially where there are additional progress achievement or staged payment implications.

There may be qualitative factors to take into account, such as the performance of tasks to a recognised or defined standard. In these circumstances it may be relevant to undertake independent inspection to confirm the required quality of work before authorising the settlement of the consultant's accounts. If adherence to quality criteria is a condition of engagement it is likely that the responsibility for correcting any errors or deviations should also be defined in the engagement documentation.

Clearly establishing the expected performance criteria will enable the subsequent ongoing monitoring of consultant performance. It will also be necessary to establish the required nature, flow and frequency of management information. Without such stable scene-setting factors in place the organisation will be unable to determine whether objectives are being satisfactorily addressed in the required timescales. The monitoring processes should incorporate the means for timely reaction to any failure to achieve the required performance and the appropriate application of any remedial action or penalties. In complex project situations where interdependencies are inevitable, delays caused by the need to correct problems may have a significant impact upon the overall project progress with time, cost and other implications. Accordingly it is essential to identify who is liable is such situations and ensure that adequate indemnity insurance or other suitable provision is arranged in advance.

Considerable amounts of resentment and negative attitude can be engendered by the employment of consultants if their engagement is poorly or insensitively handled. Existing staff can view consultants as unnecessary, excessively expensive, and with poor productivity levels. Management should have regard for staff morale, etc. when planning to involve external specialists in projects. Additionally they should, where appropriate, clearly (and honestly) communicate the necessity and justification for employing consultants to the affected staff so as to reduce any feelings of resentment or hostility. The aims should be to maintain good working relationships and facilitate the prompt and efficient completion of the related project.

PAYMENT OF ACCOUNTS

Where payment of consultants is directly related to the achievement of specified targets to a required standard in a defined timescale, all the relevant factors
will need to be confirmed before settlement is authorised. Responsibility for
confirming all the necessary elements should be allocated to a named individual, especially where matters of technical quality or standards are involved. In
the construction and public sectors there are clear lines of responsibility established and formal methods in place for recording and reporting the completion
of works. In any event, the responsible person should formally signify their satisfaction or report any shortcomings to client and consultant for rectification,
etc.

Some form of documentary evidence for the satisfactory completion of works
or services may be desirable before either interim or final accounts are paid. The
staff responsible for confirming the completion of contractual duties should be
separate from those authorising the payment of accounts and signing the appropriate cheques. Such rigid segregation of duties will, if correctly applied, further
prevent malpractice and enhance the concepts of accountability. Many organisations operate a hierarchal authority or mandate structure which may also
feature financial limitations at each stage. Such structures should be the subject
of formal procedures or financial regulations with compliance being evidenced
by the application of signatures and/or authority reference numbers.

The correct calculation of all elements of the account in accordance with the
provisions of the contract or letter of appointment should be confirmed prior to
payment. Any errors or anomalies should be referred back to the source and
satisfactorily corrected. Mechanisms should also be established to avoid the
duplication of account payments. In order to provide further assurance some
form of retention may apply to account settlement with the final proportion
being due after the expiration of a defined time period. Where contract or terms
of engagement conditions allow for the assessment and application of claims
against consultants, these should be duly accounted for, authorised and may be
taken into account against settlement invoices or accounts.

Control matrix example

The example matrix in Table 10 depicts a situation where there is a significant
consultant involvement in a project. The contents are deliberately non-sector
specific, but the relevant consultant has to be a recognised professional in order
to fulfil the client's expectations. The matrix, which is *Exposure* oriented, uses
Scale 31 as described in Appendix 7.

Table 10 Engagement of Consultants – Exposures

Overall Inherent Risk (Size) Score [5 is worst risk; 1 is best] = 2.50

A Failure to accurately identify consultant requirement(s)
B Additional cost due to inappropriate use of consultants
C Selection of inappropriate or poorly skilled consultant
D Failure to engage suitably qualified professionals
E Financially unstable or incompetent consultants engaged
F Inadequate consultant resources to cope with requirements
G Failure to engage on optimum or reasonable financial terms
H Failure to identify & agree performance requirements
I Relationship not supported by written Terms of Engagement
J Unbalanced Terms of Engagement – undue exposure to risks

K Inadequate/absence of professional indemnity insurance
L Failure to accurately communicate needs to consultant
M Failure to communicate relative responsibilities & role
N Failure to establish clear targets, objectives and goals
O Inadequate performance monitoring – delay, cost, etc.
P Failure to establish and monitor relevant cost budgets
Q Ineffective communication between consultant & client
R Failure to remedy problems/shortcomings – missed objectives
S Payment of inaccurate or inappropriate consultant accounts
T Failure to confirm that all objectives have been fully met

Scale 31 (abridged)

6 = Incorrect identification of needs, or failure to meet them
5 = Lost business; needs partly unfulfilled; or breach of rules
4 = Delay or disruption; reputation loss; minor breach of rules
(Contract auditing Exposures-oriented scale)

3 = Avoidable costs/losses; damage to contract relationships
2 = Administrative or accounting errors
1 = Detectable negative impact on the business or service

Engagement of Consultants			A	B	C	D	E	F	G	H	I	J	K	L	M	N	O	P	Q	R	S	T
		EXPOSURES																				
		=	=	=	=	=	=	=	=	=	=	=	=	=	=	=	=	=	=	=	=	=
Calculated Risk Score:	Risk		3	3	3	3	2	3	2	3	3	2	2	3	2	3	2	2	2	2	3	3
		–	–	–	–	–	–	–	–	–	–	–	–	–	–	–	–	–	–	–	–	–	–
Scale 31 (6 is most serious)	Type		6	5	6	6	5	6	3	6	5	5	5	6	6	6	6	3	6	4	5	6
Size (3 is maximum)	Size		2	2	2	2	1	2	2	2	2	1	1	2	1	2	1	2	1	2	1	2
CONTROLS	—	–	–	–	–	–	–	–	–	–	–	–	–	–	–	–	–	–	–	–	–	–
1 Project Appraisal exercise revealed positive need for a specialist contribution	Best		4	4																		
	Test	?	?	?																		
	Both																					
2 Costs of training in-house staff compared to consultancy fees – justified chosen route	Best				3																	
	Test	?			?																	
	Both																					
3 Relevant professional body was contacted for advice, prior to selection of consultant	Best				3	4	4															
	Test	?			?	?	?															
	Both																					
4 Skill requirements, etc. defined in writing as basis for selection process	Best				3	4								5								
	Test	?			?	?								?								
	Both																					
5 Only recognised professionals were engaged – qualifications confirmed beforehand	Best					4	4															
	Test	?				?	?															
	Both																					
6 Previous users/clients were contacted for comments on performance, etc.	Best						3															
	Test	?					?															
	Both																					
7 Audited accounts were examined and references obtained from bankers	Best						3															
	Test	?					?															
	Both																					
8 Resource requirements clearly established and agreed	Best							5														
	Test	?						?														
	Both																					
9 Tendering process applied to short-listed consultants	Best					3			3	4												
	Test	?				?			?	?												
	Both																					

Table 10 continued

			A	B	C	D	E	F	G	H	I	J	K	L	M	N	O	P	Q	R	S	T
			=	=	=	=	=	=	=	=	=	=	=	=	=	=	=	=	=	=	=	=
	Calculated Risk Score:	Risk	3	3	3	3	2	3	2	3	3	2	2	3	2	3	2	2	2	3	2	3
10	Professional Scale Fees used as selection benchmark	Best							4													
		Test	?						?													
		Both																				
11	All detailed requirements and timescales were documented as part of the appointment process	Best								4				4								
		Test	?							?				?								
		Both																				
12	Quality standards were clearly defined and communicated	Best								4												
		Test	?							?												
		Both																				
13	Standard Terms of Engagement issued by professional body were used	Best									5	4										
		Test	?								?	?										
		Both																				
14	Terms of Engagement examined by Legal Dept. for balance of allocated risks	Best									4											
		Test	?								?											
		Both																				
15	Evidence obtained of current level of insurance cover	Best									5											
		Test	?								?											
		Both																				
16	Project Team responsibilities documented and circulated	Best												4	5	4						
		Test	?											?	?	?						
		Both																				
17	Project Management Systems records milestones and plots actual achievements to target	Best														4	4					
		Test	?													?	?					
		Both																				
18	Project Manager responsible for monitoring progress and resolving problems, etc.	Best														4	4			4		
		Test	?													?	?			?		
		Both																				
19	Budgets established and responsibility allocated. Monitoring in place	Best															4					
		Test	?														?					
		Both																				
20	Budgets and performance problems regularly reported to management for action	Best														4	4			3		
		Test	?													?	?			?		
		Both																				
21	Regular Team meetings were held. All action points are minuted and monitored for clearance	Best																	5			
		Test	?																?			
		Both																				
22	Quality standards checked by the Project Manager for compliance. Problems referred to consultant	Best																		4		
		Test	?																	?		
		Both																				
23	All accounts are checked against time records and agreed rates, prior to payment	Best																		4		
		Test	?																	?		
		Both																				

Table 10 continued

			A	B	C	D	E	F	G	H	I	J	K	L	M	N	O	P	Q	R	S	T
			=	=	=	=	=	=	=	=	=	=	=	=	=	=	=	=	=	=	=	=
	Calculated Risk Score:	Risk	3	3	3	3	2	3	2	3	3	2	2	3	2	3	2	2	2	3	2	3
			–	–	–	–	–	–	–	–	–	–	–	–	–	–	–	–	–	–	–	–
24	Accounts are authorised by management prior to payment	Best																			4	
		Test	?																		?	
		Both																				
			–	–	–	–	–	–	–	–	–	–	–	–	–	–	–	–	–	–	–	–
25	Each significant project stage is signed off prior to account settlement	Best																			4	4
		Test	?																		?	?
		Both																				
			–	–	–	–	–	–	–	–	–	–	–	–	–	–	–	–	–	–	–	–
26	Project Manager confirms that objectives and progress are met	Best																				4
		Test	?																			?
		Both																				
			–																				

A   Failure to accurately identify consultant requirement(s)
B   Additional cost due to inappropriate use of consultants
C   Selection of inappropriate or poorly skilled consultant
D   Failure to engage suitably qualified professionals
E   Financially unstable or incompetent consultants engaged
F   Inadequate consultant resources to cope with requirements
G   Failure to engage on optimum or reasonable financial terms
H   Failure to identify & agree performance requirements
I   Relationship not supported by written Terms of Engagement
J   Unbalanced Terms of Engagement – undue exposure to risks

K   Inadequate/absence of professional indemnity insurance
L   Failure to accurately communicate needs to consultant
M   Failure to communicate relative responsibilities & role
N   Failure to establish clear targets, objectives and goals
O   Inadequate performance monitoring – delay, cost, etc.
P   Failure to establish and monitor relevant cost budgets
Q   Ineffective communication between consultant & client
R   Failure to remedy problems/shortcomings – missed objectives
S   Payment of inaccurate or inappropriate consultant accounts
T   Failure to confirm that all objectives have been fully met

Scale 31 (abridged)

6 = Incorrect identification of needs, or failure to meet them
5 = Lost business; needs partly unfilled; or breach of rules
4 = Delay or disruption; reputation loss; minor breach of rules
(Contract auditing Exposures-oriented scale)

3 = Avoidable costs/losses; damage to contract relationships
2 = Administrative or accounting errors
1 = Detectable negative impact on the business or service

11

DESIGN

Scope

The design phase is intended to take the initial project concepts and convert them into a detailed design which economically fulfils the requirements of the client, and upon which all the subsequent construction or development work can be reliably based. It is also necessary that the design addresses inter alia matters of technical quality and performance, budgetary constraints, length of construction period, and value for money issues. This chapter reviews these requirements and suggests the application of appropriate control mechanisms. Although a wide range of design administration aspects are reviewed here, the underlying target is to provide a reliable basis for the subsequent contract activities.

In the construction industry 'design and build' contracts can be applied which pass the responsibility for the design processes over to the contractor. Although the employer may in these circumstances provide a design brief, the contractor will handle the detailed design. This chapter, although not specifically dealing with the issues arising from 'design and build' contracts, incorporates some comments which would be relevant. For example the provision of an accurate design brief containing all the key requirements and performance factors.

In organisations where the levels of project and contract activity are high, there should be documented policies, procedures and standards governing all project processes. In order to remain effective such procedures should be subject to regular review and incorporate monitoring facilities so that management can be satisfied as to their correct operation. Continuity of actions throughout all stages of projects and the application of suitable authorisations are also among the essential ingredients of effective procedures.

In overview terms the design process procedures should take into account and address the following elements:

- Accurately reflect the user requirements, performance specifications, etc.
- Work in relation to a formal design brief.
- Undertake full evaluation of design and technical criteria.
- Relate design to timetable and budgetary requirements established by management.

- Generate costing information for the selected design(s). Given the refinement of the relevant project considerations this data should now be more accurately aligned with the potential final costs.
- Generate necessary design drawings and calculations.
- Take into account all the relevant standards and codes of practice, including any EC or international considerations.
- Agree the documentary basis for any related contracts, observing the appropriate formats, measuring and tendering arrangements.
- Whenever relevant consideration should be given to the associated matters of planning applications, land acquisitions and testing site conditions.

It is essential that the completed detailed design fully addresses the requirements of the end client or user. This aspect applies to most forms of project, whether they are related to construction, information technology or service provision. As previously stated, it is vital that users or commissioning clients have had sufficient input into the requirements specification processes, and that all the necessary functionality, and technical details etc. are accordingly addressed in the final designs, technical or performance specifications.

The design or specification will more likely subsequently form the basis for the contractor to prepare a tender and either provide the service, undertake the construction or develop the software. Therefore it is essential that it accurately reflects all the required parameters in order to avoid misunderstanding, delay or wastefulness. If an organisation generates either an incomplete, inadequate or inaccurate design/requirements specification, there is also the possibility of adversely affecting its reputation and credibility. Similarly, if amendments are continually made to the design this will generate delay, frustration and more importantly increase the associated costs. The simple message is to undertake thorough research and aim to get the design right first time.

It may prove necessary to undertake further investigation or research into technical matters such as emerging construction techniques or availability of specific information technology devices as part of crystallising the design requirements. Any design phase timetable should include adequate provision to effectively address such issues as they may prove to be a critical factor in the success of the eventual project.

Establishing the correct and appropriate design or specification factors at the earliest opportunity is most important as the further the project progresses the greater will be the cost of incorporating and addressing amendments and changes. However, in the real world some degree of subsequent change is inevitable on larger projects, but modifications that appear necessary should be stringently examined to ensure that they are really necessary and justifiable in cost and performance terms.

Design constraints or boundaries should be built around the project, which although permitting the generation of an adequate design will also prevent costly overstatement of requirements, etc. Such constraints may either be technical, functional or financial in nature. In commercial situations, senior management may have applied very precise financial limitations to a particular project so that it can effectively contribute to the achievement of strategically or commercially vital business objectives. There is an obvious connection with the targets established as part of strategic planning and in the public sector such constraints may be reinforced by either statutory obligations, government financial limitations, or service level expectations. As a result the products of the design process will need to be monitored against these other criteria.

The design process should be positively managed. This will include the setting of an overall design phase timetable, with mechanisms for monitoring and reporting on progress achieved. Expenditure budgets should also be established and clear responsibility allocated for completion of the design phase within both the defined cost and time limits. In the absence of these and other measures, the design phase can become a rambling, amorphous and time-consuming process.

In order that any given project can be successfully and economically completed, it is necessary to assess whether the existing staff resources within the organisation are sufficient in number, suitably skilled and appropriately competent to cope with the various identified demands. These considerations will encompass technical, administrative and operational factors, and will therefore also relate to the relative design processes. The existing workloads of in-house specialists or design staff should also be reviewed to ensure that the anticipated demands on their time can be satisfactorily met within the established design timetable. During the project appraisal stage any specific or specialist skill requirements should be identified. Additionally it will be necessary to evaluate whether such expertise already exists within the organisation and the degree to which supplementary training may be required to address any skill shortcomings in such areas.

It may prove necessary to engage the services of external consultants to handle the design and detailed specification stages. The engagement and monitoring of consultants is fully addressed in Chapter 10. However, it is important to fully assess the competence of design consultants before entering into formal relationships and to further ensure that all the requirements of the project are accurately communicated to and acknowledged by them. A further point to consider when utilising external specialists is the ability of the organisations to address future and ongoing operational needs once the consultants have discharged their responsibilities. It may prove necessary to provide suitable training for existing staff or eventually employ someone with the required knowledge if the organisation is not to be vulnerable in any way in the longer term.

In the construction project context the members of the design team, for example the technical officers of a public authority, may also have further responsibilities later in the project lifecycle for active administration of the related contract or ensuring the achievement of prevailing technical standards. It is normal practice in the public sector to name chief professional staff such as architects in the contract and thereby allocate very specific responsibilities.

It would be inappropriate for us to provide detailed analysis of the professional requirements of such officers, as these are extensively covered in the publications and codes of practice developed by the appropriate professional bodies. However, it is necessary to remind auditors responsible for reviewing systems of control that there is the potential for conflicts of interest in such situations and that suitable measures should be in place to prevent any abuses of position.

In order to effectively co-ordinate design activity and ensure the achievement of both technical and timescale targets, it will be necessary to allocate clear responsibility for leading and managing the design team (*see also* Chapter 8). In the case of external consultants the precise responsibilities may form part of specific terms or contract of engagement. Obviously the nature of the project will directly dictate the calibre and professional background of the individual team leader or project manager. For example in the public construction sector it is usual for either an architect or structural engineer to oversee the project. In any event the choice of project (or more specifically the design) manager will predominantly depend upon the suitability of skills or experience relevant to the demands of the project. There is a further important dimension to address, in that the chosen individual should also have the appropriate level of authority to maintain momentum and authorise actions within the defined cost and technical constraints, otherwise comparatively minor decisions will have to be referred to management for authorisation or sanction.

Where a project demands the skills of a range of professions or disciplines (such as a major building development) it is essential that all the specialist areas of design (e.g. electrical engineering and materials technology) are co-ordinated so that they eventually form an integrated whole. This objective can be supported by the judicious application of comprehensive design briefs, effective controls exercised over design amendments, and the free flow of relevant and accurate design information. Regular inter-discipline design meetings can also assist at the strategic level. These suggestions can also be applied to other project types, such as large-scale application software developments. Matters of technical quality may have to be related to existing or pending standards (both local and international when appropriate).

Where any team (including that relevant to project design) is formed attention will need to be paid to the interactions of all the members of the team, and this is especially true where external consultants or experts are part of the team. All manner of factors can affect the effectiveness of team performance for example either the adaptability of external consultants to the prevailing internal methods or lines of communication, or the possible disaffection of employees to the engagement of external consultants or specialists. It would be inappropriate here to explore all the potential psychological angles relevant to the performance of teams, but very often problems are in some way related to the adequacy and effectiveness of communication. This is particularly true in respect of establishing and disseminating clear objectives.

Involvement in or responsibility for the design phase does not, of course, preclude involvement at other stages in the project lifecycle, indeed there are strong arguments for such continuity, especially in large complex projects. In the construction industry there are well-developed professional protocols governing the behaviour of professionals, for example with regard to impartiality.

Whether the design process is being handled in-house or by external agents, it is essential that a sufficiently detailed design brief is provided to the design team in order that the design process is initiated upon firm and approved foundations that address all the varied requirements. The brief may be generated as part of the project appraisal phase or as the result of a separate feasibility study.

Projects can succumb to problems if the design brief is incomplete, inaccurate or fails to adequately reflect the requirements and objectives of the client department, business or authority. Prime responsibility for the brief should lie with the users or client, although design teams who accept incomplete or inadequate briefs will be likely to encounter subsequent problems or delays. The contents should not leave any avenues for doubt where either undue speculation or unauthorised assumption may be subsequently exercised by the design team. The views of users and end-clients will need to be collected, collated and refined before release of the details to the design team.

In especially complex situations or where the work is an exploratory precursor to receiving the authority to proceed, the development of a design brief may have to be a recursive process with the eventual or optimum solution having evolved into its final form. In the course of such a process certain criteria may have to be reconsidered, for example fundamental technical or financial parameters may require amendment if the detailed design analysis suggests or demands alternative solutions be applied. In the event of such changes proving necessary formal review by senior management may be required and their ratification to proceed duly obtained.

The documentary contents of a design brief will need to be defined and related to any existing or required standards or procedures, and this should apply irrespective of whether the design is being handled by in-house staff or external consultants. The requirements will vary in relation to the scale, significance, and individuality of the project.

The final brief, having met all the original or necessarily updated parameters, should be authorised for release by the appropriate committee or management group. Although it is probable that there will be a recognisable relationship between the project objectives, the design brief and the most suitable type of contract, the subject of selecting the appropriate form of contract is explored in detail in Chapter 17.

In order to avoid unnecessary delays or inefficient use of expensive resource, a timetable should be imposed for the design phase. Any such timetable should allow sufficient time for each element or stage in the design process including necessary levels of communication between designers, consultants, and users. Progress achieved against the timetable milestones should be monitored so as to allow for remedial action to be applied in good time.

Although the project management framework is discussed further in Chapter 8, the principles of project control should be addressed throughout the design phase so as to ensure that the final design is delivered in the required form at the appropriate time. Any significant shortfalls in achieving the timing deadlines and the related implications should be suitably reported to and reviewed by management.

In addressing the design criteria of all projects it is necessary to accurately consider the ongoing maintenance and running costs. This is equally true for a computer application system as it is for a building or civil engineering project. Technical decisions, taken at the earliest stage, can have a substantial impact upon the eventual operating costs and the design team should accurately establish such future costs and take account of design options with a potential impact in this area. A crude example would be the adoption of inexpensive but inferior materials which although restricting initial costs may result in substantially higher maintenance costs over the expected life of a building. Suitable forms of analysis should identify the most fitting solutions taking into account such factors as the expected life of the building, service or product, the strategic significance of the project, the level of capital expenditure and the necessary rate of return.

In technological environments, there will always be the temptation of adopting either leading-edge or emerging technologies. However, there are considerable disadvantages associated with premature adoption of new and perhaps commercially unproven systems and products. There is the danger of being the guinea-pig user of a new product and the related likelihood of acting as a form of quality control for prototype developments. Hopefully a suitable form of risk assessment at the project appraisal stage would have weeded out the more inherently risky ventures or options. Viewed rather more optimistically early involvement with emerging products can also create the environment for preferential terms of business and the potential for being seen as a 'mould-breaking' organisation. These attributes have their place, but where very firm financial constraints or profit targets apply they are generally best avoided and more established solutions sought.

Specific projects, especially those related to commercial or service provision activities, will have a related income dimension, and it will be necessary to evaluate projected income levels in light of the chosen design route. These and other factors will also need to be borne in mind when assessing the justification for subsequent design changes and modifications.

As stated earlier it is preferable to minimise design changes. However, any changes which appear vitally necessary should be subject to scrutiny and impact assessment. All changes should be referred to the controlling or responsible committee or group for approval purposes. Documentary amendments for all design changes should be effectively controlled in order to ensure that all affected parties are advised and that master copies of drawings and specifications reflect the current and authorised situation. A form of version control and referencing will need to be in place to support these objectives.

Cost and time budgets should be established for the design activities relating to important projects. Actual expenditure and progress should be progressively monitored against the budgeted targets and any substantial variations promptly highlighted, reported and reacted to.

Building developments are likely to have further dimensions in respect of the relevant site. There will be matters of land acquisition, restrictions or covenants and planning approvals to address. The site conditions may be a determinant factor in the design process, therefore it may be apt to arrange a separate contract for the investigation of the site ground conditions if this has not already been conducted at the earlier project assessment stage.

Once the design has been generated along with all the required supporting documentation and costings, it will need to be suitably approved. The whole matter should be explored and discussed so that the appropriate form of contract can be identified and the necessary documentation finalised. Whether the design is unique or one that will be applied a number of times, decisions will have to be reached as to the most apt contracting solution to apply. For example, does the nature and scale of the project lend itself either to one overall contract, a number of interrelated contracts, the appropriate involvement of the organisation's own direct labour, and so on. Such considerations, although obviously dependent upon the outcomes of the design process are more fully discussed in Chapter 17.

Where the design process has necessarily unearthed previously unforeseen factors, there may be a need to reassess the viability of the project and obtain renewed authority to proceed to the next stage. Although the design costs will be relative to the project type, aborting the project at this point is preferable in economic terms to waiting until either tendering processes have been completed or the construction work has started. In addition to the additional costs associated with the latter stages of the project, management should also consider the implications for the image and reputation of the organisation if the project is cancelled. Negative impressions of a company or authority may result in contractors being either reluctant to quote for future jobs or inclined to hike up their prices to cover the risk of subsequent cancellations.

Once approved, the design will need to be accurately incorporated into the contract documentation. Additionally, all the design material will need to be protected from loss or damage. Suitable and secure storage facilities should be provided and access controlled on a 'need to know' basis

DESIGN FAULTS AND LIABILITY

There is always the possibility that designs used for physical projects may include faults or errors. Alternatively, a design might be sound but may have been incorrectly interpreted by the construction staff, who may have utilised either incorrect or faulty materials and methods. Where a fault occurs, determining who is liable for any consequences is not always straightforward. The situation may be further exacerbated by the fact that the fault may not be apparent until some years after the construction or fabrication has been completed.

There are some basic responsibilities assigned to designers or consultants working in the field, for example to exercise reasonable care and skill and to ensure that building and planning regulations are complied with. If professional negligence can be proved, liability can be established in such situations. However, the nature of the contract, sub-contract or terms of engagement covering their employment may either diminish or modify the nature of obligations and therefore the relevant liabilities in the event of a possible design fault.

Those professionals engaged in the contract management process should ensure, in line with their respective responsibilities, that the design elements are carried out in terms of technique, material and workmanship. Where design factors play a part in contract arrangements, the employer would be wise to examine the specific interplay of the affected professionals in relation to the explicit contract terms, and ensure that the potential risks are identified, and where possible addressed.

Control matrix example

The example matrix reflects the circumstances of an important in-house design process, where there is a high level of dependency upon the related project. The context is non-sector specific and underscores the general management issues. The measures in place suggest an organisation with a well developed and professional approach to design management. The example is contained in Table 11 which is *Objectives*-oriented and uses *Scale* 30.

Table 11 Design – Objectives

Overall Inherent Risk (Size) Score [5 is worst risk; 1 is best] = 3.22

A Ensure all requirements/functionality are in chosen design
B Ensure the final design is cost effective & offers VFM
C Ensure the optimum design solution is selected & applied
D Ensure design adequately addresses the performance criteria
E Ensure that high technical & quality standards are applied
F Ensure all regulatory/technical requirements met by design
G Ensure that final design is within pre-defined cost limits
H Ensure all operational & maintenance costs are identified
I Ensure that design documentation supports subsequent stages
J Minimise need for subsequent design changes/modifications
K Ensure that all design impacts & consequences are assessed
L Ensure accuracy, completeness & standard of design documents
M Ensure that the preferred design is suitably authorised
N Ensure that the design process is completed on time
O Ensure design costs & progress are monitored/controlled
P Protect the copyright & ownership of designs
Q Determine the likely liability for any future design faults
R Ensure design elements are incorporated into the contract

Scale 30 (abridged)

6 = Strategically vital to the business or organisation
5 = Makes a contribution to business operations
4 = Contributes to reliability of data, records and information
(Contract auditing Objectives-oriented scale)
3 = Avoids disruption/meets regulatory & accountability needs
2 = Leads to administrative/operational economies/efficiencies
1 = Generates administrative economies

Design		A	B	C	D	E	F	G	H	I	J	K	L	M	N	O	P	Q	R
		=	=	=	=	=	=	=	=	=	=	=	=	=	=	=	=	=	=
Calculated Risk Score:	Risk	4	3	4	4	4	3	3	2	4	4	2	3	4	3	2	3	2	4
		–																	
Scale 30 (6 is most serious)	Type	6	6	6	6	6	5	4	5	6	5	5	6	5	6	4	5	4	5
Size (3 is maximum)	Size	3	2	3	3	3	2	2	1	3	3	1	2	3	2	1	2	1	3
MEASURES		–	–	–	–	–	–	–	–	–	–	–	–	–	–	–	–	–	–
Design brief is generated from	Best		4		3														
1 the project assessment phase.	Test	?	?		?														
Supplied to the design team	Both																		
		–	–	–	–	–	–	–	–	–	–	–	–	–	–	–	–	–	–
All requirements, functions,	Best		4		3	3													
2 and performance criteria are	Test	?	?		?	?													
documented and approved	Both																		
		–	–	–	–	–	–	–	–	–	–	–	–	–	–	–	–	–	–
Design options are fully costed	Best				3														
3 and reported to management	Test	?			?														
	Both																		
		–	–	–	–	–	–	–	–	–	–	–	–	–	–	–	–	–	–
Design process involves	Best				4														
4 examination of various options.	Test	?			?														
All consistently appraised	Both																		
		–	–	–	–	–	–	–	–	–	–	–	–	–	–	–	–	–	–
Design is chosen on basis of	Best		4	4	4	4	3		3	3									
5 costs and achievement of	Test	?	?	?	?	?	?		?	?									
defined objectives	Both																		
		–	–	–	–	–	–	–	–	–	–	–	–	–	–	–	–	–	–
	Best		3		3	4	3												
6 Designs assessed against	Test	?	?		?	?	?												
noted performance criteria	Both																		
		–	–	–	–	–	–	–	–	–	–	–	–	–	–	–	–	–	–
Choice of materials and	Best					4	3												
7 methods related to technical	Test	?				?	?												
and quality standards	Both																		
		–	–	–	–	–	–	–	–	–	–	–	–	–	–	–	–	–	–
	Best					4	3												
8 Prevailing standards observed	Test	?				?	?												
throughout the design phase	Both																		
		–	–	–	–	–	–	–	–	–	–	–	–	–	–	–	–	–	–
Compliance with prevailing	Best						4												
9 legislation confirmed by	Test	?					?												
design team manager	Both																		
		–																		

Table 11 continued

			A	B	C	D	E	F	G	H	I	J	K	L	M	N	O	P	Q	R
			=	=	=	=	=	=	=	=	=	=	=	=	=	=	=	=	=	=
	Calculated Risk Score:	Risk	4	3	4	4	4	3	3	2	4	4	2	3	4	3	2	3	2	4
			–	–	–	–	–	–	–	–	–	–	–	–	–	–	–	–	–	–
10	All operating/maintenance costs explored and documented for management consideration	Best							3	5										
		Test	?						?	?										
		Both																		
			–	–	–	–	–	–	–	–	–	–	–	–	–	–	–	–	–	–
11	Design drawings & specifications produced to recognised format and standards	Best					3				4			3						
		Test	?				?				?			?						
		Both																		
			–	–	–	–	–	–	–	–	–	–	–	–	–	–	–	–	–	–
12	Design documents checked for accuracy and completeness before release	Best									4	3		4						
		Test	?								?	?		?						
		Both																		
			–	–	–	–	–	–	–	–	–	–	–	–	–	–	–	–	–	–
13	Design options comprehensively researched	Best			4	3	2	2				5	3							
		Test	?		?	?	?	?				?	?							
		Both																		
			–	–	–	–	–	–	–	–	–	–	–	–	–	–	–	–	–	–
14	All cost, timing and practical implications are identified, documented and assessed	Best												4						
		Test	?											?						
		Both																		
			–	–	–	–	–	–	–	–	–	–	–	–	–	–	–	–	–	–
15	Preferred design option is presented to management for approval	Best													4					
		Test	?												?					
		Both																		
			–	–	–	–	–	–	–	–	–	–	–	–	–	–	–	–	–	–
16	Only Board approved designs are utilised in projects	Best													5					
		Test	?												?					
		Both																		
			–	–	–	–	–	–	–	–	–	–	–	–	–	–	–	–	–	–
17	Suitably qualified & experienced design staff are engaged on project developments	Best					3				3	3		3						
		Test	?				?				?	?		?						
		Both																		
			–	–	–	–	–	–	–	–	–	–	–	–	–	–	–	–	–	–
18	Each design project is managed by an experienced manager	Best														4				
		Test	?													?				
		Both																		
			–	–	–	–	–	–	–	–	–	–	–	–	–	–	–	–	–	–
19	Project management system is used to monitor progress against targets	Best														4				
		Test	?													?				
		Both																		
			–	–	–	–	–	–	–	–	–	–	–	–	–	–	–	–	–	–
20	Separate project design budgets are agreed, established and monitored	Best															5			
		Test	?														?			
		Both																		
			–	–	–	–	–	–	–	–	–	–	–	–	–	–	–	–	–	–
21	Budget and progress anomalies are reported to management	Best														4	4			
		Test	?													?	?			
		Both																		
			–	–	–	–	–	–	–	–	–	–	–	–	–	–	–	–	–	–
22	The company retains the copyright and ownership of all designs	Best																4		
		Test	?															?		
		Both																		
			–	–	–	–	–	–	–	–	–	–	–	–	–	–	–	–	–	–
23	Legal Dept. advice is sought to asses potential design fault liabilities	Best																	2	
		Test	?																?	
		Both																		
			–																		

Table 11 continued

			A	B	C	D	E	F	G	H	I	J	K	L	M	N	O	P	Q	R
			=	=	=	=	=	=	=	=	=	=	=	=	=	=	=	=	=	=
	Calculated Risk Score:	Risk	4	3	4	4	4	3	3	2	4	4	2	3	4	3	2	3	2	4
		–	–	–	–	–	–	–	–	–	–	–	–	–	–	–	–	–	–	–
	All designs are checked for	Best																		5
24	accuracy, prior to incorporation	Test	?																	?
	into contract documentation	Both																		
—		—	–																	

A Ensure all requirements/functionality are in chosen design
B Ensure the final design is cost effective & offers VFM
C Ensure the optimum design solution is selected & applied
D Ensure design adequately addresses the performance criteria
E Ensure that high technical & quality standards are applied
F Ensure all regulatory/technical requirements met by design
G Ensure that final design is within pre-defined cost limits
H Ensure all operational & maintenance costs are identified
I Ensure that design documentation supports subsequent stages
J Minimise need for subsequent design changes/modifications
K Ensure that all design impacts & consequences are assessed
L Ensure accuracy, completeness & standard of design documents
M Ensure that the preferred design is suitably authorised
N Ensure that the design process is completed on time
O Ensure design costs & progress are monitored/controlled
P Protect the copyright & ownership of designs
Q Determine the likely liability for any future design faults
R Ensure design elements are incorporated into the contract

Scale 30 (abridged)

6 = Strategically vital to the business or organisation
5 = Makes a contribution to business operations
4 = Contributes to reliability of data, records and information
(Contract auditing Objectives-oriented scale)

3 = Avoids disruption/meets regulatory & accountability needs
2 = Leads to administrative/operational economies/efficiencies
1 = Generates administrative economies

12

ASSESSING THE VIABILITY AND COMPETENCE OF CONTRACTORS

Scope

Prior to either inviting a contractor to submit a tender, entering into a contract, or re-employing a contractor, it is preferable to ensure that the contractor in question is financially stable and competent in relation to the employer's requirements. This chapter addresses the key issues involved in applying forms of contractor assessment and suggests appropriate measures to be employed. There are linkages between the objectives of these processes and other systems described in other chapters in this book, including tendering procedures, maintaining an approved list of contractors, insurance and bonding arrangements, performance monitoring, and review of the project out-turn.

It is in the employing organisation's best interests to ensure that any contractors engaged are financially stable, viable business concerns, technically experienced and competent in the relevant operating arena, suitably resourced and capable of achieving time and cost targets. The achievement of corporate objectives may depend, to either a lesser or greater extent, upon the performance of the contractor, and the employer will need to be satisfied that the potential contractor is both suitable and reliable before any commitment is formalised.

Employers with regular contractual involvement may be able to justify the establishment of a formal process for evaluating and assessing contractors on a range of grounds. Where this is the case, the requirements and associated methods should be encased in written procedures, capable of compliance monitoring.

Before we examine the considerations in detail, the right of access to the required information will need to be clearly established with the contractors. It can be made a condition of acceptance on to an approved list of contractors, that various forms of accounting and performance information will have to be regularly supplied in the appropriate form. In order that financial and operational assessments can be accurately conducted, the regular supply of updated information should also be arranged. The nature, form and frequency of all the required data should be clearly established, communicated to the contractor, and his agreement to the surrounding requirements and conditions obtained in writing. Where necessary, the appropriate professional or trade regulatory body may have defined guidelines on the supply of such data. For example there is a joint statement issued by CIPFA and SCQSLG on performance bonding and the financial vetting of contractors. Where such guidelines exist, and are applicable to the situation, they should be taken into account.

Deciding on whether or not to assess a contractor will be dependent on a number of factors, including the significance of the project, the overall value of the project, all the risks presented by the project or its failure, the contract period, the experiences of the organisation in similar circumstances, the costs associated with the assessment process, and so on. The value of the target contract is likely to be a major factor in risk assessment, and the decision to undertake a review of the contractor(s) may primarily stem from value consideration. For example, only applying a review where the contract value exceeds £25,000 and indemnity insurance is optional. Such considerations will clearly be tailored to the organisation's circumstances and the context of the pending contract.

The assessment of contractors can be subdivided into three areas, namely financial, technical and contract performance. Each of these is explored, in turn, in the following sections. The points noted can be suitably adapted to apply in relation to the supply of goods or services in various scenarios.

FINANCIAL

The objective here is to prove the financial stability of the contractor and thereby to minimise the probability of financial problems befalling the contractor. The process may include some or all of the following considerations:

- Examine and review the published and audited accounts for the previous three years, and beware of draft or unsubstantiated accounts.
- Obtain and examine recent interim or management accounts where the last published set are unlikely to be relevant.
- Determine and appraise selected accounting ratios and performance indicators (these may vary according to the sector of operations).
- Compare value of impending contract to level of turnover, this may result in the setting of limits to the value of the work offered to the contractor.
- Obtain and review bankers references (such references are but one part of the financial assessment and should not be solely relied upon).
- Obtain and examine business information reports from reliable sources.
- Consider the need for performance bonding or other security (*see* Chapter 16).
- Obtain (where appropriate) a written guarantee from the parent or holding company.

- Take note of comments and notes contained in annual reports or auditors certificates.
- Obtain a list of current contracts/jobs in progress to assess whether the contractor may be over-committed.
- Have regard for any other contract work currently being conducted for the organisation.
- Review any previous record with regard to contract accounts, claims, etc. if the organisation has had previous dealings with the contractor.

The information should be gathered in a uniform way for all contractors under review so that subsequent comparisons between competing contractors are meaningful. Reviews of this type should be conducted by suitably skilled staff, and any decisions and conclusions supported by reasoned arguments and facts.

TECHNICAL

The prime objective is to obtain an accurate and reliable assessment of the contractor's experience, competence, standard of work, etc. in relation to those areas of interest to the employer. If the contractor in question has been previously engaged by the organisation, the results of any previous contract performance assessments or post-completion review should also be taken into account. The following example considerations may be relevant:

- Determine the range and nature of activities conducted by the contractor.
- Note any geographic or technical limitations that apply.
- Undertake a technical interview.
- Obtain a view of the market position of the service or product.
- Record any professional or trade association affiliations.
- Obtain and review any published material on product, service, etc.
- Take note of any quality management accreditation (i.e. BS5750 or ISO9000).
- Confirm that personnel are suitably qualified and trained.
- Assess the adequacy of available resources (staff, plant, manufacturing facilities, etc.).
- Obtain a list of current contracts/jobs in progress to assess whether the contractor may be over-committed, which could lead to delays or short cuts.
- Consider contact with existing or previous clients to obtain their views.
- Take into account the contractor's commitment to after-sales service, training, and maintenance obligations.
- Ensure that any relative products conform to the required national and international standards.
- Obtain reports in trade or professional publications about contractor or current jobs.

CONTRACT PERFORMANCE

This section aims to evaluate contractors in respect of their record of previous performance and the discharge of former contractual responsibilities. Where the contractor has conducted previous work for the employer, this form of assessment can be based upon the results of a formal post completion review or project out-turn review (*see* Chapter 30). In other cases, it may be necessary to obtain the relevant observations from previous clients. Some or all of the following example points should be taken into account:

- Did the contractor meet the obligations with respect to achieving deadlines and completion dates?
- Was previous work performed to the required technical and workmanship standards?
- Did the functionality of the product or service match the defined requirements?
- Did the contractor complete the necessary work within the defined cost/budget constraints?
- What was the contractor's attitude to variations, extensions of time, contractual claims, etc.?
- Did the contractor establish good and effective working relationships with the employer's staff, sub-contractors, professionals, consultants, etc.?
- Did the contractor provide adequate numbers of suitably skilled staff to address the project requirements?
- Did the plant and equipment supplied by the contractor perform satisfactorily?
- Were delays minimised and promptly countered by the contractor's actions?
- Were the contractor's accounts accurately and correctly completed?
- Did the contractor discharge all obligations for subsequent maintenance?

In all cases, beware of unsubstantiated comments or reports, and ensure that sources of data are reliable, recognised and trailed. In larger employing organisations, where a contract or project may span and affect many different departments or disciplines, systems of liaison and communication should be established so that reliable intelligence about contractors can be accumulated and shared.

FROM THE CONTRACTOR'S VIEWPOINT

It is obviously in the contractor's best interests to present a strong and positive image to the employer when being considered for future contracts. Much will depend upon whether the contractor is truly interested in the potential work or merely wishing to maintain a connection with the client in the hope that future contracts will materialise when the level of commitments is more suitable.

Although co-operation with the potential employer is necessary, some requests for data may have previous client confidentiality or commercial sensitivity implications. It may be a wise precaution to obtain the permission of previous clients before releasing their names as references for work completed. This is especially true where the service supplied is of a potentially sensitive nature, for example IT security review or market research.

The release of current workload data may also have negative connotations, in that it may reflect a dearth of current jobs or a concentration in non-relevant areas. Contractors should be cautious before releasing such data, although also avoiding alienating potential clients by a refusal. The release of any data should be carefully controlled and suitably authorised to avoid the dissemination of inappropriate details.

Contractors will need to take a view on the impacts represented by the available contract and should honestly assess their capabilities and resources in meeting the defined requirements. There is no point in overstretching staff and other resources with the possible subsequent failure of the project. Requests for information on technical capability may be satisfied by the provision of data on the qualifications held by staff, accreditation under recognised trade proficiency schemes, demonstrable commitments to training, and so on. Finally, contractors should look to the elements of their own organisation with respect to the achievement of objectives, and draw out those aspects which can demonstrate their commitment to potential clients.

Control matrix example

The potential *Exposures* resulting from the engagement of unsuitable, unstable and incompetent contractors are contained in the example matrix provided as Table 12. This table uses *Scale* 31 which is reproduced in Appendix 7. The example data represents an organisation frequently involved in contract activities, but lacking a formal approved list of contractors. The noted controls are relatively comprehensive and suggest that the organisation has a formal procedure in place to assess potential contractors, with feedback from previous contracts being achieved through post-completion reviews. Readers requiring a detailed explanation of the theory and technique supporting the construction of matrices should refer to Chapter 32.

Table 12 Contractor Viability/Competence – Exposures
Overall Inherent Risk (Size) Score [5 is worst risk; 1 is best] = 2.45

A Financial failure of contractor – project collapse, etc.
B Ongoing disruption due to financially unstable contractor
C Engagement of generally unsuitable/unreliable contractor
D Technically incompetent/unqualified contractor engaged
E Impacts due to inadequate/overstretched contractor resources
F Delays & errors due to poorly skilled contractor employees
G Contractor engaged as result of favouritism/malpractice
H Inadequate security against breach of contract
I Absence/inadequacy of contractor's insurance cover
J Failure to maintain awareness of contractor's finances
K Delay & cost due to contractor's propensity for claims

Scale 31 (abridged)

6 = Incorrect identification of needs, or failure to meet them
5 = Lost business; needs partly unfulfilled; or breach of rules
4 = Delay or disruption; reputation loss; minor breach of rules
(Contract auditing Exposures-oriented scale)
3 = Avoidable costs/losses; damage to contract relationships
2 = Administrative or accounting errors
1 = Detectable negative impact on the business or service

Contractors Viability/Competence		EXPOSURES										
		A	B	C	D	E	F	G	H	I	J	K
		=	=	=	=	=	=	=	=	=	=	=
Calculated Risk Score:	Risk	3	3	3	3	3	2	2	3	2	3	2
Scale 31 (6 is most serious)	Type	6	6	5	5	4	6	4	5	3	6	3
Size (3 is maximum)	Size	2	2	2	2	2	1	1	2	2	2	2
CONTROLS												
1 Three years' audited accounts are examined by Finance Dept. prior to engagement	Best	3	3									
	Test	?	?	?								
	Both											
2 Key financial indicators and ratios are appraised & reported upon	Best	3	3									
	Test	?	?	?								
	Both											
3 Suitably valued guarantees are obtained from parent companies when appropriate	Best	4	4							3		
	Test	?	?	?						?		
	Both											
4 Work is allocated against maximum contract values for each contractor	Best	2	2			2						
	Test	?	?	?		?						
	Both											
5 Performance Bonds are obtained for all contacts in excess of £100,000 in value	Best	3	3						3			
	Test	?	?	?					?			
	Both											
6 Bankers references are sought for all main contractors	Best	2	2							2		
	Test	?	?	?						?		
	Both											
7 Previous clients are contacted for comments on the contractor's performance, attitudes, etc.	Best			4	4	2				2		
	Test	?		?	?	?				?		
	Both											
8 The performance of the contractor during previous contracts is reviewed	Best			4	4	2	3					3
	Test	?		?	?	?	?					?
	Both											
9 Contractors are only appointed after a review of all factors by the Development Committee	Best		4	4	4	4		2	4	3		
	Test	?	?	?	?		?	?	?			
	Both											

Table 12 continued

			A	B	C	D	E	F	G	H	I	J	K
			=	=	=	=	=	=	=	=	=	=	=
	Calculated Risk Score	Risk	3	3	3	3	3	2	2	3	2	3	2
			–	–	–	–	–	–	–	–	–	–	–
10	Contractors must provide evidence of the proficiency of their staff	Best				4		4					
		Test	?			?		?					
		Both											
			–	–	–	–	–	–	–	–	–	–	–
11	Only members of recognised professional and trade bodies are engaged	Best			3	4		3					
		Test	?		?	?		?					
		Both											
			–	–	–	–	–	–	–	–	–	–	–
12	Contractor's workloads are reviewed in light of project requirements. Evidence is sought	Best						4					
		Test	?					?					
		Both											
			–	–	–	–	–	–	–	–	–	–	–
13	Contractors are selected & appointed by independent management committee	Best							4				
		Test	?						?				
		Both											
			–	–	–	–	–	–	–	–	–	–	–
14	Key duties within the organisation are subject to strict segregation	Best							4				
		Test	?						?				
		Both											
			–	–	–	–	–	–	–	–	–	–	–
15	Liquidated damage factors are built into the applied forms of contract	Best								5			
		Test	?							?			
		Both											
			–	–	–	–	–	–	–	–	–	–	–
16	Written evidence is obtained that contractor's liability cover is valid, current & sufficient	Best								4			
		Test	?							?			
		Both											
			–	–	–	–	–	–	–	–	–	–	–
17	Insurance renewal notices and evidence of payment is sought and confirmed	Best								4			
		Test	?							?			
		Both											
			–	–	–	–	–	–	–	–	–	–	–
18	Relevant data is required to be supplied during the lifetime of long-term contracts	Best										4	
		Test	?									?	
		Both											
			–	–	–	–	–	–	–	–	–	–	–
19	Previous claims history of contractors is reviewed. Excess prevents re-engagement	Best											4
		Test	?										?
		Both											
			–	–	–	–	–	–	–	–	–	–	–
20	Post-completion reviews aim to highlight contractor's strengths and weaknesses for future work	Best			3	3							
		Test	?		?	?							
		Both											
			–										

13

MAINTAINING AN APPROVED LIST OF CONTRACTORS

Scope

The maintenance of an approved list has strong linkages with the processes for assessing contractors described in Chapter 12. Although is it probable that organisations will wish to undertake an evaluation of the contractor's competence and stability, not all can justify the upkeep of a list, therefore we have separated the subjects. This chapter explores the motivation for maintaining a list and the related procedural issues.

The mechanism of maintaining an approved list is more suited to organisations with a regular and/or high level of contracting activities. Their use is more common in the public sector, where there is a greater level of regular contracted projects and a connected requirement to demonstrate both value for money and accountability.

The approved list, if up to date and accurate, can provide a source for determining contractors with the appropriate technical experience to conduct a project. Where it is deemed necessary, perhaps for the objective of obtaining competitive quotations for work, the approved list can be used as the basis for selective tendering. (*see also* Chapter 14). In this latter context it is important to target those contractors who can match all the identified requirements.

The nature of the procedures required to administer and maintain the approved list will vary in relation to the operating sector of the organisation. For example, in the public sector the procedures should take account of the need to ensure impartiality, and provide for adequate controls over the inclusion of contractors on the list. This chapter explores the subject with this more demanding environment in mind. However, readers from other operating backgrounds may, understandably, find such an approach either too cumbersome for their needs, or not justifiable on cost grounds.

Before examining in detail the key issues, it is stressed that written procedures should be provided as the basis for allocating responsibilities and defining the discrete processes to cater for the establishment and maintenance of an approved list. These procedures, which may be further necessitated by the statutory requirements in selected environments, may also have to be supported by authorised corporate policies.

The responsibility for the administration of the approved list, in accordance with the established procedures, should be clearly allocated to a nominated individual or group. In sectors where segregation of key duties is deemed necessary, as a means of providing both assurance and impartiality, the person(s) responsible should be completely independent from those functions and departments with front-line responsibilities for initiating and controlling the related works or services.

The approved list, which may take the form of a computer database, should incorporate appropriate details, including:

- indication of whether the entry is current or inactive
- key contacts
- the categories or types of work handled by the contractor
- geographic area covered
- limitations on the value of contracts to be tendered for
- references to previous contract involvement with the organisation
- date placed on approved list
- date of last data review
- date when the next review is due
- comments regarding previous failures to respond to tender invitations
- date removed from active list and reason for removal.

The list or database should be capable of efficient analysis so that suitable potential candidates for selective tendering processes can be extracted in accordance with the established requirements.

All additions, amendments and deletions should be routed via the person or committee charged with responsibility for maintaining the list. Due regard should be given to the needs for commercial confidentiality and access to the list data will need to be controlled accordingly. Prior to the use of the list for selecting candidates to be invited to submit tenders, the accuracy of the list and whether it is up to date should be positively confirmed. Applying such a check will ensure that no contractors are disadvantaged due to error or omission.

A policy or procedure should be in place to ensure that selections made from the list are fair and equitable. Any decisions to exclude apparently valid contenders from the tendering process should be documented, supported by comments and independently authorised.

ADDITIONS TO THE LIST

The grounds for accepting a contractor on to the approved list should be judged on a number of different elements, some of which may be very specific to the nature and scale of the related activities. These factors may be summarised as either financial, technical or performance-related in nature. The explicit processes for determining the viability and competence of a contractor are fully explored in Chapter 12. However, the procedures employed should form the basis for assessing whether the contractor is financially stable, has the requisite technical experience for the nature of work envisaged, has a reliable track record, and the capacity and resources to cope with the demands of the work in question.

The factors used to assess the overall suitability of a contractor will vary both in terms of the demands of the organisation and the degree to which the contractor can fulfil those demands. For example, the capacity of the contractor will vary in relation to the current workload and staffing levels, and their financial strength will be linked to both macroeconomic and microeconomic considerations. In light of this proclivity for variation of degree, the employing organisation should ensure that the relevant data and assessment is progressively reviewed and updated. Correspondence with applicant contractors should clearly define the nature, form and frequency of information required if they are to be considered for future project involvement. The intention to create, update or maintain an approved list within a public sector organisation may require the appropriate placing of a public announcement or notice.

The procedures should clearly define the circumstances and criteria that apply to permitting new entries to be made to the list. In simple terms admission to the list should only be permitted when all the defined qualifying criteria have been satisfied, and the authority of the governing individual or committee has been obtained in writing. Rejection of an applicant should be supported by a suitable rationale, as the decision may have to be explained to the applicant, if only for the sake of courtesy. The mechanism employed should prevent the unauthorised inclusion of contractors on the list, and to this end, all the appropriate supporting documentation, including the required written authorities, should be securely retained on file.

AMENDING AND UPDATING THE LIST

In association with those responsible for conducting the assessment of contractors' suitability, regular reviews of contractors should be applied, with the aim of updating the relative data and ensuring that only contractors who continue to achieve the required standards are featured on the approved list. The date and nature of any reviews should be recorded and documented, and the objective should be to ensure that tendering processes and management decisions are applied on the basis of current and accurate contractor data.

DELETIONS FROM THE APPROVED LIST

Decisions to remove contractors from the list should be adequately documented, supported and authorised. Some deletions may, for example, be necessary because the contractor is no longer trading, is in liquidation, is currently fully committed, or has failed to react to previous invitations to tender.

If the list is held as a database, the deletion date and reason should be recorded. In any case, the relevant documentation supporting the removal of a contractor should be retained. In specific instances it may be necessary to advise the contractor of his removal from the approved list.

Control matrix example

The key *Exposures* relative to the maintenance of an approved list of contractors are recorded in the example matrix featured in Table 13. The data are intended to represent the requirements of an organisation with regular mid-range contract activities where a pool of reliable contractors is required. Formalised methods are employed in the selection of contractors for appearance on the approved list, and care is taken to maintain the integrity and accuracy of the data. This scenario could also represent the basic requirements of a public sector operation. Appendix 7 contains details of *Scale* 31 which has been used in this example.

Table 13 Maintaining an Approved List – Exposures
Overall Inherent Risk (Size) Score [5 is worst risk; 1 is best] = 2.05

A Inability to select the most suitable & optimum contractor
B Listing/selection of financially unsuitable contractors
C Listing/selection of technically incompetent contractors
D Listing/selection of unreliable/unproven contractors
E Listing/selection of under-resourced contractors
F Listing/selection of previously unsatisfactory contractors
G Criteria too liberal to avoid inappropriate decision
H Unfair conditions for inclusion on to approved list
I Unauthorised inclusion on to approved list
J Contractor data no longer valid or out of date
K Contractor data subject to unauthorised amendment or update
L Inclusion/selection of contractor as result of malpractice
M Selection data in error – disruption of contract awards
N Unauthorised/invalid deletion from approved list
O Regulatory or legislative requirements not addressed
P Incorrect use and interpretation of approved list
Q Failure to allocate responsibility for maintenance of list
R Award of contract to non-listed contractor
S Breach of confidentiality with sensitive contractor data

Scale 31 (abridged)

6 = Incorrect identification of needs, or failure to meet them
5 = Lost business; needs partly unfulfilled; or breach of rules
4 = Delay or disruption; reputation loss; minor breach of rules
(Contract auditing Exposures-oriented scale)

3 = Avoidable costs/losses; damage to contract relationships
2 = Administrative or accounting errors
1 = Detectable negative impact on the business or service

Maintaining an Approved List		A	B	C	D	E	F	G	H	I	J	K	L	M	N	O	P	Q	R	S
		=	=	=	=	=	=	=	=	=	=	=	=	=	=	=	=	=	=	=
Calculated Risk Score:	Risk	3	3	3	3	3	3	3	2	3	3	3	2	3	2	3	3	2	2	2
Scale 31 (6 is most serious)	Type	6	5	4	4	4	4	5	5	4	5	4	4	4	3	5	4	5	4	3
Size (3 is maximum)	Size	2	2	2	2	2	2	2	1	2	2	2	1	2	1	2	2	1	1	1
CONTROLS																				
1 Register of Approved Contractors maintained on personal computer database	Best		4																	
	Test	?	?																	
	Both																			
2 Policy & procedure in place governing the conditions for inclusion and selection	Best	3	3	3	3	3	2	2	4	4	2	2	2	2	3	4	3	3		
	Test	?	?	?	?	?	?	?	?	?	?	?	?	?	?	?	?	?		
	Both																			
3 Full financial appraisal is conducted by the Finance Dept.	Best		4																	
	Test	?	?																	
	Both																			
4 Three years of audited accounts are examined and key ratios and indicators are analysed	Best		4																	
	Test	?	?																	
	Both																			
5 Bankers references are obtained and reviewed	Best		2																	
	Test	?	?																	
	Both																			
6 Technical interview and questionnaire utilised to assess ability/proficiency	Best			4																
	Test	?		?																
	Both																			
7 Only members of recognised professional and trade bodies are listed and engaged	Best			4																
	Test	?		?																
	Both																			
8 Previous clients are contacted for their comments	Best				3															
	Test	?			?															
	Both																			
9 Newly listed contractors are subject to a low contract value limitation until proven	Best			2	2	2	2													
	Test			?	?	?	?													
	Both																			

Table 13 continued

			A	B	C	D	E	F	G	H	I	J	K	L	M	N	O	P	Q	R	S
			=	=	=	=	=	=	=	=	=	=	=	=	=	=	=	=	=	=	=
	Calculated Risk Score:	Risk	3	3	3	3	3	3	3	2	3	3	3	2	3	2	3	3	2	2	2
10	Ongoing review and update of key data is applied per defined procedures	Best								3		3										
		Test	?							?		?										
		Both																				
11	Previous involvement with the organisation is reviewed and data updated on list	Best						4														
		Test	?					?														
		Both																				
12	Contractors' current workload is reviewed in relation to demands of pending contracts	Best						4														
		Test	?					?														
		Both																				
13	Contractors obliged to provide ongoing workload, financial and commitment data	Best						3														
		Test	?					?														
		Both																				
14	Listing/selection criteria are defined in procedures, as approved by committee/Board	Best		4	3	3	3	3	3	3	4		3	2	3							
		Test	?	?	?	?	?	?	?	?	?		?	?	?							
		Both																				
15	Listing conditions comply with best practice, EC and other regulations where necessary	Best								4						4						
		Test	?							?						?						
		Both																				
16	Conditions of listing are circulated to all applying contractors	Best								3												
		Test	?							?												
		Both																				
17	All supplied details are reviewed against requirements & listing approved by management	Best		4	3	3	3	3	3	4												
		Test	?	?	?	?	?	?	?	?												
		Both																				
18	Date of last entry/update is recorded and used to trigger contract for current data	Best										4										
		Test	?									?										
		Both																				
19	Access to system is protected by use of password and user ID	Best										4	4									
		Test	?									?	?									
		Both																				
20	Responsibility for maintaining the register is allocated to an independent employee	Best										4	4	2		3			5			
		Test	?									?	?	?		?			?			
		Both																				
21	All amendments are recorded on the PC activity log	Best										3										
		Test	?									?										
		Both																				
22	Management seek clarification or support of doubtful data entries	Best												2								
		Test	?											?								
		Both																				
23	All list entries and details are authorised by the management committee	Best											4		3							
		Test	?										?		?							
		Both																				

Table 13 continued

#	Description			A	B	C	D	E	F	G	H	I	J	K	L	M	N	O	P	Q	R	S
				=	=	=	=	=	=	=	=	=	=	=	=	=	=	=	=	=	=	=
	Calculated Risk Score:	Risk	–	3	3	3	3	3	3	3	2	3	3	3	2	3	2	3	3	2	2	2
			–	–	–	–	–	–	–	–	–	–	–	–	–	–	–	–	–	–	–	–
24	Printouts of key data are sent to contractors for verification and correction	Best														4	3					
		Test	?													?	?					
		Both																				
			–	–	–	–	–	–	–	–	–	–	–	–	–	–	–	–	–	–	–	–
25	The contents of the register are subject to periodic review and editing via the committee	Best												3	3							
		Test	?											?	?							
		Both																				
			–	–	–	–	–	–	–	–	–	–	–	–	–	–	–	–	–	–	–	–
26	Unsuitable/unsatisfactory contractors are removed from the list after review/authority	Best			3	3		4		3												
		Test	?		?	?		?		?												
		Both																				
			–	–	–	–	–	–	–	–	–	–	–	–	–	–	–	–	–	–	–	–
27	Award of contracts only normally permitted to listed contractors per tendering procedures	Best																3	4		4	
		Test	?															?	?		?	
		Both																				
			–	–	–	–	–	–	–	–	–	–	–	–	–	–	–	–	–	–	–	–
28	Exceptional/non-standard contracts approved for award to non-listed contractors	Best																			4	
		Test	?																		?	
		Both																				
			–	–	–	–	–	–	–	–	–	–	–	–	–	–	–	–	–	–	–	–
29	Circulation of list data is restricted on a 'need to know' basis	Best																				3
		Test	?																			?
		Both																				
			–	–	–	–	–	–	–	–	–	–	–	–	–	–	–	–	–	–	–	–
30	Printouts are kept in a lockable cupboard	Best																				2
		Test	?																			?
		Both																				
			–																				

A Inability to select the most suitable & optimum contractor
B Listing/selection of financially unsuitable contractors
C Listing/selection of technically incompetent contractors
D Listing/selection of unreliable/unproven contractors
E Listing/selection of under-resourced contractors
F Listing/selection of previously unsatisfactory contractors
G Criteria too liberal to avoid inappropriate decision
H Unfair conditions for inclusion on to approved list
I Unauthorised inclusion on to approved list
J Contractor data no longer valid or out of date
K Contractor data subject to unauthorised amendment or update
L Inclusion/selection of contractor as result of malpractice
M Selection data in error – disruption of contract awards
N Unauthorised/invalid deletion from approved list
O Regulatory or legislative requirements not addressed
P Incorrect use and interpretation of approved list
Q Failure to allocate responsibility for maintenance of list
R Award of contract to non-listed contractor
S Breach of confidentiality with sensitive contractor data

Scale 31 (abridged)

6 = Incorrect identification of needs, or failure to meet them
5 = Lost business; needs partly unfulfilled; or breach of rules
4 = Delay or disruption; reputation loss; minor breach of rules
(Contract auditing Exposures-oriented scale)

3 = Avoidable costs/losses; damage to contract relationships
2 = Administrative or accounting errors
1 = Detectable negative impact on the business or service

14

TENDERING PROCEDURES

Scope

This chapter examines the motivation for applying a tendering approach, and then moves on to discuss the different forms of tendering and the related procedural issues and requirements. In defining possible tendering procedures, we have applied a comprehensive view of the requirements which is only likely to apply in very large organisations with a correspondingly high level of contracting activity. In areas where the contracting activities are less significant, some of the suggested procedures may be either omitted or reduced appropriately.

Having established, during the appraisal and design phases of the project, all the detailed requirements, specifications, performance criteria, etc., the organisation then has to seek out the most suitable and appropriate contractor or supplier to fulfil the identified requirements. Tendering, in its various forms, is a process which seeks to identify the optimum match between requirement and provider. As a process it is most common in the public sector which has an established convention for seeking value for money and for having to openly demonstrate accountability. Therefore, it is within the public sector that tendering procedures are most developed, indeed they normally form part of the formal documented standing orders or financial regulations of public authorities.

Outwith the public sector, with its need to reflect an independent and unbiased standpoint, there is not a universal justification to apply the techniques of tendering. For example, the requirement for a specialised service or product may automatically limit the source suppliers or contractors to one. This form of supply limitation can of course also apply to the public sector, for example in the defence procurement arena. Additionally in the wider commercial world, where there is a healthy regard for the bottom line, the costs that can be associated with an effective and fair tendering process would perhaps rule it out. If an organisation is not obliged to go out to tender, it may elect to negotiate directly with contractors especially where the new requirement is akin to a previous contract arrangement. It is also worth mentioning that tendering can be a time-consuming procedure. However, all factors should be relative to the end-product, i.e. the achievement of the objective by using the appropriate contractor at a price which offers value for money.

Assessing whether tendering is either a necessary or effective method of identifying a contractor or supplier is dependent on a number of factors, including:

- the scale of the related project and its significance to the organisation
- whether the organisation is conversant with the nature of the project or service
- the competence of in-house staff in relation to the project or service
- whether the related market is narrow or broad in nature
- the costs and time delay that may be associated with a tendering process
- whether the related market is currently particularly competitive and therefore whether any appreciable benefits may result from putting the project out to tender
- the general economic conditions and the trading environment.

Even within the public sector it is not always obligatory to go through the tendering process in certain situations, and the responsible officers may have some leeway in this regard. This flexibility or discretion needs to be applied in an informed way and obviously should not contravene either recognised codes of practice, statutory regulations or relevant European Directives (*see* Chapter 1). Special arrangements may be necessary to cater for the supply of goods and services in emergency situations, for example undertaking essential repairs to storm damaged structures. Much work has been done by the NJCC (National Joint Consultative Committee, for Building) in the area of developing tendering best practice for the building sector, and they publish relevant codes of practice for the various basic tendering methods.

One of the outcomes of the tendering process is to enable management to make more informed decisions on a consistent basis. Where management has to support or justify its decision, for example in a local authority, tendering can provide the mechanism for logically arriving at the optimum solution. Alternatively the process can result in tenders being received for substantially higher sums than the employer's estimate, which may give cause for second thoughts. Abandoning projects at this stage will avoid commitments and the greater costs associated with the development, provision or construction phases. Preparing tender documentation and bids is a time-consuming and costly process for contractors, and employers should avoid getting a reputation for not proceeding with projects after such time and effort has been expended.

However, before we delve more deeply into the detail of tendering processes, it is prudent to point out that the lowest price tender may not automatically be the best choice for the organisation. The process may reveal factors beyond cost which will rightly influence the selection of the contractor, these may include quality of work, proven ability to meet deadlines, relevant spare capacity, etc.

If the organisation has regular recourse to tendering, the related processes should be subject to formal documented policies and procedures. Mechanisms will need to be in place to ensure that all affected staff are fully aware of their responsibilities under the auspices of the procedures. Additionally, the procedures should incorporate review and monitoring processes which enable either the confirmation of compliance or the detection of non-compliance in relation to key factors or processes.

THE FORM OF CONTRACT

Selecting the most appropriate form of contract is a critical process. (Please note that this subject is more fully discussed in Chapter 17). A number of standard forms of contract are available although they mostly address the needs of the building, and civil, mechanical and electrical engineering sectors. The use of a standard form of contract may offer the advantages of being recognised and acceptable, but they may not be capable of suitable amendment to meet your specific needs.

Most standard forms of contract relevant to construction have established common elements which cater for both tendering and forming the subsequent basis for the work required. In the preparation of all the tendering documentation, compliance with the requirements of the relevant form of contract should be confirmed before release.

When preparing tender documents, care should be taken to ensure that the approved details of the design and technical requirements are accurately reflected. Any modifications or amendments applied to the designs, drawings, etc. will need to be updated on the relevant tender documentation before release. The tender documents will need to be checked for accuracy and completeness prior to copying and despatch.

CATEGORIES OF TENDERING

There are a number of different forms of tendering.

Selective tendering

This is where the employing organisation invites a number of nominated contractors or suppliers to submit bids for the available activity, work, etc. The process is usually related to the maintenance of an approved list of contractors (*see* Chapter 13 for more details). If the procedures surrounding the maintenance of the approved list are sound, the contractors should have satisfactorily achieved a number of target criteria such as financial stability, proven technical ability, acceptable levels of performance during previous projects, and so on. The tendering procedures should define the required sample of tenderers applicable to the value and nature of the available contract. A further practical method is to either rotate or systematically vary the selection of those invited, although it would still be necessary to ensure that they possessed the appropriate degrees of experience and competence. The approved list should be subject to periodic review and unsuitable or generally unresponsive contractors removed under controlled conditions.

Two-stage selective tendering

This form of tendering is normally applied to complex projects and is useful in selecting appropriate contractors and involving them in the early stages of the project so that the finalisation of all the pre-contract documentation is a collaborative process. The first stage is therefore related to selecting the contractor based upon a limited amount of project design data, and the second is the refinement of that basic information into all the necessary designs, bills of quantity, etc. which will eventually support the execution of the contracted work or activity.

Open tendering

As the name suggests this method supports the principles of open and fair submission of tenders. However, the applicants are likely to be an unknown quantity and further assessment of their technical and financial suitability would have to be undertaken before progressing with any formal relationship. Open tendering involves the employing organisation advertising in the press, sector, or trade publications, etc., the fact that a particular job or project is open for tendering. Consideration will need to be given to the selection of the most suitable media for the advertisement. Basic details only are provided and suitably qualified or experienced contractors are invited to apply for the necessary documentation. Care should be taken in the preparation of the advertisement, in order that it conforms to any prevailing statutory requirements. It is normal practice to ask for a refundable deposit to be paid when issuing the tender documents; this will hopefully prevent the receipt of false or time-wasting requests.

Negotiated tendering

Where a forthcoming project is similar to a previous one and the performance of the initial contractor proved to be satisfactory, it may be appropriate to use the negotiated tendering approach. The process involves direct contact with either a specific or previously used contractor and therefore eliminates free and open competition of available work. Although this approach would present problems for organisations obliged to demonstrate accountability and impartiality, it does allow for prompt and cost-effective agreements to be reached. On the distaff side, precautions need to be in place to prevent the abuse of responsibility or a cult of favouritism being developed, and to counteract the danger that quoted contract prices will be unnecessarily high as a result of reducing competition.

Single or restricted tendering

Where the target market or requirement is very specialised (for example in advanced technology defence equipment) and therefore the potential suppliers are restricted, it may be acceptable to invite a single contractor to bid for the work. Caution is required in such instances so that the system cannot be abused.

Serial tendering

Where it is necessary either to conduct a number of similar projects perhaps phased over a long timescale, or to break down an especially large project into a number of discrete but comparable contracts, this category of tendering may be appropriate. The process should ensure that the basis for the required range of contracts is consistent, especially the pricing structure, although allowance should be made for any unavoidable price variations over long time periods by the use of agreed price formulae.

Design and build

In this type of contract, which is fully described in Chapter 15, contractors normally bid competitively for a construction project where they will also provide (directly or indirectly) the necessary designs. Unless the employer has the ability to clearly specify any quality, workmanship or technical standards, the contractor may only be able to accommodate or contain cost targets within the quoted price by reducing the quality of finish and materials. Please note that this form of tendering is the subject of a specific NJCC code of practice.

TENDERS – EUROPEAN DIRECTIVES

The following EEC Directives, which only refer to the public and utilities* sectors, all relate to the award of either supply, works or service contracts:

Directive reference	*Date*
77/62/EEC	21 December 1976
80/767/EEC	22 July 1980
88/295/EEC	22 March 1988
89/440/EEC	18 July 1989
90/531/EEC*	17 September 1990 (refers to energy, water, transport and telecommunications)
92/50/EEC	18 June 1992

Full title descriptions of these Directives are provided, under the heading HMSO, in the Bibliography contained in Appendix 4. Their applicability is related to comparatively low-contract-value thresholds which are defined in European Currency Units (ECU).

When formulating and applying tendering procedures, the affected public bodies will have to ensure that they conform to the appropriate EEC requirements, which include, *inter alia*, the following elements:

• advertising the contract details in the *Official Journal of the European Communities*

- defined timetable for advertising, receiving and processing tenders
- defined contents and formats for notices and communications
- various financial limits for eligible contracts expressed in ECU.

On the matter of assessing contractors submitting tenders, the Directives specify that proof of the supplier's financial standing may be furnished by either bankers reference, accounting information, or turnover statements.

TENDERING – DEFINING THE PROCEDURAL REQUIREMENTS

Tendering procedures should be in place within the employing organisation which should, among other factors, address the following where applicable:

- allocating specific responsibilities to named employees or officers
- reinforcing segregation of key duties and responsibilities by ensuring that impartial members of staff are involved in the receipt, opening and storage of tenders submitted
- conditions under which tenders are sought and the minimum number of tenders required in relation to the material value of the contract
- determining the optimum method of tendering to utilise in specific situations
- establishing a clear and realistic timetable for the tendering process, defining the date and time by which tenders should be returned
- the requirements of any relevant EEC Directives
- those invited to submit tenders should be given clear and unambiguous instructions regarding the details required, the forms to be used, the standards to be adopted, timescales, etc.
- guidelines as to the use of approved lists of contractors as means of selecting contractors to receive invitations to tender
- providing linkages to the assessment of financial and technical suitability of contractors prior to selection for tendering
- arrangements for dealing with queries from contractors and ensuring that all those invited to tender are treated equally and fairly. This includes ensuring that any subsequent amendments of the tendering conditions are provided to all affected contractors at the same time
- matters regarding the extension of the original tendering timetable
- determining how tender submissions should be clearly identified (per contract/project reference) so as to ensure correct handling, storage, opening, etc.
- the impartiality of the submission process can be enhanced by a requirement that the envelope or package containing the tender should be devoid of any identifying marks linking it with the contractor
- avoiding the inadvertent opening of tenders by ensuring that they are suitably labelled and identified

- defining the action to be taken where incorrectly identified tender submissions were opened by unauthorised staff
- procedures for the opening and examination of tenders (see below for more details) NB: Tenders should be kept sealed until the deadline is reached so that no relevant information is prematurely revealed, thus avoiding either the release or misuse of such data
- an independent custodian (who is not involved in any other aspect of the tendering process) should be nominated and made responsible for receiving, recording and storing all the submissions prior to the opening process. The custodian has no reason to know the identity of contractors invited to submit tenders
- in organisations where invitations to tender are regularly issued, the custodian will need to be kept advised of all those expected (i.e. contract references, number of invitations issued, timetable and deadline details, etc.)
- the recipient/custodian should maintain a record, by contract, of all tenders received within the defined timescale, which can be used subsequently when the tenders are opened to ensure that all have been appropriately examined
- the date and time of receipt should be endorsed on the envelope or package containing the tenders, and the recipient should also initial the package
- action to be taken on tenders that were either received after the deadline, were incorrectly identified per the instructions, or bore some mark which enabled the identification of the submitting organisation
- secure (and fire-proof) storage conditions should be provided and access controlled until the tenders are opened
- where submissions do not conform to the instructions (e.g. late arrivals or inappropriately labelled) the means by which they should be returned to the sender should be prescribed.

This list is not intended to be definitive in all cases and does reflect a deliberate bias towards the additional principals of good practice that are specifically relevant to the public sector. It is recognised that in the private sector and organisations where the incidence of contract tendering is low key, some of the above elements may not be cost justified. However the list is intended to alert readers to some of the surrounding factors which can be evaluated in the context of their situations. Readers working in the public sector will no doubt be aware of the relevant comprehensive guidelines issued and promoted by CIPFA.

In the case of a building project, an organisation should ensure that the requisite land is in their ownership and all the required planning permissions are obtained before instigating the tendering process.

The recurring issue running through the optimum processes is that key areas of responsibility are subject to strict segregation of duties. This is primarily designed to ensure that the tender submission process cannot be unduly influenced or the target of malpractice. Such considerations are of particular significance in the public sector where equality, accountability and scrupulous fairness need to be proactively demonstrated.

The tendering conditions should include a provision requiring the contractor to supply relevant financial and workload information which can be used by the organisation to adequately assess the financial standing of applicants for either a particular contract or for inclusion on to an approved contractor list.

OPENING SUBMITTED TENDERS

As noted above, this phase of the process should also be subject to formal written procedures. Whether all the conditions noted in the following section will be applicable in your specific arena will depend upon a range of factors including the level of contract letting activity, the need to openly demonstrate fair play and accountability, the potential for either staff or contractor malpractice, etc. We recognise that not all the mechanisms will apply in every case, but our objective is to provide comprehensive guidance.

The tendering instructions relevant to the particular contract or project should specify the date when all the tenders will be opened. In order to impartially control the opening, all submissions should be opened at the same time and in the presence of at least two members of staff. The first question to address is, who should be involved in the opening and review processes? In most cases, whether impartiality is a major issue or not, the actions of opening and reviewing should be separated, so as to ensure that all submitted bids are accurately and completely recorded before they are assessed in detail. Such an approach prevents members of staff directly involved in the awarding of contracts from either deliberately excluding or amending submissions as a means of either unfairly promoting or disadvantaging specific contractors. Therefore, if circumstances require, the opening of the tenders should be undertaken by staff who have no active involvement whatsoever in the subsequent processes and who are accordingly authorised by senior management. Such precautions will accurately establish the facts for each submission before the tender documentation is handed over to the individuals responsible for detailed assessment of the tender.

The first task is to ensure that all the tenders recorded as received by the custodian are accounted for and have not been tampered with. The written procedures should provide clear guidance as to the actions required in the event of missing documents or evidence of prior unauthorised opening.

A register should be maintained (where appropriate) with sections for each defined contract or project. It is important that the staff performing the opening of tenders accurately record the key data in this register before passing on the documents for assessment. The recorded details should include, the names of all contractors invited to submit tenders, the date and time when the tenders were opened and by whom, and the amount of each tender received. In order that the approved list of contractors can be maintained up to date, the fact that tenders have been submitted can also be noted on the approved list database. Note should certainly be taken of tenders expected but not received. The register can be subsequently updated with the details of any late tender submissions and the action taken in such circumstances (e.g. the return of the documents, investigation of the receiving process if the contractor disputes the dispatch and receipt details, etc.).

In order to ensure that all the 'key' documents and relevant correspondence are present and accounted for, it may be necessary (dependent upon the prevailing regulations) for the persons opening the tenders to initial the relevant pages and note in the register that all the expected documents were present. This process should ensure that subsequent appraisal of the tender can be undertaken and also avoid any disputes about the contents with those performing the detailed evaluation.

Having opened all the tenders received and recorded the salient factors, all the documents need to be passed over to the staff responsible for detailed evaluation. A signature should be obtained (on the register) from the person receiving the documents on behalf of the review group.

THE REVIEW OF TENDERS

The purpose of the review process is to select and recommend the tender which most appropriately meets the objectives of the project on the most economic terms for the employer. The basis for evaluation should not be restricted purely to the lowest costs.

A prime question for this stage is 'Who should perform the evaluation?' The question, in audit terms, implies a requirement for impartiality, but adequately assessing the submissions may also presuppose a high degree of specific technical knowledge, which can only be supplied by staff who will otherwise be actively involved in the project and therefore who cannot be described as totally objective. This situation can be tempered by the involvement of a detached individual, for example a member of the finance or accounting department. In quoting this example we do *not* imply the proactive involvement of internal auditors as they must be seen to remain completely objective in the performance of their duties, and it would be difficult (if not impossible) to remain objective during subsequent reviews if the auditor concerned had actively assisted in the initial selection process.

The review team should be adequately representative of the project, balanced in composition and not so large as to unduly hinder the required rate of progress. They should exercise adequate security over the documents and be able to account for all the originals. It may be prudent to take photocopies for use by the team and securely store the originals. However, the copies should be checked for completeness before use. The review team should be acting under the auspices of an appropriate senior management committee or the responsible sponsoring group. Where either the organisational environment or the nature of the project demands it, there may be a case for the issue of written terms of reference to the review team. Such terms should clearly establish the key objectives of the task without introducing bias and undue prejudice.

In order to minimise subsequent impacts, the submissions should ideally be examined for arithmetic accuracy. This can be a time-consuming task, but it is preferable to reveal any significant errors at the earliest stage. Any significant problems should be referred back to, and agreed with, the contractor and there should be documented procedures as to how such communication should be handled without the dangers of either implying undue influence, contravention of internal protocols on staff independence, the possibility of staff and contractor malpractice, and so on. There may be circumstances where contact with the tenderer is required in order to discuss or negotiate possible reductions. These activities will need to be carefully considered if all tenderers are to be treated fairly and equitably.

If the design process was suitably comprehensive, all the key cost, technical, and performance criteria should have been identified and incorporated into the tendering documentation requirements. The relative values for each tender will need to be dispassionately considered and compared. Additionally, the organisation (or the sponsoring department) may have established critical capital and running-cost targets, against which the tenders will need to be compared on a consistent basis. Before approaching the review process, all these key components should have been revealed so that the reviewers could construct the methods appropriate to fully appraising them. The reviewers should be especially aware of any qualifying statements or alternatives submitted by the tenderer which may have a material effect on the achievement of the organisation's various aspirations for the project. Where necessary, the tendering documentation should make clear that under no circumstances will any deviations from the design specification be permitted in the interests of either commercial equanimity or technical standards.

Of key interest will be the relative unit prices or rates applied to elements of the project. Any abnormal items should be catalogued and used to support decision making where necessary. The reviewers will need to be assured about the capacity and capability of the tenderers with regard to the contract. In this regard they will need to be supplied with sufficient relevant data for analysis if their assessment is to be accurate and reliable. For example, the tenderer may be required to submit some indication of his present workload, available resource capacity, etc. in order that the evaluation can take account of his ability to meet all the obligations of the job in question.

It is not our intention to go into an exploration of every plausible basis for reviewing tenders as this will fluctuate and be dependent on innumerable variables (for example strict cost constraints, the requirement for technical excellence, the criticality of achieving deadlines, etc.). However, given the specifics of the environment applicable to the review team, they will need to actively and clearly demonstrate to management the reasoning behind their decision to recommend a particular tender.

A report should be prepared for management briefly setting the scene, outlining the key factors for each tender received, indicating the recommended option and the reasons for its selection over the others. The report should also feature any relevant comparisons between the preferred solution costs and the targets established at the appraisal and design stages. It should be obligatory (within the prevailing procedures) to provide a reasoned argument why the lowest tender was not recommended. The circumstances which conceivably affect decisions can change over time, and what appeared logical and justifiable may become difficult to fathom after the event. Therefore it is prudent to note or report upon any influencing factors so that decisions can be adequately trailed.

The appropriate management or sponsoring committee or Board should assess the reviewer's report and if necessary request further information until they are satisfied about the effectiveness of the review process and the recommendation. In certain environments, more notably in the private sector, management may not be obliged to accept the recommended option, but in any situation they should document the reasons for their eventual decision. The auditor, during his assessment of the current mechanisms, should ensure that the relevant board or committee minutes adequately support all decisions. Auditors should not be intimidated into having to readily accept that senior management have made a decision without having sight of the supporting justification, this would be an abdication of audit responsibilities.

Having received management assent to the recommendation, the successful contractor will need to be promptly informed of the outcome by the issue of a letter of acceptance which may, in itself, form the contract (*see also* Chapter 17). Advising the successful contractor will need to be effected within the time limits defined in the tendering process procedures. Similarly, and as a matter of courtesy, the unsuccessful applicants will also need to be informed, but only after the successful tenderer has confirmed his acceptance. In order to maintain commercial confidentiality, care needs to be exercised over the information provided to unsuccessful contractors, especially with regard to how their quotation compared with the others received.

ACTIONS REQUIRED BY CONTRACTORS INVITED TO SUBMIT A TENDER

Contractors who are invited to submit a tender initially face a seemingly simple choice of whether or not to enter a bid. This decision will be dependent upon a range of factors, including the workload and capacity during the intended project timescale, the nature and scale of the project, previous experience with the employer if appropriate, and whether or not the submission of a bid will affect the contractor's chance of remaining on the employer's approved list. Where the contractor was not interested in taking the job, but wanted to remain on the approved list, one tactic would be to submit a deliberately inflated bid, although this may also discourage the employer from issuing future invitations. Irrespective of the outcome, the contractor is still obliged to expend effort in creating the bid, and therefore all such decisions should be carefully considered.

The preparation of a bid is often time-consuming and involves considerable paperwork. The tender documentation may, as in the case of a building project, take the form of a series of detailed bills of quantity, each of which will require completion in terms of providing raw material cost, labour rates, periods of time required, allowances for necessary plant, supervision and overheads, and so on. Using this data, cost extensions are calculated and eventually the total bid value generated. In considering all the data elements, the contractor will also have to take into account other factors such as logistics, previous experiences with similar projects, the likely price sensitivity tolerances of the employer, etc. All these factors should ideally be documented so that the basis of the bid is fully supported, and could be subjected to subsequent analysis if this proved necessary.

In responding to either an invitation to tender or an open tender advertisement, contractors should ensure that they receive all the appropriate documentation, and clear instructions governing such matters as the form of contract to be used, the basis for measuring and calculating, the timetable for submitting tenders, and so on. Acknowledgement of receipt of the tender may be required under the administration procedures. Additionally, after initial consideration, it is good practice to confirm to the employing organisation whether or not a tender is to be submitted.

The contractor's administrative processes should include provisions to ensure that the completion of the tender documentation is accurate, complete, in accord with the employer's instructions, and reflects any internal policy decisions. Documents will need to be independently checked and copies taken for retention.

The contractor will also, from a practical viewpoint, need to identify the effects of potential projects on his cashflow, resources, skill availabilities, current and committed workloads, effects on profitability, etc. The financial implications of the overall bid should be reviewed at a senior level, and may require appropriate senior management approval prior to release. Any amendments applied in the course of such a review should also be authorised.

The bid preparation process should be monitored so as to ensure that the submission deadline is met. Very often public sector employers will require that the external packing used for tender documents is devoid of any marks identifying the submitting organisation. Therefore the package should be checked prior to dispatch to confirm that it does not bear any company logo or identifying postal franking impressions. Dispatch should be by a secure means and the details recorded.

An assessment of the risks associated with the possible project should also be undertaken. This process should include judgements on how the conditions of the intended form of contract will either exacerbate or disperse the contractor's proportion of risk exposure. Records reflecting summary details of all tenders submitted should be maintained, monitored, and updated with events and decisions. Where events dictate the withdrawal of a bid, care should be taken to avoid any repercussions, especially for the contractor's reputation.

Where the tender is accepted, it will be necessary to initiate the appropriate planning and administrative processes. It is not our intention to explore such requirements further, partly because of the huge variation of requirements that could apply in relation to the nature of the project. Of key significance will be the eventual formalising of the contract with the employer (*see* Chapter 17).

Clearly not all tenderers will be successful, and the losers will normally have to bear the considerable costs involved in researching, compiling and presenting tenders. It is possible that employers will offer to meet, albeit only some, of the costs involved. Where this situation is implied, the contractor should obtain written confirmation of the arrangement and take note of any limitations before submitting a suitable account. It would also be prudent for bidders to maintain a record of the costs associated with submitting tenders, and where appropriate link this to the calculation of overheads to be applied to the generation of tender valuations.

Where the tender has not been accepted and the contractor was especially keen to obtain the business, a follow-up review may be justified so that valuable lessons can be learnt and applied to improve future tendering. In some cases, the employing organisation may be willing, where they are permitted to do so, to provide details of the other quotes received for the specific contract. These details, which do not normally reveal the identities of the submitting companies, may be used as part of the internal review and post-mortem. Where a contractor is known to feature on an employer's approved list, and provides the required information, he should react accordingly to his removal from the list (*see* Chapters 12 and 13).

Control matrix example

An *Exposures*-oriented example matrix is provided as Table 14. The scenario depicted refers to an organisation regularly involved in contract tendering and with a need to actively demonstrate accountability and fairness. Many of the suggested *Controls* are aimed at selecting the optimum solution and ensuring the impartiality of the surrounding procedures. *Scale* 31, as described in Appendix 7, has been used to support the *Type* score data.

Table 14 Tendering Procedures – Exposures

Overall Inherent Risk (Size) Score [5 is worst risk; 1 is best] = 1.75

A Inappropriate form of tendering applied – cost, delay, etc.
B Inaccurate/incomplete tendering documentation – error, delay
C Inappropriate/invalid selection of tenderers – no competition
D Failure to comply with regulations & EEC Directives
E Failure due to unrealistic/inappropriate tender timetable
F Tendering not consistent with chosen form of contract
G Possibility of fraud, collusion or malpractice
H Limited sample of tenderers – limited competition, poor VFM
I Ambiguous/inadequate tendering instructions – delay, error
J Failure to deal fairly, impartially & consistently

K Ineffective receipt, recording, opening & handling of tenders
L Inadequate security exercised over storage of tenders
M Unauthorised or premature opening of tenders
N Inadequate handling of late tenders – unfair advantage
O Failure to independently capture all data upon opening
P Inadequate evaluation of tenders received – additional cost
Q Failure to select the optimum tender based on price, etc.
R Failure to detect errors or qualifications in tenders
S Failure to obtain management approval of recommended tender
T Failure to correctly advise successful & failed tenderers

Scale 31 (abridged)

6 = Incorrect identification of needs, or failure to meet them
5 = Lost business; needs partly unfulfilled; or breach of rules
4 = Delay or disruption; reputation loss; minor breach of rules
(Contract auditing Exposures-oriented scale)

3 = Avoidable costs/losses; damage to contract relationships
2 = Administrative or accounting errors
1 = Detectable negative impact on the business or service

#	Tendering Procedures	Metric	A	B	C	D	E	F	G	H	I	J	K	L	M	N	O	P	Q	R	S	T
			=	=	=	=	=	=	=	=	=	=	=	=	=	=	=	=	=	=	=	=
	Calculated Risk Score:	Risk	3	3	3	3	3	3	3	2	2	2	2	2	2	2	2	2	3	2	2	2
	Scale 31 (6 is most serious)	Type	4	4	5	5	4	4	4	4	5	3	4	4	3	3	3	4	6	5	6	3
	Size (3 is maximum)	Size	2	2	2	2	2	2	2	1	2	1	1	1	1	1	1	1	2	1	1	1
	CONTROLS																					
1	Tendering Policy and Procedures are documented and in place	Best	4	3	3	4	2	3	3	3	2	2	3	3	3	3	3	3	3	3	3	3
		Test	?	?	?	?	?	?	?	?	?	?	?	?	?	?	?	?	?	?	?	?
		Both																				
2	Project appraisal process recommends appropriate form of tendering to apply	Best		3																		
		Test	?	?																		
		Both																				
3	Tendering approach agreed and authorised by management	Best		4																		
		Test	?	?																		
		Both																				
4	Tendering documentation is generated from Design phase – checked for accuracy & content	Best		4				4														
		Test		?				?														
		Both																				
5	All elements are subject to documented specification	Best		4				3														
		Test		?				?														
		Both																				
6	Responsibilities for tendering allocated to independent individual	Best							3													
		Test	?						?													
		Both																				
7	Based on either open tenders per advertising or selected from approved list of contractors	Best			4					3												
		Test	?		?					?												
		Both																				
8	Optimum sample of tenderers agreed and selected per driving requirements	Best			3					3												
		Test	?		?					?												
		Both																				
9	Where appropriate relevant EEC Directives are complied with. Confirmed by Legal Dept.	Best				4																
		Test	?			?																
		Both																				

Table 14 continued

			A	B	C	D	E	F	G	H	I	J	K	L	M	N	O	P	Q	R	S	T
			=	=	=	=	=	=	=	=	=	=	=	=	=	=	=	=	=	=	=	=
Calculated Risk Score:	Risk		3	3	3	3	3	3	3	2	2	2	2	2	2	2	2	2	3	2	2	2
			–	–	–	–	–	–	–	–	–	–	–	–	–	–	–	–	–	–	–	–
10 Tendering timetable as per the adopted standard form of contract	Best						4															
	Test		?				?															
	Both																					
			–	–	–	–	–	–	–	–	–	–	–	–	–	–	–	–	–	–	–	–
11 Timetable for submission is incorporated into the instructions issued to tenderers	Best						3				3											
	Test		?				?				?											
	Both																					
			–	–	–	–	–	–	–	–	–	–	–	–	–	–	–	–	–	–	–	–
12 Timetable may be extended if significant problems apparent – subject to relevant authority	Best						2															
	Test		?				?															
	Both																					
			–	–	–	–	–	–	–	–	–	–	–	–	–	–	–	–	–	–	–	–
13 Tender documentation is checked for consistency with form of contract & measurement method	Best			3					4													
	Test		?	?					?													
	Both																					
			–	–	–	–	–	–	–	–	–	–	–	–	–	–	–	–	–	–	–	–
14 Strict segregation of duties applied to key stages of contract	Best								4			3										
	Test		?						?			?										
	Both																					
			–	–	–	–	–	–	–	–	–	–	–	–	–	–	–	–	–	–	–	–
15 Independent and balanced representation on tender review panel	Best								4			3						3	3			
	Test		?						?			?						?	?			
	Both																					
			–	–	–	–	–	–	–	–	–	–	–	–	–	–	–	–	–	–	–	–
16 Detailed & explicit instructions issued to all tenderers	Best											4										
	Test		?									?										
	Both																					
			–	–	–	–	–	–	–	–	–	–	–	–	–	–	–	–	–	–	–	–
17 Any additional data, etc. is supplied equally to all tenderers	Best											3										
	Test		?									?										
	Both																					
			–	–	–	–	–	–	–	–	–	–	–	–	–	–	–	–	–	–	–	–
18 No other direct contact or negotiations are permitted – disciplinary offence	Best								2			2										
	Test		?						?			?										
	Both																					
			–	–	–	–	–	–	–	–	–	–	–	–	–	–	–	–	–	–	–	–
19 Procedures are subject to periodic review re effectiveness and relevance, etc.	Best			3		3	2		2		3	2	2	2	2	2	2	2	2	2	2	2
	Test		?	?		?	?		?		?	?	?	?	?	?	?	?	?	?	?	?
	Both																					
			–	–	–	–	–	–	–	–	–	–	–	–	–	–	–	–	–	–	–	–
20 Staff are suitably trained and supervised	Best								2			3										
	Test		?						?			?										
	Both																					
			–	–	–	–	–	–	–	–	–	–	–	–	–	–	–	–	–	–	–	–
21 Tender envelopes have to be identifiable as such, whilst not revealing identity of tenderer	Best											3										
	Test		?									?										
	Both																					
			–	–	–	–	–	–	–	–	–	–	–	–	–	–	–	–	–	–	–	–
22 All receipts are recorded in register & stored unopened in safe until deadline	Best											3	4									
	Test		?									?	?									
	Both																					
			–	–	–	–	–	–	–	–	–	–	–	–	–	–	–	–	–	–	–	–
23 Nominated individual is responsible for safe custody & storage of tenders	Best											3										
	Test		?									?										
	Both																					
			–																				

Table 14 continued

#			A	B	C	D	E	F	G	H	I	J	K	L	M	N	O	P	Q	R	S	T
			=	=	=	=	=	=	=	=	=	=	=	=	=	=	=	=	=	=	=	=
	Calculated Risk Score:	Risk	3	3	3	3	3	3	3	2	2	2	2	2	2	2	2	2	3	2	2	2
24	Tenders are only opened at the appointed time by at least 2 employees – details recorded	Best													5							
		Test	?												?							
		Both																				
25	All tenders are subject to arithmetic check and review for qualifications or amendments	Best										3				4			4			
		Test	?									?				?			?			
		Both																				
26	Late submissions are returned to tenderer with covering letter	Best													5							
		Test	?												?							
		Both																				
27	All queries pursued with the tenderers	Best																			5	
		Test	?																		?	
		Both																				
28	Tenderers are evaluated by the review panel per established objectives and procedures	Best															4	4	3			
		Test	?														?	?	?			
		Both																				
29	Management report circulated, summarising all tenders and making recommendation	Best															4					
		Test	?														?					
		Both																				
30	Recommended tender is subject to senior management review and authority	Best															4		5			
		Test	?														?		?			
		Both																				
31	Rationale provided if the recommended tender is not the lowest or other option selected	Best															4					
		Test	?														?					
		Both																				
32	Successful tenderer is advised in writing and his or her confirmation is sought	Best																				4
		Test	?																			?
		Both																				
33	Unsuccessful tenderers advised after acceptance is received	Best																				4
		Test	?																			?
		Both																				
34	Contracts who were invited but did not submit are noted on approved list/register	Best										3										2
		Test	?									?										?
		Both																				
35	Anonymous details of all tenders received are circulated to tenderers if requested	Best										3										3
		Test	?									?										?
		Both																				

A Inappropriate form of tendering applied – cost, delay, etc.
B Inaccurate/incomplete tendering documentation – error, delay
C Inappropriate/invalid selection of tenderers – no competition
D Failure to comply with regulations & EEC Directives
E Failure due to unrealistic/inappropriate tender timetable
F Tendering not consistent with chosen form of contract
G Possibility of fraud, collusion or malpractice
H Limited sample of tenderers – limited competition, poor VFM
I Ambiguous/inadequate tendering instructions – delay, error
J Failure to deal fairly, impartially & consistently

K Ineffective receipt, recording, opening & handling of tenders
L Inadequate security exercised over storage of tenders
M Unauthorised or premature opening of tenders
N Inadequate handling of late tenders – unfair advantage
O Failure to independently capture all data upon opening
P Inadequate evaluation of tenders received – additional cost
Q Failure to select the optimum tender based on price, etc.
R Failure to detect errors or qualifications in tenders
S Failure to obtain management approval of recommended tender
T Failure to correctly advise successful & failed tenderers

Scale 31 (abridged)

6 = Incorrect identification of needs, or failure to meet them
5 = Lost business; needs partly unfulfilled; or breach of rules
4 = Delay or disruption; reputation loss; minor breach of rules
(Contract auditing Exposures-oriented scale)

3 = Avoidable costs/losses; damage to contract relationships
2 = Administrative or accounting errors
1 = Detectable negative impact on the business or service

15

CONTRACT AND TENDER DOCUMENTATION

Scope

This chapter is concerned with the completion, accuracy and security aspects of contract and tendering documentation. Descriptions of the documents normally forming the contract are provided. The objectives are to ensure that all the relevant documentation is accurately generated, appropriately distributed, and securely stored.

Please note that this chapter does not address all matters relating to either interim and final accounts documentation, or all the necessary site and administrative documents. The explicit subject chapters incorporate, where necessary, references to documentation requirements. However, it is obviously necessary to support all contractual matters and events with the prescribed or accepted form of documentation, and to provide adequate and secure document storage facilities.

Before we examine the main issues relative to contracts and tender documents, there are a number of general matters to consider. In the context of a significant project, the documentation reflects real events or actions such as the physical design of a structure or the precise methods of calculating payments due. They are not esoteric administrative procedures which can be lightly dismissed or disregarded. The contents of contracts and tenders form the basis for all the physical and financial actions that follow and therefore their material accuracy and completeness is of prime importance. Additionally, of course, they are legally binding agreements with obligations, liabilities and roles defined for all parties. The consequences of errors are potentially disastrous, extremely expensive and, in some cases, even life threatening. Subsequently correcting errors and omissions can lead to delays which may have repercussions on other dependent projects or mean that expensive resources are idle whilst possible solutions are formulated.

The real enemy in relation to documentation errors is additional cost. The cost of correcting errors increases exponentially the further into the project they are discovered. In complex construction developments the detection of errors could have repercussion on technical areas which fundamentally affect the progress of the project. The legal implications of error and related delay can also be pivotal, especially where the contract conditions establish clear cut responsibility and liability.

In order that all the necessary factors are considered and adequately catered for, the organisation should have established formal written procedures in place. Such procedures should where required, as in the public sector, form part of any standing orders or financial regulations.

The main countermeasure to avoiding the above noted problems is the early involvement of, or consultation, with all the affected professional and specialist staff or advisers. However, unless this multiskill review process is handled efficiently, it too can become a source of procrastination, delay and additional cost. In a complex or long-term contract, there is considerable scope for discrepancies between the various related documentary elements. During the course of the contract, there should be a clear mechanism for reporting and resolving matters of documentary discrepancies.

CONTRACTS

Types

There are many different forms of contract. Some of the more common types of construction, civil engineering, mechanical and electrical contracts are summarised in Appendix 2. Although there are natural linkages between certain types of works or project and the most suitable form of contract, the selection of the most appropriate type is of paramount importance if the interests of all the affected parties are to be protected and the most advantageous terms agreed. In this context the selection of the most suitable contract is as critical as choosing the right calibre of contractor (*see also* Chapter 12).

The terms and conditions of these various forms are rather complex and we do not intend to examine any of them in great detail. Appendix 6 contains cross-references to key contract clauses for four of the commonly used standard forms of contract, and Appendix 4 lists publications which provide more detailed commentaries upon specific contract types. Readers are also referred to Chapter 17 which deals with the selection of the form of contract.

Contract documents

Although the legal term 'contract documents' can relate to a limited number of documents, which may vary between operational sectors, we are using the broader meaning in this chapter. For example the term as applied to a building contract characterises those documents which define the contractor's obligations. Irrespective of the nature of the contract there will be certain constant elements within contractual documentation, such as the articles of agreement. Additionally, we have included some of the key documents which will be generated during the life of a contract, such as the interim valuation certificates, on the basis that all related documents should eventually be brought together for trailing, filing and archiving purposes.

Dependent upon the form of contract to be used it is likely that there will be a number of other related documents which either support the contract provisions or provide more detailed information so that contractors can fulfil their obligations. As stated above some of this supporting documentation will also be used in the tendering process as a means of providing a common basis for communication, etc. The following notes include brief descriptions of various types of contract documents. However, it should be stressed that not every contract will contain the items noted. Additionally not all the listed documents are issued at the same time, for example the certificates provided by the architect support interim payments.

Articles of agreement – These bring together the key elements of the agreement, including:

- the parties to the contract
- what service is to be provided (or what goods are to be supplied, or what is to be built or constructed)
- the amount to be paid (also referred to as the consideration, the contract sum, or the contract price).

Some articles include a section making reference to the receipt and acceptance of tenders. The parties normally sign the articles as acceptance of the details and conditions contained in the contract documents.

Conditions of contract – These are formed by the detailed clauses which define, normally in great detail, the obligations of the parties to the contract and the rules by which certain subsequent actions can take place. For example, the rules for declaring an extension of time.

Appendix – Even in standard forms of contract, there can be factors which will either vary between contracts or not apply in every case. Such factors can be recorded in the appendix. For example the completion date, the base for the purpose of calculating price fluctuations, and the agreed value of liquidated damages.

Drawings – These need to be complete, accurate and up to date if they have been subject to progressive revision during the design process. After the construction or development work has commenced, the contractor may file claims if the drawings contain errors or omissions. The drawings should be prepared using the accepted symbols and terminology and to the required professional standard. They may have to be correlated to the bills of quantity. Drawings start out as representing the designer's intentions, but they may be amended in the course of the project and the final versions become 'as built'. In any event, the final form should be secured and distributed accordingly for maintenance, etc. Parties should be clear as to the copyright of drawings.

Specifications – The degree of detail provided in the specification will depend upon the nature of the project, for example, in the instance of a computer software application development the specification may describe, among other factors, the type of computer platform to be utilised, all the required functionality, the maximum response times, the reporting facilities, access security arrangements, and so on. In a building project the specification may include the technical specifications and standards of the required materials, the tolerances for quality of finish or workmanship, the operating parameters of installed plant and equipment, and so on. The contents of the specification are also likely to form part of the basis of any subsequent measurement and assessment of contractor performance. There is some degree of data exchangeability between specifications and bills of quantity.

Schedules – These may be used in support of either drawings or specifications. Schedules may contain the dimensions and quantities of regular items or components as a means of providing a simplified form of data presentation. Alternatively, they can be used to summarise the type and quantity of goods to be supplied, for example laser printers, office furniture, or window frames.

Bills of quantity – These are mainly relevant to building or civil engineering projects and summarise the quantification of materials and work operations, required for each defined stage (or sub-stage) of the project. There is a variant available referred to as the bill of approximate quantities. In the tendering process, the potential contractor will cost out each item of material and work required as the basis for calculating an overall bid price. The breakdown and pre-definition of each stage of the works thereby provides a standard basis for all bidding contractors. Where applicable, the standard method of measurement to be adopted will need to be defined in the contract terms. Bills are also used in the measurement of work completed, and in this role they act as support for the interim accounts.

Instructions to tenderers – In the public sector such instructions may relate to the requirements of any standing orders or financial regulations. They need to provide clear and fair guidance to the bidding contractors and include such details as the timetable for completing and submitting the tender documents, the fact that no qualifications to the presented conditions will be accepted, the method of return for the documents so as to ensure due impartiality, and so on. (Tendering processes are more fully explored in Chapter 14).

Form of tender – This element varies between types of contract, but is normally a signed and dated summary of the tender addressed to the employer. It will generally include the overall tender value, the period of the contract, and any specific undertakings. Additional details may also apply with certain forms of contract, these include the name of the architect or engineer responsible for the project, the details of the contractor's parent company or bankers.

Performance bonds – Such bonds are optional and some organisations prefer to make their own insurance arrangements. Most bonds are provided by banks, surety or insurance companies, and basically they are undertakings to accept the responsibility for the discharge of a specified contractual obligation in the event that the responsible person defaults on that obligation. (*see* Chapter 16 for full details).

Insurance – This section should include the details of the relevant insurance cover to be provided in order to protect the associated property, works, persons, etc. (*see also* Chapter 16).

Certificates – Here we are referring specifically to construction contracts. The following types of certificate may apply, and they are usually completed by a responsible supervising professional such as an architect or engineer. The collective term 'event certificates' is our own and generally relates to the professional signifying whether defined stages have been achieved:

- Interim certificate are issued in support of work completed by the contractor and detailed on the relevant interim account, which may have been amended by the Architect.
- 'Events certificates' will vary between types of works and contract, but may include:

  - certificate of practical completion
  - certificate of final completion
  - certificate of non-completion
  - certificate of completion of making good defects.

Other documents – In a building project, the contract may permit the issue of authorised instructions which cover such situations as variations from the contracted design, an extension of time, or certification of a contractor's claim. Copies of all such additional documents especially those that affect, in some way, the cost of works should be securely filed with all other contract documents, to form a consolidated record of the progress of the contract.

General matters

Outwith the standard forms of contract there are those, predominantly in the general private and service sectors, which are applied to more specific activities. A service supplier may have their own form of contract honed over the years, but perhaps mainly geared to their interests rather than those of the customer. The effects of general consumer, business-related, and EC legislation should have had an impact on the terms of these special contracts so that they also provide basic protection for either the client, purchaser or employer. The onus is very much on the 'employer' to adequately review the relevant contract and assess the effects and obligations of all the clauses. Unless the manager possesses a suitable grasp of the legal framework, most organisations prefer to let their legal representatives review contracts and report to them on the potential areas of concern. It may be necessary to insist upon the insertion of additional clauses which provide greater flexibility, assurance, control, or balance of risk. The amendment of contracts is a balanced process requiring both the requisite legal knowledge and effective negotiating skills.

In very large or long-running projects it may prove necessary to break down the work into a series of individual contracts which may take different forms. Where this is necessary but there is an allied need to interface all the work in a consistent way, care should exercised in ensuring that the related contracts reflect the required consistency where necessary.

Where an organisation is regularly involved in the letting of contracts, a form of contracts register should be maintained, indeed in the public sector such a register may be required as a condition of the prevailing financial regulations. The contracts register should summarise *inter alia* for each contract, the principal financial implications, the prevailing contractual provisions, and the details of interim and other payments made, so as to enable a determination of the current financial status of each contract. In this latter context, the register can perform an enhanced control and management information function and provide a linkage between the contract status and the processing of payments due through the creditors ledger. Other relevant details, such as those members of staff responsible for certain aspects of the contract may also be included in the register, which may take the form of a computer-based database system.

Any correspondence between the contracted parties should be appropriately routed, dealt with and then securely retained for future reference. This and other documentation should be capable of providing an accurate and comprehensive picture of the contract and the key events that have taken place during the contract lifecycle.

Given the possibility that a dispute related to the contract could arise, care should be taken to ensure that all the necessary documentation is securely retained, and in a form that enables prompt recovery of the appropriate documents. Access to the prime copies of contract documents will need to be controlled and suitably restricted, taking into account any commercial sensitivity dimensions.

TENDERS

The tendering process is fully described in Chapter 14. We are more concerned here with the integrity, accuracy and security of tender documents as part of the wider contract scenario. Having accepted a particular tender, it will be necessary to incorporate the relevant documents into the contract arrangements.

When initially formulating the tendering documentation care should be taken to ensure that the format corresponds with that required by the chosen form of contract. Additionally the documentation will need to address all the defined stages and requirements, and accurately reflect same using the agreed measurement and technical formats. All the relative points of synergy between the design, specification and tender documentation will need to be checked for accuracy and completeness prior to the release to candidate contractors. A master set of tender documentation should be held at all times, with amendments subject to appropriate version control and approval. When copying the final and accepted version of tender documents, care should be taken to ensure that all the copy sets are both legible and complete prior to dispatch.

A register of all tenders received should be maintained, and all those submitted should be capable of being accounted for. This will necessitate the secure retention of all tenders for trailing purposes, and where either appropriate or required the retention period for such documents should be specified in the organisation's procedures or regulations.

The accuracy and completeness of the tender(s) will need to be verified prior to formal acceptance and incorporation into the relevant contract. Once confirmed and accepted, the relevant documents should be securely retained as the basis of subsequent key operations. Copies may have to be made and circulated to affected personnel, in which case care should be taken to ensure the completeness of the document sets and that they have been based upon the approved and agreed versions. The number of pages constituting the complete set should be recorded and suitable page numbering applied and checked.

Access to the original copies of tendering documents should be controlled. Copies should be used in preference, and again the copy sets should be checked to ensure that they correspond to the contents of the original. Alterations and amendments should not be permitted, but handled and documented separately on an agreed basis. The disposal of both submitted and accepted tenders should be in accordance with a defined document destruction policy linked to any statutory or defined retention periods.

Control matrix example

An example matrix, which is *Exposures*-oriented, is provided as Table 15. The table includes references to both contract and tender documentation, although not every organisation will necessarily use the tendering approach. The disposal or destruction of documentation is incorporated in the example as a reminder that care should be taken in the determination of destruction dates given that the product of the contract may remain relevant (in a legal sense) for many years. *Scale* 31 has been used in the example, and this is described in Appendix 7. The matrix theory is explored in Chapter 32.

Table 15 Contract and Tender Documentation – Exposures

Overall Inherent Risk (Size) Score [5 is worst risk; 1 is best] = 2.61

A Incomplete contract documents created and distributed
B Failure to protect contract documents from loss, damage, etc
C Delay and costs due to errors and omissions in contact
D Failure to record the status of all contracts
E Delay in tracing documents due to inadequate filing
F Failure to retain complete master set of documents
G Unauthorised amendments applied to contract documents
H Incomplete or illegible copies of documents – reputation
I Outdated/invalid supporting documents provided (drawings)
J Failure to correctly incorporate amendments
K Incorrect form of documentation used – delay, reputation, etc
L Insecure/inappropriate storage of Bonds – loss, delay, etc.
M Inadequate filing of certificates, correspondence, etc.
N Premature disposal or destruction of contract documents
O Inaccurate or incomplete Tender documentation – error, delay
P Loss of selected Tender documents – unable to confirm a/c's
Q Unauthorised amendment of Tender documents
R Premature disposal or destruction of Tender documents

Scale 31 (abridged)

6 = Incorrect identification of needs, or failure to meet them
5 = Lost business; needs partly unfulfilled; or breach of rules
4 = Delay or disruption, reputation loss; minor breach of rules
(Contract auditing Exposures-oriented scale)

3 = Avoidable costs/losses; damage to contract relationships
2 = Administrative or accounting errors
1 = Detectable negative impact on the business or service

	Contract and Tender Documentation		A	B	C	D	E	F	G	H	I	J	K	L	M	N	O	P	Q	R
			EXPOSURES																	
			=	=	=	=	=	=	=	=	=	=	=	=	=	=	=	=	=	=
	Calculated Risk Score:	Risk	3	3	2	3	3	3	3	2	3	3	3	3	2	4	3	2	3	4
			−	−	−	−	−	−	−	−	−	−	−	−	−	−	−	−	−	−
	Scale 30 (6 is most serious)	Type	4	4	3	4	4	5	4	3	5	5	4	4	3	5	4	5	5	5
	Size (3 is maximum)	Size	3	3	2	2	2	2	2	2	2	2	2	2	2	3	3	1	2	3
	CONTROLS	−	−	−	−	−	−	−	−	−	−	−	−	−	−	−	−	−	−	−
1	Procedures in place which define documentary requirements – staff suitably trained	Best	3	3	3	3		3	2			3	2	2	2	2	2	2	2	2
		Test	?	?	?	?	?		?	?		?	?	?	?	?	?	?	?	?
		Both																		
			−	−	−	−	−	−	−	−	−	−	−	−	−	−	−	−	−	−
2	Contract completion checked by Legal Dept. prior to copying and release	Best		4		3		3	3		2	2	3			3				
		Test	?	?		?		?	?		?	?	?			?				
		Both																		
			−	−	−	−	−	−	−	−	−	−	−	−	−	−	−	−	−	−
3	All original contracts are stored in fire-proof strongroom	Best		4		3														
		Test	?	?		?														
		Both																		
			−	−	−	−	−	−	−	−	−	−	−	−	−	−	−	−	−	−
4	Access to the strongroom is restricted and a record kept of the contents	Best		4				2										3		3
		Test	?	?				?										?		?
		Both																		
			−	−	−	−	−	−	−	−	−	−	−	−	−	−	−	−	−	−
5	Original documents not released from Legal Dept. Copies are taken and used by other staff	Best		3				2	2									3		
		Test	?	?				?	?									?		
		Both																		
			−	−	−	−	−	−	−	−	−	−	−	−	−	−	−	−	−	−
6	In addition to 2 above, user departments also review the contents of contract documents	Best				4			3											
		Test	?			?			?											
		Both																		
			−	−	−	−	−	−	−	−	−	−	−	−	−	−	−	−	−	−
7	Contracts register is maintained and updated with status details, payments made, etc.	Best					5													
		Test	?				?													
		Both																		
			−	−	−	−	−	−	−	−	−	−	−	−	−	−	−	−	−	−
8	Contracts documents are filed in separate and labelled storage cases	Best						4												
		Test	?					?												
		Both																		
			−	−	−	−	−	−	−	−	−	−	−	−	−	−	−	−	−	−
9	Contents of secure store are checked and confirmed on a monthly basis	Best		4				4										4		
		Test	?	?				?										?		
		Both																		
			−																		

Table 15 continued

			Risk	A	B	C	D	E	F	G	H	I	J	K	L	M	N	O	P	Q	R
				=	=	=	=	=	=	=	=	=	=	=	=	=	=	=	=	=	=
	Calculated Risk Score:	Risk		3	3	2	3	3	3	3	2	3	3	3	3	2	4	3	2	3	4
10	Any alterations or clause deletions are signified	Best								3											
		Test	?							?											
		Both																			
11	Photocopies of contracts are checked for completeness and legibility before release	Best									4										
		Test	?								?										
		Both																			
12	Version control exercised over supporting documents. Records kept and contents agreed	Best										4									
		Test	?									?									
		Both																			
13	All amendments are confirmed by the Legal Dept.	Best										4									
		Test	?									?									
		Both																			
14	Standard contract sets utilised	Best												5							
		Test	?											?							
		Both																			
15	All performance bonds are retained with contracts in the strongroom	Best												5							
		Test	?											?							
		Both																			
16	All correspondence etc. is coded with contract ref. and filed with main papers	Best													4						
		Test	?												?						
		Both																			
17	At conclusion of the contract a destruction date is applied and recorded in the register	Best													3						
		Test	?												?						
		Both																			
18	Tender documentation is checked by the relevant Engineer prior to release	Best															4				
		Test	?														?				
		Both																			
19	Tenders are stored in the strongroom and details are registered	Best															4				
		Test	?														?				
		Both																			
20	Amendments to tenders received are only applied following correspondence with contractors	Best																	3		
		Test	?																?		
		Both																			
21	Tender documents are marked with a destruction date per prevailing policy	Best																			3
		Test	?																		?
		Both																			
22	Legal documents are held for the statutory retention periods	Best																			3
		Test	?																		?
		Both																			
23	Advice is sought before documents are destroyed. Authority is sought/recorded	Best																			2
		Test	?																		?
		Both																			

A Incomplete contract documents created and distributed
B Failure to protect contract documents from loss, damage, etc
C Delay and costs due to errors and omissions in contact
D Failure to record the status of all contracts
E Delay in tracing documents due to inadequate filing
F Failure to retain complete master set of documents
G Unauthorised amendments applied to contract documents
H Incomplete or illegible copies of documents – reputation
I Outdated/invalid supporting documents provided (drawings)
J Failure to correctly incorporate amendments

K Incorrect form of documentation used – delay, reputation, etc
L Insecure/inappropriate storage of Bonds – loss, delay, etc.
M Inadequate filing of certificates, correspondence, etc.
N Premature disposal or destruction of contract documents
O Inaccurate or incomplete Tender documentation – error, delay
P Loss of selected Tender documents – unable to confirm a/c's
Q Unauthorised amendment of Tender documents
R Premature disposal or destruction of Tender documents

Scale 31 (abridged)

6 = Incorrect identification of needs, or failure to meet them
5 = Lost business; needs partly unfulfilled; or breach of rules
4 = Delay or disruption, reputation loss; minor breach of rules
(Contract auditing Exposures-oriented scale)

3 = Avoidable costs/losses; damage to contract relationships
2 = Administrative or accounting errors
1 = Detectable negative impact on the business or service

16

INSURANCE AND BONDING

Scope

In this chapter we discuss methods of providing security in the event of problems occurring which affect either the continuation or completion of the project as planned.

INSURANCE

It is necessary to initially clarify the distinction between liability insurance and loss insurance. Under a liability insurance policy, the insured person is indemnified by the insurer for the value of damages and/or legal costs associated with specified actions or failures, which are due to another person or organisation. In the case of a loss policy, the insurers will compensate the insured person for any loss or damage suffered by that person either as a result of an accident or another person's negligence. This simple view is often, in practice, blurred by the imposition of cover limits, complex interactions which may have a bearing on the degree of liability, and all manner of subtleties relating to specific contract clauses.

There are four principal areas of audit concern with regard to contract-related insurance cover, namely:

- What discrete areas or matters require to be insured?
- What level and type of cover is adequate?
- Are the insurance companies employed stable and reliable?
- Is the cover actually in place and renewed as necessary?

In circumstances where project related insurance requirements are commonplace, formal procedures should be established and monitored. Insurance requirements should be incorporated into the contract conditions as a means of formalising the arrangements. Where standard forms of contract are utilised, care should be taken to either conform to the required clauses or ensure that irrelevant clauses are excluded.

As regards what aspects of the project require to be insured, this will obviously depend upon the nature and scale of the project. There are established protocols and responsibilities for the construction industry and for public sector projects. However the wider commercial and private sectors are less well defined, possibly given the potentially broader range of implications. An organisation may have to consider the impact upon their ability to trade if a project is delayed or collapses (e.g. in the event that marketing opportunities are lost due to a computer application system being delivered late from the software developers).

The factors to be insured in a given project are likely to be a mixture of 'hard' and 'soft'. Hard factors include such items as damage to equipment, buildings and materials, whereas soft factors may be lost revenue, market reputation, and so on. Under the conditions of the current forms of standard building, civil engineering and other engineering contracts, the contractor is obliged to provide insurance cover for the works and property and persons other than the works. Appendix 6 summarises the relevant clauses for four of the commonly used standard forms of contract.

The amount of cover should be accurately, economically and realistically assessed in light of established facts, and the enabling conditions of the applied form of contract. The type of cover has logical associations with inherent risks and the degree of likelihood. Some form of prior assessment of risks may be desirable in order to set the scene and the relevance of insurance requirements.

Employers should satisfy themselves that the choices of insurance companies, levels and types of cover are adequate and reliable. It is obviously in their best interests for employers to approve the choice of insurance companies as is required in particular circumstances in the construction industry. In some instances, the contract may permit the employer to recover the cost of providing cover where the contractor has failed to make the necessary arrangements as required by the contract in place.

Employers should obtain evidence that the requisite policies are in force, and some contracts bestow the right to request such evidence as copy policies and premium receipts issued by the insurers. For example, both the JCT80 and ICE conditions of contract contain such clauses (*see* Appendix 6 for details). A record should be maintained of the renewal dates that apply during the currency of the contract, and evidence obtained that the contractor has paid the appropriate premiums. Account should be taken of any special considerations such as the use of hazardous materials, use of explosives for site clearance, etc.

Contractors should have mechanisms in place to ensure that the required levels of relevant cover are in place for each active project and that all policies are subject to renewal and review as necessary. Conditions, such as the level of work currently active may radically change and a process of continual assessment of the adequacy of cover should be applied.

Where the contractor provides the required insurance cover, the costs are obviously passed on to the employer, and in some instances (e.g. where the employer is regularly involved in projects and can negotiate very competitive premiums) the employer may opt to arrange and administer the necessary cover. If this approach is adopted, the contract conditions should reflect the appropriate liabilities and responsibilities.

Where the employer has engaged a professional consultant for significant involvement in a project or contract, he should ensure a suitable form of professional indemnity insurance is in place, and that it provides adequate and relevant cover. Not all of the terms of engagement endorsed by the appropriate professional bodies stipulate insurance requirements in respect of professional negligence. In any event, such policies normally have financial limits, and once exceeded the professional's own funds are at stake. In the case of substantial claims, where both the insured person's own funds and policy limits have been exceeded, the client may have to bear the remaining costs himself.

Patently, providing all-singing-and-dancing insurance cover can be prohibitively expensive, and one must not lose sight of the probability of certain events occurring. Identified risks should also be sensibly assessed in light of the cost of providing cover for the related eventuality.

BONDING

Performance bonds are normally provided by either banks, insurance companies or companies specialising in surety matters. They are formal 'guarantees' whereby the guarantor undertakes to accept the liabilities of the person(s) responsible under the terms of a contract if that person defaults against their contractual obligations and responsibilities. Although such an arrangement can provide a further degree of assurance, in the event of having to invoke the bond, there could be considerable delay in achieving the appropriate settlement during which time costs and other implications would have been accumulating. The person issuing the bond will, in the event of a claim, want to be satisfied that there is no other possible source of appropriate compensation available to the claimant. Therefore proving any entitlement could be a long-winded affair.

Given that the employer has to pay the bond premium, which therefore adds to the up-front contract costs, and that he should also be undertaking an adequate form of contractor assessment before letting the contract, there is a persuasive school of thought that suggests that bonds should be unnecessary if the assessment is thorough and properly conducted. In the public sector or where an organisation is regularly involved in the letting of contracts, the assessment of contractors is likely to be part of the prevailing culture. However, where seeking a stable and reliable contractor is a less frequent occurrence a suitable bond may be viewed as a justified additional form of security for the organisation. In any event the use of bonds is essentially a matter of policy linked to the relevant degree of risk.

It is also logical to argue that banks and others issuing bonds will be unlikely to indulge in risky situations and provide a bond for a doubtful or dubious contractor. In this respect the bank's willingness to issue a bond is an indicator of the calibre of the contractor. However, in an uncertain world, perhaps reliance on such a view should be appropriately tempered by the application of other evaluations of a contractor's financial status. Expressed in simplistic terms it may be more effective to route the costs of providing bonds into a more thorough investigation and assessment of the contractor's financial condition. In any case, circumstances can change rapidly and overtake the situation that applied when the bond was issued or the view of the contractor's stability was formed.

Some organisations, notably in the public sector, have dispensed with the use of bonds and choose to fund their own insurance protection schemes augmented by rigorous vetting of potential contractors. If an approved list or register of contractors is maintained, a formal process of appraisal should be applied to the technical and financial suitability of contractors in order to justify their continued inclusion on the list (*see also* Chapters 12 and 13). It is logical to suggest that comprehensive and effective financial and technical assessment procedures should be applied in any case.

If your organisation is regularly involved in contracting matters and has a history of requiring performance bond cover, it is logical to review the track record of this mechanism, taking into account the costs of provision and the instances when it has been necessary to make a claim against the bond. Just because a practice has become an established part of the culture does not necessarily guarantee that it is still relevant and effective. Applying such a review may reveal that continuing to use bonding as a form of assurance is not justified and that expenditure can be accordingly reduced without further undue risk. Where a contractor is part of a larger parent organisation, it may be preferable to obtain a suitably protective guarantee from the parent company.

The Chartered Institute of Public Finance and Accountancy (CIPFA) has undertaken considerable work in developing areas of best practice in the public sector, often in collaboration with other affected professional bodies. In 1980, CIPFA in conjunction with the Society of Chief Quantity Surveyors in Local Government (SCQSLG) issued a statement on performance bonding and financial vetting, which explores the key issues and the form of measures that can be applied to counter associated concerns and risks.

In any event the use of bonds is also dependent upon a number of factors over and above the financial and technical competence of the contractor concerned including the following which should be taken into account during a formal review of risks and controls:

- the scale and commercial significance of the related project
- whether the contract is of a specialist nature representing greater degrees of risk
- the overall scale of liabilities that could fall upon the organisation and the effects upon reputation and public image in the event of failure
- the relationship between the scale of liabilities and the anticipated cost of providing adequate bonding coverage
- the criticality of factors such as timescale and target completion date
- previous claim experiences
- any extended areas of potential liability (e.g. where there are implications for trading partnerships)

- the degree of work currently being handled by the potential contractor (e.g. he could be severely overstretched and elements of his workload could fail due to inadequate resources or financial backing).

Management may conclude that performance bonding in only effective in selected situations, for example either where contracts are above a certain critical value or in relation to particular unproven contractors.

If the organisation uses bonding as a means of protection, records of costs, claims and recovered values should be maintained as a means of permitting ongoing review of the advantages and disadvantages of the mechanism. Such records and related analysis can be used to support strategic-level decisions or policies as to whether or not bonding should continue to be applied to projects, thus avoiding unsubstantiated decision making.

It is important to ensure that any bond considered for use in a project will remain in force for the appropriate project period, and does not expire before all the contractor's obligations are discharged. There are standard forms of bond in use, for example those relevant to the building industry, and they will normally remain effective up to and including the maintenance period. The bond conditions, including any timing considerations should be subject to scrutiny before terms are formally accepted.

Assuming that all the relevant conditions support the requirement for bonding cover, work should only be allowed to commence once the bond arrangements are active and when management are satisfied that the party acting as surety is reliable and financially stable. Bonds will need to be securely stored whilst in effect. A form of register of bonds held may prove necessary where a number of contracts are in progress concurrently. The register can be updated when bonds are either awaited at the commencement of a contract or are authorised for release upon the satisfactory completion of same.

The authority to release bonds should be limited, and only applied when all the relevant professionals are satisfied that the contractor has discharged his contractual responsibilities. Due attention should also be given to ensuring that there are no outstanding claims against the contractor and that he has fully complied with the requirements of any maintenance period. Contractors may press the employer for release from a bond to avoid the bonding organisation applying a financial limit to the bonds outstanding on the contractor which might otherwise prevent him from pursuing further business opportunities and thereby possibly overstretching his resources. Such requests should be cautiously reviewed by the employer with a natural bias towards the interests of their organisation and the risks represented by the outstanding contractual matters and obligations. In practice the value of these obligations may be covered by the value of any retention still held over by the employer. Each case for the release of a bond should be considered on its merits and only after having consulted with the responsible professionals.

The requirement for contractors to provide adequate and up-to-date financial data in support of their tender, should be incorporated into the tendering terms and conditions. Where a contractor is a subsidiary of a holding company, suitable forms of guarantees should be obtained following a comprehensive financial assessment of that holding company.

Control matrix example

Table 16 contains an example matrix incorporating both insurance and bonding considerations. All aspects are covered including the assessment of risks and the provision of suitable secure storage facilities. The table uses *Scale* 30 as featured in Appendix 7, and is *Objectives*-oriented.

Table 16 Insurance and Bonding – Objectives

Overall Inherent Risk (Size) Score [5 is worst risk; 1 is best] = 2.10

A Develop a strategy for minimising exposures to risk(s)
B Ensure all relevant cover & security is provided & adequate
C Ensure accurate & complete records of cover are maintained
D Ensure that cover conditions are appropriate and relevant
E Ensure that cover/bond remains in force throughout contract
F Clearly establish & justify the costs of providing cover
G Ensure the selected insurance/surety companies are stable
H Ensure the contractor fulfils his insurance obligations
I Ensure cover is current & renewed during life of contract
J Ensure cover accords with he contract terms/conditions

K Ensure third party liabilities are appropriately addressed
L Ensure conditions for making claims are clearly defined
M Ensure that claims are made as & when appropriate
N Ensure claim values are realistic & adequately supported
O Ensure values due from contractor's insurance are received
P Ensure all claims are promptly & satisfactorily settled
Q Ensure consultants have sufficient Indemnity cover in place
R Ensure bonds & guarantees are obtained when appropriate
S Ensure that Bonds and Policies are securely stored
T Ensure Bonds are only released when all obligations are met

Scale 30 (abridged)

6 = Strategically vital to the business or organisation
5 = Makes a contribution to business operations
4 = Contributes to reliability of data, records and information
(Contract auditing Objectives-oriented scale)

3 = Avoids disruption/meets regulatory & accountability needs
2 = Leads to administrative/operational economies/efficiencies
1 = Generates administrative economies

Insurance and Bonding			A	B	C	D	E	F	G	H	I	J	K	L	M	N	O	P	Q	R	S	T
			=	=	=	=	=	=	=	=	=	=	=	=	=	=	=	=	=	=	=	=
Calculated Risk Score:	Risk		3	3	2	3	3	2	2	3	2	2	2	2	2	2	2	2	2	2	2	2
Scale 30 (6 is most serious)	Type		6	6	3	5	6	3	6	6	6	4	5	3	5	3	5	5	3	5	3	5
Size (3 is maximum)	Size		2	2	2	2	2	1	1	1	2	1	1	2	1	2	1	1	1	1	2	1
MEASURES																							
1 Policy defined and documented for providing insurance and security cover for contracts	Best		5	3	2	3	2	1	2	2	2	2	3								2	2
	Test		?	?	?	?	?	?	?	?	?	?	?								?	?
	Both																					
2 Each contract/project assessed for security and insurance requirements	Best			3	4		2		2			3	2									
	Test			?	?		?		?			?	?									
	Both																					
3 Cover is related to contract conditions where possible	Best				3		3					4	2									
	Test		?		?		?					?	?									
	Both																					
4 Required values of cover are determined by use of Risk Analysis	Best			3	4		3		2			2										
	Test		?	?	?		?		?			?										
	Both																					
5 All policies and bonds are recorded in register with premiums, claim & renewals	Best					5	2			2								2				
	Test		?			?	?			?								?				
	Both																					
6 Legal Dept. undertakes a review of proposed securities prior to arrangements being finalised	Best			2	3		4					2										
	Test		?	?	?		?					?										
	Both																					
7 Periods of cover/bond are confirmed as correct and noted in the register	Best				3	4	4															
	Test		?		?	?	?															
	Both																					
8 All related costs are recorded against budget and reported to management	Best							4														
	Test		?					?														
	Both																					
9 Management approval is obtained prior to confirming cover arrangements	Best							4														
	Test		?					?														
	Both																					

Table 16 continued

#	Description		A	B	C	D	E	F	G	H	I	J	K	L	M	N	O	P	Q	R	S	T
			=	=	=	=	=	=	=	=	=	=	=	=	=	=	=	=	=	=	=	=
	Calculated Risk Score:	Risk	3	3	2	3	3	2	2	2	3	2	2	2	2	2	2	2	2	2	2	2
			−	−	−	−	−	−	−	−	−	−	−	−	−	−	−	−	−	−	−	−
10	Only recognised & established sources are used for providing cover and bonds	Best							4													
		Test	?						?													
		Both																				
			−	−	−	−	−	−	−	−	−	−	−	−	−	−	−	−	−	−	−	−
11	Contractors are required to confirm in writing their cover arrangements & provide evidence	Best					3		3	3												
		Test	?				?		?	?												
		Both																				
			−	−	−	−	−	−	−	−	−	−	−	−	−	−	−	−	−	−	−	−
12	Contractors are required to provide evidence of renewals when appropriate	Best								3	3											
		Test	?							?	?											
		Both																				
			−	−	−	−	−	−	−	−	−	−	−	−	−	−	−	−	−	−	−	−
13	In-house renewals are triggered by report generated from PC register	Best								4												
		Test	?							?												
		Both																				
			−	−	−	−	−	−	−	−	−	−	−	−	−	−	−	−	−	−	−	−
14	Third party requirements are accounted for in Controls 2 and 4 noted above	Best										4										
		Test	?									?										
		Both																				
			−	−	−	−	−	−	−	−	−	−	−	−	−	−	−	−	−	−	−	−
15	Policy terms are linked to the obligations, etc. included in the contact	Best										4	2									
		Test	?									?	?									
		Both																				
			−	−	−	−	−	−	−	−	−	−	−	−	−	−	−	−	−	−	−	−
16	Legal Dept. provides guidance on claim conditions whenever necessary	Best												4								
		Test	?											?								
		Both																				
			−	−	−	−	−	−	−	−	−	−	−	−	−	−	−	−	−	−	−	−
17	All claim situations reported to management for approval to proceed	Best												3	3	3						
		Test	?											?	?	?						
		Both																				
			−	−	−	−	−	−	−	−	−	−	−	−	−	−	−	−	−	−	−	−
18	All claims are calculated on the agreed basis & supported by relevant accounting data	Best															4					
		Test	?														?					
		Both																				
			−	−	−	−	−	−	−	−	−	−	−	−	−	−	−	−	−	−	−	−
19	All claims are logged and regularly progressed for settlement	Best															3	3				
		Test	?														?	?				
		Both																				
			−	−	−	−	−	−	−	−	−	−	−	−	−	−	−	−	−	−	−	−
20	Values due from contractor's insurance are pursued. Other payments withheld if not settled	Best															3					
		Test	?														?					
		Both																				
			−	−	−	−	−	−	−	−	−	−	−	−	−	−	−	−	−	−	−	−
21	All outstanding claims are reported to management	Best															3	3				
		Test	?														?	?				
		Both																				
			−	−	−	−	−	−	−	−	−	−	−	−	−	−	−	−	−	−	−	−
22	Alternative solutions are sought for unsuccessful claims – subject to authority	Best																3				
		Test	?															?				
		Both																				
			−	−	−	−	−	−	−	−	−	−	−	−	−	−	−	−	−	−	−	−
23	Senior management authority is obtained to write off unsuccessful claim costs/losses	Best																2				
		Test	?															?				
		Both																				
			−																				

Table 16 continued

			A	B	C	D	E	F	G	H	I	J	K	L	M	N	O	P	Q	R	S	T
			=	=	=	=	=	=	=	=	=	=	=	=	=	=	=	=	=	=	=	=
	Calculated Risk Score:	Risk	3	3	2	3	3	2	2	2	3	2	2	2	2	2	2	2	2	2	2	2
			–	–	–	–	–	–	–	–	–	–	–	–	–	–	–	–	–	–	–	–
24	It is a condition of engagement that consultants must have adequate indemnity cover	Best																	5			
		Test	?																?			
		Both																				
			–	–	–	–	–	–	–	–	–	–	–	–	–	–	–	–	–	–	–	–
25	Bonds are only used following a full assessment of contractor and project requirements	Best																		4		
		Test	?																	?		
		Both																				
			–	–	–	–	–	–	–	–	–	–	–	–	–	–	–	–	–	–	–	–
26	Guarantees from parent companies are used for contracts over a specified value limit	Best																		3		
		Test	?																	?		
		Both																				
			–	–	–	–	–	–	–	–	–	–	–	–	–	–	–	–	–	–	–	–
27	The costs of arranging Bonds are assessed in light of the protection provided	Best																		3		
		Test	?																	?		
		Both																				
			–	–	–	–	–	–	–	–	–	–	–	–	–	–	–	–	–	–	–	–
28	All bonds/policies are stored in fire-proof strongroom with contract documentation	Best																			5	
		Test	?																		?	
		Both																				
			–	–	–	–	–	–	–	–	–	–	–	–	–	–	–	–	–	–	–	–
29	Bonds are released in accord with contract conditions and sector best practice	Best																				4
		Test	?																			?
		Both																				
			–	–	–	–	–	–	–	–	–	–	–	–	–	–	–	–	–	–	–	–
30	Bonds are only released when all contractual obligations have been met as per Project Manager	Best																				4
		Test	?																			?
		Both																				
			–																			

A Develop a strategy for minimising exposures to risk(s)
B Ensure all relevant cover & security is provided & adequate
C Ensure accurate & complete records of cover are maintained
D Ensure that cover conditions are appropriate and relevant
E Ensure that cover/bond remains in force throughout contract
F Clearly establish & justify the costs of providing cover
G Ensure the selected insurance/surety companies are stable
H Ensure the contractor fulfils his insurance obligations
I Ensure cover is current & renewed during life of contract
J Ensure cover accords with he contract terms/conditions

K Ensure third party liabilities are appropriately addressed
L Ensure conditions for making claims are clearly defined
M Ensure that claims are made as & when appropriate
N Ensure claim values are realistic & adequately supported
O Ensure values due from contractor's insurance are received
P Ensure all claims are promptly & satisfactorily settled
Q Ensure consultants have sufficient Indemnity cover in place
R Ensure bonds & guarantees are obtained when appropriate
S Ensure that Bonds and Policies are securely stored
T Ensure Bonds are only released when all obligations are met

Scale 30 (abridged)

6 = Strategically vital to the business or organisation
5 = Makes a contribution to business operations
4 = Contributes to reliability of data, records and information
(Contract auditing Objectives-oriented scale)

3 = Avoids disruption/meets regulatory & accountability needs
2 = Leads to administrative/operational economies/efficiencies
1 = Generates administrative economies

17

THE SELECTION AND LETTING OF CONTRACTS

Scope

This chapter includes an examination of the issues surrounding both the selection of the most appropriate form of contract, and the correct letting of contracts. Chapter 15 discusses the contract documentation requirements, and the various operational matters arising from contractual relationships and obligations are addressed in separate subject or system level chapters.

In reading this chapter, it is necessary to bear in mind that some organisations have their own in-house legal department, or at least access to an external legal consultant who provides advice on appropriate matters. In order to obtain the appropriate degree of assurance, management would be wise to seek professional legal advice on contract matters, so that potential risks are sufficiently catered for in contract conditions and protocols. Chapter 1 provides some, albeit brief, guidance to the general principles of contract law.

SELECTING THE APPROPRIATE FORM OF CONTRACT

Companies and authorities with a high incidence of contracted activities, will usually have a procurement policy in place which defines the type(s) of contract to be commonly used. Adoption of a particular form of contract may be as a result of either the availability of a standard form which addresses the sector needs of the organisation, or the refinement over time of a specialised and modified form of contract which more precisely matches the identified requirements and sphere of business. For example, in the former situation a public authority may adopt the use of a standard building contract such as the JCT80. The latter requirements are normally dictated by the strength of market or negotiating position occupied by either the employer or the contractor. In all other general cases, an employer may have to accept the form of contract proffered by the contractor, which may have been developed to meet the specific requirements of the contractor's business environment. Independent prior review of this type of contract is always prudent, and any contentious clauses discussed and a compromise reached.

Whatever the scenario, the organisation should periodically review the appropriateness of the form of contract to be used. Market conditions will be subject to change, the balance of power between employer and contractor may alter. These, and other factors should be taken into account when assessing the choice of contract to apply. Decisions to change the form of contract in use should be supported by a rationale and the evidence of appropriate specialist legal advice. Implementing the change should incorporate any related changes to documentation supporting the contract and the surrounding administration procedures.

Forms of contract, even those of a standard nature, will have optional elements associated with them. Careful selection of options or caveats and the way in which they are applied may offer greater flexibility and protection against problems or breach of contract. The employer should, in the case of significant contractual arrangements, undertake a prior risk assessment of the project and aim to minimise the identified exposures as far as possible. This risk containment approach should, where practical or permissible, include the tailoring of contractual arrangements. However, contracts are two-way mechanisms, and the contractor will also be seeking the protection of his own position. Mutual agreement to the conditions will still be required so that the contract can be formed, and the adoption of unrealistic or unreasonable views by either party may lead to a failure in concluding any arrangements. Considerable cost and delay can be generated by the overzealous pursuit of the achievement of zero risk.

Once selected, the form of contract adopted will dictate and direct the other documentary and procedural requirements. Suggested systems of control for the management of contract processes are provided in other specific chapters. The procedures and measures in place should be appropriate to both the situation and the form of contract. Regular review of all procedures is a necessary and positive way of ensuring the ongoing effectiveness of administration. However, implementing administrative changes will require authorisation.

The type and nature of a project will generally direct the choice of contract to be used. The professional bodies, (such as those representing civil engineers, surveyors, consulting engineers, electrical or mechanical engineers) have been proactive in developing forms of contracts suited to the requirements of activities performed by their members. Many of these forms have been developed as joint ventures under the auspices of related professional bodies with common or shared interests. These standard forms of contract are now widely accepted and are available in various forms to more readily suit particular types of project or client, the main division being between the public and private sectors. There are also selected versions which specifically address the requirements of the Scottish legal system. Within this broad correlation between contract and project type, there are further sub-types which more precisely address the financial and other considerations.

The development of standard forms of contracts is an ongoing process and many have been progressively revised and updated in light of prevailing conditions and the wider needs of a pan-European scenario. Conditional or additional sections have also been created to address variable aspects such as sub-contractors, suppliers and price fluctuations.

Appendix 2 lists some of the more commonly used standard forms of contract in the construction, civil engineering, and electrical and mechanical engineering fields. Appendix 6 summarises the key elements in contractual arrangements cross-referred to the relevant clauses in selected standard forms of contract. The reader can use this table to identify the contract contents that address any of his or her concerns. The table is provided for general guidance only, and is no substitute for examining in detail the text of the required contract.

The more widespread the use of standard contracts the more generally acceptable they become. Where disputes have arisen and the matters have been addressed by the courts, more precise legal interpretations are generated from case law which further aid subsequent users of that form of contract. Additionally, some professional bodies (for example, the Chartered Institute of Building) publish regular reviews of relevant case law which summarise the effects of recent legal actions.

An important consideration when either choosing a form of contract or tailoring the conditions, is the basis upon which the pricing is to be established. Noted below are some pricing variants, not all will apply in every case, some are specific to either a sector or industry.

Firm or fixed price

These contract values are, as the name suggests, fixed in relation to the amount tendered or estimated and are not subject to amendment in line with the actual costs incurred by the contractor. In the case of long projects, for example over 12 months duration, a fixed price contract may not be the best option. Contractors in such instances will be inclined to include contingent inflation, pay awards, etc. in order to protect their interests. Alternatively if the contractor allows insufficient flexibility for future costs, he may either have to take short cuts or risk financial problems.

Variable price

The contractor's accounts can, in this instance, be subject to change. Contracts allowing for the application of price fluctuations are generally more costly to administer.

Lump sum

This is where the work (or identified sections of it) are priced as entities without the need to account for all the elements involved.

Measured work

Some contracts (for example in the building industry) allow for tenders based on estimated quantities, with the eventual accounts being based on the measurement of the actual work at appropriate rates.

Cost reimbursement

In this case contractor's accounts are calculated by adding an oncost to the actual costs incurred. The oncost element represents agreed allowances for profit, etc.

Target price

Accounts are based on actual costs incurred. Additionally a target price would have been previously agreed by the employer and contractor, and any difference between the target price and actual costs will be apportioned between the parties on an agreed basis.

Guaranteed maximum price (GMP)

This method is used more commonly in design and build forms of contract as a ceiling figure for the project. Employers can draw some assurance in respect of cost control.

In the construction industry there is a type of contract referred to as design and build. In such contracts it is still usual for the employer to provide an initial design brief, but the bidding contractors will present their own design solutions to the brief as part of the contract. They may either utilise their own design staff, or sub-contract the work to appropriate professionals. With design and build projects, the contractor will take responsibility for all aspects and they are normally empowered to complete the project as they see fit. However, the employers can elect (by an appropriate inclusion in the design brief) to employ their own consultant to monitor essential technical matters. Design and build contracts can also be applied to other activities such as shipbuilding. The benefits of this category of contract are that responsibility is devolved, timescales can be reduced and cost containment becomes the concern of the contractor. On the distaff side, the employer has limited influence over the quality of work, and subsequent negotiation opportunities are restricted.

As can be seen, selecting an inappropriate contract type can have very real disadvantages perhaps in the form of additional costs for example by reason of applying an inappropriate formula for the length of the project. In the construction sector, the form of contract may have a direct relationship to the tendering process in that both the contract and the tender will have a common documentary basis in the form of specifications, drawings and bills of quantities. For example the bill of quantity sent to contractors invited to tender will be used by the contractor for calculating parts of their eventual tender, and subsequently by the client (or employer) for determining the value of work completed.

INTERNATIONAL IMPLICATIONS

Where contracts, procurement or projects have an international dimension due consideration should be given to the choice of national law for the contract. Some of the potential legal implications are further discussed in Chapter 1. However aspects affecting this choice may include:

- currency considerations
- nature, form and scale of contracted activity
- previous trading or contract experience with the country in question
- EEC Directives affecting the award of public sector contracts
- level of in-house knowledge of the market
- knowledge of, and familiarity with, language, customs and business culture
- logistical factors, such as the movement of goods across borders
- whether or not the target country is a member of the EC
- advice and assistance available about legal, trading and cultural relationships.

Agreeing a form of contract may present problems in that forms recognised in the UK may be either inapplicable or inappropriate. However there has been some work undertaken by selected professional bodies in the development of more flexible and internationally acceptable forms of contract, for example the New Engineering Contract (NEC) formulated by the Association of Consulting Engineers (ACE). Further advice on overseas contracts and financial arrangements may be available from Central Government departments.

The language to be used in the contract will also have to be considered against the background of familiarity. Reliable sources of translation should be used perhaps in association with legal advisers based in the appropriate country. If the contracted work is to be undertaken outside the UK the need for reliable and competent local representatives or project managers becomes vital in order that close monitoring of progress and developments is possible. The specification aspects of international contracts will need be accurate and capable of local interpretation.

Last but not least the relevant financial arrangements will have to be researched. The timing and form of financing arrangements may be critical factors which are partly driven by the scale of the relevant currency transfers. Obviously the choice of currency, and the prevailing exchange rates will have a considerable bearing for all parties. Procedures should be in place to ensure that the relevant accounts are settled at the most opportune time after being both fully verified and authorised.

THE LETTING OF CONTRACTS

Once the most suitable form of contract has been chosen, and all the preceding formalities of tendering, and selecting the contractor have been performed, it is necessary to ensure the contract is correctly and accurately completed and appropriately enacted. All the relevant key dates and parameters will have to be accurately incorporated into the contract documents, and checked prior to signatures being applied. The correct and complete versions of all the supporting contract documents will also need to be made available, copied and checked.

The signing, and where necessary the sealing, of contracts will have to be correctly applied at the appropriate management level. Witnessing and document exchange formalities will also have to be correctly completed. Positive confirmation of the completion of all the necessary formalities should be noted, received and documented. Chapter 15 incorporates the issues surrounding the secure retention of all contract documents.

Control matrix example

Table 17 is an *Objectives*-oriented example utilising *Scale* 30. The data indicates relatively high levels of risk and significance that could be associated with regular contract activities. Some of the risks are mitigated by the use of standard forms of contract and the application of extensive measures.

Table 17 Selection and Letting of Contracts – Objectives

Overall Inherent Risk (Size) Score [5 is worst risk; 1 is best] = 2.61

A Ensure the most appropriate form of contract is utilised
B Ensure that the organisation's objectives will be achieved
C Ensure adoption of optimum contract pricing method
D Ensure chosen contract balances the risks between parties
E Ensure contract offers adequate protection if breached
F Ensure contract conditions are suitably tailored to risks
G Ensure all contract procedural requirements are addressed
H Aim to use contract conditions for settlement of disputes
I Minimise probability of costly & time-consuming litigation
J Ensure European & international implications are addressed
K Ensure the most suitable & reliable contractor is selected
L Ensure key values are correctly incorporated into contact
M Ensure that the parties obligations are clearly defined
N Ensure all contingent matters & obligations are addressed
O Ensure the contract is accurately & fully completed
P Ensure the contract is correctly authorised & enacted
Q Ensure that all the necessary formalities are observed
R Ensure contract documents are securely stored and protected

Scale 30 (abridged)

6 = Strategically vital to the business or organisation
5 = Makes a contribution to business operations
4 = Contributes to reliability of data, records and information (Contract auditing Objectives-oriented scale)
3 = Avoids disruption/meets regulatory & accountability needs
2 = Leads to administrative/operational economies/efficiencies
1 = Generates administrative economies

Selection and Letting of Contracts		OBJECTIVES																	
		A	B	C	D	E	F	G	H	I	J	K	L	M	N	O	P	Q	R
		=	=	=	=	=	=	=	=	=	=	=	=	=	=	=	=	=	=
Calculated Risk Score:	Risk	3	4	3	3	3	3	3	3	3	2	3	3	2	2	3	3	3	2
		–	–	–	–	–	–	–	–	–	–	–	–	–	–	–	–	–	–
Scale 30 (6 is most serious)	Type	6	6	6	4	5	6	4	4	4	5	6	4	6	5	5	5	5	5
Size (3 is maximum)	Size	2	3	2	2	2	2	2	2	2	1	2	2	1	1	2	2	2	1
MEASURES	—	–	–	–	–	–	–	–	–	–	–	–	–	–	–	–	–	–	–
1 Legal advice obtained to determine the most suitable form of contract in each case	Best	5	4	4	4	4	3	3	3	4	4		4						
	Test	?	?	?	?	?	?	?	?	?	?	?	?						
	Both																		
		–	–	–	–	–	–	–	–	–	–	–	–	–	–	–	–	–	–
2 Objectives are clearly defined as part of the project brief & reflected in choice of contract	Best		4																
	Test	?	?																
	Both																		
		–	–	–	–	–	–	–	–	–	–	–	–	–	–	–	–	–	–
3 Legal and Finance Depts. report upon optimum pricing method for the circumstances	Best				4														
	Test	?			?														
	Both																		
		–	–	–	–	–	–	–	–	–	–	–	–	–	–	–	–	–	–
4 Risk Analysis is applied to project and contractual matters	Best				4	3				2									
	Test	?			?	?				?									
	Both																		
		–	–	–	–	–	–	–	–	–	–	–	–	–	–	–	–	–	–
5 Standard forms of contract are used as a preference in most situations	Best		3			3	3		3	3			4	4					
	Test	?	?			?	?		?	?			?	?					
	Both																		
		–	–	–	–	–	–	–	–	–	–	–	–	–	–	–	–	–	–
6 Clause additions, deletions & amendments are negotiated & applied per Measure 1 above	Best					5			3	3									
	Test	?				?			?	?									
	Both																		
		–	–	–	–	–	–	–	–	–	–	–	–	–	–	–	–	–	–
7 Responsibilities and actions required are documented and allocated	Best							4											
	Test							?											
	Both																		
		–	–	–	–	–	–	–	–	–	–	–	–	–	–	–	–	–	–
8 Tendering & contractor assessment procedures are applied	Best											5							
	Test											?							
	Both																		
		–	–	–	–	–	–	–	–	–	–	–	–	–	–	–	–	–	–
9 Draft contract details are scrutinised by User and Legal Departments	Best												4		4				
	Test												?		?				
	Both																		
		–																		

Table 17 continued

			A	B	C	D	E	F	G	H	I	J	K	L	M	N	O	P	Q	R
			=	=	=	=	=	=	=	=	=	=	=	=	=	=	=	=	=	=
	Calculated Risk Score:	Risk	3	4	3	3	3	3	3	3	3	2	3	3	2	2	3	3	3	2
			–	–	–	–	–	–	–	–	–	–	–	–	–	–	–	–	–	–
10	Final contract is reviewed before signing	Best															4			
		Test	?														?			
		Both																		
			–	–	–	–	–	–	–	–	–	–	–	–	–	–	–	–	–	–
11	Only authorised/mandated managers permitted to sign on behalf of organisation	Best																	5	
		Test	?																?	
		Both																		
			–	–	–	–	–	–	–	–	–	–	–	–	–	–	–	–	–	–
12	All supporting documents are checked for accuracy, etc. before signing of contract	Best							4							3				
		Test	?						?							?				
		Both																		
			–	–	–	–	–	–	–	–	–	–	–	–	–	–	–	–	–	–
13	Witnessing, exchanging & sealing are undertaken by the Legal Dept.	Best																	5	
		Test	?																?	
		Both																		
			–	–	–	–	–	–	–	–	–	–	–	–	–	–	–	–	–	–
14	All contract documents are stored in fire-proof strongroom	Best																		5
		Test	?																	?
		Both																		
			–																		

A Ensure the most appropriate form of contract is utilised
B Ensure that the organisation's objectives will be achieved
C Ensure adoption of optimum contract pricing method
D Ensure chosen contract balances the risks between parties
E Ensure contract offers adequate protection if breached
F Ensure contract conditions are suitably tailored to risks
G Ensure all contract procedural requirements are addressed
H Aim to use contract conditions for settlement of disputes
I Minimise probability of costly & time-consuming litigation
J Ensure European & international implications are addressed
K Ensure the most suitable & reliable contractor is selected
L Ensure key values are correctly incorporated into contact
M Ensure that the parties obligations are clearly defined
N Ensure all contingent matters & obligations are addressed
O Ensure the contract is accurately & fully completed
P Ensure the contract is correctly authorised & enacted
Q Ensure that all the necessary formalities are observed
R Ensure contract documents are securely stored and protected

Scale 30 (abridged)

6 = Strategically vital to the business or organisation
5 = Makes a contribution to business operations
4 = Contributes to reliability of data, records and information
(Contract auditing Objectives-oriented scale)

3 = Avoids disruption/meets regulatory & accountability needs
2 = Leads to administrative/operational economies/efficiencies
1 = Generates administrative economies

Part III

DURING THE CURRENCY
OF THE CONTRACT

18

MANAGEMENT INFORMATION AND REPORTING

Scope

In this chapter we examine the role of management information during the currency of a project or contract. The fundamental concerns are that the relevant data is accurate, complete, relevant and timely. Particular mechanisms could be of equal interest to employer and contractor, and the general information needs of contractors are implied in the text. Matters of contractor performance are more fully examined in Chapter 19, but are included here in the overall context of a project and as a constituent part of the complete management information system.

The flow of accurate, complete and timely information is vital to the effective management of a project and a suitable range of systems should be in place to support the management information requirements. Such requirements can be relative to progress, technical, financial and performance matters. In all cases measures should be in place (and monitored) which progressively ensure the integrity and appropriateness of data and related processing mechanisms.

In selected scenarios, such as a building scheme, the accuracy and reliability of management information may be heavily dependent upon the quality of records created and maintained at site level. As part of a review of the management information system, the auditor may need to undertake a site visit to assess the effectiveness of controls exercised at the source. The planning and undertaking of audit site visits is explicitly explored in Chapter 6.

The sophistication and nature of management information and reporting systems will be dependent upon the contract-related culture of the organisation and the relative significance of the contract(s) concerned. There is a natural balance to be sought in the provision of data between the level that is required to enable effective management to be exercised and the associated overheads in recording, analysing and reporting same. In this respect the inclusion of such data should be justified so as to avoid the clouding of the key issues and enabling the containment of the costs associated with its preparation.

A further general factor to determine is the appropriate frequency for the preparation and presentation of management information. It is necessarily quite difficult to set universal rules for this element. Much depends upon the pace at which the project naturally flows, and this in turn is perhaps linked to the business or operating cycle of the underlying business or service. The hackneyed answer to the question is that information should be provided on a timescale that enables the accurate detection and prompt resolution of any significant problems, while minimising the associated implications. However, this stance presupposes that the nature of all potential problems can be predicted. An intuitive solution may be to link the frequency of project reporting to the financial accounting reporting cycle, for example on a month-end basis, but this might not be best placed to arrest the development of practical problems. A separate and open-ended reporting channel might be required for alerting management to momentous problems as they arise, for example contractors claims, the need to vary the specification, cost implications of unavoidable delays, and so on.

The needs of the different recipients of data will vary. For example, the project manager will be likely to require greater degrees of detail compared to a member of senior management. In a similar vein the nature of critical data will be linked to the specialist activity of an individual. The information requirements of the project should be determined, albeit perhaps only approximately, before work starts. This will enable the appropriate documentary and analysis framework to be in place. Where contract or project related activity is commonplace within the organisation, a policy and procedure on information requirements should be agreed and established as part of the administrative infrastructure.

The recording, analysis and presentation of the required data may be, in part or wholly, aided by the use of computer systems such as databases, spreadsheets, accounting packages, and desktop publishing. Where this is the case, great reliance may be placed upon both the hardware and software system elements. Adequate precautions should be in place to guard against the loss, corruption, and leakage of data. The necessary measures should include regular backing up of data, controls preventing unauthorised access to applications and data, and procedures for reconciling and agreeing the accuracy of data. Auditors may elect to examine the general use of computers in the project as a free-standing audit exercise.

The following headed sections aim to address the key issues for the probable subdivisions of management information. However, there should ideally be a form of co-ordinating process which brings together all the required data and ensures, *inter alia*, that all the items are present, that the data represents the same point of time, that matters of accuracy and completeness are satisfactorily addressed and that the data is distributed to all authorised recipients with regard to confidentiality requirements.

FINANCIAL

One of the key classifications of project information will be the financial interpretation of the situation. Up-to-date and accurate cost data becomes crucial not only as a means to determine the impact upon the organisation in terms of cash flow and commitment, but also to ensure that the project costs are in accord with those established at the outset. There is a need to accurately identify significant cost variations and to promptly and effectively react to them.

The overall financial status of a project should be regularly summarised and provided to senior management for their consideration. The most apt frequency for providing such information will depend upon the scale of the project, the related investment, the natural cycles of project disbursements, and so on. Any financial reporting has to set in the context of the actual progress achieved with the project. For example, if the project is actually 50 per cent completed, the actual cost data available from the feeding accounting systems may not represent the equivalent point in time. In this instance the actual costs should be projected, based on pending accounts and other calculable costs so that any staged budget comparisons can be meaningful and realistic. This requirement is additional to the concurrent necessity to estimate and project the overall final completed costs incorporating the predicted effects of permitted price fluctuations. The amount of analysis and cost breakdown will again be relative to the project type, but the accuracy of any analysed data should be confirmed back to a reliable source by applying suitable reconciliations.

It would be unwise to suggest that one method of presenting or summarising financial data for projects could be applicable in all situations, but aspects of the following elements may be relevant. The methods of presenting such data are numerous, but in all cases the key words are accuracy and completeness.

Budget

This should represent the original budget set for the project or a staged part thereof. Amendments applied to budgets should be appropriately controlled and subject to documented authority.

Amount disbursed to date

The value should represent the actual payments made to date via the appropriate accounting system. Further details may be provided on a supporting schedule which could reflect constituent details.

Commitments

This element can represent the financial value of various commitments or work completed but not yet paid. It may be desirable to separate these two elements as a means of determining those services and goods that are to be provided against those which already have been.

Future expenditure

A further consideration may be elements which have yet to be committed. Such costs may have to be based upon original tenders and quotations, etc.

Price fluctuations

Where the contract conditions permit the update of prices in accordance with an agreed basis, allowance for the likely uplift (or reduction) in costs should be made.

Total estimated final cost

This is the total of all the actual and potential costs, taking into account work yet to be completed and charged for. It should provide a meaningful comparison with the budget established for the equivalent stage of project work.

Variations between budget and final costs

This could also relate to comparisons at key stages or sections of the overall project where appropriate budgets have been established. Significant variations should be supported by narrative outlining the relevant circumstances and consequences. For example, for a construction project management should be informed of any significant variations to the work as suggested by the supervising professional, or any cost implications of claims lodged by the contractor within the terms of the contract where there are additional cost implications. In some cases, the relevant budgets may already include a value for unforeseen contingencies.

A number of factors included in the cost and progress reporting, such as the basis for calculating price fluctuations, may require further explanation in the form of accompanying notes or schedules.

The auditor's concern will naturally extend beyond the accuracy and reliability of the financial information presented to management. He will also want to see a suitable mechanism for ensuring that significant variations or problems reflected in the accounting data, were in fact acted upon by management. Capital projects may generate the need for additional data, perhaps incorporating the drawing upon external funds or the implications of variable interest rates.

PROGRESS

In this section we are referring to two fundamental elements 'expectation' versus 'actuality'. In order to measure the extent of progress, it is necessary to determine a baseline against which actual events can be measured. In the case of a hypothetical project, the expectations could fall into the following example categories and be further related to time:

- physical construction
- availability of facilities
- delivery and commissioning of equipment
- ability to operate or trade.

The overall project management systems and techniques should aim to clearly identify the key milestones, interdependencies, timescales, resource planning requirements, and so on. Critical path analysis will hopefully flush out all the key relationships and determine the timebase for each element (*see also* Chapter 8).

Obviously there should also be workable mechanisms for accurately plotting the progress achieved and the comparison of these results with the appropriate targets, in terms of timing. Project control and management systems, running on personal computers, can be employed to contain all the relevant target and actual data. Furthermore they can hold and summarise the time expended by members of the team. These tools normally have flexible report generators and can also highlight potential conflicts, overdue actions, and resourcing problems. Interactive project management systems can support management in assessing the validity and effectiveness of alternative solutions and scenarios.

Programmes of work, progress charts, gantt charts, etc. can all be used as aids to reflect the progress being made against expectations. Whatever form is used, the messages should be clear and only events which have a significant impact upon the achievement of the project in the required timescale should be reported. Otherwise, recipients become bombarded with excessive amounts of data and this can affect their ability to subsequently detect real problems. Reporting should aim to be clear and unambiguous.

The progress being achieved also has a strong relevance to the perceived performance of the contractor, especially where there are established key target dates reflected in the contract. The contract conditions may facilitate a relevant claim for damages in certain specified circumstances, and progress reporting supported by accurate data should clarify such situations.

The reasons behind the reported delays or problems will need to be determined, and the level and detail of source records should be appropriately pitched and trailed. This trailing should be effective in both directions. There is no point in detecting a problem at the top-level of project control if it takes many hours of analysing the underlying data to determine the nature and source of the cause.

PROBLEMS

One has to understand the nature and extent of a problem before determining the optimum solution. Detecting and reporting problems should be included in the overall management information strategy. There is a synergy between problems and the monitoring and reporting of progress as mentioned in the previous section.

The precise nature of potential problems will be project dependent. Accordingly, the source records maintained and the monitoring process applied will differ considerably in practice. For example where a project or contract is labour intensive, being able to detect manpower shortfalls, excessive absenteeism, or idle time caused by lack of materials will all be relevant factors to record, monitor and report upon.

There are some consistent types of problems that are likely to apply to most contract situations, these include:

- the need to fundamentally change the design or specification of a contract element
- the impact of the weather on progress
- failure of external suppliers
- industrial disputes and strikes
- criminal acts such as theft or vandalism
- the liquidation or bankruptcy of contractors, sub-contractors or suppliers
- acts of God.

Some problems have obvious antidotes, whereas others require due consideration and planning to resolve them. The common enemy is usually time, and therefore the quicker they can be detected and reported, the sooner they can be resolved.

Communication channels should be established as part of the project framework so that potential problem situations can be promptly and accurately brought to the attention of contractors, employers, key professionals and staff. Procedures should define the key personnel to contact in the event of problems, serious events or disaster, and the responsibilities of those individuals in such events.

The highlighting, assessment and resolution of problems should be consistently documented so that subsequent review of the circumstances can be undertaken and lessons learned for future projects. The maintenance of a project or site diary summarising key events can be useful in this respect. Where a problem can be addressed by an appropriate clause in the contract, compliance with all the required conditions should be monitored and confirmed.

Control matrix example

The *Objectives*-oriented example matrix contained in Table 18 examines the key issues affecting the establishment of a reliable management information system for a contract or project. The *Type* data (which uses *Scale* 30 per Appendix 7), characterises significant implications for the organisation. In the example *Measures,* a personal computer is utilised to store the management data, and access control and back-up processes are applied to provide the required security and resilience.

Table 18 Management Information and Reporting – Objectives
Overall Inherent Risk (Size) Score [5 is worst risk; 1 is best] = 3.18

A Enable appropriate & informed management decision making
B Ensure that management information is complete & accurate
C Ensure management is timely/promptly circulated
D Ensure that information is appropriate & accordingly routed
E Prevent the leakage, loss or corruption of project data
F Ensure all significant events are reported to management
G Ensure the financial implications of problems are provided
H Provide up-to-date information on all contractual claims
I Ensure that information systems are resilient and secure
J Ensure the final projected costs are accurately determined
K Ensure the responsibilities & accountabilities are allocated

Scale 30 (abridged)

6 = Strategically vital to the business or organisation
5 = Makes a contribution to business operations
4 = Contributes to reliability of data, records and information
(Contract auditing Objectives-oriented scale)
3 = Avoids disruption/meets regulatory & accountability needs
2 = Leads to administrative/operational economies/efficiencies
1 = Generates administrative economies

Management Information and Reporting		OBJECTIVES										
		A	B	C	D	E	F	G	H	I	J	K
		=	=	=	=	=	=	=	=	=	=	=
Calculated Risk Score:	Risk	4	4	3	3	3	3	3	3	4	3	3
		–	–	–	–	–	–	–	–	–	–	–
Scale 30 (6 is most serious)	Type	5	5	5	5	5	5	5	4	5	6	5
Size (3 is maximum)	Size	3	3	2	2	2	2	2	2	3	2	2
MEASURES		–	–	–	–	–	–	–	–	–	–	–
1 Management information reporting requirements were defined prior to start of project	Best		3	2	2	3		3	2	2		
	Test	?	?	?	?	?		?	?	?		
	Both											
		–	–	–	–	–	–	–	–	–	–	–
2 Data is obtained from agreed and reliable sources	Best		3	4								
	Test	?	?	?								
	Both											
		–	–	–	–	–	–	–	–	–	–	–
3 Data is reconciled to source before circulation	Best		3	4			2					
	Test	?	?	?			?					
	Both											
		–	–	–	–	–	–	–	–	–	–	–
4 Information flows have been established. Weekly timetable applied and monitored	Best				4							
	Test	?			?							
	Both											
		–	–	–	–	–	–	–	–	–	–	–
5 Responsibilities for producing accurate data on time have been defined and allocated	Best		3	4	4		3					4
	Test	?	?	?	?		?					?
	Both											
		–	–	–	–	–	–	–	–	–	–	–
6 Agreed circulation lists in place. Operated by Post Room staff	Best					4						
	Test	?				?						
	Both											
		–	–	–	–	–	–	–	–	–	–	–
7 Data is held on a dedicated PC protected by password access controls	Best					4				4		
	Test	?				?				?		
	Both											
		–	–	–	–	–	–	–	–	–	–	–
8 Circulation of sensitive data is restricted and in sealed 'addressee only' envelopes	Best					3						
	Test	?				?						
	Both											
		–	–	–	–	–	–	–	–	–	–	–
9 All events (i.e. claims) are summarised for circulation and discussion at project meetings	Best						4					
	Test	?					?					
	Both											
		–											

Table 18 continued

			A	B	C	D	E	F	G	H	I	J	K
			=	=	=	=	=	=	=	=	=	=	=
	Calculated Risk Score:	Risk	4	4	3	3	3	3	3	3	4	3	3
			–	–	–	–	–	–	–	–	–	–	–
10	Project/Contract accounts are maintained on agreed basis Monthly reports generated	Best							3				
		Test	?						?				
		Both											
			–	–	–	–	–	–	–	–	–	–	–
11	Financial implications are accordingly projected using agreed methods/formulae	Best							4		4		
		Test	?						?		?		
		Both											
			–	–	–	–	–	–	–	–	–	–	–
12	Claims status reports are produced and circulated to Project Team	Best							5				
		Test	?						?				
		Both											
			–	–	–	–	–	–	–	–	–	–	–
13	All data is backed up to disk on daily basis. Alternative PC is available for use	Best									4		
		Test	?								?		
		Both											
			–	–	–	–	–	–	–	–	–	–	–
14	Copies of source documents are filed centrally. Data back-up stored off-site	Best									3		
		Test	?								?		
		Both											
			–	–	–	–	–	–	–	–	–	–	–
15	Management responsibilities allocated and actions monitored by project committee	Best											4
		Test											?
		Both											
			–	–	–	–	–	–	–	–	–	–	–

A Enable appropriate & informed management decision making
B Ensure that management information is complete & accurate
C Ensure management is timely/promptly circulated
D Ensure that information is appropriate & accordingly routed
E Prevent the leakage, loss or corruption of project data
F Ensure all significant events are reported to management
G Ensure the financial implications of problems are provided
H Provide up-to-date information on all contractual claims
I Ensure that information systems are resilient and secure
J Ensure the final projected costs are accurately determined
K Ensure the responsibilities & accountabilities are allocated

Scale 30 (abridged)

6 = Strategically vital to the business or organisation
5 = Makes a contribution to business operations
4 = Contributes to reliability of data, records and information (Contract auditing Objectives-oriented scale)

3 = Avoids disruption/meets regulatory & accountability needs
2 = Leads to administrative/operational economies/efficiencies
1 = Generates administrative economies

19

PERFORMANCE MONITORING

Scope

This chapter examines the requirements associated with conducting ongoing performance monitoring of contractors, consultants, and others involved in the project or contract. The application of such processes is more usual during the currency of a project in order to ensure that all the requirements are being addressed. Such processes can also generate useful data that can be used both in improving the organisation's approach to future contracts, and ensuring that the relevant professionals are worthy of future re-employment.

The contents have a natural affinity with aspects reflected in Chapters 8, 18, and 30 which examine project management, management information, and project reviews respectively. Liquidated damages are also explored in this chapter, as they reflect directly upon the failure of a contractor in the construction sector to fulfil contractual obligations.

PERFORMANCE MONITORING

In this chapter we address all aspects of performance monitoring including that related to the contractor. Some aspects of performance are normally explicitly defined in the contract, for example the specification of the required product or service, and the timescale in which the contract should be completed. Alternatively performance can be defined in terms of required technical standards or quality of workmanship, and these too can be explicitly incorporated into the contract conditions.

If the contract defines various performance criteria or benchmarks, it generally follows that any failure, on the contractor's part, to achieve such targets can be construed as a breach of the contract. In order to avoid lengthy and costly court actions for breaches of contract, some forms will incorporate conditions and mechanisms designed to resolve disputes between parties on an agreed basis. For example, the contracts used for building projects normally incorporate liquidated damages conditions, which define in monetary terms an assessment of the losses that could be payable to the employer if the contractor fails to complete the contract on schedule in the absence of an authorised reason and just cause for the delay. A separate section at the end of this chapter examines liquidated damages in detail.

Performance monitoring can be justified for a number of reasons, including the following:

- to ensure that each stage of the project is achieved on time and within budget
- to ensure that the product of the contract (e.g. the building, the computer system or the nuclear submarine) conforms to the required technical and performance standards
- to assess whether the contractor should be considered for future contract work on behalf of the employing organisation
- to assess the effectiveness of the organisation's own management in the conduct of the project and contract
- to assess the effectiveness, relevance and cost-justification of existing contract and project administration procedures
- to confirm that the chosen form of contract was appropriate, sufficiently flexible and in the organisation's best interests for use in relation to similar projects in the future
- to identify any element in the management of contracts that should be revised and improved for future situations.

The ability to accurately assess performance in a contract will be to a greater or lesser extent dependent upon the effectiveness of project and general management controls in place. These should be organic in that they are regularly reviewed in relation to their effectiveness and practicality in application, and any required changes are duly authorised and incorporated.

The processes to follow in the course of performance assessment may benefit from being formalised in writing where this is justified in respect of contract activity or project scale. The post-completion or project out-turn review process (*see* Chapter 30) should incorporate elements covering contractor performance.

Preventing unreasonable levels of subjectivity from creeping into review processes can be difficult to legislate for in procedures, and it is impossible to remove it completely. In the case of project post-completion reviews, we would suggest that some members of the review group are outwith the relevant project team or end-users, this will hopefully inject a moderating element of objectivity into the process.

Where the organisation maintains an approved list of contractors, it can be useful to appraise the performance of contractors and their attitude to claims, changed priorities, variation orders and other problems. The reliability, competence and professionalism of the contractor can be more effectively and objectively appraised during an actual project, and the knowledge gained during this period can be incorporated into the overall evaluation of the suitability of the contractor (*see also* Chapters 12 and 13). The performance of a contractor may continue to be relevant during any period of maintenance beyond either the supply, development or construction phase of the contract.

LIQUIDATED DAMAGES

In the construction sector, it is usual to incorporate into the tender and contract a value referred to as either liquidated damages or liquidated and ascertained damages. This represents an assessment of losses that could be genuinely due to the employer if there is breach of the contract conditions such as an unauthorised delay in the completion of the contract caused by the contractor. The relevant rules of eligibility are normally defined in the contract conditions. However, it is stressed that the application of liquidated damages should not be regarded as the application of a penalty clause.

Liquidated damages will normally be payable if the contractor fails to complete the contract on or by the defined date. However, there are possible circumstances, for example where the employer's action causes delay in the contractor getting possession of the site, when the employer's rights to claim liquidated damages may be lost. This is further justification for ensuring that the contract project management methods exercise adequate control over key milestones and dates.

Under the conditions of the JCT80 standard contract (clause 24.1), the supervising professional will signify the failure of the contractor to meet the required deadline by issuing a certificate of non-completion. This action instigates the payment of liquidated damages. The overall liquidated damages method of assessing damages due has the advantages of being capable of prompt and efficient resolution without the need to refer the matter to the courts, which process can absorb both time and costs in alarming amounts.

Separate amounts of liquidated damages may be calculated for phases of contracts which are progressively completed in sections; as the final completion point is approached the overall amount of liquidated damages would be reduced. Once agreed and incorporated into the contract, the value of liquidated damages should be recorded together with other key contract data in a contract register or other permanent record. The nature of 'losses' that can be included in the calculation are clearly defined, especially in relation to local government developments.

The inclusion of liquidated damages into a contract should be based on an acceptable method of calculation. This may be related, in the case of delays in completing specified work, to the number of days or weeks the actual completion exceeded the defined completion date. A periodic rate of liquidated damages would then be applied for each day or week of delay.

The commonly used forms of building and construction contract permit the supervising architect or engineer to instruct the contractor with respect to changes, amendments, etc. and these in turn may have a logical effect on the timing of the project programme of work which requires a suitably authorised extension of time. Amending or postponing the expected completion date in this authorised way, will have an effect on the appropriate determination of liquidated damages, and may result in the return of previously paid damages if subsequent extensions of time are granted.

As can be seen from the previous example, it is necessary to maintain up-to-date and accurate records of all extensions of time, revised completion dates, effects on programmes of work, impacts of events upon the completion dates for sections of the project, claims for liquidated damages and their status, monies received in respect of claims, etc. All the facts should be at hand when claims are considered and prepared, as valuable time can otherwise be wasted.

In some cases the value of liquidated damages contained in the contract documentation becomes absolute, in that it is due from the contractors irrespective of whether the actual losses are either greater or less than the estimated value. Liquidated damages can be deducted from sums due to the contractor if the contractor has not completed the project by the defined completion date. This approach also applies to any agreed extension of the completion date as instigated by the architect or engineer responsible for the project. It should be noted that, in the construction industry context, it is the employer who deducts any liquidated damages from sums due, and it is not the responsibility of either the architect or engineer to certify the situation. Where, after due review, the decision is taken not to deduct liquidated damages, the reasons should be documented and authorised. Measures should be in place to ensure that all proven and substantiated liquidated damages are taken into account during account settlement.

Control matrix example

The example matrix featured in Table 19 examines a broad range of contract performance-related matters and their remedies. The *Exposures*-oriented matrix, which uses *Scale* 31, is non-sector specific, but includes reference to liquidated damages in *Measure* number 4. Most of the contents relate to the effectiveness (or otherwise) of project management monitoring. The matrix has been constructed using the techniques described in Chapter 32.

Table 19 Performance monitoring – Exposures

Overall Inherent Risk (Size) Score [5 is worst risk; 1 is best] = 2.80

A Failure to achieve overall project/contract objectives
B Failure to control project/contract costs within budget
C Failure to complete project/contract on time
D Failure to achieve required technical & quality standards
E Failure to comply with regulatory/legislative requirements
F Unsatisfactory contractor performance – delay, costs, etc.
G Unsatisfactory consultant performance – delay, costs, etc.
H Contractor failed to fulfil contractual obligations
I Excessive number of contractual claims – costs & delays
J Numerous design changes & modifications – additional cost
K Inadequate project management – failed objectives

L Inadequate, inappropriate or unworkable procedures
M inappropriate form of contract – inflexible and unbalanced
N Inadequate/ineffective monitoring of progress
O Inadequate/inaccurate project documentation
P Failure to allocate clear roles & responsibilities
Q Insufficient or inappropriate forms of insurance/security
R Uncontrolled variations and extensions of time
S Inadequate resources and skills – error, cost, delay
T Costly & time-consuming litigation required to seek redress

Scale 31 (abridged)

6 = Incorrect identification of needs, or failure to meet them
5 = Lost business; needs partly unfulfilled; or breach of rules
4 = Delay or disruption; reputation loss; minor breach of rules
(Contract auditing Exposures-oriented scale)

3 = Avoidable costs/losses; damage to contract relationships
2 = Administrative or accounting errors
1 = Detectable negative impact on the business or service

Performance Monitoring			A	B	C	D	E	F	G	H	I	J	K	L	M	N	O	P	Q	R	S	T
		EXPOSURES																				
			=	=	=	=	=	=	=	=	=	=	=	=	=	=	=	=	=	=	=	=
	Calculated Risk Score:	Risk	4	3	3	3	2	3	3	3	3	3	3	2	3	3	3	3	2	3	3	2
	Scale 31 (6 is most serious)	Type	6	5	4	6	5	6	5	5	3	5	6	3	6	6	4	6	3	5	4	5
	Size (3 is maximum)	Size	3	2	3	2	1	2	2	2	3	2	2	2	2	2	2	2	2	2	2	1
	CONTROLS	–																				
1	Project Management System & procedures in place with defined roles & responsibilities	Best	4	3	4		2	3	3	2			5			3		4				
		Test	?	?	?	?	?	?	?	?			?			?		?				
		Both																				
2	Objectives and requirements clearly communicated in contract/project documentation	Best		4														4				
		Test	?	?														?				
		Both																				
3	Budgets agreed & monitored. Project Manager responsible for day-to-day a/c confirmation	Best			4																	
		Test	?		?																	
		Both																				
4	Contract allows for Liquidated Damages if contractor fails to complete on time	Best			4				3	4												
		Test	?		?				?	?												
		Both																				
5	Technical & workmanship standards are defined in the contract	Best				3																
		Test	?			?																
		Both																				
6	All work is signed-off by the Engineer for compliance with standards. Errors are referred	Best				4				4												
		Test	?			?				?												
		Both																				
7	Achievement of regulatory requirements confirmed by the Legal Dept.	Best					3															
		Test	?				?															
		Both																				
8	MIS in place to ensure management awareness of problems progress, costs, etc.	Best	4	4	3	2	2	2	2	2	2									3		
		Test	?	?	?	?	?	?	?	?	?	?								?		
		Both																				
9	Contractor's obligations clearly defined in contract and specifications	Best		3	3	3	3		3	4												
		Test	?	?	?	?	?		?	?												
		Both																				

Table 19 continued

			A	B	C	D	E	F	G	H	I	J	K	L	M	N	O	P	Q	R	S	T
			=	=	=	=	=	=	=	=	=	=	=	=	=	=	=	=	=	=	=	=
	Calculated Risk Score:	Risk	4	3	3	3	2	3	3	3	3	3	3	2	3	3	3	3	2	3	3	2
10	Contractor's performance subject to ongoing monitoring – Regular meetings to resolve problems	Best						4		4												
		Test	?					?		?												
		Both																				
11	Consultant's role defined in the Terms of Engagement – monitored by Project Manager	Best								3												
		Test	?							?												
		Both																				
12	All claims reviewed by the Engineer in charge against contract conditions	Best							3													
		Test	?						?													
		Both																				
13	Thorough design phase restricted need for subsequent changes and modifications	Best							4													
		Test	?						?													
		Both																				
14	All variations/design changes have to be approved by management	Best							4											4		
		Test	?						?											?		
		Both																				
15	Project is subject to monitoring by senior management – Problem's solutions are quickly applied	Best		3	3	3						4		3								
		Test	?	?	?	?						?		?								
		Both																				
16	Procedures are developed and enhanced over time. Previous experiences taken into account	Best										3										
		Test	?									?										
		Both																				
17	Procedures periodically reviewed and amended after management authority received	Best										4										
		Test	?									?										
		Both																				
18	Form of contract selected after comprehensive review of project requirements, legal factors, etc.	Best												5								
		Test	?											?								
		Both																				
19	Contract documentation checked for accuracy & completeness prior to letting of contract	Best														3						
		Test	?													?						
		Both																				
20	Ongoing admin. documentation is produced to defined standards. Subject to quality reviews	Best														3						
		Test	?													?						
		Both																				
21	Insurance & Bonding arrangements applied per Risk Analysis. Premiums justified & authorised	Best																	3			
		Test	?																?			
		Both																				
22	Evidence obtained of currency and validity of Contractor's insurance requirements	Best																	3			
		Test	?																?			
		Both																				
23	Resource assessment undertaken at Project Appraisal phase	Best																			3	
		Test	?																		?	
		Both																				

Table 19 continued

				A	B	C	D	E	F	G	H	I	J	K	L	M	N	O	P	Q	R	S	T
				=	=	=	=	=	=	=	=	=	=	=	=	=	=	=	=	=	=	=	=
	Calculated Risk Score:	Risk		4	3	3	3	2	3	3	3	3	3	3	2	3	3	3	3	2	3	3	2
			–	–	–	–	–	–	–	–	–	–	–	–	–	–	–	–	–	–	–	–	–
24	Contractors have to confirm availability of sufficient & suitably skilled resources	Best																				3	
		Test	?																			?	
		Both																					
			–	–	–	–	–	–	–	–	–	–	–	–	–	–	–	–	–	–	–	–	–
25	Organisation's resource requirements defined and provided per Board authority	Best																				3	
		Test	?																			?	
		Both																					
			–	–	–	–	–	–	–	–	–	–	–	–	–	–	–	–	–	–	–	–	–
26	Contract conditions aim to settle most disputes by mutual agreement outwith courts	Best																					3
		Test	?																				?
		Both																					
			–																				

A Failure to achieve overall project/contract objectives
B Failure to control project/contract costs within budget
C Failure to complete project/contract on time
D Failure to achieve required technical & quality standards
E Failure to comply with regulatory/legislative requirements
F Unsatisfactory contractor performance – delay, costs, etc.
G Unsatisfactory consultant performance – delay, costs, etc.
H Contractor failed to fulfil contractual obligations
I Excessive number of contractual claims – costs & delays
J Numerous design changes & modifications – additional cost
K Inadequate project management – failed objectives

L Inadequate, inappropriate or unworkable procedures
M inappropriate form of contract – inflexible and unbalanced
N Inadequate/ineffective monitoring of progress
O Inadequate/inaccurate project documentation
P Failure to allocate clear roles & responsibilities
Q Insufficient or inappropriate forms of insurance/security
R Uncontrolled variations and extensions of time
S Inadequate resources and skills – error, cost, delay
T Costly & time-consuming litigation required to seek redress

Scale 31 (abridged)

6 = Incorrect identification of needs, or failure to meet them
5 = Lost business; needs partly unfulfilled; or breach of rules
4 = Delay or disruption; reputation loss; minor breach of rules
(Contract auditing Exposures-oriented scale)

3 = Avoidable costs/losses; damage to contract relationships
2 = Administrative or accounting errors
1 = Detectable negative impact on the business or service

20

ARRANGEMENTS FOR SUB-CONTRACTORS AND SUPPLIERS

Scope

The involvement of sub-contractors in a project can further complicate the legal interrelationships. Additionally, there is the concurrent objective of ensuring that any work conducted by, or materials supplied by, sub-contractors is of an acceptable quality. This chapter explores the issues relative to the selection, monitoring and payment of sub-contractors and suppliers, with the intention of reducing the attendant risks.

Existing contract law also allows, under specific circumstances, for the transfer of contractual rights and obligations. These factors are not discussed in the following text, but readers should be aware that such assignments are permitted. For example all the forms of contract analysed in Appendix 6 contain clauses specifying the required actions and stressing the need for written consent of the other affected parties.

In order to fulfil the objectives of a project it may be necessary to involve sub-contractors and suppliers. If there is a contractual relationship established between the employer and contractor, the performance of the sub-contractor(s) will normally be the responsibility of the main contractor. The contractor is also primarily responsible for settling the accounts of the sub-contractor, and the employer has no formal contractual relationship with the sub-contractor.

SUB-CONTRACTORS

Sub-contracting part or all of project activity is not uncommon, indeed it is a very prominent feature of the UK construction industry. The nature and scope of sub-contracted work varies considerably and can be broken down as follows:

- *The supply of materials only* This is where the sub-contractor provides the required items or materials and delivers them to the site or warehouse. Such arrangements will be subject to the *Sale of Goods Act 1979*.

- *Labour only* This is where specialist, skilled or general staff are provided to perform either a defined or general function. The *Supply of Goods and Services Act 1982 Part II* which relates to the provision of services will have a bearing on such activities.
- *Supply and fix or supply and fit* This is a hybrid of the two previous forms, and relates to the one sub-contractor providing both the materials and the staff to assemble and install them. Parts I and II of the *Supply of Goods and Services Act 1982 will both be applicable in this context.*

In the case of a major project, perhaps with complex sub-contracting arrangements, it is likely that the success or failure of the project will be heavily dependent upon the performance and quality of sub-contractors. In the event of either the main contractor or any of the sub-contractors experiencing financial or trading difficulties, there could be serious repercussions for the end-client or employer. In order to maintain an overall awareness of the situation, it may be prudent (within the confines of the relevant contract arrangements) for the employer to carefully monitor progress achieved and obtain evidence that sub-contractors have been correctly and promptly paid by the main contractor. In the construction sector this latter point can be catered for in respect of sub-contractors initially nominated by the architect or engineer and it provides further reassurance against future financial problems which could adversely affect the project. However, if the architect or engineer reveals that the appropriate payments have not been made, there are circumstances where such settlement can be made directly by the employer on the understanding that appropriate recovery will be made from the main contractor in due course.

In the case of either liquidation or bankruptcy of the main contractor there are different arrangements with regard to settling sub-contractor's outstanding accounts (*see* Chapter 27). However, if the completion of a project affected by a liquidation is crucially dependent upon the continued involvement of affected sub-contractors, it may prove expedient, subject to certain precautions, for the employer to enter into a direct relationship with a previous sub-contractor in order that the project can continue. In such a situation, the employer should ensure that the sub-contractor is financially stable, and it may be necessary to secure a suitable bond as further assurance before formalising the relationship.

With regard to building and construction projects it is in order for the architect or engineer to nominate the engagement of a specific sub-contractor, in which case he is referred to as a nominated sub-contractor. Because the main contractor would be responsible for the activities and work quality of the nominated sub-contractor, the relative forms of contract can make allowance for him to object to a suggested appointment. For the employer there will be natural concerns about the quality, reliability and stability of selected sub-contractors, especially where their role is crucial to the successful completion of the project. By electing to use a form of contract permitting the nomination of sub-contractors, the employer can exercise some control over their selection based upon quality and performance factors. In construction projects, the supervising professional should ensure that all the contractors are of a suitable standard and reliable.

In the case of nominated sub-contractors in the construction sector, the contract between the employer and the main contractor will be likely to include the cost of sub-contracted work under either 'Provisional Items' or 'Prime Costs'. Such costs to the employer can include elements representing the main contractor's profit, supervision costs, etc. When the main contractors accounts are submitted, it is normal practice to separately schedule the costs for nominated sub-contractors. The relevant supervising architect or engineer should also have separately identified such costs on the appropriate certificates. The employer can therefore confirm, prior to payment being made, that the amounts are both in accord with those included in the relevant tender documentation and have been confirmed by the supervising professional as valid for payment.

Where the main contractor makes all the necessary arrangements for sub-contracting, and the employer has no involvement, the arrangements are classified as 'domestic', and the accordingly the sub-contractors are referred to as domestic sub-contractors. In such instances, the supervising engineer or architect should, where the contract conditions permit, provide prior written consent to their engagement, thus ensuring that the subsequent work will meet quality and other requirements. In this situation, where the employer's representatives have limited involvement in the engagement of sub-contractors, the contractual relationships are clear, in that the sub-contractor recovers any monies due from the main contractor, who in turn is paid directly by the employer or end-client. No contractual relationships, duties, rights, etc. exist between the employer and the sub-contractor(s).

As mentioned elsewhere in this book, in the case of civil engineering and building projects the supervising professional is, throughout the course of a project, responsible for ensuring that work is undertaken to the required standard. He regularly certifies the successful completion of the work, and this process provides the employer with the necessary evidence to support payment of either interim or final accounts. For the most part the main contractor is obliged to settle sub-contractor's accounts directly, but employers should be satisfied that this has been done before themselves paying the main contractor for the relevant part of the works.

Outwith the construction sector, the same general principal applies to the settlement of sub-contractor's accounts by the main contractor, but without the equivalent of the architect's monitoring role. It would be wise for the employer to ensure that the form of contract to be used clearly states the responsibilities, rights, duties, etc. with respect to the engagement, monitoring and payment of sub-contractors. Legal advice and assurances should be sought about the degree to which the employer could be liable for sub-contractor accounts in the event of the main contractor defaulting or going into liquidation.

SUPPLIERS

In some projects, the main contractor may also be the prime supplier, for example in the case of commissioning a new computer installation. The relevant contract may specify staged payments, and employers should be able to confirm that the relevant goods have been delivered and installed in working condition before sanctioning payment of the relevant account. End-users should signify their satisfaction with the relevant items and confirm that all their functional and performance requirements have been correctly addressed. For example, the modification of a software application by an external contractor as part of a larger system implementation should involve extensive testing of the delivered system by the users in a realistic situation before the accounts are authorised for settlement. There may also be a strong case for including a retention arrangement in the contract until the relevant system has been proven in a live usage scenario.

Payment of supplier's accounts should only be made when there is reliable evidence of either the goods or services having been appropriately provided in accordance with the specified requirements. Additionally, the payments should be authorised at the appropriate level within the organisation. Due regard should be given to the need to prevent malpractice by the application of adequate segregation of duties and responsibilities.

Control matrix example

Table 20 contains an example *Exposures*-oriented matrix representing a contract situation with a relatively high level of sub-contractor involvement. Appendix 7 contains details of *Scale* 31 which has been applied in this case.

Table 20 Sub-contractors and Suppliers – Exposures
Overall Inherent Risk (Size) Score [5 is worst risk; 1 is best] = 1.86

A Use of financially unstable or incompetent sub-contractors
B Failure to achieve required technical & quality standards
C No influence over selection of suitable sub-contractors
D Inadequate communication with sub-contractors – error, delay
E Financial failure of sub-contractors – delay, costs
F Failure of main contractors to settle sub-contract accounts
G Goods/services not available at the correct time
H Insufficient sub-contract resources - programme delayed
I Insufficiently skilled sub-contract employees – error etc.

J Additional costs & delay due to poor project planning
K Payment of invalid Prime Cost charges for sub-contract work
L Financial failure of main contractor-unpaid sub-contractors
M Sub-contract costs paid where faults/problems are apparent
N Costs related to subsequent problems with sub-contract work

SCALE 31 (abridged)

6 = Incorrect identification of needs, or failure to meet them
5 = Lost business; needs partly unfulfilled; or breach of rules
4 = Delay or disruption; reputation loss; minor breach of rules
(Contract auditing Exposures-oriented scale)

3 = Avoidable costs/losses; damage to contract relationships
2 = Administrative or accounting errors
1 = Detectable negative impact on the business or service

Sub-contractors & suppliers		EXPOSURES													
		A	B	C	D	E	F	G	H	I	J	K	L	M	N
		=	=	=	=	=	=	=	=	=	=	=	=	=	=
Calculated Risk Score:	Risk	3	3	2	2	3	2	3	3	3	3	2	2	2	2
Scale 31 (6 is most serious)	Type	5	4	3	4	5	3	4	4	4	4	3	5	3	3
Size (3 is maximum)	Size	2	2	2	1	2	1	2	2	2	2	2	1	1	1
CONTROLS															
1 Sub-contractors nominated by mutal agreement with the Main contractor	Best		4	3	4		4		3	2					
	Test	?	?	?	?		?		?	?					
	Both														
2 Finances and track record of sub-contractors formally assessed	Best		4	4			4								
	Test	?	?	?			?								
	Both														
3 Only members of recognised trade and professional bodies are engaged	Best		3	4					3						2
	Test	?	?	?					?						?
	Both														
4 Regular team meetings held to discuss progress and reslove problems	Best				3			3			2				
	Test	?			?			?			?				
	Both														
5 Evidence of payments made by main contractor provided before settlement of Prime Cost items	Best						4					3			
	Test	?					?					?			
	Both														
6 Contract Administrator confirms workmanship/material standards prior to payment being made	Best			4								3		3	2
	Test	?		?								?		?	?
	Both														
7 Employer has no direct contractual obligation to settle unpaid sub-contractor accounts	Best						2								
	Test	?					?								
	Both														
8 Programme of works is circulated to all parties with key dates specified	Best							3			3				
	Test	?						?			?				
	Both														
9 Main contractor is responsible for ensuring that sub-contract work is completed on time	Best							3			3				
	Test	?						?			?				
	Both														

Table 20 continued

			A	B	C	D	E	F	G	H	I	J	K	L	M	N
			=	=	=	=	=	=	=	=	=	=	=	=	=	=
	Calculated Risk Score:	Risk	3	3	2	2	3	2	3	3	3	3	2	2	2	2
			–	–	–	–	–	–	–	–	–	–	–	–	–	–
10	Resource/skill requirements identified by main contractor – written confirmation sought	Best								3	3					
		Test	?							?	?					
		Both														
			–	–	–	–	–	–	–	–	–	–	–	–	–	–
11	Contract administrator certifies the completion of all work for account payment	Best											4			
		Test	?										?			
		Both														
			–	–	–	–	–	–	–	–	–	–	–	–	–	–
12	Legal advice sought – no direct obligation to pay	Best											2			
		Test	?										?			
		Both														
			–	–	–	–	–	–	–	–	–	–	–	–	–	–
13	Management authority required to pay outstanding accounts if critical to project success	Best											3			
		Test	?										?			
		Both														
			–	–	–	–	–	–	–	–	–	–	–	–	–	–
14	All work is subject to twelve month maintainance cover – completion is certified	Best														4
		Test	?													?
		Both														
			–	–	–	–	–	–	–	–	–	–	–	–	–	–

21

MATERIALS, PLANT AND PROJECT ASSETS

Scope

This chapter, which is intentionally biased towards the construction sector, addresses the issues surrounding materials, items of plant and the assets acquired specifically for the project in question. Some of the contents, especially that related to project assets, could be readily construed to apply to non-construction scenarios. We discuss matters relative to the security, ownership and recording of items procured for a project or contract.

MATERIALS AND GOODS

The responsibility for the supply of materials during the project can either be vested with the contractor or the employer. Either party can initiate the procurement of materials or goods to fulfil the contracted work (or a part of it) as defined in the contract documentation. Additionally the materials concerned can either be delivered to and stored on the site, or held elsewhere until they are required for use. The latter option may be relevant in the case of items required later on in the project timetable or where site storage could lead to the damage, deterioration or loss of the relevant items especially where they were relatively high in value.

Materials could relate to tasks where the contractor has tendered on the basis of providing and utilising the items, for example laying a driveway where the contractor quotes on the basis of both labour and materials. Alternatively, the items could have been subject to separate costing within the contract, perhaps as prime cost sums, for example specialist lighting equipment.

In considering the rest of this section, it is important to establish the ground rules about the ownership of materials. In the case of a building project, materials delivered to the site and awaiting incorporation into the structure remain the property of the contractor, until such time as they become part of the building, when they are the employer's property. In the case of materials provided by a supplier, they legally remain the property of the supplier until full payment for them has been made. For the most part these definitions are academic, but they take on renewed significance if either party to a contract becomes insolvent. In the event of this unfortunate occurrence, the creditors of the insolvent person are entitled to a share of that person's assets, which would include materials in the situations described above.

It can be seen that the question of who owns what materials and goods on the site need not be straightforward. From a practical point of view the appearance of materials and goods on the site also raises questions of timing, for example the premature delivery of goods before they are required by the tradesmen may cause problems of storage or deterioration. The call-off of materials from the source suppliers should be subject to controls linked to the progress of the work and the supply lead times. The following audit and review considerations will vary slightly in application in relation to who has claim to ownership.

The auditor will be interested in ensuring that the ordering process is subject to suitable authorisation and that the correct items are ordered at the correct prices where a definite need is established. Ensuring that the appropriate delivery dates and call-off arrangements are requested may also be critical to avoid the disruption of project progress.

Documentary trails incorporating orders, delivery notes, stock records and invoices should be in place, with checks to ensure accuracy and completeness. All the documents should be appropriately filed and accessible.

Quality control checks conducted on material deliveries should be suitably evidenced together with confirmation that the correct items and quantities have been supplied in accordance with the contract specifications. Rejected, damaged, sub-standard or incorrect goods should be recorded and accounted for, with relevant correspondence available. Where items are damaged on the site, the liability should be clearly established in association with the responsibilities defined in the contract or administrative procedures.

Stock and material records should be maintained which reflect all movements of goods including:

- deliveries from suppliers
- returns or rejected deliveries
- transfers or movements between sites or back-up stores
- issues to the contractor's or sub-contractor's staff for project work.

Stock and material records should be up to date and reflect the current level of holdings available with an indication of outstanding or pending orders and deliveries. The balance held should be apparent and subject to regular stock checking with supporting evidence. This also holds true for any items held off-site, for example by the manufacturer in which case any confirmatory documentation should be readily available. Details of significant stocktaking variations should be recorded, reported to the appropriate level of management and subject to investigation. The liability for losses and shortfalls should be established and either insurance claims confirmed or evidence of required action cited.

Invoices received should be capable of linkage with the relevant delivery documentation, and the details confirmed as correct before payment is effected. Those accounts to be paid by the employer should be suitably confirmed and authorised before payment is effected. There will also need to be suitable linkages established between the creditor and project accounting systems, so that all project-related costs are accurately encoded and reported. Where the contractor is entitled to seek payment for specific items before they are utilised in the project, the invoice and proof of payment should both be available. In the construction site context, the usage of materials and the items remaining will have a relevance to the calculation of interim valuations by the supervising professional where this is called for.

Adequate and secure site storage facilities should be provided to protect materials and goods from damage, theft, and pilferage. Auditors may, in the course of their site visits observe the security arrangements in force. Accounting records and ongoing management information should accurately reflect the authorised costs of materials and goods supplied to date. Comparisons of the actual costs to predetermined budgets should also be available and reviewed by management in order to ensure that adverse variations are detected and reacted to.

PLANT AND EQUIPMENT

In practice the nature of plant and equipment employed on the site will be driven by the type of development, but it generically relates to the machinery and other items required to undertake or assist in the work. Therefore it obviously excludes any items which will be permanent features of the completed works (*see* 'project assets' below).

The plant may be owned by either the contractor or, more rarely, the employer. Alternatively, it may be on hire or lease. Where the contractor has the responsibility for obtaining the necessary equipment, the associated costs will usually have been incorporated within his tender. However, where some action by the employer or his agents has necessitated the contractor to undertake additional work which may be the subject of either a variation order or contractual claim, additional plant may be necessary. In this instance and in the case of dayworks, the costs associated with the provision and use of the relevant equipment will have to be accurately estimated so that the eventual costs can be appropriately determined.

In any event, there should be up-to-date and comprehensive records available of all the plant, with clear distinctions between that owned, on hire or leased. Supporting documentation should also be available, including copies of hire or leasing agreements. The main records should identify each item with a suitable description so that it can be easily identified. The responsibility for providing suitable insurance cover for plant should be defined and the appropriate arrangements confirmed.

Records of equipment usage should also be available, indicating the hours used in relation to specific or identifiable tasks. The details of any time or productivity lost due to faults and problems should also be recorded as these may have further relevance to either claims against the plant hire company or those made subsequently by the contractor.

Idle or unnecessary plant and equipment should be identified, especially where costs are being incurred. The key issue here is that such equipment should be available on site at the appropriate times. Arrangements with plant hire companies should be clear in respect of the required delivery dates, with any problems and claims being actively pursued. Conversely, any equipment on site which is no longer required should be returned to the supplier. Of course, all action taken with regard to plant should be within the confines of any contract or agreement with the plant hire company or supplier.

The issue of a variation order by the supervising engineer or architect may generate the requirement for additional plant. This course of action should be sanctioned by the engineer and once again suitably detailed records maintained to support any subsequent additional costs submitted by the contractor. Such records should be cross-referred to the details of the job or variation order.

The auditor may decide to confirm the existence of selected items of plant, for example any which is either owned or supplied by the employer. This task will obviously require suitably accurate records which signify ownership. Where the usage of plant is a significant cost factor, perhaps charged separately, the project accounting records should permit accurate reporting of the related costs.

PROJECT ASSETS

Broadly speaking we are using the term 'project assets' to mean any piece of equipment or capital item which will form part of the project structure or project. For example, this could be a bespoke public address and sound system for a new building, a specialist pumping system for a civil engineering project, or the computer hardware for an office automation system.

Initially such items may have been subject to the requirements generally applied to all project materials and goods, as described in the first section of this chapter. However, there are additional issues to address as these items may have a critical significance to the project and will certainly have additional accounting significance. In the context of practical considerations, it may be relevant to undertake very precisely defined installation, testing and commissioning of such items. For example either the provision of a suitably controlled environment for a new mainframe computer system, the satisfaction of defined performance and functionality criteria for a software application, or the operational reliability of air conditioning equipment in a new building.

The achievement of these elements in a project will ideally be addressed in accordance with predetermined standards and requirements. For instance, the testing of software applications according to an agreed test plan with target performance limits and response times. This sub-element of the overall project plan, will likely require the establishment of documented requirements, responsibilities, procedures, and objectives. The project management system should specifically cater for these activities and monitor progress against any and all of them.

Having successfully passed through the appropriate appraisal, testing, modification and commissioning stages, the relevant items will normally have to be formally accepted (or handed over) to the employer or client. There is an obvious need at this stage, for the employer to be fully satisfied with all aspects of the item(s) concerned, before officially accepting same. The auditor will be looking for supporting evidence of the previous activities which should positively indicate the acceptability of the item concerned and authorise its acceptance on behalf of the organisation.

Measures should be in place which accordingly identify items (or project elements) which require specific accounting treatment, such as fixed assets, and ensure that they are applied. The organisation's accounting policies may well dictate the action to take in such cases. Factors such as the application of appropriate accounts systems coding, the depreciation period and rates to be applied, etc. should all hopefully be clearly defined. The appraisal phase of the project could incorporate the required financial treatment of selected elements and have been used as the basis for defining specific procedures governing subsequent accounting actions.

Accounting information generated from the project should take account of any particular requirements and management should be in receipt of regular and accurate financial and accounting data. A true financial representation of the project should be further supported by the existence and application of general accounting controls within the organisation.

Control matrix example

The contents of the example matrix supplied as Table 21 relate to materials and plant on a conventional construction site, but the underlying principals of accountability and security will apply in most other instances. The matrix, which is *Exposures*-oriented, utilises *Scale* 31 as described in Appendix 7. Readers are referred to Chapter 32 for an account of the theory applied to the construction of all matrix examples.

Table 21 Materials, Plant and Project Assets – Exposures

Overall Inherent Risk (Size) Score [5 is worst risk; 1 is best] = 1.40

A Incorrect, inappropriate or insufficient materials supplied
B Materials supplied at the wrong time – delay/deterioration
C Goods/materials not to required standard or quality
D Inaccurate/inadequate material and stock records
E Loss of materials due to inadequate or insecure storage
F Theft or pilferage of materials – further cost, disruption
G Damage or deterioration of materials – inadequate storage
H Unauthorised orders for goods – incorrect payment of invoices
I Payment for goods not received and/or returned to supplier

J Failure to accurately account for material usage
K Payment for materials not yet incorporated into the project
L Incorrect accounting treatment of project assets
M Inadequate insurance cover for materials and plant
N Insufficient/inadequate plant for the work in hand
O Loss or damage to plant due to inadequate security
P Costs due to hire or retention of unnecessary/idle plant
Q Failure to account for own plant and equipment
R Payment of invalid plant hire and usage charges
S Inadequate records of plant and usage
T Delays caused by faulty or unreliable plant and equipment

SCALE 31 (abridged)

6 = Incorrect identification of needs or failure to meet them
5 = Lost business; needs partly unfulfilled; or breach of rules
4 = Delay or disruption; reputation loss; minor breach of rules (Contract auditing Exposures-oriented scale)

3 = Avoidable costs/losses; damage to contract relationships
2 = Administrative or accounting errors
1 = Detectable negative impact on the business or service

Materials, Plant & Project Assets		A	B	C	D	E	F	G	H	I	J	K	L	M	N	O	P	Q	R	S	T
		=	=	=	=	=	=	=	=	=	=	=	=	=	=	=	=	=	=	=	=
Calculated Risk Score:	Risk	3	3	3	3	2	3	2	2	2	2	2	2	3	2	2	2	2	2	2	2
Scale 31 (6 is most serious)	Type	4	4	4	4	3	4	4	3	3	3	2	2	4	4	3	3	3	3	2	4
Size (3 is maximum)	Size	3	2	2	2	1	2	1	1	1	1	1	2	2	2	1	1	1	2	1	2
CONTROLS																					
1 Official orders clearly specify requirements, delivery dates, etc.	Best		2	2	2																
	Test	?	?	?	?																
	Both																				
2 All deliveries are examined for quality, type & quality – problems are escalated	Best		3	3	3																
	Test	?	?	?	?																
	Both																				
3 Overdue deliveries are progressed by Clerk of Works	Best		3																		
	Test	?	?																		
	Both																				
4 Premature deliveries are rejected if materials would deteriorate on site	Best		3					2													
	Test	?	?					?												
	Both																				
5 All materials are inspected for quality – substandard items are rejected	Best			5																	
	Test	?		?																	
	Both																				
6 Computerised stock records are maintained with full documentary trail	Best				2						2										
	Test	?			?						?										
	Both																				
7 Stock balances are confirmed on weekly basis – variances are reported to management	Best				4		3				2										
	Test	?			?		?				?										
	Both																				
8 Lockable storage buildings are provided. Main site perimeter is fenced & guarded at night	Best					4	4	3								4					
	Test	?				?	?	?								?					
	Both																				
9 All official orders are subject to authority signature before release	Best								3												
	Test	?							?												
	Both																				

Table 21 continued

			A	B	C	D	E	F	G	H	I	J	K	L	M	N	O	P	Q	R	S	T
			=	=	=	=	=	=	=	=	=	=	=	=	=	=	=	=	=	=	=	=
	Calculated Risk Score:	Risk	3	3	3	2	3	2	2	2	2	2	2	3	2	2	2	2	2	2	2	2
			–	–	–	–	–	–	–	–	–	–	–	–	–	–	–	–	–	–	–	–
10	Deliveries/invoices are checked to authorised orders prior to payment	Best								3	3											
		Test	?							?	?											
		Both																				
			–	–	–	–	–	–	–	–	–	–	–	–	–	–	–	–	–	–	–	–
11	All rejections/returns are documented. Records checked prior to payment authority	Best									4											
		Test	?								?											
		Both																				
			–	–	–	–	–	–	–	–	–	–	–	–	–	–	–	–	–	–	–	–
12	All invoices and charges are authorised before settlement	Best								3	3											
		Test	?							?	?											
		Both																				
			–	–	–	–	–	–	–	–	–	–	–	–	–	–	–	–	–	–	–	–
13	All usage is supported by site documentation. Confirmed by measurement of work for payment	Best										4	4									
		Test										?	?									
		Both																				
			–	–	–	–	–	–	–	–	–	–	–	–	–	–	–	–	–	–	–	–
14	All project asset orders are identified for application of relevant account coding	Best												2								
		Test												?								
		Both																				
			–	–	–	–	–	–	–	–	–	–	–	–	–	–	–	–	–	–	–	–
15	Contractor is responsible for site insurance matters, evidence of current cover is obtained	Best												4								
		Test												?								
		Both																				
			–	–	–	–	–	–	–	–	–	–	–	–	–	–	–	–	–	–	–	–
16	Plant requirements confirmed by Engineer in charge. Contractor responsible for fulfilment	Best													3							
		Test													?							
		Both																				
			–	–	–	–	–	–	–	–	–	–	–	–	–	–	–	–	–	–	–	–
17	Engineer identifies surplus plant & initiates return to the hire/rental company	Best															3					
		Test															?					
		Both																				
			–	–	–	–	–	–	–	–	–	–	–	–	–	–	–	–	–	–	–	–
18	Site records maintained for own plant – physically confirmed during weekly stock counts	Best																		4	3	
		Test																		?	?	
		Both																				
			–	–	–	–	–	–	–	–	–	–	–	–	–	–	–	–	–	–	–	–
19	Schedule of plant/equipment is maintained and used to confirm charges	Best																		4	3	
		Test																		?	?	
		Both																				
			–	–	–	–	–	–	–	–	–	–	–	–	–	–	–	–	–	–	–	–
20	Erroneous charges are rejected or investigated	Best																		4		
		Test																		?		
		Both																				
			–	–	–	–	–	–	–	–	–	–	–	–	–	–	–	–	–	–	–	–
21	Usage records maintained for plant to support interim accounts, dayworks, etc.	Best																			4	
		Test																			?	
		Both																				
			–	–	–	–	–	–	–	–	–	–	–	–	–	–	–	–	–	–	–	–
22	Plant failure or faults covered by same day call-out service from hire company	Best																				4
		Test																				?
		Both																				
			–	–	–	–	–	–	–	–	–	–	–	–	–	–	–	–	–	–	–	–

A Incorrect, inappropriate or insufficient materials supplied
B Materials supplied at the wrong time – delay/deterioration
C Goods/materials not to required standard or quality
D Inaccurate/inadequate material and stock records
E Loss of materials due to inadequate or insecure storage
F Theft or pilferage of materials – further cost, disruption
G Damage or deterioration of materials – inadequate storage
H Unauthorised orders for goods – incorrect payment of invoices
I Payment for goods not received and/or returned to supplier

J Failure to accurately account for material usage
K Payment for materials not yet incorporated into the project
L Incorrect accounting treatment of project assets
M Inadequate insurance cover for materials and plant
N Insufficient/inadequate plant for the work in hand
O Loss or damage to plant due to inadequate security
P Costs due to hire or retention of unnecessary/idle plant
Q Failure to account for own plant and equipment
R Payment of invalid plant hire and usage charges
S Inadequate records of plant and usage
T Delays caused by faulty or unreliable plant and equipment

SCALE 31 (abridged)

6 = Incorrect identification of needs or failure to meet them
5 = Lost business; needs partly unfulfilled; or breach of rules
4 = Delay or disruption; reputation loss; minor breach of rules
(Contract auditing Exposures-oriented scale)

3 = Avoidable costs/losses; damage to contract relationships
2 = Administrative or accounting errors
1 = Detectable negative impact on the business or service

22

VALUING WORK FOR INTERIM PAYMENTS

Scope

Effecting staged or interim payments during the life of a contract or project may be required. For the employer the key questions will be: 'Are the costs claimed relevant to work actually completed or services received?' and 'Are the charges correctly calculated on the basis prescribed in the relevant contract?' This chapter examines measures relevant to satisfactorily answering these and other questions.

Where such ongoing and regular valuations are relevant there is an obvious synergy with the preparation of the final account. Readers are also referred to Chapter 28 which explicitly examines the issues surrounding the final account. Duplications in coverage between this chapter and Chapter 28 are intentional.

In the event of a long-term or staged completion contract there may be the need to undertake an interim valuation of the work completed so that a suitable account can be prepared and presented. This sort of approach is common in the construction world and the contents of this chapter will deal predominantly with matters and issues relevant to that sector.

The terms of the contract and the period of the contract will have a bearing, among other factors, on the need and desirability of interim account payments. Where there is a measurable progression to the associated work, as typified by the building industry, then the relevant mechanisms are easier to address. In other contexts, staged payments may be relevant, for example in the supply of Electronic Funds Transfer at Point Of Sale (EFTPOS) terminals to a large high street retailer, where the project may run over several months and the calculation of amounts due for the equipment supplied is fairly straightforward to determine so long as actual progress is accurately monitored and recorded.

In any case it will be necessary to ensure that any proportions or values due during the lifetime of the contract are clearly defined in the contract conditions or appendices. Additionally, the method of measurement and pricing basis to be employed will also need to be appropriately defined, so as to allow for subsequent verification of submitted accounts. It follows therefore that procedures should be in place to ensure that any accounts submitted are checked for accuracy and compliance with the defined rules before settlement is both authorised and effected. A further dimension to the process, may be the definition, within the contract, of timetables for actioning interim accounts, with a limit to the period permitting any challenge to the amounts submitted.

Where the scale of contract-related activities is significant, appropriate procedures should be established which address all the key issues and enable compliance with all relevant contract conditions to be both monitored and confirmed. Responsibility should be clearly allocated for the examination and checking of submitted accounts. Compliance with the agreed and defined rules of account completion should be positively confirmed and the overall arithmetic accuracy of the account verified. Quantities should be supported and the rates applied agreed to the contents of any bills of quantity or contract definitions.

Contracts in use in particular sectors may define specific responsibilities and protocols governing the completion, submission, verification and certification of accounts. This is certainly true for the common standard forms of contract in use in the construction industry, where the engineer or architect is normally charged with certifying that the completion of interim accounts is correct before they are passed on to employers for payment. In such instances the responsible professional should ensure that the measurement of work, the determination of the work completed and the pricing basis are all satisfactorily undertaken per the relevant sections of the contract governing the works.

The contractor submitting interim accounts should provide the required supporting information to enable the architect or engineer to discharge his responsibilities in the prescribed timescale. Any amendments applied by the supervising professional should be supported and advised to the contractor.

All manner of factors may be taken into consideration when compiling an account and they should be supported by the stipulated documents, such as bills of quantity, effects of claims and variation orders, invoices submitted by suppliers and sub-contractors, records of materials held on site or remotely, dayworks records, price fluctuation schedules, engineers' certificates, and so on. These specific elements are addressed in detail in separate chapters. Copies of the relevant documents should be retained, and may have to be held at the appropriate site. The auditor will be concerned about the adequacy and completeness of documentary trails and the security of key documents.

Evidence of account review should be recorded and any errors or necessary amendments promptly reported and dealt with. Amendments applied to the account should be clearly marked.

In certain situations the determination of a suitable retention value may apply to interim accounts. The calculation of the relevant retention value is normally liable to change (i.e. reduce) the further the work progresses. Measures should be in place to confirm that retention has been correctly calculated per the provisions of the contract.

Within the employer's organisation best practice techniques should be applied to the verification of all creditors' accounts. Suitable prior authorisation to pay the account should be obtained and clearly evidenced. In order to reduce the potential for fraud or malpractice, adequate segregation of key

duties and appropriate spheres of influence should be in place. The maintenance of separate records of all interim accounts received, by project, should
also enable the confirmation that all charges received are duly paid.

Control matrix example

Table 22 contains an example matrix reflecting the *Exposure* issues relative to
interim payments in the construction context. The value data related to *Scale*
31 (*see* Appendix 7) suggests a medium to high level of contract significance,
and the suggested controls understandably concentrate upon the validity and
accuracy of submitted accounts.

Table 22 Interim Payments – Exposures

Overall Inherent Risk (Size) Score [5 is worst risk; 1 is best] = 1.86

A Payments made for either incomplete or unsatisfactory work
B Payments made for goods/services not received
C Payments made for unauthorised activities
D Payment for work outwith contractual requirements
E Incorrect measurement of work or calculation of account
F Payment of duplicated accounts or work previously paid for
G Unable to substantiate work included on invoice
H Failure to settle accounts in stipulated time period
I Failure to settle account – effect on contract relationship
J Payments made without required authority
K Payments made that are outwith budgeted figures
L Incorrect treatment & payment of variations and other costs
M Incorrect calculation of retention – overpayment
N Errors due to inadequacy/inaccuracy of contract accounts

SCALE 31 (abridged)

6 = Incorrect identification of needs, or failure to meet them
5 = Lost business; needs partly unfulfilled; or breach of rules
4 = Delay or disruption; reputation loss; minor breach of rules
(Contract auditing Exposures-oriented scale)

3 = Avoidable costs/losses; damage to contract relationships
2 = Administrative or accounting errors
1 = Detectable negative impact on the business or service

Interim Payments			EXPOSURES													
			A	B	C	D	E	F	G	H	I	J	K	L	M	N
			=	=	=	=	=	=	=	=	=	=	=	=	=	=
Calculated Risk Score:	Risk		3	3	2	3	3	2	3	2	2	2	2	2	2	2
			–	–	–	–	–	–	–	–	–	–	–	–	–	–
Scale 31 (6 is most serious)	Type		5	5	3	5	4	2	4	4	4	5	5	5	3	3
Size (3 is maximum)	Size		2	2	2	2	2	2	2	1	1	1	1	1	1	1
CONTROLS		–	–	–	–	–	–	–	–	–	–	–	–	–	–	–
1 All work is certified by the Architect as complete and to required standard	Best		5	5	4	4	3	3	3				4		
	Test		?	?	?	?	?	?	?	?			?		
	Both														
		–	–	–	–	–	–	–	–	–	–	–	–	–	–
2 Documentary evidence provided in support of invoices	Best			3	3			3	3						
	Test		?	?	?			?	?						
	Both														
		–	–	–	–	–	–	–	–	–	–	–	–	–	–
3 All charges are supported by either contract specification or authorised orders/instructions	Best			2		4	4		2	3					
	Test		?	?		?	?		?	?					
	Both														
		–	–	–	–	–	–	–	–	–	–	–	–	–	–
4 Measurement of work is confirmed within certification process on agreed basis	Best						4	3	3						
	Test		?				?	?	?						
	Both														
		–	–	–	–	–	–	–	–	–	–	–	–	–	–
5 All interim charges are arithmetically checked. Errors are suitably adjusted	Best						4								
	Test		?				?								
	Both														
		–	–	–	–	–	–	–	–	–	–	–	–	–	–
6 Register of all payments is maintained and examined prior to payment being authorised	Best								4	2					
	Test		?						?	?					
	Both														
		–	–	–	–	–	–	–	–	–	–	–	–	–	–
7 Once a certicate is obtained & details confirmed, payment is made within 14 days per contract	Best									5	3				
	Test		?							?	?				
	Both														
		–	–	–	–	–	–	–	–	–	–	–	–	–	–
8 All accounts are logged and progressed for payment per agreed timetable	Best									4					
	Test		?							?					
	Both														
		–	–	–	–	–	–	–	–	–	–	–	–	–	–
9 Account queries are pursued and resolved	Best									4					
	Test		?							?					
	Both														
		–														

Table 22 continued

			A	B	C	D	E	F	G	H	I	J	K	L	M	N
			=	=	=	=	=	=	=	=	=	=	=	=	=	=
	Calculated Risk Score:	Risk	3	3	2	3	3	2	3	2	2	2	2	2	2	2
			–	–	–	–	–	–	–	–	–	–	–	–	–	–
10	All payments have to be authorised in writing by management	Best										5				
		Test	?									?				
		Both														
			–	–	–	–	–	–	–	–	–	–	–	–	–	–
11	Budget variances are reported. Explanations are documented for management information	Best										4				
		Test	?									?				
		Both														
			–	–	–	–	–	–	–	–	–	–	–	–	–	–
12	All variation orders are documented and authorised in advance of work	Best											4			
		Test	?										?			
		Both														
			–	–	–	–	–	–	–	–	–	–	–	–	–	–
13	Retention figure is confirmed by Architect prior to payment being made	Best												4		
		Test	?											?		
		Both														
			–	–	–	–	–	–	–	–	–	–	–	–	–	–
14	Management Account reports are circulated for comments, etc. Errors/omissions are corrected	Best														2
		Test	?													?
		Both														
			–														

A Payments made for either incomplete or unsatisfactory work
B Payments made for goods/services not received
C Payments made for unauthorised activities
D Payment for work outwith contractual requirements
E Incorrect measurement of work or calculation of account
F Payment of duplicated accounts or work previously paid for
G Unable to substantiate work included on invoice
H Failure to settle accounts in stipulated time period
I Failure to settle account – effect on contract relationship
J Payments made without required authority
K Payments made that are outwith budgeted figures
L Incorrect treatment & payment of variations and other costs
M Incorrect calculation of retention – overpayment
N Errors due to inadequacy/inaccuracy of contract accounts

SCALE 31 (abridged)

6 = Incorrect identification of needs, or failure to meet them
5 = Lost business; needs partly unfulfilled; or breach of rules
4 = Delay or disruption; reputation loss; minor breach of rules
(Contract auditing Exposures-oriented scale)

3 = Avoidable costs/losses; damage to contract relationships
2 = Administrative or accounting errors
1 = Detectable negative impact on the business or service

23

CONTROLLING PRICE FLUCTUATIONS

Scope

This chapter addresses the implications of subsequently amending the contract price with the effects of certain defined price fluctuations. Of crucial importance is the need to ensure that the appropriate price fluctuation approach is adopted and correctly applied.

With contracts that apply to projects running over protracted periods it is likely that all manner of factors will affect related costs. These factors will include external influences beyond the control of the parties to the contract. Obviously, if related costs rise significantly the profitability or cost-effectiveness of the project can be affected for either of the parties.

It is normal practice in instances of long-term or protracted contracts to incorporate some form of price fluctuation mechanism into the conditions. For example in the following standard forms of contract, there are specific clauses governing this eventuality:

Contract	*Clause ref.*
JCT80	37, 38, 39, or 40
ICE 6th Edition	69
C1030 (version of GC/Works1)	9
MF/1	6.2

Most fluctuations in the building, engineering and civil engineering sectors are calculated in accordance with an agreed and proven formula. This type of approach creates adjustments to prices based upon changes that are apparent from an agreed base date. The following examples are three recognised formulae in common use:

Formula	*Relevant form(s) of contract*
OSBOURNE	Building works (JCT and GC Works 1)

BAXTER   Civil engineering schemes (ICE and GC Works 1)

BEAMA*   Electrical and mechanical engineering

* British Electrical and Allied Manufacturers Association

Fluctuation formulae will either generate justifiable increases payable to the contractor or more rarely overall cost reductions due to the employer in some form (i.e. to be taken against payments due or in the form of refund payments).

If actual cost variations had to be accurately calculated, the necessary work would be both exacting and time-consuming. Additionally, the employer or client would have to commit resources to checking and confirming both the applicability and accuracy of such financial adjustments. The use of a mutually acceptable index-based formula method of calculating price fluctuations should significantly reduce the administrative overhead, although the questions of accuracy and relevance will still apply. The calculations concerned can be supported by the use of computer-based techniques, and if these are used care should be taken to ensure that the correct parameters and data have been entered, that the correct version of the program or formula has been applied, and that the interpretation of the computed results is correct.

In determining the applicable driving parameters for calculating cost variations, it is normal practice to refer to a proven and reliable data source. The required data may be obtainable from recognised and respected professional, trade and government sources. Account may have to be taken of a number of factors including, the relevant cost indices, the date to be used as the basis for the calculation, the cost elements to be excluded, etc.

A contractor may wish to impose a form of contract allowing for the calculation of price variations in the appropriate circumstances. In such situations, clients or employers should satisfy themselves that the relevant formula is fair, generally recognised, or adopted by the relevant professional body governing that sector. In the case of all projects with significant cost implications, employers should seek legal advice on the matter of price fluctuations prior to committing themselves to the proffered terms and conditions. If the contract calls for staged payments, which may be in themselves subject to amendment by the application of a price fluctuation formula, the employer should ensure that the calculation and application of the additional charges has been accurately handled before payment is sanctioned.

Responsibility should be allocated for checking and confirming the accuracy of price fluctuation calculations including the use of the appropriate parameters and coefficients. The incorporation of fluctuation calculations into either interim or final accounts should also be confirmed. Errors or omissions should be promptly referred back to the contractor for rectification. The contractor should supply all the required supporting information, and retain the relevant working papers, such as computer model printouts. In the construction context, price fluctuations could have an effect on either the interim or final accounts submitted by the contractor (*see* Chapters 22 and 28 for further details).

reflectsthekey*Objectives*whenconsideringtheuseandmonitoringofapricefluctuationmethod.Thevaluesofthe*Type*dataarerelatedto*Scale*

Controlling Price Fluctuations 209

Control matrix example

Table 23 reflects the key *Objectives* when considering the use and monitoring of a price fluctuation method. The values of the *Type* data are related to *Scale* 30 which is reproduced in Appendix 7. The example data generally reflects a high level of significance for the application of price adjustments.

Table 23 Controlling Price Fluctuations – Objectives
Overall Inherent Risk (Size) Score [5 is worst risk; 1 is best] = 2.57

A Ensure adoption of the optimum price fluctuation approach
B Only use price fluctuation approach when risks are balanced
C Provide maximum protection from unreasonable price impact
D Achieve the contract/project objectives within budget
E Ensure fluctuation formula is restricted to permitted items
F Confirm correct calculation of price adjustments
G Ensure the relevant conditions are included in the contract

Scale 30 (abridged)

6 = Strategically vital to the business or organisation
5 = Makes a contribution to business operations
4 = Contributes to reliability of data, records and information
(Contract auditing Objectives-oriented scale)

3 = Avoids disruption/meets regulatory & accountability needs
2 = Leads to administrative/operational economies/efficiencies
1 = Generates administrative economies

Controlling Price Fluctuations		OBJECTIVES							
			A	B	C	D	E	F	G
			=	=	=	=	=	=	=
Calculated Risk Score:	Risk		3	3	3	3	3	3	3
			–	–	–	–	–	–	–
Scale 30 (6 is most serious)	Type		5	5	4	4	4	4	5
Size (3 is maximum)	Size		2	2	2	3	2	2	2
MEASURES		–	–	–	–	–	–	–	–
1 Price fluctuation options were reviewed as part of selecting the appropriate contract	Best			4					4
	Test	?	?						?
	Both								
		–	–	–	–	–	–	–	–
2 Standard form of contract adopted with proven Price adjustment method incorporated	Best			4	4				
	Test	?	?	?					
	Both								
		–	–	–	–	–	–	–	–
3 Price fluctuation formula is index linked to reliable and acceptable data source	Best				3				
	Test	?			?				
	Both								
		–	–	–	–	–	–	–	–
4 Price fluctuation impact was projected during preparation of project budgets	Best			2		2	4		
	Test	?	?		?	?			
	Both								
		–	–	–	–	–	–	–	–
5 All price fluctuation adjustments are reviewed, checked, confirmed & authorised	Best						5	5	
	Test	?					?	?	
	Both								
		–	–	–	–	–	–	–	–

24

MONITORING AND CONTROLLING VARIATIONS

Scope

Although careful attention to the specification and design stages of a project should ensure the integrity of the following work, it often proves necessary to apply changes or variations at later stages. This chapter examines the implications of such variations and the contractual and procedural measures aimed at controlling their impact.

In the context of this chapter the term 'variations' can relate to two basic situations. The first is specific to construction contracts where the supervising architect or engineer authorises necessary changes to the work stipulated in the contract. The second scenario is broader in nature and covers any form of subsequent modification or change to the general contract requirements. This could, for example, relate to justified changes to the functionality of a software application or the technical criteria of hardware vindicated by a need to provide improved response times. In any case the key word is justified.

Applying changes after the appraisal and design phases is progressively more expensive. Great emphasis should be placed upon adequately researching the requirements and the means to provide the most apposite solution before embarking upon construction or development. If the appraisal and design phases are limited, prejudged or inadequate, the need to apply subsequent change may be exacerbated with the result that delays and additional costs may follow. We address the issues relevant to both the construction and general environments in the following separate sections.

CONSTRUCTION PROJECTS

It is recognised that construction project amendments, additions, and substitutions, will often be necessary. Some instances of required change are only apparent when work is under way or where actual site conditions create unexpected problems for the contractor.

In the case of the construction industry, the standard forms of contract provide mechanisms to cater for changes, and professional practice dictates the responsibilities for assessing and authorising the application of modifications.

The commonly used standard forms of contract reflect clauses which allow for variations to be applied:

Contract form	Clause(s)
JCT80	13 (updated per amendment 12)
ICE 6th Edition	51 and 52
C1030 (GC/Works 1)	8
MF/1	27

Any deviation from the work as specified in the contract will need to be assessed and authorised by the supervising architect or engineer. The modification may be justified on technical grounds or necessary to ensure that the client's usage and performance requirements are met. Matters relevant to safety and technical standards may also have a bearing upon the need to incorporate changes. The thoroughness and effectiveness of project appraisal and design phases will have a bearing on the necessity for subsequent change, but cannot, in reality, completely guarantee that none will be required.

The contractor will normally only react to amendments upon receipt of an official variation order completed by either the architect or engineer supervising the works. Where any initial instructions have been verbal, the requirement to accordingly document them is crucial. It is also likely that authorised changes will generate the need to amend and update design drawings or specifications, and all such modifications should be applied and the master set updated. The impact of necessary changes should be appropriately documented so as to provide a suitable trail for those involved in subsequent review and maintenance of projects.

The financial implications of changes should be accurately assessed before the issue of the relevant variation order. Additionally, the methods of measurement and payment should both be determined and agreed at the earliest opportunity. The accuracy of such assessments is important, not least as they should provide an agreed basis for subsequent related charges from the contractor. The basis upon which the additional work should be costed will be dependent upon specific situations, but any work of comparable nature to that already applied will normally be costed on a like basis, perhaps in the form prescribed in the bill of quantities. Alternatively a revised cost calculation base will have to be agreed. Any additional or different materials required should be identified and costed. In some cases there may also be the need to acquire or hire specific pieces of plant and machinery. There may also be implications for subsequent maintenance costs and these too should be assessed and calculated. The end-client or employer should be kept advised of necessary changes, the associated costs, and any contingent delays. Significant variations may generate interactions with other programmed parts of the works, and the full implications on progress should be identified, reported and authorised accordingly. All the pertinent site-level records should suitably and specifically identify activities relevant to each variation, and thereby provide a documentary trail in support of subsequent charges or claims.

Accurate and permanent records of all authorised changes should be maintained so that subsequent accounts can be examined and their accuracy confirmed. Checks should be conducted to ensure that submitted accounts are correctly calculated in the agreed and specified fashion. This is particularly important where the contract does not permit certain specified categories of work to be included in accounts. Any additional work undertaken without either written or verbal instructions having been issued should be identified and the associated costs investigated. Where monthly or other interim valuations are presented, the costs of any variations are likely to be included.

GENERAL PROJECTS

All projects where there is a deliverable end product should all share the objective of 'getting the design right before commencing the work'. This certainly applies to software development where the synergy between the user's required functionality and the eventual performance of the developed system is of paramount importance. The ability to deliver the proposed design should, in most cases, be capable of assessment before commencing either the development or manufacturing stages. As discussed in Chapter 11, one of the essential ingredients of successful specification and design is the active involvement of end-users in the process, so that the final design adequately reflects all their needs. However, in the real world subsequent changes can prove to be necessary and any project should have defined methods of dealing with them effectively if excessive costs, delays and frustration are to be avoided.

Before considering the procedural aspects of handling changes to project specifications, let us briefly consider the contract implications. Away from the construction scenario discussed in the preceding section, where the standard forms of contract cater for the inevitable changes, the structure of contracts is generally more fluid.

In necessarily simplistic terms, any deviation (by either party) from the route prescribed in a contract can be regarded as a breach of that contract, with the resulting implications of legal action against the offending party. The parties are normally bound to the stated terms and conditions of the contract, and unless there are specific clauses catering for the handling and application of change, this situation is set in concrete.

The general constraints placed upon parties to contracts, reinforce the need to accurately encapsulate and document all the relevant requirements, specifications, and performance criteria, before finalising the contract. The logical and economic arguments for ensuring a stable basis for subsequent activities are clear, however some projects, by their very nature, are more susceptible to subsequent modifications. For example in the application of leading edge or emerging technologies, where some of the ground rules and economic bases have yet to be firmly established. Such variables can be major deterrents to becoming 'guinea pig' clients for the application of new products or technologies.

It may prove to be desirable in appropriate projects, for all parties, to incorporate specific contract clauses to handle subsequent changes and modifications. They should be so constructed as to avoid their deliberate use as generators of additional income for the contractor or as justification for the employer to constantly shift the goalposts. There needs to be a formal mechanism for identifying, documenting and communicating potential change. The assessment of all financial and technical implications should be undertaken and impartially reported upon. The impact of change upon the required or defined timescales will also need to be evaluated.

Some organisations have formal review and authorisation procedures which are applied to all proposed changes to projects. For example, an information technology Steering Committee will evaluate significant changes to software development projects and either authorise their progress within designated financial limits or reject them as not justified. However, such a mechanism presupposes that all the related factors have been accurately (and impartially) identified and presented. The influences of internal politics will also have a bearing on most aspects of a project, although we do not intend to further discuss this necessary evil.

In identifying changes to the specification, it is critical that all the key details are documented and accurately costed on an agreed basis. Such documentation can then form an agreed basis for all parties to proceed. It is obviously incumbent upon the employer to ensure that all the identified changes are actually effected and that any subsequent accounts accurately reflect the agreed costs.

Control matrix example

A range of potential *Exposures* that could apply with regard to variations from the contracted design are featured in Table 24. The score data represents a middle-level significance assigned to the cost and disruption aspects of variations, the *Type* values are based upon *Scale* 31 as featured in Appendix 7. A full explanation of the matrix theory is provided in Chapter 32.

Table 24 Controlling Variations – Exposures
Overall Inherent Risk (Size) Score [5 is worst risk; 1 is best] = 2.29

A Unnecessary/unauthorised work conducted at additional cost
B Failure to meet contract objectives within budget
C Excessive number of variations leading to increased costs
D Ineffective/inadequate design resulting in many variations
E Failure to accurately assess justify & authorise variations
F Absence of variation orders or inadequate instructions
G Failure to ensure variations correctly applied/to standard

H Failure to confirm accuracy & validity of variation charges
I Contract does not permit or define variation conditions
J Inappropriate charging basis adopted for variations
K Adverse implications for other contracts – i.e. interfacing
L Failure to satisfactorily fulfil variation requirements
M Failure to assess effects upon operating/maintenance costs
N Failure to clearly communicate requirements to contractor

SCALE 31 (abridged)

6 = Incorrect identification of needs, or failure to meet them
5 = Lost business, needs partly unfulfilled, or breach of rules
4 = Delay or disruption; reputation loss, minor breach of rules
(Contract auditing, Exposures-oriented scale)

3 = Avoidable costs/losses; damage to contract relationships
2 = Administrative or accounting errors
1 = Detectable negative impact on the business or service

Controlling Variations		EXPOSURES													
		A	B	C	D	E	F	G	H	I	J	K	L	M	N
		=	=	=	=	=	=	=	=	=	=	=	=	=	=
Calculated Risk Score:	Risk	3	3	3	2	3	3	3	2	2	2	2	3	2	3
		–	–	–	–	–	–	–	–	–	–	–	–	–	–
Scale 31 (6 is most serious)	Type	5	6	5	6	5	4	4	5	6	3	6	4	3	4
Size (3 is maximum)	Size	2	2	2	1	2	2	2	1	1	2	1	2	2	2
CONTROLS		–	–	–	–	–	–	–	–	–	–	–	–	–	–
1 Contract design produced after a thorough exploration of options. Aim to minimise variations	Best	4	4	4	5										
	Test	?	?	?	?	?									
	Both														
		–	–	–	–	–	–	–	–	–	–	–	–	–	–
2 All variations have e to be assessed, costed, justified & authorised	Best		4	3	3		5						3		
	Test	?	?	?	?		?						?		
	Both														
		–	–	–	–	–	–	–	–	–	–	–	–	–	–
3 Overall budget contains 8% contingency factor for the construction phase	Best		4												
	Test	?	?												
	Both														
		–	–	–	–	–	–	–	–	–	–	–	–	–	–
4 All variations subject to specification and official variation orders as per contract	Best						5								5
	Test	?					?								?
	Both														
		–	–	–	–	–	–	–	–	–	–	–	–	–	–
5 Initial verbal instructions followed up by Control 4 above	Best						3								3
	Test	?					?								?
	Both														
		–	–	–	–	–	–	–	–	–	–	–	–	–	–
6 All workmanship standards are defined and communicated to the contractor	Best							3				3			
	Test	?						?				?			
	Both														
		–	–	–	–	–	–	–	–	–	–	–	–	–	–
7 Completed work is examined & tested to ensure compliance with standards	Best							4				3			
	Test	?						?				?			
	Both														
		–	–	–	–	–	–	–	–	–	–	–	–	–	–
8 Variation costing methods are agreed per the prevailing contract conditions	Best		3								4				
	Test	?	?								?				
	Both														
		–	–	–	–	–	–	–	–	–	–	–	–	–	–
9 All variation charges confirmed to the agreed cost basis prior to settlement	Best		3			3					4				
	Test	?	?			?					?				
	Both														
		–														

Table 24 continued

		A	B	C	D	E	F	G	H	I	J	K	L	M	N
		=	=	=	=	=	=	=	=	=	=	=	=	=	=
Calculated Risk Score:	Risk	3	3	3	2	3	3	3	2	2	2	3	3	2	3
		–	–	–	–	–	–	–	–	–	–	–	–	–	–
10 Standard form of contract used which incorporates mechanism for handling variations	Best									5	5				
	Test	?								?	?				
	Both														
		–	–	–	–	–	–	–	–	–	–	–	–	–	–
11 All impacts and dependencies are assessed & decisions taken to minimise any disruption	Best										3				
	Test	?									?				
	Both														
		–	–	–	–	–	–	–	–	–	–	–	–	–	–
12 The contractor's failure to fulfil requirements is subject to contract remedy	Best												3		
	Test	?											?		
	Both														
		–														

A Unnecessary/unauthorised work conducted at additional cost
B Failure to meet contract objectives within budget
C Excessive number of variations leading to increased costs
D Ineffective/inadequate design resulting in many variations
E Failure to accurately assess justify & authorise variations
F Absence of variation orders or inadequate instructions
G Failure to ensure variations correctly applied/to standard
H Failure to confirm accuracy & validity of variation charges
I Contract does not permit or define variation conditions
J Inappropriate charging basis adopted for variations
K Adverse implications for other contracts – i.e. interfacing
L Failure to satisfactorily fulfil variation requirements
M Failure to assess effects upon operating/maintenance costs
N Failure to clearly communicate requirements to contractor

SCALE 31 (abridged)

6 = Incorrect identification of needs, or failure to meet them
5 = Lost business, needs partly unfulfilled, or breach of rules
4 = Delay or disruption; reputation loss, minor breach of rules
(Contract auditing, Exposures-oriented scale)

3 = Avoidable costs/losses; damage to contract relationships
2 = Administrative or accounting errors
1 = Detectable negative impact on the business or service

25

EXTENSIONS OF TIME

Scope

Amending the target completion date of a contract or related project can have a significant impact upon costs and management objectives. The granting of extensions of time should follow an accurate assessment of the impact, and this chapter examines the related implications and procedural requirements.

Most projects and contract-related activities are likely to be time critical. The determination of a target completion, commissioning or delivery date may be driven by critical strategic factors for the organisation. The dates concerned may, for example, relate to the launching of a new business venture or a statutory requirement to provide either a service or facility at a defined point in time.

Hopefully, from the earliest stages of the project or contract, the time factors will have been clearly established, and suitable planning and management processes applied to confirm the practicality of addressing all the dependent activities in relation to the required timetable. There is no point in launching a project and seeking contractual commitments unless the timescale is realistic and achievable. Additionally, thorough prior examination of the requirements and the means to address them, should have enhanced the probability of achieving the desired goals.

The ongoing project management and monitoring mechanisms should enable the constant assessment of the progress being made against the required deadlines and the application of any necessary interventions to secure the successful conclusion of the project. Speed of reaction here is critical and partly dependent upon the flow of accurate and reliable information.

All such preparation and forethought is very well, but in the real world there are still going to be unexpected events and unforeseen circumstances which will have a bearing on project progress, such as difficult ground conditions on a construction site, the failure of leading edge technology to fulfil its promises, exceptional weather conditions, or the issue of variation orders where these are permitted. Such events will perhaps necessitate the amendment or extension of the completion date of the overall contract or a section thereof.

Granting extensions of time should be a tightly controlled process, and carefully applied within the enabling clauses or appendices of the contract concerned. The protocol for assessing and permitting extensions of time is, for example, well established in the civil engineering and construction sectors, where the common forms of contract clearly define the requirements, as in the following clauses:

Contract form	Clause
JCT80	25 (updated per amendment 12)
ICE 6th Edition	44
C1030 (GC/Works 1)	22
MF/1	33

Viewed from the employer's standpoint, extensions of time may create additional costs, although it is true to say that not every extension automatically entitles contractors to apply extra charges. The impact of extensions will need to be considered in the broader context of the project and its relevance to the achievement of the relative commercial or service-oriented objectives. Where the contract concerned is one of a number of interrelated sub-projects, the overall timing and financial implications of amending the timetable should be fully examined. The contractor may instigate the process by bringing to the attention of the relative person the details of a problem which in his view, and within the conditions of the contract, could relate to the need to extend the completion date(s).

The combination of a sense of urgency and mounting costs may restrict the opportunities for a detailed examination of all the facts, but these constraints should not absolve management from their responsibilities for effective decision making in the best interests of the organisation. It is necessary, therefore, that any decisions about extensions are duly authorised. The form of contract in effect, may clearly define who is responsible for initiating and authorising extensions. For example, the engineer in charge of a civil engineering scheme will, under the terms of the ICE form of contract, be charged with assessing the situation and declaring an extension, which should be accordingly advised to both the contractor and employer.

Outwith the construction arena, employers should carefully examine the contract for clauses governing subsequent revision of timescales. If the related project or product has time-critical connotations, advice should be sought and agreed amendments to the contract applied that allow for the required flexibility. The objective should be to predetermine the likely need for extensions of time and incorporate a suitable and balanced mechanism in the relevant contract, rather than trust to resolving the basis for any such need when the event occurs. Attempt to remove some of the uncertainty beforehand.

There is an obvious need to support any extension consideration with all requisite information and evidence. The person charged with assessing the situation will need to be satisfied that all the evidence has been made available and reviewed in the light of all the known circumstances. The decision process itself should be adequately supported by relevant calculations and rationale. There may be prescribed requirements governing the acknowledgement, rejection or acceptance of claims for extension, within a permitted timetable.

Measures should be in place to ensure that all such claims are processed in accordance with defined requirements, for example the need to communicate the decision to grant an extension with reference to the empowering contract clauses.

An accurate assessment of the cost implications should be undertaken. The basis of such costings will have to be in accordance with the relevant contract clauses, defined measurement methods and pricing scales. This is especially true if the work required is similar in nature to that previously conducted by the contractor. All the costing working papers, supporting data, related correspondence, etc. should be securely retained for future reference purposes.

Where relevant, the determination of any extension of time should take into account the effects on any related contract mechanisms, such as price fluctuation or liquidated damage clauses. Repositioning the completion date will have an effect on the application of this type of process and a clear agreed understanding of the revised situation should be established.

From the contractor's perspective, any indication that the workload, progress and other conditions may have an effect on achieving the target completion dates should be swiftly reacted to. He may be severely disadvantaged if a suitable approach is not agreed with the employer, albeit that any extension of time will have to be relative to the enabling conditions in the contract. It will be necessary for him to clearly demonstrate the context of the request for an extension, and in particular any actions on the employer's part which may have contributed to such a requirement.

Control matrix example

Table 25 contains an *Exposures*-oriented example matrix incorporating a sample of controls designed to combat the implications and effects of extending contract completion dates. The value data reinforces the significance of amending target completion dates in respect of ensuring the achievement of corporate objectives. Appendix 7 includes details of *Scale* 31 which has been used in this example.

Table 25 Extensions of Time – Exposures

Overall Inherent Risk (Size) Score [5 is worst risk; 1 is best] = 3.46

A Failure to achieve objectives due to invalid extensions
B Contract not completed on time with adverse implications
C Contract does not permit/ specify conditions for extensions
D Incorrect/inadequate assessment of extension implications
E Unqualified acceptance of contractor's extension request
F Failure to accurately assess cost implications of extension
G No compensation where extension is due to contractor breach
H Failure to advise management of extension & implications
I Extensions not subject to authorisation
J Unable to support extension due to inadequate documentation
K Failure to clearly establish revised completion date
L Failure to reflect effects of extension in the project plan
M Failure to achieve revised completion date

SCALE 31 (abridged)

6 = Incorrect identification of needs, or failure to meet them
5 = Lost business; needs partly unfulfilled; or breach of rules
4 = Delay or disruption; reputation loss; minor breach of rules
(Contract auditing Exposures-oriented scale)

3 = Avoidable costs/losses; damage to contract relationships
2 = Administrative or accounting errors
1 = Detectable negative impact on the business or service

#	Extensions of Time		A	B	C	D	E	F	G	H	I	J	K	L	M
			=	=	=	=	=	=	=	=	=	=	=	=	=
	Calculated Risk Score:	Risk	4	3	3	4	3	4	3	3	3	3	3	3	4
	Scale 31 (6 is most serious)	Type	6	6	4	6	5	5	3	6	6	4	6	6	6
	Size (3 is maximum)	Size	3	2	3	3	2	3	3	3	2	2	2	2	3
	CONTROLS														
1	Ongoing monitoring of progress and early detection of possible failure to complete on time	Best	2	3											4
		Test	?	?	?										?
		Both													
2	All extensions are assessed, costed, documented, agreed & authorised per procedures	Best	4			4	3	4		3	5				
		Test	?	?		?	?	?		?	?				
		Both													
3	Chosen form of contract incorporates conditions for revising completion dates	Best			5										
		Test	?		?										
		Both													
4	All contractor submissions are fully assessed & reacted to. Unjustified requests rejected	Best				3									
		Test	?			?									
		Both													
5	Full costing is produced, circulated to management for information and approval	Best						4		4					
		Test	?					?		?					
		Both													
6	Contractor's performance and progress constantly monitored. Shortcomings subject to remedy	Best							4						
		Test	?						?						
		Both													
7	Liquidated damages sought when relevent per contract conditions	Best							4						
		Test	?						?						
		Both													
8	All activities are supported by documents per procedures. Subject to complance checks	Best										5			
		Test	?									?			
		Both													
9	Authorised extensions incorporate an agreed revised completion date	Best											3		
		Test	?										?		
		Both													

Table 25 continued

			A	B	C	D	E	F	G	H	I	J	K	L	M
			=	=	=	=	=	=	=	=	=	=	=	=	=
	Calculated Risk Score:	Risk	4	3	3	4	3	4	3	3	3	3	3	3	4
		———	–	–	–	–	–	–	–	–	–	–	–	–	–
10	Revised completion date generated by analysis of updated project planning data	Best											4	4	
		Test											?	?	
		Both													
		———	–	–	–	–	–	–	–	–	–	–	–	–	–
11	All interactions/implications of revised date computed and planning amended accordingly	Best											4	4	
		Test											?	?	
		Both													
		———	–												

26

CONTROLLING CONTRACTUAL CLAIMS

Scope

Contractors may feel entitled to make a claim for the effects of situations beyond their control, and the form of contract in use may reinforce this position by providing clauses which specify the range of situations that could form the basis for claims. This chapter discusses the issues with regard to both the employer's inclination for controlling contractual claims, and the contractor's desire to be treated fairly.

This chapter is generally geared to the construction industry, but some of the principles explored can also relate to more general forms of contract. Readers are also referred to Chapter 29 which deals with the recovery of damages.

In general terms, any party to a contract can make a claim against the other under the terms permitted within the contract. This may be as a result of a suspected breach of the terms or in respect of an unforeseen event which puts the claiming party at some form of disadvantage. In the course of exploring a wide range of potential scenarios for contractual claims, it would usually be necessary to address all the probable forms of contract that could apply. In order to avoid this degree of bewildering detail, we have elected to base most of this chapter upon the forms of contract and practice extant in the construction sector. However, where appropriate, general themes, issues and points will be highlighted.

Within the existing legal framework there are three categories of claim, as follows:

- *Contractual claims* This category relates to claims permitted within the scope of the conditions contained in the form of contract in force. The main advantage of this category of claim is that settlement can normally be achieved between the parties without the necessity to refer the matter to court. For example the standard forms of contract used in the building industry define the framework for making and dealing with claims. In these processes the engineer or architect plays a key role.

- *Common law damages claims* Claims falling into this category relate to situations where there has been a breach of contract which entitles the claiming party to sue the party in breach of contract using the principle of tort (*see* Chapter 1). This situation may apply when the parties have been unable to agree a settlement within the provisions of the conditions of contract. However, all the benefits of containing the assessment of claims within the terms of the contract and between the affected parties, without redress to the legal system are lost. Additionally, the costs and delays associated with pursuing this route through the courts can be considerable.
- *Ex-gratia claims* Such claims relate to circumstances which are not specifically addressed by the prevailing contract conditions and consequently they have no contractual status. The contractor may elect to make a claim in respect of any additional costs necessitated by the circumstances. The employer, who may be bound by strict government-imposed rules preventing such payments, may be able and feel inclined to make an ex-gratia payment to the contractor where this does not conflict with the statutory obligations.

Claims are obviously a two-way process, and the motivation for one party is unlikely to be readily acceptable to the other. The claimant may see his claim as justifiable because he has incurred additional costs either for reasons beyond his direct control or as a consequence of action taken by the other party to the contract. The recipient may view the claim as unfounded or as an obstacle to completing the project within the established cost and time limits. In the interests of continued good relations and for the sake of the related project, some form of compromise between these two simplistic views may have to be logically achieved. In any event, all parties will be bound by the conditions and provisions of the chosen form of contract. The common forms of building, civil engineering and other engineering contracts contain clauses relevant to contractor claims. Claims should exclude situations which are adequately provided for within other areas of the contract, for example price fluctuations addressed by the agreed formula arrangements.

The following analysis indicates the various key clauses in four commonly applied forms of contract which define the determination of claims by either party:

Contract form	*Clause(s)*
JCT80	26, 27, 28 and 28A
ICE 6th Edition	12 and 63
C1030 (GC/Works 1)	7, 8.3, 34.5, 35 and 47
MF/1	25, 27.4, 33, 41, 49 and 51

Before considering the general issues, it is worth mentioning the tactical dimension of contractual claims. Although we are not suggesting that the motivation for invoking the claim clauses is as frenzied as the American penchant for litigation, there is the possibility that contractors may submit an attractively low tender with the subsequent intention of overtly using the permitted claim processes to augment their rewards, perhaps using the services of individuals with a speciality for claims. However, that practice aside, we will assume for our examples that the claims are legitimate and have some justification.

There can be all manner of reasons that generate claims, such as:

- changes to the design requirements applied by the employer or his consultant (although in construction and civil engineering contracts such situations are handled specifically as variations)
- necessary amendments to the technical or material specifications due to unforeseen site conditions
- impact on the intended programme of work, perhaps as the result of either of two above noted points
- the granting of an extension of time by the architect or engineer where additional costs may be incurred.

The type of contract in use will usually define the rules of eligibility, associated processes, responsibilities and timetable to be adopted for claims. Due to the variety of contract forms that could apply, the points that appear in this chapter may not apply in every case, but are provided for guidance purposes.

It is usual practice to present claims in writing, perhaps in a prescribed form. The claim will have to be supported with pertinent facts, measurements, costings, and so on. Contractors should also ensure that they address claims to the appropriate and responsible person. The receipt of the claim should be acknowledged in writing without prejudicing the subsequent review process. The allocation of a sequential claim reference number should be considered as a means of appropriately identifying all related correspondence and documentation. Copies of the relevant correspondence should be retained in an accessible manner.

In all claims it is necessary to clearly establish whether the associated costs are due to factors or actions which are the other party's responsibility. The exact nature of the amounts that can be claimed for reimbursement are usually defined in the contract conditions. These conditions may only allow the payment of actual costs, the inclusion of a profit element in claims is not universally permitted. Eligibility for inclusion in any price fluctuation arrangements should be clearly determined during the claim valuation and review processes, whether or not the contractor has assumed that they are applicable. Any such implications should be both recorded and reported.

A mechanism should be in place to examine and validate claims. If the contract defines the ground rules for this, the requirements should be suitably followed. Beyond determining the admissibility of the claim, the associated costs should be thoroughly scrutinised for relevance and reasonableness. The accuracy and reliability of either project or site records will have a direct bearing on the assessment processes.

Acceptance or rejection in principle, wholly or in part, of a claim will need to be made in writing, supported by a suitably detailed rationale related to the enabling clause in the contract. In order to avoid costly debate and delay, it is preferable to aim to settle claims within the contract conditions.

The architect or engineer, in the case of a construction project, will normally initially receive contractor's claims, and it is his responsibility to assess the claim for validity. This is an area where the contractual impartiality of the supervising professional is also called into play. Given all the variables that could theoretically apply, it is impossible to predefine ground rules for every eventuality and thereby totally guard against subjectivity in any assessment process. However, it is necessary that each claim be dispassionately reviewed.

The contract may contain requirements governing the timing and form of the correspondence concerning claims, and mechanisms should be established to ensure that all such elements are correctly handled. Incorrect or overdue responses may affect the legality of the claim or the relevant liabilities. The recipient's evaluation of the claim should initially confirm that the relevant contract permits such a claim to be made. Beyond this the facts will need to be precisely established, and here the accuracy and currency of the site and project documentation will play a key role.

The processing of claims should be well-supported by documentation, thus enabling subsequent review of all aspects of the situation. This is especially critical when the project may extend over a long time period, where changes of staff may be frequent and there is the need for adequate documentary support and trailing of actions and decisions. The 'assessor' may have to apply a particular method of claim assessment and the basis of this should be adequately communicated. Where a decision has been reached the contractor should be informed in writing. Copies of all such correspondence should be retained.

Settlement of the claim amount may be made through the interim valuation process and added to any other sums due. Payment should only be effected if the person responsible for reviewing claims has communicated acceptance both in relation to principal and content. If the claim is to be paid in stages, perhaps because the effects of the claim are ongoing, records of payments should be kept and final clearance recorded.

The details of all claims received should be reported to employer management, ideally as part of the periodic management information reports on the project. The anticipated costs of pending claims should also be reported to the employer at the earliest opportunity. Accounting and budgetary updates may be necessary in the event of substantial claim values. All outstanding claims or partially cleared claims will need to be taken into account on the contractor's final account.

From the claimant's point of view, it is important that their claim is adequately documented in accordance with both the relevant contract conditions and any additional requirements specified by the employer if they are binding. Quoting, on the claim, the specific contract clause under which the claim is made may assist the recipient in dealing promptly with the situation. There may be time limits within which it necessary to submit such claims. Records should be kept of all claims submitted and the progress and status of each.

EX-GRATIA CLAIMS AND PAYMENTS

Ex-gratia payments are those that are made outwith the terms and conditions of the contract. Such payments may be made by employers to contractors following receipt of claims in respect of general matters. Consideration of ex-gratia claims may avoid a more costly settlement route for a problem or dispute. However, all parties will need to ensure that the particular circumstances are not catered for by either existing contract conditions or common law solutions. Generally speaking these defined courses of action will usually suffice. This advice should apply to claimants and recipients alike. In the normal course of business, such payments should be rare, and in any event subject to stringent examination and authorisation processes. Furthermore, in the public sector, established codes of practice or government rules may prevent such payments, and auditors working in this sector will need to be aware of the specific rules that apply.

Claims may be in the context of problems that may, sooner or later, affect the successful completion of the contract. It may be preferable, dependent upon the precise nature of the circumstances, to invoke another established mechanism in preference to the ex-gratia route in situations where the related project is threatened. The employer should be assured that the settlement of an ex-gratia claim will totally resolve the problem, and that further claims will not be either necessary or forthcoming.

Appropriate legal advice should be sought before any commitment is given. Claims should be thoroughly examined and all the appropriate and obligatory information should be obtained from the claimant. The accuracy and relevance of any supporting accounting and financial data should be scrutinised, and the calculations of any contract dependent losses sustained verified. Details of any other recent or pending claims made by the contractor should be obtained and viewed in context.

Documented assurances should be obtained from the claimant's auditors and/or legal representatives that their client will be able to continue trading and remain solvent following any payments. Having taken account of the effects of probable ex-gratia payments on the contract costings, etc., high-level authority to make the payment should be obtained and documented.

Control matrix example

Table 26 contains an *Exposures*-oriented example matrix utilising *Scale* 31 values as defined in Appendix 7. The data suggests a middle to low-level significance and a fairly pessimistic view of the effectiveness of some of the controls in counteracting the exposures.

Table 26 Controlling Contractual Claims – Exposures
Overall Inherent Risk (Size) Score [5 is worst risk; 1 is best] = 2.25

A Acceptance and payment of invalid claims – increased costs
B Acceptance of unsubstantiated or unproven claims
C Acceptance of claims submitted outwith permitted timetable
D Inability to support/prove claim due to poor records
E Settlement of incorrectly or unreasonably costed claims
F Unauthorised settlement of claims
G Excessive costs as a result of litigation
H Unreasonable frequency of claims submitted by contractor

I Failure to complete contract within budget due to claims
J Inadequate procedures contributing to claims activity
K Inability to resolve claims/damages by mutual consent
L Administrative delay in receiving and processing claims
M Failure to settle agreed and authorised claims
N Inadequate claims records – loss of control of status etc.
O Unauthorised settlement of Ex-gratia claims
P Failure to comply with regulatory requirements

SCALE 31 (abridged)

6 = Incorrect identification of needs or failure to meet them
5 = Lost business; needs partly unfulfilled; or breach of rules
4 = Delay or disruption; reputation loss; minor breach of rules (Contract auditing Exposures-oriented scale)
3 = Avoidable costs/losses; damage to contract relationships
2 = Administrative or accounting errors
1 = Detectable negative impact on the business or service

Controlling Contractual Claims		EXPOSURES															
		A	B	C	D	E	F	G	H	I	J	K	L	M	N	O	P
		=	=	=	=	=	=	=	=	=	=	=	=	=	=	=	=
Calculated Risk Score:	Risk	3	3	2	2	3	3	3	3	3	3	2	2	2	2	2	3
		–	–	–	–	–	–	–	–	–	–	–	–	–	–	–	–
Scale 31 (6 is most serious)	Type	3	3	3	3	3	4	5	5	6	4	5	3	4	4	3	5
Size (3 is maximum)	Size	3	3	2	2	3	2	2	2	2	2	1	1	1	1	2	2
CONTROLS	–	–	–	–	–	–	–	–	–	–	–	–	–	–	–	–	–
1 All claims are independently assessed in relation to the relevant contract conditions	Best	4	4	3						2	2		2				
	Test	?	?	?	?					?	?		?				
	Both																
2 Claims are only settled after assessment, justification and authorisation	Best		4	4	3		3	4							2		
	Test	?	?	?	?		?	?							?		
	Both																
3 All claims must be appropriately supported with evidence and documentation	Best			4		3	3										
	Test	?		?		?	?										
	Both																
4 Unproven or ill-founded claims are rejected by the Contract Administrator with reasons	Best		4	4			2										
	Test	?	?	?			?										
	Both																
5 Contract conditions define the timetable for action. Procedures & monitoring ensure compliance	Best				3												
	Test	?			?												
	Both																
6 Contract records established per written requirements. Quality checks applied periodically	Best					2											
	Test	?				?											
	Both																
7 All claims are subject to authorisation prior to settlement	Best							4									
	Test	?						?									
	Both																
8 The objective is to settle all claims within the contract conditions or mutual consent	Best							4				4					
	Test	?						?				?					
	Both																
9 Recourse to Arbitration per contract if parties are unable to reach agreement	Best							4									
	Test	?						?									
	Both																
		–															

Table 26 continued

			A	B	C	D	E	F	G	H	I	J	K	L	M	N	O	P
			=	=	=	=	=	=	=	=	=	=	=	=	=	=	=	=
	Calculated Risk Score:	Risk	3	3	2	2	3	3	3	3	3	3	2	2	2	2	2	3
			–	–	–	–	–	–	–	–	–	–	–	–	–	–	–	–
10	Contractor's claim activity is monitored and reported to management	Best								3								
		Test	?							?								
		Both																
			–	–	–	–	–	–	–	–	–	–	–	–	–	–	–	–
11	Discussions held with the contractor if claims activity is viewed as unreasonable	Best								3								
		Test	?							?								
		Both																
			–	–	–	–	–	–	–	–	–	–	–	–	–	–	–	–
12	Claim damages have to be authorised & total costs are monitored to budget	Best									3							
		Test	?								?							
		Both																
			–	–	–	–	–	–	–	–	–	–	–	–	–	–	–	–
13	Procedures & policies reviewed for effectiveness. Amendments are authorised & implemented	Best									3							
		Test	?								?							
		Both																
			–	–	–	–	–	–	–	–	–	–	–	–	–	–	–	–
14	Post-completion review examines adequacy of procedures, and recommends update	Best									2							
		Test	?								?							
		Both																
			–	–	–	–	–	–	–	–	–	–	–	–	–	–	–	–
15	Procedures aim to provide the maximum control, and minimise costs and disruption	Best									3	3						
		Test	?								?	?						
		Both																
			–	–	–	–	–	–	–	–	–	–	–	–	–	–	–	–
16	Litigation is considered as last resort after frank review of case. Authority required	Best							4			4						
		Test	?						?			?						
		Both																
			–	–	–	–	–	–	–	–	–	–	–	–	–	–	–	–
17	Once agreed & authorised claims should feature in next monthly account for payment	Best													5			
		Test	?												?			
		Both																
			–	–	–	–	–	–	–	–	–	–	–	–	–	–	–	–
18	All claims values contained in accounts are checked for authority before payment	Best						4							3			
		Test	?					?							?			
		Both																
			–	–	–	–	–	–	–	–	–	–	–	–	–	–	–	–
19	Register of all claims & related costs is maintained as the basis for control, analysis & reporting	Best														4		
		Test	?													?		
		Both																
			–	–	–	–	–	–	–	–	–	–	–	–	–	–	–	–
20	Ex-gratia claims are subject to strictly observed procedures and high-level authorities	Best														4		
		Test	?													?		
		Both																
			–	–	–	–	–	–	–	–	–	–	–	–	–	–	–	–
21	Regulatory obligations are addressed in procedures – Legal Dept. monitor compliance	Best															3	5
		Test															?	?
		Both																
			–															

A Acceptance and payment of invalid claims – increased costs
B Acceptance of unsubstantiated or unproven claims
C Acceptance of claims submitted outwith permitted timetable
D Inability to support/prove claim due to poor records
E Settlement of incorrectly or unreasonably costed claims
F Unauthorised settlement of claims
G Excessive costs as a result of litigation
H Unreasonable frequency of claims submitted by contractor

I Failure to complete contract within budget due to claims
J Inadequate procedures contributing to claims activity
K Inability to resolve claims/damages by mutual consent
L Administrative delay in receiving and processing claims
M Failure to settle agreed and authorised claims
N Inadequate claims records – loss of control of status etc.
O Unauthorised settlement of Ex-gratia claims
P Failure to comply with regulatory requirements

SCALE 31 (abridged)

6 = Incorrect identification of needs or failure to meet them
5 = Lost business; needs partly unfulfilled; or breach of rules
4 = Delay or disruption; reputation loss; minor breach of rules
(Contract auditing Exposures-oriented scale)

3 = Avoidable costs/losses; damage to contract relationships
2 = Administrative or accounting errors
1 = Detectable negative impact on the business or service

27

LIQUIDATIONS AND BANKRUPTCIES

Scope

A contract and the related project can be severely disrupted by the financial failure of a contractor. This chapter reviews the precautionary measures that employers can apply prior to forming a contractual relationship, and the actions required in the event of the contractor suffering financial problems. The key factors for the employer are the containment of effects and costs, the application of effective solutions, and the achievement of established targets.

Whenever there are severe economic conditions or when trading conditions are difficult, there is always the possibility of companies and other concerns succumbing to either liquidation or bankruptcy. In some cases there are few overt indications or advance warnings of such events, whereas it is possible that the cracks will either be on public display or the subject of general speculation, perhaps in the media. In the context of a contractor the impacts of financial failure and collapse can have drastic effects upon those depending on the successful completion of active contracts. The project in question may have vital significance in terms of the survival of the employer's business, or may be directly linked to the achievement of expected or statutory service levels in the public sector.

It would of course be improbable to suggest that clients should be able to unswervingly detect the impending financial problems of all those they deal with. Although the benefits of hindsight can offer few crumbs of reassurance, it is preferable to limit the potential for subsequent problems by undertaking an effective and wide-ranging review of the financial standing and general reliability of a contractor before entering into a formal contractual relationship. The subject of assessing the viability and competence of contractors is more fully explored in Chapter 12, but it is possible that clear messages about the current status of contractors will be revealed by the application of a realistic and comprehensive assessment procedure. The initial assessment of a contractor should have also incorporated the setting of a limit of contract activity placed with him. This mechanism, in relation to the contractor's resources, aims to restrict the level of the employer's exposure in the event of financial failure of the contractor.

In practice, and in an uncertain business world, financial problems will occur for all manner of reasons, not least due to over commitment of resources, encountering problems affecting the progress of current projects, delays beyond the control of any party, disputes over contract matters and the settlement of accounts due. It is very difficult, if not impossible, to reliably predict the likely eventuality and impact of all such factors.

Although an organisation would aim to reduce the prospects of financial difficulties leading to either liquidation or bankruptcy, they can strike. It is not our intention to provide guidance to the contractor unfortunate enough to become the victim of either event, as there are other more fitting sources of reference available. Our emphasis will be placed on the actions required to be taken by the employer or client in such situations during the currency of a contract relationship in order to control and minimise the relevant implications.

Initially let us identify the most likely top-level effects upon the employer when a contractor is placed in the hands of a liquidator. The first is the realisation that settlement of the situation may take years to finalise. The main preoccupations of the employer will be how the project is to be completed and at what eventual cost? The employer will be obliged to pay over to the appointed liquidator or receiver any monies owed to the contractor for work completed so far. Unless the progress so far in the project has been subject to effective control and documentation, it may be difficult to accurately assess the stage of development reached and thereby determine what requires to be done and what payments may be due.

The nature of the project will determine the options available for its completion. For example very specialised or niche activities may only be performed by a relatively few contractors. Additionally there may be crucial time-related criteria for the project perhaps linked to the successful achievement of corporate objectives. In any event a comprehensive appraisal of the status of the project will be necessary. All the available and practical options for continuing the project will also need to be identified and suitably appraised.

From a practical point of view the relative site(s) should be secured and any project assets protected.

All financial aspects will need to be identified, including:

- costs to date
- anticipated costs for the completion of the project, comparing the merits of a range of potential solutions
- the effects of calling in any relevant bonds or guarantees, taking account of the length of time to extract settlement
- the overall implications if the contractor is engaged on more than one contract for the employer (for instance, common law set-off rights may apply in such circumstances)
- the level and status of any retention monies.

It will also be necessary to accurately determine the value of work completed to date, as this may be claimable by the receiver, if not already paid by the employer. The employer should ensure that his property, equipment and plant on the affected site is suitably secured, identified and listed. This will also apply, where relevant, to any items that have become the employer's property by virtue of either incorporation into the scheme or the settlement of the relevant supplier's accounts. Separate accounting records will need to be established, so that all the related liabilities, costs, etc. can be reliably identified.

The contract may feature the actions permitted and the rights applicable to affected parties in the event of the contractor having financial difficulties and either going into liquidation or being declared bankrupt. The more common standard forms of contract have clauses relevant to such situations, for example clause 27 in the JCT80 conditions.

The situation can become more complex if sub-contractors are involved in the project. This is especially true if the completion or success of the project is heavily dependent upon sub-contractors. There are two broad scenarios that could apply. First where the main contractor is affected by financial difficulties and these affect his contractual relationship with sub-contractors. Second, where the sub-contractor is declared bankrupt or faces liquidation.

The optimum action for the employer to pursue will vary with regard to the specific circumstances, but it usual in the case of sub-contracting for the main contractor to have the prime responsibility for monitoring the work of sub-contractors and directly settling their accounts. The employer has no direct contractual relationship with sub-contractors, but may generally elect to ensure that the main contractor has settled relevant accounts before, in turn, making payments for the relative work to the main contractor. The available options will depend upon the nature and form of contract in place. In the construction sector, for example, the protocols are well established and involve the supervising engineer or architect confirming the validity of payments to the main contractor both with regard to certifying the completion of the relevant work to the required standard and that the sub-contractor's accounts have been duly settled by the main contractor.

Where the involvement of a sub-contractor is critical to the project, there may be few alternatives to the employer directly engaging them to complete their portion of the work if the main contractor is severely affected by financial problems. This is particularly true in specialised areas, where the choice of potential or alternative sub-contractors may be severely limited. Furthermore, the contract may define rules or limitations on the subsequent assignment of arrangements to another party, an example would be clause 19 of the JCT80 contract.

The resolution of the problems associated with the liquidation, etc. may take years, and the employer may be compelled, for commercial or statutory reasons, to ensure that the project is promptly completed. If the contract provisions allow, there may be scope for subsequently reclaiming the cost of completing the contract from either the receiver of the original main contractor, the guarantor, insurer, or against any relative performance bonds.

Responsibility for the settlement of earlier sub-contractor accounts for work completed will still lie with the main contractor through the auspices of the appointed receiver or liquidator. Whatever action the employer takes, it should not prejudice the legal requirements governing the amounts owed to the main contractor, which in turn affect the payments that can be made by the receiver or liquidator to affected creditors including the sub-contractors. Appropriate legal advice should be sought to ensure that the action taken maximises the ability to complete the project and minimises the potential financial implications for the employer.

Control matrix example

Table 27 explores the key in the form of an example matrix related to a construction sector situation where the main contractor has gone into liquidation. The suggested controls generally aim to allow the recovery of the situation and facilitate the completion of the contract. The matrix is formed using the techniques examined in Chapter 32. The value data is related to *Scale* 31 as described in Appendix 7.

Table 27 Liquidations and Bankruptcies – Exposures
Overall Inherent Risk (Size) Score [5 is worst risk; 1 is best] = 2.56

A Failure to complete project or fulfil objectives
B Additional financial burden due to contractor's liquidation
C Delay/disruption due to contractor's liquidation/bankruptcy
D Inability to continue with completion of project
E Inability to accurately identify amounts owed to contractor
F Inadequate bonding and guarantee arrangements in place
G FInancial loss due to inadequacy of retention
H Loss due to failure to secure materials & plant on site
I Further disruption due to related failure of sub-contractor

J Additional costs of seeking/engaging alternative contractor
K Restrictions on ability to assign contract
L Failure to establish adequate accounts to reflect situation
M Additional costs due to settlement of sub-contractor's a/c
N Failure to lodge accurate claims for outstanding damages
O Failure to obtain legal advice & adopt optimum solution
P Previous overpayment of contractor – inability to recover

SCALE 31 (abridged)

6 = Incorrect identification of needs, or failure to meet them
5 = Lost business; needs partly unfulfilled; or breach of rules
4 = Delay or disruption; reputation loss; minor breach of rules
(Contract auditing Objectives-oriented scale)

3 = Avoidable costs/losses; damage to contract relationships
2 = Administrative or accounting errors
1 = Detectable negative impact on the business or service

#	Liquidations & Bankruptcies		EXPOSURES															
			A	B	C	D	E	F	G	H	I	J	K	L	M	N	O	P
			=	=	=	=	=	=	=	=	=	=	=	=	=	=	=	=
	Calculated Risk Score:	Risk	4	3	3	3	2	3	3	2	3	2	3	3	2	2	3	2
	Scale 31 (6 is most serious)	Type	6	5	6	6	3	5	5	3	4	3	4	4	3	3	6	3
	Size (3 is maximum)	Size	3	2	2	2	2	2	2	2	2	2	3	2	2	1	2	2
	CONTROLS																	
1	Project records & other data is sufficient to enable the formulation of a recovery plan	Best	3		2	3	2											
		Test	?	?	?	?	?											
		Both																
2	Contract documents still form a valid & accurate foundation for seeking alternative contractor	Best	3		2	3												
		Test	?	?	?	?												
		Both																
3	Invoking the performance bonds & other securities will reduce the financial impact	Best		3														
		Test	?		?													
		Both																
4	Contingency planning procedures established to aid recovery in such circumstances	Best			3	3												
		Test	?		?	?												
		Both																
5	All possible recovery options considered, costed & management authority obtained to proceed	Best		4		4	4											
		Test	?	?		?	?											
		Both																
6	Progress measurement and certification of previous a/cs used to prove values paid/due	Best						4										
		Test	?					?										
		Both																
7	Current data combined with new measurements used to confirm the current status of the works	Best		4		4	3											
		Test	?	?		?	?											
		Both																
8	Bond & surety values initially set per approved risk-related approach	Best						4										
		Test	?					?										
		Both																
9	Validity & currency of bonds & securities confirmed at the outset & during the project	Best						4										
		Test	?					?										
		Both																

Table 27 continued

		A	B	C	D	E	F	G	H	I	J	K	L	M	N	O	P
		=	=	=	=	=	=	=	=	=	=	=	=	=	=	=	=
Calculated Risk Score:	Risk	4	3	3	3	2	3	3	2	3	2	3	3	2	2	3	2
10 Retention value progressively reduced in accord with sector best practice	Best							4									
	Test	?						?									
	Both																
11 Permission to visit site sought. All employer's plant & goods identified, agreed & valued	Best							4									
	Test	?						?									
	Both																
12 Management authority obtained to directly settle sub-contractor a/c where vital for project	Best								3				3				
	Test	?							?				?				
	Both																
13 Records of additional costs are maintained in case they can be subsequently reclaimed	Best								2								
	Test	?							?								
	Both																
14 Form of contract utilised that enables assignment in case of liquidation. Permission obtained	Best										5						
	Test	?									?						
	Both																
15 All accounts authorised, certified and maintained up to date	Best			3								4					
	Test	?		?								?					
	Both																
16 All outstanding claims (less amount payable) lodged with liquidator/receiver	Best														4		
	Test	?													?		
	Both																
17 Legal Dept. activity involved in the formulation of a suitable recovery plan	Best															4	
	Test	?														?	
	Both																
18 All previous payments subject to certification & authorisation. Reduces chances of overpayment	Best																3
	Test	?															?
	Both																

Part IV

UPON AND AFTER CONTRACT COMPLETION

28

CONTRACTOR'S FINAL ACCOUNT

Scope

This chapter examines the key issues relating to the verification and agreement of the contractor's final account. In practice there may have been staged or interim accounts submitted in line with either the completion of discrete phases of the project or in support of work completed at agreed time intervals (e.g. monthly). The issues specific to interim accounts are noted in Chapter 22.

The contents gravitate towards the construction sector. However, the underlying principles can be applied to most situations, and the relevant audit concerns are universal in nature.

In relation to the processing of contractor's accounts, the auditor will need to review the established systems of control and assess their effectiveness. Historically, auditors in the public sector may have been too actively involved in examining final accounts, indeed the relevant financial procedures may have precisely defined their role in this respect. The dangers of auditors becoming too active in any control environment are well known, it encourages those with the relevant responsibilities to rely too heavily upon audit examination. Additionally, it puts the auditor in the impossible situation of trying to objectively review and report upon a system in which he or a colleague takes an active part.

If the related project was a complex one, the subject of authorised modifications, or the victim of delay, etc., it is probable that the final account will be quite complicated, perhaps incorporating some (or all) of the following elements:

- effect of interim payments*
- permitted retention monies
- costs related to authorised variations and specification changes*
- effects of agreed price fluctuations*
- effects of claims submitted by contractors for additional costs, etc.*
- values of liquidated damages permitted by the conditions of contract*
- costs of authorised Dayworks.

The items marked with an * are the subject of comment in chapters elsewhere in this book.

The main objectives to consider are that the final total costs are in accord with the terms of the contract, suitably authorised, and that the project has been achieved within the agreed financial constraints.

The nature of the contract in use will regulate the contents of the final account. Most of the above noted elements are likely to be the subject of specific conditions and clauses, and the inclusion of such charges will need to be substantiated in relation to the appropriate enabling contract conditions. Appendix 6 provides a summary of key clause references for some of the more common standard forms of contract. Those factors arising as a result of earlier disputes or contractual claims should have been identified, reviewed and acted upon before the submission of the final account.

Before we examine, in more detail, the specific considerations of the various elements of contract final accounts, it is necessary to take a view of the prevailing culture of the employing (or client) organisation with respect to the payment of creditors. The degree of control exercised will depend on the nature and scale of the organisation. In the public sector, for example, where accountability and cost control feature strongly in the culture, it is probable that there will be written procedures covering the authorisation and payment of accounts, perhaps in the form of standing orders or financial regulations. The principles applied will vary between sectors, but may be based upon a hierarchical management structure with authority rights granted on a progressive financial scale.

A further dimension is represented by the protocols applicable to the construction and civil engineering sectors, where it is usual practice for the supervising architect or engineer to play an active role in signifying the validity and accuracy of the submitted accounts. The inclusion of additional costs relative to variations from the contracted design requirements will normally, in construction projects, be as a result of formal instructions issued by the architect or engineer to the contractor. Employer management should have been informed of all such variation orders and the related cost implications.

If all the other preceding stages of the project have been subject to effective control measures, then it follows that the examination of the final account will normally be made easier. For the most part, the accurate completion of all accounts is dependent upon the quality of measurements of the work completed. Suitable documentation will hopefully have been established in relation to changes and other events likely to affect the final accounts. Any disputes that have arisen in the course of the project should also have been suitably addressed and documented. However, all the appropriate precautions do not necessarily prevent problems occurring with the final account.

The degree to which the recipient examines the final account will, in part, be relevant to the extent and effectiveness of the procedures applied at the earlier stages in the project/contract lifecycle. The degree of effectiveness is partially relative to the quality and frequency of management information; this should be established so that there are no surprises when the final account is received and management are fully aware of the outstanding issues. In any event, the final account should be supported by adequately detailed schedules. Checking a complex final account can be time-consuming and account needs to be taken of the effectiveness of preceding control checks when considering the amount of final checking to apply.

The timing of the submission of the final account will vary with the nature of the project and may be subject to a timescale incorporated into the contract conditions. For example, the supply of computer hardware and a related bespoke application system may require final settlement of the capital sums upon delivery or shortly thereafter. In the construction sector, the contractor may not be eligible to submit his final account until after the expiration of the maintenance period during which he is responsible for correcting any defects. In some cases the retention of a defined percentage of the contract value is permitted until the maintenance period has elapsed. Where contract conditions permit the contractor to adjust values in respect of permitted profit, the calculation of such oncosts should be verified for both eligibility and accuracy.

For illustrative purposes, provided below are the elements likely to be contained in a construction sector final account:

- *Preliminaries or general items* This category would include general site-establishing activities, the provision of site facilities, etc. The items may have been specified in the bills of quantity and the final account should be examined to ensure that the relevant services were actually provided.
- *Quantities* As the name suggests these are charges relative to the measurement of work completed using the agreed method. The estimated quantities would have featured in the tender documents and any notable differences should be scrutinised and verified. The application of the agreed methods of measurement and pricing should be confirmed and checked for accuracy. Supporting evidence should be available, when applicable, from the site-level or quantity surveyor's records.
- *Prime cost sums* In the course of the project it may be necessary to obtain either materials or services from suppliers or sub-contractors. Such items or services are noted in the bills of quantity provided with the tender documents. The contractor initially provides estimated costs for such items including allowances for profit, etc. See Chapter 20 for full details of arrangements with (and accounts from) nominated sub-contractors and suppliers.
- *Provisional sum* As it is not always possible to state all the required goods, services or materials in the tender documents a provisional value is entered to cater for this contingency.
- *Variation orders or instructions* As discussed in Chapter 24 it is accepted practice that the supervising architect or engineer can, during the project, instruct the contractor to undertake work outwith the contracted design, methods or construction programme. All these instructions should be subject

to cost estimation and formally documented and signed by the supervising professional. The basis for calculating the relevant costs will be dependent upon a number of factors including whether or not the nature of the new work is similar to that already applied and therefore subject to the same charging mechanism. Where the variation order involves prime cost (PC) items, the entries on the final account should be supported by supplier's or sub-contractor's invoices.

- *Dayworks* Some activities are not conducive to costing using the measurement-based and other methods of pricing. In such circumstances it may be necessary to charge for work based on the number of hours applied by the affected tradesmen and the permitted hourly rates of pay. This method is referred to as dayworks. The rates used to calculate the amount due may either be determined nationally or recorded in the contract on a daywork schedule. The supervising architect or engineer should signify, in writing, that specific work should be completed as dayworks. Site-level records should detail the hours worked, any equipment or materials used, and be scrutinised and agreed by the appropriate supervising professional.
- *Adjustment item* These can be variously applied by the contractor, as directed by the contents of the contract.
- *Retention* This is a mechanism designed to provide greater assurance for the employer in the event that a contractor defaults on his contractual obligations. It operates by the employer withholding a defined percentage of the contract value as various stages of the project are completed. One half of the retained value is normally released when the works are substantially completed, and the remaining balance is released when a maintenance certificate is duly issued.
- *Tax fluctuation clause* Such clauses are designed to permit the adjustment of the contract value in the event of changes being applied to the taxation matters affecting labour where there is an effect upon the profitability of the contract. The types of taxation matters permitted under such clauses are very clearly specified and exclude, for example, value added tax.
- *Value added tax (VAT)* It is normal practice to assume that VAT has been excluded from the relevant tender prices. Therefore, it has to be applied when appropriate. Please note that payments of liquidated damages are not currently subject to VAT.
- *Income tax deductions* As required by the prevailing revenue legislation.
- *Previous payment(s) made* Details of previous interim and other payments should be recorded and reconciled by the employer. Some organisations active in the placement of contracts maintain a contracts register which reflects the current status of contracts including payments made and the outstanding commitments.
- *Contract price fluctuations* As noted in Chapter 23, most long-term contracts have provisions for applying the effects of price fluctuations on some form of agreed basis. The schedules supporting the price fluctuation entries should be agreed in line with the formula and index base used. The requirements of any applicable government guidelines should be observed where applicable.

- *Contractors' claims* The methods of assessing and controlling contractors' claims are discussed in Chapter 26. The relevant entries on the final account should be examined to confirm their appropriateness and accuracy. The existing records should aid the determination of the current status of all claims and assist in the confirmation that the relevant payments are valid and appropriately authorised.

SETTLEMENT OF LIQUIDATED DAMAGES

In the course of considering the completeness of accounts submitted by a contractor, any outstanding claims for liquidated damages should be taken into account. Although the subject of liquidated damages is fully detailed in Chapter 19, they generally arise in the event of the contractor defaulting in respect of defined contractual obligations, such as completing works by the required date. The determination of whether such damages can be claimed will partly depend on the reliability of the relevant site records.

Liquidated damages are calculated on a sum specified in the contract documents and may be applied as a daily rate in relation to the number of days the completion date is exceeded. There should be a mechanism which alerts the employer to the applicability of invoking this facility and confirming that the appropriate deduction has been correctly calculated and applied to the submitted accounts.

OTHER DIRECT PAYMENTS MADE BY THE EMPLOYER

The necessity to make direct payments may arise because of the default of the contractor who would normally be responsible for them, for example to subcontractors or suppliers. The requirement to effect such payments may be expedient in order to achieve the objectives of the project. It may also be possible for the employer to subsequently claim reimbursement of these costs from the defaulting contractor under the terms of the contract where this is prescribed. The reasons for taking this route will vary, and not all forms of contracts will permit this course of action, therefore care needs to be exercised by the employer in order to avoid contravening the legal protocols.

In a similar vein, the employer may elect at the outset of the project to meet certain specified associated costs. For example, he may wish to directly arrange suitable insurance cover for the works in a building project and bear the associated costs. In other circumstances, the main contractor would normally be expected to arrange for suitable cover, and only in the case of failure to meet his obligations would an employer arrange the appropriate cover and seek reimbursement of the cost from the defaulting contractor under the terms of the contract where applicable. There are other potential items of expenditure which are normally regarded as the responsibility of the employer and these should be allowed for in any budgeting and payment authority arrangements.

PAYMENT OF EXTERNAL CONSULTANTS OR SPECIALISTS

It may have been necessary to engage the services of a suitably experienced consultant or expert to either assist with or control the project. The issues surrounding the selection and engagement of consultants are featured in Chapter 10. Many professional bodies promote standard forms of contract and scales of fees. Where these have been used the verification of the relevant fee accounts should be straightforward, so long as adequate records have been maintained of the consultant's activities during the project.

The members of some professions are now permitted to submit competitive quotations for their services and not be tied, in every situation, to the fee scales established by their representative bodies. Where this 'free market' situation applies, employers should ensure that the relevant agreement clearly specifies how the charges will be applied in practice. Once again, the maintenance of records throughout the period of the project will assist in the checking and verification of consultant's accounts. All accounts received should be examined for accuracy, relevance, etc. before being duly authorised for payment. Employers must coincidently ensure that all the consultant's obligations have been appropriately discharged.

ACCOUNTING FOR PROJECT-RELATED GRANTS, SUBSIDIES, ETC.

Certain categories of project may attract government or other forms of grant or subsidy. This is particularly true of the public sector, and may also apply to the private sector, for example with regard to developments in a designated business enterprise area. The financial implications of available grants should have been fully researched and considered during the project assessment and justification processes. The project should have been suitably tailored in order to qualify for the relevant assistance, and any specific requirements identified and incorporated into the project administration infrastructure. Before commencing the project, written confirmation of eligibility and the value of the assistance applicable, should have been received.

In order to maximise the benefits of such contributions, compliance with any qualifying conditions should be subject to ongoing monitoring throughout the project lifecycle, and any possible problems suitably averted. There may also be the need to provide regular reports to the appropriate authority or government ministry in order to remain eligible for assistance.

Upon successful completion of the project, the appropriate form of claim should be submitted in the required timescale. Any supporting financial and other information should be checked for accuracy and completeness before submission. All pending claims should be appropriately progressed and the funds received applied in the required and appropriate manner. Evidence of the related internal financial transactions should be retained in accordance with any specified procedures.

LINKAGES WITH LIQUIDATION AND BANKRUPTCY

There may be some natural linkages between the settlement of accounts and the events surrounding the liquidation or bankruptcy of a main contractor. Although this chapter is primarily targeted at the final account, these related matters will be briefly explored. More details of liquidations and bankruptcies are supplied in Chapter 27.

Where a project has been affected by contractors having financial difficulties, the prime concern of the employer will be how to ensure that the project is duly completed within the established cost and time constraints. Clearly, the settlement of complex financial problems and the associated contractual liabilities may take many years, and the employer is unlikely to be able to await the conclusion of the related legal processes. Therefore it may be necessary to make alternative arrangements, perhaps with affected sub-contractors in order to maintain the required momentum of the project. In such instances due regard should be paid to the legal implications of directly engaging key sub-contractors, and the settlement of valid accounts with the liquidator appointed to oversee the affairs of the troubled main contractor.

Within the employing organisation, it will be necessary to ensure that adequate control is exercised over any additional expenditure incurred as a consequence of completing a project by alternative means. The accuracy and completeness of associated records may be crucial when subsequently attempting to recover such costs if the contractual provisions allow. It will also be necessary to ensure that the commitment to such additional costs is suitably authorised, and the same is true of accounts presented for settlement. Of course, the role of the supervising professional in construction contracts provides further control where the amounts due are usually certified in advance.

GENERAL BUDGETARY AND ACCOUNTING CONTROL

At the outset of the project appraisal process, certain expectations and objectives would have been established for the project. These would have undoubtedly included the setting of the required financial criteria, such as overall cost constraints, level of capital investment, cash flow predictions, and so on. Once the project had been authorised and permitted to commence, these hard factors would have provided points of comparison against which to register actual progress and costs. In the course of the project, some of these parameters may have been the subject of change in light of any unforeseen problems or situations, although thorough preparation should limit the scope of such changes.

Throughout the project lifecycle, the management information system should have provided accurate and up-to-date financial data. Management should have been alerted to any significant variations from the expected criteria, allowing them to take the necessary action. Those responsible for the management and day-to-day control of the project should have kept management informed of any problems. Explicit authority may have to be obtained to permit the project to continue with amended goals or objectives.

During the project, interim accounts may have been presented. Procedures should be in place to ensure that payment of all such accounts have been preceded by checks for relevance, accuracy and authority to pay.

At the end of the project, the final account(s) data can be incorporated into the accounting system and the final overall appraisal of the financial performance of the project undertaken. For the most part this will take the form of measuring actual achievements against the key expectations and objectives established for the project. Various measures may be applied in practice. It is obviously important to ensure that any significant variations or trends are thoroughly investigated, and corrected if necessary. In certain situations it may be necessary to seek senior management sanction to the acceptance of same.

Where the completion of a project leads into the operation of a business activity, it may be necessary to wait until the venture is under way before assessing the overall effectiveness and performance of the project and its application. Examining all aspects of the project and measuring its relevant success may take the form of a full post-completion review which process is fully considered in Chapter 30.

Control matrix example

The example matrix provided as Table 28 deliberately incorporates a comprehensive range of final account elements. While realising that not every situation in practice would require all the noted points, they are provided as a full illustration of the key issues. In the example much reliance is placed upon the accuracy and integrity of supporting contract records and documents as reflection of previous key events. The example matrix is *Exposures*-oriented and uses *Scale* 31 which is defined in Appendix 7.

Table 28 Contractor's Final Account – Exposures

Overall Inherent Risk (Size) Score [5 is worst risk; 1 is best] = 1.84

A Payment of inaccurate final account – error overstatement
B Payment for goods/services not received or incomplete work
C Incorrect valuation or measurement of work
D Inaccurate valuation based upon non-contract rates
E Significant variation between account and contract amounts
F Failure to react to variations and overspends
G Outstanding workmanship and quality issues
H Inaccurate/inadequate calculation of retained value
I Overpayment due to error in previous payments
J Inaccurate application of price fluctuation adjustments

K Inclusion of values for unresolved contractor's claims
L Inaccurate reflection of costs for variations/modifications
M Inaccurate/inappropriate deduction of Liquidated Damages
N Cost or adjustments not previously certified/authorised
O Unauthorised settlement of final account
P Incorrect treatment of VAT and other taxation matters
Q Verification of account delayed due to inadequate records
R Failure to settle account in stipulated timescale
S Failure to correctly deduct agreed damages due to employer

SCALE 31 (abridged)

6 = Incorrect identification of needs or failure to meet them
5 = Lost business; needs partly unfulfilled; or breach of rules
4 = Delay or disruption; reputation loss; minor breach of rules
(Contract auditing Exposures-oriented scale)

3 = Avoidable costs/losses; damage to contract relationships
2 = Administrative or accounting errors
1 = Detectable negative impact on the business or service

Contractor's Final Account		EXPOSURES	A	B	C	D	E	F	G	H	I	J	K	L	M	N	O	P	Q	R	S
			=	=	=	=	=	=	=	=	=	=	=	=	=	=	=	=	=	=	=
Calculated Risk Score:	Risk		3	3	2	2	2	2	2	2	2	2	2	2	2	2	3	3	2	2	2
Scale 31 (6 is most serious)	Type		5	5	3	3	3	5	4	3	2	3	3	3	5	3	6	5	3	3	3
Size (3 is maximum)	Size		2	2	2	2	2	1	1	2	2	1	1	1	1	2	2	2	1	1	2
CONTROLS																					
1 All accounts are subject to a comprehensive review and reconciliation to source records	Best		3	3	3	3	3			3	3	2	2	2	2	2		2			2
	Test		?	?	?	?	?			?	?	?	?	?	?	?		?			?
	Both																				
2 All completed work is certified as the basis for confirming account charges	Best		3	3	3	3			2												
	Test		?	?	?	?	?		?												
	Both																				
3 Measurement and value elements are defined in the contract - account detail checked/confirmed	Best				3		4	4	2												
	Test		?		?		?	?	?												
	Both																				
4 Errors are highlighted, adjusted and referred to contractor	Best			3	3	3	3			3		2									
	Test		?	?	?	?	?			?		?									
	Both																				
5 Costs versus budget are monitored throughout project. Action is authorised & taken	Best								3	3											
	Test		?						?	?											
	Both																				
6 All significant variations are reported to management for decision and action	Best								3	3											
	Test		?						?	?											
	Both																				
7 All work is certified. Faults are highlighted & required corrective action is defined	Best									3											
	Test		?							?											
	Both																				
8 Project Manager is responsible for confirming/certifying that all faults are resolved	Best									3											
	Test		?							?											
	Both																				
9 Maintenance retention value is applied and confirmed in accordance with contract conditions	Best										4										
	Test		?								?										
	Both																				

Table 28 continued

		A	B	C	D	E	F	G	H	I	J	K	L	M	N	O	P	Q	R	S
		=	=	=	=	=	=	=	=	=	=	=	=	=	=	=	=	=	=	=
Calculated Risk Score:	Risk	3	3	2	2	2	2	2	2	2	2	2	2	2	2	3	3	2	2	2
		–	–	–	–	–	–	–	–	–	–	–	–	–	–	–	–	–	–	–
10 Register of previous accounts, claims & payments is maintained & used to confirm balance due	Best									4										
	Test	?								?										
	Both																			
		–	–	–	–	–	–	–	–	–	–	–	–	–	–	–	–	–	–	–
11 Contract conditions define basis of price fluctuations. Entries verified by Finance Dept.	Best										5									
	Test										?									
	Both																			
		–	–	–	–	–	–	–	–	–	–	–	–	–	–	–	–	–	–	–
12 All claims received are registered. Accepted claims are coded & verified for payment	Best											4								
	Test											?								
	Both																			
		–	–	–	–	–	–	–	–	–	–	–	–	–	–	–	–	–	–	–
13 Records maintained of all variations. Valuation of work is verified to agreed terms	Best												5							
	Test												?							
	Both																			
		–	–	–	–	–	–	–	–	–	–	–	–	–	–	–	–	–	–	–
14 Validility of Liquidated Damages verified by Legal Dept. and applied per contract conditions	Best													4						
	Test													?						
	Both																			
		–	–	–	–	–	–	–	–	–	–	–	–	–	–	–	–	–	–	–
15 All other account items are checked to supporting records/ documents for validity, etc.	Best														4					
	Test														?					
	Both																			
		–	–	–	–	–	–	–	–	–	–	–	–	–	–	–	–	–	–	–
16 Following checking all accounts are authorised for payment by senior management	Best															5				
	Test															?				
	Both																			
		–	–	–	–	–	–	–	–	–	–	–	–	–	–	–	–	–	–	–
17 All taxation entries are checked by Finance Dept. in accordance with contract & taxation regulations	Best																5			
	Test																?			
	Both																			
		–	–	–	–	–	–	–	–	–	–	–	–	–	–	–	–	–	–	–
18 Records established & used during life of contract to verify interim a/cs and claims	Best																	3		
	Test																	?		
	Both																			
		–	–	–	–	–	–	–	–	–	–	–	–	–	–	–	–	–	–	–
19 Verification/authorisation is applied per documented policies including payment timetable	Best																		4	
	Test																		?	
	Both																			
		–	–	–	–	–	–	–	–	–	–	–	–	–	–	–	–	–	–	–
20 Account is checked to records of Employer's claims to ensure inclusion of correct value(s)	Best																			5
	Test																			?
	Both																			
		–																			

A Payment of inaccurate final account – error overstatement
B Payment for goods/services not received or incomplete work
C Incorrect valuation or measurement of work
D Inaccurate valuation based upon non-contract rates
E Significant variation between account and contract amounts
F Failure to react to variations and overspends
G Outstanding workmanship and quality issues
H Inaccurate/inadequate calculation of retained value
I Overpayment due to error in previous payments
J Inaccurate application of price fluctuation adjustments
K Inclusion of values for unresolved contractor's claims
L Inaccurate reflection of costs for variations/modifications
M Inaccurate/inappropriate deduction of Liquidated Damages
N Cost or adjustments not previously certified/authorised
O Unauthorised settlement of final account
P Incorrect treatment of VAT and other taxation matters
Q Verification of account delayed due to inadequate records
R Failure to settle account in stipulated timescale
S Failure to correctly deduct agreed damages due to employer

SCALE 31 (abridged)

6 = Incorrect identification of needs or failure to meet them
5 = Lost business; needs partly unfulfilled; or breach of rules
4 = Delay or disruption; reputation loss; minor breach of rules
(Contract auditing Exposures-oriented scale)
3 = Avoidable costs/losses; damage to contract relationships
2 = Administrative or accounting errors
1 = Detectable negative impact on the business or service

29

RECOVERY OF DAMAGES

Scope

During the course of a contract, events and circumstances may have generated claims by either party. The possible and probable circumstances for such claims have been included in other chapters, such as extensions of time (Chapter 25) and contractor's claims (Chapter 26). This chapter looks at the aftermath of establishing such claims and the settlement processes in more detail. We also include comments upon the available solutions including arbitration.

The contents of this chapter do not discriminate between all the possible parties to a dispute. For example, the parties referred to in the text could in reality be the main contractor, the end-employer, nominated or domestic sub-contractors, and so on. Although each of these parties may have a different motivation for recovering damages, the elements described here should be generally applicable.

As can be seen from the contents of earlier chapters, there are many reasons for claims to be made against either party during the lifetime of the contract and indeed beyond. In this chapter we aim to bring into focus the necessity to ensure that all claims (and counter-claims) are accordingly followed up in the most appropriate way. Before examining the various key options and procedures, it should be stressed that the contents of this chapter are not meant to be a definitive statement on matters of law. Given the enormous variety of possible interplays that could apply in the contracting environment, every case is virtually unique and should be correspondingly subjected to examination by suitably skilled legal advisers.

Most claims revolve around the issue of money, and are expressed in terms of damages against the defaulting party. Damages can be awarded or obtained by a number of routes which we explore subsequently, but the value of them is generally geared to ensuring that the plaintiff (or claimant) ends up in the same financial position he or she would have occupied had the contract (or part thereof) been performed properly. Damages can relate to either hard or soft factors, for example the actual cost of making good a defect could be regarded as a hard factor, whereas the loss of income due to a delay caused by the contractor will usually be a soft quantification.

There are a variety of bases for establishing a claim for damages, these include:

- breach of contract (i.e. failure to comply with the contract conditions)
- contractual claims (i.e. within the scope of the conditions of contract, this includes liquidated or liquidated and ascertained damage claims)
- common-law claims (i.e. under the principle of tort)
- ex-gratia claims (i.e. those without contractual status).

These classifications are defined more fully in Chapter 26.

Perhaps unfairly one normally thinks of breach of contract being perpetrated mainly by the contractor. However, employers can also be the offending party in that, for example, they may cause undue hindrance or delay, may not make the necessary payments for work completed at the appointed time, or may fail to give the contractor possession of the relevant site at the defined time.

The need to apply effective ongoing monitoring of contract performance is critical in both ensuring that contracts are satisfactorily executed and detecting any problems in good time. Although monitoring will not necessarily prevent breaches of contract conditions, the process should enable a prompt and effective response to either avoid or divert claims activity.

The requirement for accurate and comprehensive project and contract-related performance documentation also plays an important role in damage claims. For the employer and contractor alike, the establishment of clear and complete records of activities will support the factual requirements of subsequent claims. Equally their absence or inaccuracy may present the opposing party with a case for an unchallengeable claim. Other chapters discuss the merits of establishing the necessary administrative and documentary processes.

Claims can be resolved in a number of ways, which can be summarised as follows:

- by mutual consent and agreement between the parties
- by conciliation or mediation
- by court action
- by arbitration.

The last two are obviously adversarial in nature and prone to be expensive processes. We will examine the related issues in subsequent paragraphs.

From the claimant's point of view, there is a need to establish the accurate and justifiable basis for a claim, and subsequently ensure that all claims are settled. However, this is a very simplistic view, because in reality there may be all manner of conflicting claims and factors which will need to be jointly considered so that an overall claims recovery strategy can be formulated.

We are not, in this chapter, necessarily concerned with whether or not a particular claim is valid, but more focused on the need to pursue and resolve damage claims. We have assumed that a combination of appropriate legal advice and supporting evidence has concluded that a particular claim is worth pursuing. On this deliberately broad basis the contents can apply to either the employer or contractor in their respective submissions.

MUTUAL CONSENT

The success or otherwise of claims will in part depend on the conditions contained in the specific contract. If, at the formulation of the contract, the parties reached a balanced view of the apportionment of relative risks reflected in the conditions, most eventualities should have been expressly catered for. For example the use of one of the common standard forms of construction contracts does generally afford the achievement of such a balance, as the conditions have been refined over many years and are based upon transitional case law.

Specific conditions (or clauses) may present opportunities to either party to establish the basis for a claim. Additionally, as in the case of construction contract liquidated damages, there is the possibility of agreeing the financial value of potential claims in advance. Such processes can not only hasten the resolution of appropriate claims but avoid altogether the requirement to refer such matters to the courts.

There is obviously benefit in amicably resolving claims and disputes between the parties without the need to refer the matter to the courts or arbitration. Contract conditions should include the definition, in appropriate situations, of the required form of claims to be made under certain defined conditions. For example contractor's claims submitted when an action by the employer has caused the contractor to incur additional costs outwith the original requirements. There should be mechanisms in place to handle the submission of the relevant claim, the fair assessment of the claim, the communication of the decision about the validity and acceptance of the claim, and the subsequent settlement of same where proven valid.

CONCILIATION AND MEDIATION

Both of these processes involve the services of a third party with the intention of providing an independent but knowledgeable review of the circumstances leading towards an agreed settlement. They differ in that conciliation is normally conducted with both parties present during the review, while mediation normally involves the mediator initially meeting the parties separately.

In both processes the parties to the contract in question are not bound by the suggestions of either the conciliator or mediator, and resolution is still dependent upon mutual agreement and acceptance. If agreement cannot be achieved by these processes, the parties may consider the alternatives of litigation or arbitration.

COURT ACTION

Where prior mutual consent or arbitration processes are neither possible nor successful, referring the matter of damage claims to law may be necessary.

However, the costs of this route are extremely high and should be considered in relationship to the value of damages sought, the need to maintain ongoing relationships with the contractor (especially if the project is yet to be finalised), and the perceived strength of the claimant's case.

Decisions to take claims through the legal process should be made at a high level within the organisation and only after a full and balanced evaluation of all the relevant factors. Legal advice should be sought and heeded, especially where the situation is either technically or commercially complex in nature. All the attendant risks and potential costs should be carefully weighed against the assessment of the likely success of the case.

Particular attention should be paid to the accuracy, completeness and relevance of any required supporting contract or project documentation. Having reached this stage of events, the organisation may realise that the procedural and documentary arrangements are somewhat inadequate. Key events and occurrences will need to be accurately and reliably supported by documentary and factual evidence if the inherent strengths of the case are to be maximised.

In addition to justifying the case on legal grounds, management should also take account of the effects of exposing all relevant matters to public gaze, and consider the possible effects of this on their reputation and sector standing. The public washing of dirty linen and the revelation of significant inadequacies in internal control mechanisms will not serve to enhance the image of either the employer or contractor in such situations.

Chapter 1 highlights some of the legal considerations relevant to contracts with an international dimension. When applicable, the further complications represented by matters of international law will need to be thoroughly researched, and the additional costs estimated.

ARBITRATION

Arbitration is a process applied to resolve a conflict or dispute. The framework applied to such processes is normally determined with the mutual consent of the parties involved, indeed they may have defined the relevant arbitration protocols in advance and incorporated them into the contract conditions, for example, some of the standard forms of contract incorporate or refer to defined arbitration processes.

Taking into account the contents of any contract conditions which specify the arbitration rules to be applied in case of disputes, it should be noted that arbitration does not operate outwith the confines of the established law. In fact arbitration processes themselves are the subject of specific legislation in the form of the *Arbitration Acts of 1950, 1975 and 1979.* In Scotland different arrangements exist under the contents of the *(Scotland) Arbitration Act of 1894.*

Although arbitration can be regarded as a process built upon agreed terms and methodologies, the process will draw heavily upon the contents of the contract existing between the parties and actions taken in relation to the contractual provisions during the operation of the contract. Let us initially examine the advantages and disadvantages of arbitration before briefly discussing the relevant processes:

Advantages

- consent of parties to the arbitration process and the choice of arbitrator
- potential for lower costs when compared to court actions
- existence of various forms of arbitration process in relation to the value of the contract and the specific conditions, thus enabling the tailoring of facilities
- potential for expediency in resolving disputes, partly due to the involvement of arbitrators with the requisite knowledge of the speciality or technical area under review
- conduct of proceedings in private, away from the public gaze thereby avoiding potential reputation or image problems
- findings are binding.

Disadvantages

- the cost of arbitration, although potentially less than an equivalent court case, can still be significant in nature
- competence of arbitrators.

It should be clearly stressed that the quality and competence of arbitrators is generally not a major problem, partly because of the work of the Chartered Institute of Arbitrators in the development of appropriate standards and professional practices. Additionally, it is the practice to select an arbitrator with knowledge and experience relevant to the matter under review. In any event the parties to an arbitration process should satisfy themselves that the choice of arbitrator is relevant, perhaps by reference to an established register of arbitrators with the requisite experience of their sphere of operations. Additionally there are safeguards in place within the legislation to ensure that the arbitrator has no current material connection with either party to the dispute.

The particular form of contract in place may incorporate or define the nature and form of arbitration process to apply in the event that certain types of insoluble dispute arise. Some form of prior agreement to refer disputes to a defined form of arbitration may be established between contracted parties, and care should be taken to ensure that the interests of the organisation are best served by the prescribed form of arbitration. In practice there is no automatic constricting requirement to only apply arbitration, the matter can still be, if necessary and prudent, referred to the courts for resolution.

Under the legislation, the arbitrator is empowered in many respects, such as:

- with authority that is legally recognised, but which can be subject to High Court review
- to direct an award of damages, costs and interest (where appropriate)
- the power to order that errors and mistakes are corrected, and to order performance of specific actions.

The legislation combined with the practices promoted by the Chartered Institute of Arbitrators, defines the form of arbitration proceedings. There are all manner of mechanisms aimed at fairness and balance in the proceedings, especially in the required form and nature of evidence presented. This evidence is often based upon the documentation of events created during the contract activity. Therefore it is crucial for the success of the case that the procedures in place to gather, record and interpret such data are reliable and accurate.

Agreement to partake in arbitration, as compared to pursuing the matter through the courts, should be ratified by senior management following a full review of the constituent facts, including reference to appropriate legal advice, and a full assessment of the probable costs. The arbitration process requires a range of defined documents to be completed at appropriate stages. Advice should be obtained so that all of the procedural requirements are correctly addressed. All costs incurred during the process should be recorded as they may be subsequently recovered if the award is in the organisation's favour.

Generally speaking the award arising from an arbitration hearing is binding upon the losing party, and therefore failure to make the appropriate settlement can be referred to the High Court for judgement. However, appeal processes are provided in the arbitration procedure. From an accounting point of view, the value of any award made together with reimbursement of costs, should be agreed to the arbitrator's ruling upon settlement.

OVERALL CONTROL

Management should be kept informed of the extent of current outstanding damage claims, both against the organisation and in its favour. This implies that adequate and accurate management information systems are in place. This form of top-level data should be supported by comprehensive and up-to-date supporting records, so that the status of each claim, in both financial and legal terms, can be promptly and reliably ascertained. Controls should be in place to ensure that such records are complete and that all claims issued and received are captured and their significance reflected in the information system.

Records of the costs of pursuing and/or defending damage claims should be maintained and reported progressively in relation to amounts of damages awarded. The recovery of related costs may be permitted in certain circumstances. Amounts either received or paid in relation to claims should be confirmed as correct and to include all the required elements, for example the value of previous retention.

Damage claims should only be abandoned after careful analysis and appropriate senior management approval. Write off of costs should be subject to any prevailing accounting entry authority limits and conditions, and the relevant effects reported to management.

Control matrix example

An example *Objectives*-oriented matrix is provided as Table 29. The contents aim to represent a comprehensive examination of the relative issues, and the score data suggests a middle-level of significance. The example is not sector specific but an amalgam of general factors. *Scale* 30 has been used to support the *Type* scores, descriptions of the relative values are provided in Appendix 7. Chapter 32 provides the reader with a full explanation of the underlying matrix theory.

Table 29 Recovery of Damages – Objectives
Overall Inherent Risk (Size) Score [5 is worst risk; 1 is best] = 2.07

A Ensure that all damages due are recorded and recovered
B Ensure that all claims are accurate and realistic
C Ensure that all claims accord with contract/legislation
D Ensure claims are presented in the correct format/timescale
E Provide accurate & adequate supporting records
F Ensure that claims are settled economically & promptly
G Ensure that claims are subject to management authorisation

H Minimise the necessity to take claims through the courts
I Ensure contract conditions offer balanced claims approach
J Ensure conciliation or arbitration options are provided
K Ensure that the costs of pursuing claims are recovered
L Ensure working relationship is maintained with other party
M Provide accurate & timely management information
N Ensure decisions to abandon claims are valid and authorised

SCALE 30 (abridged)

6 = Strategically vital to the business or organisation
5 = Makes a contribution to business operations
4 = Contributes to reliability of data records and information
(Contract auditing Objectives-oriented scale)

3 = Avoids disruption/meets regulatory & accountability needs
2 = Leads to administrative/operational economies/efficiencies
1 = Generates administrative economies

Recovery of Damages		OBJECTIVES													
		A	B	C	D	E	F	G	H	I	J	K	L	M	N
		=	=	=	=	=	=	=	=	=	=	=	=	=	=
Calculated Risk Score:	Risk	3	3	3	3	2	3	2	3	3	3	2	2	2	2
Scale 30 (6 is most serious)	Type	5	4	4	4	3	4	3	5	5	4	4	5	5	4
Size (3 is maximum)	Size	2	2	2	2	2	2	2	2	2	2	1	1	1	1
MEASURES															
1 Records of all claims maintained as the basis for progressing and confirming settlement	Best	4					2								
	Test	?	?				?								
	Both														
2 All claims are assessed and valued by Contract Administrator per contract conditions/records	Best			5	4	3									
	Test	?		?	?	?									
	Both														
3 If necessary, claim circumstances are checked by Legal Dept. for validity of points, etc.	Best				4										
	Test	?			?										
	Both														
4 Procedures define the admin. requirements for preparing and presenting claims per contract	Best			3	4										
	Test	?		?	?										
	Both														
5 All claims are supported by relevant documentation, which is confirmed for accuracy	Best		2			4									
	Test	?	?			?									
	Both														
6 The status of all claims is regularly progressed by the Contract Administrator	Best						4								
	Test	?					?								
	Both														
7 Optimum method of progressing claims is chosen. Aim to settle by mutual agreement	Best						4					3			
	Test	?					?					?			
	Both														
8 Facts for all claims are presented to management for written authority to proceed	Best							4							
	Test	?						?							
	Both														
9 Failing mutual agreement, significant claims are referred for conciliation or arbitration	Best							3	4	4					
	Test	?						?	?	?					
	Both														

Table 29 continued

			A	B	C	D	E	F	G	H	I	J	K	L	M	N
			=	=	=	=	=	=	=	=	=	=	=	=	=	=
	Calculated Risk Score:	Risk	3	3	3	3	2	3	2	3	3	3	2	2	2	2
			–	–	–	–	–	–	–	–	–	–	–	–	–	–
10	Claims only taken to court if significant damages involved and case is strong	Best								4						
		Test	?							?						
		Both														
			–	–	–	–	–	–	–	–	–	–	–	–	–	–
11	Additional authority is required for court action to pursue claim	Best								4						
		Test	?							?						
		Both														
			–	–	–	–	–	–	–	–	–	–	–	–	–	–
12	Standard form of contract is utilised incorporating arbitration rules	Best								5	4					
		Test	?							?	?					
		Both														
			–	–	–	–	–	–	–	–	–	–	–	–	–	–
13	All associated costs are identified and recorded for each claim	Best										3				
		Test	?									?				
		Both														
			–	–	–	–	–	–	–	–	–	–	–	–	–	–
14	Costs for successful claims are recovered per contract conditions or via court	Best										4				
		Test	?									?				
		Both														
			–	–	–	–	–	–	–	–	–	–	–	–	–	–
15	Best interests of project taken into account during claim negotiations with other party	Best												4		
		Test	?											?		
		Both														
			–	–	–	–	–	–	–	–	–	–	–	–	–	–
16	Monthly management report is created from established claims records	Best													4	
		Test	?												?	
		Both														
			–	–	–	–	–	–	–	–	–	–	–	–	–	–
17	Claims only aborted when success is unlikely. Management authority required to abandon	Best														5
		Test	?													?
		Both														
			–	–	–	–	–	–	–	–	–	–	–	–	–	–

30

REVIEW OF PROJECT OUT-TURN AND PERFORMANCE

Scope

The process of undertaking a form of post-project review, is referred to by various terms, such as 'post-completion review', 'post-implementation review', 'project out-turn review', and so on. We are aware that some operational differences apply to these terms when applied by specific groups. However, for the sake of convenience, we have regarded all the relevant terms as being interchangeable throughout this text. In this chapter we discuss the justification, methods and benefits of conducting such a review.

Persuading management to undertake a post-completion review of a project can be difficult as they may adopt the view that the priorities lie with planning and applying new projects and ventures, not rummaging over the bones of past ones. Although acknowledging that resources can be limited and there is an overhead in undertaking such a review, the benefits can be considerable. This is especially true in organisations where the level of contract-related activity is either high or critical for successful operations. However, it is also necessary to consider the necessity for such reviews in relation to size and value of projects, and the costs associated with applying the review process.

Significant amounts of effort are expended in initially assessing the need for a project. Hopefully all this activity will be driven by realistic and critical business or operational objectives (*see also* Chapter 9 on project appraisal). In the commercial world, the continued existence of a company may be dependent upon the successful implementation of revised business operations linked to major projects or developments. If all this initial analysis and appraisal was deemed either necessary or crucial for the sake of the organisation, it logically follows that management should ensure that all their expectations and likely success factors were in fact achieved. Additionally, by examining the operation and results of projects, lessons can be learned which can be applied to subsequent projects to provide greater efficiency, improved control, etc. in the future. This latter point obviously has greater significance in organisations regularly involved in similar projects.

The success or otherwise of a review process can, in part, be dependent upon the spirit in which it is conducted and the management style in evidence within the organisation. The review should present a positive image, whereby lessons can be learnt and procedures can be enhanced. Staff morale can be adversely affected if the management tone determines that the review should be a post-mortem intended to root out errors and apportion blame. This type of negative approach is as self-defeating as the (hopefully) historical view of internal auditors as 'those sent in by management after the battle to bayonet the wounded'. The positive benefits of such reviews should be emphasised and the creation of a contributive environment encouraged. This does not preclude the honest appraisal of faults and a determination to avoid repeating the same mistakes again.

The critical factors that apply to the operations of one organisation are not automatically applicable to another. If these specific crucial elements are not clearly established and promoted as part of the corporate culture, the organisation has real problems. They can be linked intrinsically to all manner of sector specific matters, such as the market position occupied by the organisation, the prevailing economic conditions, or the sense of direction promoted by the government of the day.

Procedures may already exist which govern the complete project lifecycle, including the conduct of post-completion reviews. These frameworks should be organic in nature, that is progressively under review, subject to revision in light of changed business needs or experiences. The aim should be to enhance, refine and improve internal procedures so that future activities are more efficiently handled with the application of sensible and realistic controls. Additionally, in selected sectors compliance with statutory requirements forms part of the culture and therefore existing procedures should adequately address the current requirements.

Written policies and procedures for the conduct of post completion reviews should ideally be in place. These should define the conditions when a review is applicable. This may be determined with respect to the relative value of a project or its strategic importance to the organisation. In organisations with a formal approach to project assessment, projects may be stratified in proportion to the type and value of assets involved. In any event, where there is wide range of projects in evidence with limited review resources, the application of post completion reviews will need to be targeted in accordance with some form of stable policy perhaps driven by risk analysis considerations.

In summary terms, the prime purposes in undertaking a review of projects following their implementation are:

- to ensure that the project in question successfully achieved all the established performance, financial and timescale targets. These may include financial targets such as return on capital allocated or budgeted levels of revenue, etc. Alternatively, in the public services sector, the crucial measurements may relate to levels of service provision or the reduction in waiting time, etc.
- to reveal areas where existing practices may be improved so that future projects will benefit in terms of efficiency, value for money, control, regulatory compliance, and so on.

Before turning our attention to the type of processes that can be incorporated into post-project reviews, it should be stressed that the effectiveness of monitoring and management information systems in place during the lifetime of the project will also play an important role in ensuring that target objectives are attained (*see also* Chapter 18). The appraisal of project activities and performance should not be solely left to the end, it must be an ongoing process if adequate control is to be exercised over the project. This approach will avoid the discovery of matters of significance at the eleventh hour, when it is too late to effect adequate corrective action. In a perfect world, there should be no 'nasty surprises' revealed during the post-completion review if the preceding events have been subject to effective review, monitoring and control.

The quality of project documentation will play a crucial role in the smooth application of a review. Once the project team has been disbanded, accurately recreating previous situations can be impossible without supporting documentary trails. Operational, financial and other distinctive components will have a bearing on the optimum approach to post-completion reviews, for example whether all projects are examined, or only those exceeding a defined capital cost ceiling.

In the following sections we examine the areas and issues for possible inclusion into a project out-turn review. However, not all the factors listed will apply to every organisation or every project or contract. Therefore readers should have regard for their own operating environment when selecting the pertinent points. The headings below should not, in appropriate circumstances, be viewed in isolation, there are interrelated contents, therefore any duplication of the noted points is intentional on our part.

INTEGRITY OF INFORMATION

The availability of accurate and reliable data about a project is crucial, not only for the purposes of undertaking a post-completion review of the relevant project, but in order to monitor progress of key elements or indicators throughout the project lifecycle. If the required information is not created during the course of the project, there can be considerable problems (and costs) in generating it after the project has been concluded. This is especially true if the original project team has been disbanded.

It is possible that during the course of the review, questions are raised about the integrity and accuracy of project information. Findings of this sort should logically lead to improvements in the relevant record keeping, data analysis or management information processes. In the course of developing the necessary management information framework for the lifetime of the project, due regard should be paid to the back-end information needs. Such requirements may go beyond the simple analysis of existing data, and additional elements, such as the relative income created as a result of the project, may be essential.

It is vital that the sources of any information are reliable and complete, especially when management decisions may rest on the relevant data. Furthermore, the application of analysis techniques should incorporate safeguards over the continued accuracy of the data. Reconciling data back to the reliable source will partly serve this latter purpose, for example in the case of budget and financial data. The use of spreadsheets should be subject to controls ensuring that the information so presented is reliable and accurate.

It is equally important to ensure that the appropriate information is provided and that recipients are not overburdened with either an excess of data or irrelevant information. This can not only cloud the real issues but waste time. Both throughout the project lifecycle and during the post-completion review, information should be current and up to date. Arrangements should be established to provide any specific areas of information required for the post-review processes.

TIMING OF POST-PROJECT REVIEWS

The matter of timing will be conditional upon a number of factors, which may include the following:

- the timing of the income cycle for the related business or service activity
- the extent of capital investment and the anticipated pay-back period if relevant
- the period required to accrue sufficient data for appraisal
- the extent to which projects are subject to effective ongoing review during their lifecycle
- the level of resources available to undertake the review
- the degree of importance to the organisation represented by the relevant project
- whether a similar project is about to be initiated and the gathering of relevant facts may be especially pertinent
- the requirement to provide data to external bodies, for example in support of claims for financial assistance, grants, etc.
- any statutory reporting requirements.

There is no point in undertaking an extensive review of project out-turn unless the timing is correct, for example it may be true that insufficient performance information will be available for a meaningful review.

Where projects run over long periods, and the sums involved are significant, there may be a case for interim project reviews based upon updated assumptions and financial data. Although projects are unlikely to be abandoned as a consequence of such reviews, subtle changes may be incorporated which can improve the longer-term viability or profitability of the related activities. The application of this form of interim assessment should be conducted by management, and not internal audit. The work of internal audit should be independent of that applied by management, although audit review and system testing work may lead to recommendations being made to management for their consideration.

Where an organisation is regularly involved in projects, perhaps of a common type, the timing of reviews may take on additional significance if systems and procedures can be progressively improved and refined. For example, design processes may benefit from the changes that proved necessary during a previous project, especially where projects are similar in nature.

When considering the timing of reviews, account should be taken of appropriateness of timescale relevant to the business cycle of the related activities, and the standard forms of measurement that can be applied. Interwoven with this aspect, is the determination of a suitable period when suggested changes and modifications to all manner of factors can still be realistically incorporated. There is no point in reviewing the operation of a system, product or building, if it is too late to cost-effectively apply any lessons learnt from the review process.

In assessing when to undertake the review, management should consider all the appropriate and discrete factors. Once the optimum timing has been established, they also need to ensure that they provide a suitable documented procedural framework for the review process.

WHO SHOULD UNDERTAKE REVIEWS ?

The key issue here is whether the members of the review team should have been actively involved in the project under scrutiny. It boils down to objectivity versus knowledge of the specific project, and how the best interests of the organisation are to be served during the review process.

It is, of course, possible that those actively involved in the project will have fixed and potentially biased views of it. They may also be seen to have vested interests in the maintenance of certain viewpoints or situations. In practical terms, not all those actively involved in the project will still be available for the review process. For example, internal specialists may have been redeployed on other current projects or external consultants may no longer be engaged by the organisation. A key factor is whether or not it is essential for members of the review team to possess appropriate specialist knowledge in order to contribute effectively to the process. Alternatively, fresh and unbiased views may be more readily represented by members of staff outwith the project group. In the public sector, the inclusion of such individuals can further demonstrate a required degree of accountability.

Setting aside the above issues for a moment, the composition of the review team should attempt to strike a balance across the affected departments or disciplines and to involve all the required areas of expertise, such as finance, information technology, operations, and human resources. When forming the review team and examining the related procedures, it is necessary to ensure that the team is neither too large nor unwieldy, as this can prolong the timescale and generate irrelevant debate. The procedures should be clear as to the allocation of responsibilities and the definition of objectives for the review process. Needless to say positive management of the group will further support the efficient discharge of the defined responsibilities. Irrespective of the membership of the review team, they should be empowered to examine all the relevant documents and co-opt individuals with specific skills or knowledge.

Internal auditors should be primarily concerned with the effectiveness of management review systems in place and should resist becoming too willing to undertake a role in the control processes. If this were to be the case, management may rely on the auditor and abdicate their own prime responsibility to provide adequate control mechanisms. This proviso does not prevent auditors undertaking their own independent review of aspects of the project as a means of verifying the effectiveness of the established control systems.

FINANCIAL ASSESSMENT

If a controlled and prescribed project lifecycle is in evidence, the determination at an early stage of the relevant costs, benefits, investment levels, anticipated income, and so on should have been undertaken. As part of the process of justifying a project, all manner of key financial factors will have been identified, most of which are critical to either the success of the project or the achievement of strategically important corporate objectives.

Hopefully, adequate monitoring of the key financial aspects would have been in evidence throughout all the discrete stages of the project. Regular management information reports should have highlighted variations, trends, additional costs, etc. so that relevant action could be applied. If this ongoing process is effectively applied there should be no great surprises at the conclusion of a project. However, it may only be possible to bring together all the required financial data either at the conclusion of the project or after the resultant scheme, business or service has been in operation for a time. Actual cash flows and amended payback periods may exert an influence on embarking upon similar projects in the future.

In addition to the review of the up-front project costs, many projects relate to activities which have notable subsequent running costs. Once again, such costs may have been the subject of detailed appraisal prior to the project commencing and the design and solution selection procedure may have taken full account of running costs. Targets may have been established for running costs, and specific designs and technology applied to their achievement. For example, a building project may have to conform to energy usage or defined maintenance criteria. Whereas a software development project may have the objective of reducing staffing or training costs within a given timescale.

Actual running costs should be determined and compared to the expectations established at the initiation of the project. Action may be required if there are significant variations in achieving the targets. A contribution to additional costs, may be the failure of systems and equipment to either achieve the required performance level or to remain reliable in use. It may prove necessary to approach the supplier and obtain some form of redress if maintenance requirements are excessive.

The organisation may only be permitted to secure the payment of grants and other aid at the conclusion of the contracted stages. Alternatively, only after a period of operation, during which income is being generated, can meaningful measurement of success (or otherwise) be practical. The reasons behind cost over-runs may point to the need to improve procedures and controls, and there should be a feedback loop into the review or strengthening of existing procedures.

Where net running costs are affected by levels of usage or patronage, and these have fallen below the anticipated levels determined at the feasibility stage, management may need to take action. The ability of the organisation to accurately predict all manner of key statistics may be called into question when assessing the actual data against expectations, therefore it may be necessary to revise the planning procedures so that trends can be more accurately predicted in future.

REVIEWING CHANGES APPLIED DURING THE PROJECT

At the commencement of a project involving contracted elements, the organisation may be assured that they have accurately prepared the necessary designs, specifications and associated costings as a suitable foundation for all that follows. However, there is a certain inevitability about subsequent change, especially in complex or innovative projects. It is not always possible to predetermine all eventualities, and some changes may be brought about by forces beyond the control of either the employer or contractor. As discussed elsewhere (*see* Chapter 24) changes should be carefully controlled, costed, justified and implemented. Documentary trails should be provided incorporating the necessary evidence of authorisations and implications upon the targeted objectives of the project including financial considerations. Any unexplained variances will require investigation, but not purely in the context of apportioning blame.

Are there any lessons to be learnt from analysing the changes that had to be applied? Can future occurrences be avoided by improving the procedures governing the design and specification stages of comparable projects?

THE ACHIEVEMENT OF KEY PROJECT OBJECTIVES

Each project will have a number of defined target objectives identified at the outset. The way in which an organisation signifies their objectives will depend upon their sector or sphere of operations. A limited company may regard the achievement of the project within tightly defined cost constraints as a key objective. A public authority, although no doubt also having due regard for cost containment, may be statutorily obliged to effectively address the provision of a prescribed level of service by means of a contracted development. The forms of measurement that can be applied to determining the success or otherwise of a project will be variable and sector specific.

In the public sector the review should identify if all the required performance, service provision, financial, and other targets will be achieved following the completion of the relevant project. In addition, it may also be necessary to ensure that the assumptions and driving criteria which supported the initiation of the project or scheme are accurate and justified.

The criteria for instigating a project may have included an objective to reduce operational costs by providing either a new facility, building or computer system. In this context it is necessary to subsequently assess whether the proposed savings are actually being achieved.

Project objectives may be time critical, for instance the necessity to launch a business venture supported by a new computer system before a competitor can enter the same market, or in the public sector where one of a number of like building projects has to be available for occupation by a specified time in order to be eligible for development grants. A review of the performance of the contractor in this regard may result in influencing decisions about either continuing with the similar projects or utilising the services of the same supplier or contractor in the future. The review should compare the intended timetable for key events against that achieved, documentation should already exist which provides explanation and support for failure to meet deadlines. The reasons will need to be analysed and any necessary administrative improvements recommended and implemented.

There is a probability that during the course of longer projects and developments, some of the critical driving factors may have changed, perhaps beyond the control of both the employer and the contractor. There is no substitute for ongoing monitoring of key business and service provision criteria which would enable organisations to maintain a flexibility in their planning. A consequence of such monitoring may be that project plans are put on ice until the conditions once again become more suitable for the relevant project to proceed. However, it may transpire that significant changes may be apparent at the conclusion of the project which will have a bearing upon the ongoing performance of the scheme. Such influences may require management action to ensure that the current situation is maximised.

Predictions of revenue generation and income forecasts with a bearing upon projects can be subject to grave overestimation, unless they are based upon reliable and relevant sources. Grossly different figures or projections at the conclusion of a project can suggest that the in-house research facilities need to be reviewed.

Where a project has implications for customers or others outwith the organisation, their views may have to be taken into account when assessing the success factors. In situations where services are being provided to end-users or customers, the quality of that service may be critical to the ongoing viability of the venture. Finally in this section, the findings relevant to meeting the objectives of a specific project may be pertinent to other project proposals in the pipeline, and there should be an obvious connection established so that any lessons learnt are passed on and heeded.

REVIEWING CONTRACTUAL MATTERS

Whether or not the organisation is regularly involved in the use of contracts, it is possible that particular experiences with a form of contract may influence the future choice of contracts, for example, if it is concluded that there could be improvements in the manner that the contractor's responsibilities are defined based upon recently encountered difficulties. Management will be interested to assess the flexibility and effectiveness of contract conditions and clauses in light of specific incidents such as contractual claims, and price fluctuation adjustments. They may conclude that it is preferable to utilise different forms of contract in the future.

The contract administration requirements, for example in relation to handling tendering processes or documentation trails, may have to be considered as a means of improving future efficiency. In addition to assessing the 'performance' of the type of contract in the particular project, management may also seek reassurance that the existing internal contract administration arrangements ensure, *inter alia*, that their obligations are correctly discharged in accordance with the prescribed timetables.

PERFORMANCE OF PROJECT TEAM AND EXTERNAL CONSULTANTS

This part of the review should not be approached in a punitive context, but in a positive way as a means to improve procedures and identify either training or personal development needs. The specific points relevant to external consultants are addressed separately below.

The approach to adopt when reviewing this aspect will depend on whether project management was a recurring requirement within the organisation and members of staff were regularly involved in like activities. The existence and application of project management procedures will also have a significant bearing, especially if they cater for ongoing monitoring of progress by management. The relevance and effectiveness of existing procedures should be questioned where necessary, and suitable revisions implemented if required. Alternatively, staff may not be correctly applying the required procedures, suggesting the need for appropriate training.

Where the project involves a multidisciplined team, perhaps involving external consultants and professionals, the maintenance of good working relationships can be crucial to progress. In the case of building or civil engineering projects, relationships with the contractor's staff are often pivotal.

With regard to external consultants, the degree to which they are subject to performance review should be relative to the extent of their role in the project (*see also* Chapter 10 for more details concerning the engagement of consultants). In the case of a construction project, perhaps on behalf of a public authority, the consultant can play a key role in the design and management of the development or scheme. Given his pivotal role in such cases the consultant, who may be an engineer or architect, should be the subject of a similar review to that applied to the contractor.

The consultant has the ability to ensure that a project runs on time, within cost, with the minimum of changes to the design, and conforms to the required technical and workmanship standards. Besides his obvious technical competence, the consultant also requires excellent communication and interpersonal skills. He needs to establish good working relationships with employers, their representatives, the contractor and his staff. The ability to meet deadlines is crucial, especially when others, such as tradesmen, are dependent upon the consultant providing the relevant directions, drawings, and specifications. The performance of the consultant may be further justified if he is to be considered for any future project assignments.

ASSESSING THE PERFORMANCE OF CONTRACTORS

Any assessment of a contractor should include both operational and financial considerations. Most of the key operational issues are normally defined in the contract, such as target completion/delivery dates, costs, required technical standards, required functionality, quality of workmanship or finish, and so on. Assessment can, in part, be a matter of measuring actual performance as supported by site records, project management documentation, etc. against the specified expectations in the contract.

Events that occurred during the course of the project which either had some form of notable impact or were abnormally frequent should also be taken into account. The employer's representatives, such as the project manager, should apply ongoing monitoring of key processes and participants throughout the project.

Financial consideration will often be consequent upon either failures to achieve operational targets or compliance with technical requirements. Ongoing management monitoring throughout the project should identify shortcomings or problems, and contain any related effects.

In appropriate organisations, notably in the public sector, approved lists of contractors are maintained. Although inclusion on such a list should be conditional on a range of parameters, the performance of a contractor during a previous contract may have a bearing on whether the contractor continues to be included (*see* Chapters 12 and 13 regarding the assessment of contractors and the maintenance of approved lists respectively). Any relevant points should be documented and taken into account when assessing whether a contractor is suitable for consideration for similar or future projects.

Other questions may also apply:

- Within the confines of the contract, did the contractor appear to overindulge in proposing claims?

- Were good working relationships apparent between the contractor, the employer and any supervising professional (e.g. the consulting engineer)? On construction projects, the contractor should ensure that staffing levels and site supervision are adequate.
- Was there evidence of frequent or unreasonable delays being caused by the contractor or his staff?
- Were there delays in the supply of necessary contract information?
- Was the plant and equipment provided by the contractor reliable and suitable for the purpose?

ASSESSING THE EFFECTIVENESS, PRACTICALITY AND EFFICIENCY OF ALL PROCEDURES

One spin-off of the review process is that any shortcomings in the existing procedures can be pinpointed, so enabling them to be improved. Some processes or procedural requirements may prove to be non-starters in terms of the cost of application, the effectiveness of the process, or the absence of the required data. This offers the opportunity to rationalise and improve procedures and guidelines. A particular procedure may be very worthwhile if correctly applied, the problem may be that staff are not correctly applying it. This could suggest that further training is required.

The overall review of projects can flush out all manner of procedural matters which can be improved, supplemented or even disregarded. The review of the organisation's procedures should be a continuous process and take account of all the environmental, commercial and economic changes that are taking place. Procedures that are out of date or out of touch can be disregarded by staff along with those that are still relevant and important; they can create a stale and ineffective control environment. Take steps to cut out the dead wood and nurture a core of good practices.

The administrative processes should be appraised for their effectiveness. Considerable administrative activity is associated with contracting, much of it related to adequacy, availability and accuracy of documentation such as technical drawings and supporting specifications. Inaccuracies and delays in preparing these documents can obviously affect the progress of the contract. Throughout the lifetime of the contract significant administrative problems or delays should be noted, and the related procedures earmarked for review.

CONCLUSIONS AND REPORTING METHODS

If the prevailing project reporting arrangements are adequate throughout the life of a project, and management are regularly supplied with accurate and up-to-date management information about progress, costs, etc. there should be no cataclysmic revelations emerging from the post-project review. However, important lessons for the future can be revealed.

Management will need to know whether the project 'hit the targets' or not. If not, they also need to know by what extent did they fail, and what is being done about the problems that have been revealed. Recommendations may need to be addressed to management for ratification and subsequent action. A mechanism should be in place to ensure that accepted recommendations are, in fact, actioned correctly. Specific sectors may have further statutory reporting obligations to consider.

Control matrix example

The example matrix provided as Table 30 features the likely *Objectives* that would be set by management for undertaking a post-completion review. Basically they are seeking to confirm that the contract/project attained the relevant targets and that the prevailing administrative mechanisms positively contributed to that process. Where shortcomings are apparent they should be addressed by refining the related procedures. *Scale* 30 has been used in the example and the contents of this ladder are contained in Appendix 7.

Table 30 Out-turn and Performance Review – Objectives

Overall Inherent Risk (Size) Score [5 is worst risk; 1 is best] = 2.83

A Ensure the achievement! of all contract/project objectives
B Ensure procedures & policies are optimised & up to date
C Ensure procedures are modified to cater for shortcomings
D Ensure contract obligations are satisfactorily discharged
E Confirm the accuracy & suitability of accounting system
F Confirm the accuracy/reliability of management information
G Confirm the adequacy of project/contract management methods
H Ensure that contracts are completed on time & within budget
I Ensure quality & standards issues are correctly addressed
J Ensure that non-standard events were justified & authorised
K Ensure the most appropriate form of contract is utilised
L Ensure legal & regulatory requirements are correctly met
M Enable comprehensive appraisal of contractor performance
N Enable comprehensive appraisal of consultant performance
O Ensure that records & documentation are accurate & adequate
P Ensure all findings are reported, authorised & implemented
Q Ensure that all outstanding contract matters are resolved
R Identify staff training and development requirements

Scale 30 (abridged)

6 = Strategically vital to the business or organisation
5 = Makes a contribution to business operations
4 = Contributes to reliability of data, records and information
(Contract auditing Objectives-oriented scale)

3 = Avoids disruption/meets regulatory & accountability needs
2 = Leads to administrative/operational economies/efficiencies
1 = Generates administrative economies

Out-turn/Performance Review			OBJECTIVES																	
			A	B	C	D	E	F	G	H	I	J	K	L	M	N	O	P	Q	R
			=	=	=	=	=	=	=	=	=	=	=	=	=	=	=	=	=	=
	Calculated Risk Score:	Risk	4	3	3	3	3	3	3	3	3	2	3	3	3	3	3	3	3	2
			–	–	–	–	–	–	–	–	–	–	–	–	–	–	–	–	–	–
	Scale 30 (6 is most serious)	Type	6	3	3	5	6	6	5	6	6	4	5	4	4	4	5	5	4	3
	Size (3 is maximum)	Size	3	3	3	2	2	2	2	2	1	2	2	3	2	2	2	2	3	2
	MEASURES	—	–	–	–	–	–	–	–	–	–	–	–	–	–	–	–	–	–	–
1	Contract outcomes compared to objectives & targets. Achievement confirmed & shortcomings noted	Best	4																	
		Test	?	?																
		Both																		
		—	–	–	–	–	–	–	–	–	–	–	–	–	–	–	–	–	–	–
2	Procedures reviewed for their effectiveness. Improvements proposed where justified	Best			4	4														
		Test	?		?	?														
		Both																		
		—	–	–	–	–	–	–	–	–	–	–	–	–	–	–	–	–	–	–
3	Monitoring applied during life of contract to ensure that all obligations are met	Best		3			4		3	4	3									
		Test	?	?			?		?	?	?									
		Both																		
		—	–	–	–	–	–	–	–	–	–	–	–	–	–	–	–	–	–	–
4	Problems/shortfalls reported to management for authority and resolution	Best					3													
		Test	?				?													
		Both																		
		—	–	–	–	–	–	–	–	–	–	–	–	–	–	–	–	–	–	–
5	Claims raised & damages sought in respect of contractor's failure to meet obligations	Best					4													
		Test	?				?													
		Both																		
		—	–	–	–	–	–	–	–	–	–	–	–	–	–	–	–	–	–	–
6	Performance & reliability of accounting data assessed. Improvements suggested	Best					4													
		Test	?				?													
		Both																		
		—	–	–	–	–	–	–	–	–	–	–	–	–	–	–	–	–	–	–
7	Data reconciled to source and entry input is subject to appropriate authorisation	Best					4	4												
		Test	?				?	?												
		Both																		
		—	–	–	–	–	–	–	–	–	–	–	–	–	–	–	–	–	–	–
8	Problems/shortcomings with management processes reported and improvements applied	Best								5										
		Test	?							?										
		Both																		
		—	–	–	–	–	–	–	–	–	–	–	–	–	–	–	–	–	–	–
9	Progress of contract is monitored & managed. Problems are reported and solved	Best								4										
		Test	?							?										
		Both																		
		—	–																	

Table 30 continued

#	Description	Type	A	B	C	D	E	F	G	H	I	J	K	L	M	N	O	P	Q	R
			=	=	=	=	=	=	=	=	=	=	=	=	=	=	=	=	=	=
	Calculated Risk Score:	Risk	4	3	3	3	3	3	3	3	2	3	3	3	3	3	3	3	3	2
			–	–	–	–	–	–	–	–	–	–	–	–	–	–	–	–	–	–
10	The possibility of excess costs is identified at the time and authority obtained to proceed	Best								4										
		Test	?							?										
		Both																		
			–	–	–	–	–	–	–	–	–	–	–	–	–	–	–	–	–	–
11	Requirements are clearly defined in contract. Project Manager to certify satisfaction	Best	3			3				3	3									
		Test	?	?		?				?	?									
		Both																		
			–	–	–	–	–	–	–	–	–	–	–	–	–	–	–	–	–	–
12	Technical & Quality matters are subject to inspection & sign off by experienced manager	Best								4										
		Test	?							?										
		Both																		
			–	–	–	–	–	–	–	–	–	–	–	–	–	–	–	–	–	–
13	All variations, extensions of time, etc. are subject to reporting and authorisation	Best									5									
		Test	?								?									
		Both																		
			–	–	–	–	–	–	–	–	–	–	–	–	–	–	–	–	–	–
14	Suitability of form of contract is assessed in light of problems & approach modified as required	Best										5								
		Test	?									?								
		Both																		
			–	–	–	–	–	–	–	–	–	–	–	–	–	–	–	–	–	–
15	Legal Dept. monitors/manages all compliance issues. Problems are reported for action	Best											4							
		Test	?										?							
		Both																		
			–	–	–	–	–	–	–	–	–	–	–	–	–	–	–	–	–	–
16	All relevant events are assessed including meeting targets, etc. Approved list amended	Best											4	4						
		Test	?										?	?						
		Both																		
			–	–	–	–	–	–	–	–	–	–	–	–	–	–	–	–	–	–
17	Delays & errors caused by the inadequacy of documentation are reviewed. Amendments suggested	Best														4				
		Test	?													?				
		Both																		
			–	–	–	–	–	–	–	–	–	–	–	–	–	–	–	–	–	–
18	Documentation requirements and standards defined in contract administration procedures	Best														4				
		Test														?				
		Both																		
			–	–	–	–	–	–	–	–	–	–	–	–	–	–	–	–	–	–
19	Report issued to management. Recommendations considered, approved & implemented	Best															5			
		Test															?			
		Both																		
			–	–	–	–	–	–	–	–	–	–	–	–	–	–	–	–	–	–
20	Records maintained of all outstanding issues for subsequent management attention	Best																	5	
		Test																	?	
		Both																		
			–	–	–	–	–	–	–	–	–	–	–	–	–	–	–	–	–	–
21	Resource/training needs are identified & plans drawn up and authorised by management	Best																		5
		Test																		?
		Both																		
			–																		

31

MAINTENANCE OBLIGATIONS

Scope

This chapter relates to the contractor's obligations after the completion of the project to address any shortcoming, faults, or defects in his work and to make good any problems with workmanship. Although the contents concentrate upon examples relative to the building industry, similar arrangements could be applied to other activities.

As a building project progresses, each significant or defined stage is certified as correctly and appropriately completed in accordance with the requirements of the design and the contract. The performance of the contractor is monitored and the quality of all work, including that undertaken by sub-contractors, is checked for compliance with the technical specification and the required standards of workmanship and finish. This principle of ongoing quality review and control can also apply to non-construction scenarios, and may be very relevant when staged payments are to be made.

The tender documentation and the relative form of contract employed will inevitably contain references to the maintenance (or defects liability) period. The maintenance period is the period running from the date of substantial or practical completion, and usually lasts between six and twelve months. The date of substantial or practical completion is determined and certified by either the architect or engineer.

If there are any outstanding works or matters requiring the contractor's attention, these are noted by the architect on the certificate. The contractor is normally obliged to attend to these listed matters as soon as possible or within any defined timescales permitted within the conditions of contract. When the matters are satisfactorily addressed, the architect will issue a certificate of completion of making good defects.

A non-building sector example would be the development of a bespoke software application development, during which the employer or project team representative should record any shortcomings or problems related to the agreed specification of requirements. Any remedies or solutions to the recorded problems should be adequately tested and their effectiveness confirmed. The creation of such solutions should be at the contractor's expense as part of his contractual obligation to deliver a system in accordance with the base specification. This assumes that any new or amended user requirements have been separately dealt with. At the point of completion or when the contractor submits his account, it is possible that there will still be some outstanding matters. In this case the employer should withhold full settlement until such time as all anomalies have been resolved.

It should also be noted that a percentage of the contract value may be retained by the employer until all the maintenance obligations of the contractor have been discharged. This provides further security for the employer against the risks of the contractor defaulting with regard to the contract conditions.

The liability for the costs of identified work may be in question. The architect or engineer will determine if the problem, defect or shortcoming is due either to the failure of the contractor to conform to the contract requirements, the workmanship of the tradesmen employed by the contractor, the inappropriate or incorrect use of materials, or some other reason beyond the control and influence of the contractor. Where the cause of the problem requiring rectification is due, in some part, to the failure of the contractor, the costs of remedying the situation are borne by the contractor. Alternatively, if the cause is outwith the responsibility of the contractor, for instance action taken by the architect, the employer will have to meet the additional costs himself. Where there is evidence that faulty or substandard materials or goods had been provided by suppliers, consideration should be given to obtaining appropriate reparation from the supplier.

The more common standard forms of contract contain a number of clauses appertaining to matters of completion, maintenance obligations, and related protocols, as follows:

Contract form	*Clause(s)*
JCT80	17 (Clause 17.4 specifically relates to the certificate of completion of making good defects)
ICE 6th Edition	49, 50 and 61
C1030 (GC/Works 1)	32 and 34.2
MF/1	26, 28 and 36.

When invoking the mechanisms permitted under the above-noted clauses, the relevant party should ensure that all the necessary conditions have been met.

The benefits of having comprehensive and accurate design and specification documentation are obvious when commencing a project, as they can provide the basis for assessing the contractor's compliance in the course of construction. Additionally, all manner of prescribed site and project records will, if adequately maintained, aid the process of determining the stage of progress achieved and those matters that are outstanding.

During any period of maintenance there should be ongoing communication between the contractor and the supervising professional as to progress and problems. Without this form of dialogue, outstanding items and problems may only be apparent at the eleventh hour.

If there are still outstanding works remaining at the end of the maintenance period, an estimate of the costs associated with addressing such items will be made by the architect, consultant or engineer. This value can then be deducted by the employer from any retention sums due to the contractor. Unless all the required work is conducted by the contractor in the permitted timescale, the employer can legitimately arrange for this work to be conducted and the costs recovered subsequently from the contractor.

Beyond the satisfactory rectification of defects, there may be the necessity to arrange some form of ongoing maintenance cover. These matters are not further discussed here, but Chapter 3 looks at the general issues surrounding service contracts, and Chapter 5 includes comments concerning information technology maintenance topics.

Control matrix example

Table 31 contains an *Exposures*-oriented example matrix reflecting the potential risks associated with maintenance obligations together with some sample controls designed to counter or reduce the related effects. In common with most other exposure-oriented matrices, not all the consequences of the exposure are defined. This is partly due to limited space in the appropriate text field, but most of the consequences are self-evident and relate to additional costs, disruption or general failure to achieve the required functionality or performance to support a business activity.

The example utilises *Scale* 31 values for the *Type* score. Descriptions in support of *Scale* 31 values are contained in Appendix 7.

Table 31 Maintenance Obligations – Exposures

Overall Inherent Risk (Size) Score [5 is worst risk; 1 is best] = 2.36

A Failure to rectify fault, defects, performance shortcomings
B Costs of engaging other contractors to resolve defects
C Failure to clearly identify all faults & advise contractor
D Form of contract does not cater for rectification of faults
E Failure to ensure achievement of technical/quality standard
F Outstanding problems at the end of the maintenance period

G Failure to establish the liability for rectification costs
H Additional faults apparent during subsequent occupation/use
I Failure to retain adequate value during maintenance period
J Failure to seize retention when contractor defaults
K Costs arising from inadequate specification or materials

SCALE 31 (abridged)

6 = Incorrect identification of needs, or failure to meet them
5 = Lost business; needs partly unfulfilled; or breach of rules
4 = Delay or disruption; reputation loss, minor breach of rules
(Contract auditing Exposures-oriented scale)

3 = Avoidable costs/losses; damage to contract relationships
2 = Administrative or accounting errors
1 = Detectable negative impact on the business or service

Maintenance Obligations		EXPOSURES										
		A	B	C	D	E	F	G	H	I	J	K
		=	=	=	=	=	=	=	=	=	=	=
Calculated Risk Score:	Risk	3	2	3	3	3	3	3	2	2	2	3
Scale 31 (6 is most serious)	Type	6	3	4	6	6	4	5	3	3	3	5
Size (3 is maximum)	Size	2	2	2	2	2	2	2	1	2	2	2
CONTROLS												
1 Contract used incorporates conditions for rectifying faults in specified maintenance period	Best	4			5			3		2	2	
	Test	?	?		?			?		?	?	
	Both											
2 If contractor fails to rectify faults, contract allows costs to be recovered from contractor	Best		4				4					
	Test	?	?				?					
	Both											
3 Faults & problems are documented throughout project & officially reported to contractor to action	Best			5								
	Test	?		?								
	Both											
4 All technical/quality matters are monitored & signed off by Engineer during the project	Best					5						
	Test	?				?						
	Both											
5 Contract conditions clearly specify liability for rectifying faults in various circumstances	Best							4	2			
	Test	?						?	?			
	Both											
6 Significant problems are assessed & liability defined (i.e. design, materials. etc.)	Best								2			3
	Test	?							?			?
	Both											
7 Action taken to seek redress from the responsible party	Best								3			
	Test	?							?			
	Both											
8 Retention value calculated per contract conditions & sector best practice	Best									3		
	Test	?								?		
	Both											
9 Additional costs are offset by retention value	Best		3				3				4	
	Test	?	?				?				?	
	Both											

Table 31 continued

			A	B	C	D	E	F	G	H	I	J	K
			=	=	=	=	=	=	=	=	=	=	=
	Calculated Risk Score:	Risk	3	2	3	3	3	3	3	2	2	2	3
			–	–	–	–	–	–	–	–	–	–	–
10	Action is taken to recover damages from relevant party. (designer, architect, builder)	Best											4
		Test											?
		Both											
—			–										

A Failure to rectify fault, defects, performance shortcomings
B Costs of engaging other contractors to resolve defects
C Failure to clearly identify all faults & advise contractor
D Form of contract does not cater for rectification of faults
E Failure to ensure achievement of technical/quality standard
F Outstanding problems at the end of the maintenance period
G Failure to establish the liability for rectification costs
H Additional faults apparent during subsequent occupation/use
I Failure to retain adequate value during maintenance period
J Failure to seize retention when contractor defaults
K Costs arising from inadequate specification or materials

SCALE 31 (abridged)

6 = Incorrect identification of needs, or failure to meet them
5 = Lost business; needs partly unfulfilled; or breach of rules
4 = Delay or disruption; reputation loss, minor breach of rules
(Contract auditing Exposures-oriented scale)

3 = Avoidable costs/losses; damage to contract relationships
2 = Administrative or accounting errors
1 = Detectable negative impact on the business or service

Part V

RISK ANALYSIS TECHNIQUES IN CONTRACT AUDITING

32

UNDERSTANDING CONTROL MATRICES

Scope

In Chapter 33 we will examine the development of audit risk formulae to assist in determining the appropriate amount of audit resource to be allocated to each contracting auditable unit, that is to each potential audit of a contract or contract sub-system. That would be the technique we would recommend to be used when drawing up a future programme of audits to be conducted. In this chapter we explain the theory and practice of the matrix technique which we have applied in Chapters 7 to 31 – each of those chapters includes an example control matrix. In working through this chapter readers may wish to refer to some of those control matrices. The control matrix technique can be used as an aid within *any audit in order to identify the principal risk areas within the activity which is subject to audit so as to enable the audit resources being expended on that auditable unit to be applied to best effect.*

Perhaps the easiest way to understand the purpose of this matrix technique is to consider that it replaces the internal control questionnaire (ICQ) or internal control evaluation questionnaire (ICEQ). It is ideally designed before the audit fieldwork commences and completed early in the fieldwork so as to provide a means of assessing the control problems and determining the further audit work to be done and the points to be made to management in the audit report.

Control matrices may be designed so that they are oriented positively *in that they are addressing management's* objectives; *alternatively they may be oriented* negatively *in that they address* exposures. *We explain the distinctions between these two styles of matrix later in this chapter. Due to limitations of space within this book we have restricted ourselves to one matrix for each of Chapters 7 to 31 – either* objectives *or* exposures *oriented.*

Audit resources are invariably scarce. This is partly because the scope of auditing has broadened and partly the complexity and scale of businesses has increased. It is also to do with the accelerating pace of change in modern businesses. It may also be because audit resources have been scaled down – even though in many cases there are now regulatory requirements for internal audit where there were none before. Whether or not this means that auditing is less effective today depends in part upon whether audit professionalism has improved so as to rise to these challenges. Certainly auditors need effective techniques to identify high risk areas so as to be able to focus their scarce resources where the potential to benefit from audit is greatest, and in order to be able to quickly draw to management's attention where improvements are most needed. In times when auditors have to be highly selective in what they review, it is also helpful to have documented justification for their assessment of risk which determined the focus of their work.

INTERNAL CONTROL QUESTIONNAIRES

Within an audit auditors have traditionally used the internal control questionnaire to point up the areas of control weakness. In essence the ICQ was a list of 'key' questions, the answers to which could be interpreted by the auditor to indicate whether there were control weaknesses. So the questions were answered early in the audit fieldwork and the remainder of the audit time would be spent probing the identified areas of weakness and working up recommendations for improving control to put before management.

The ICQ was a vague and voluminous tool. The technique of the ICQ generally did not address effectively any of the following which the control matrix technique explained later in this chapter has been designed to achieve:

- The ICQ did not specifically relate particular controls to particular objectives or exposures.
- The ICQ did not show that individual controls have a different potential degree of effectiveness.
- The ICQ forced yes/no answers about compliance with controls when in reality partial compliance is more common, and partial compliance is better than no compliance at all.
- The ICQ did not combine the potential for a control to be effective with the extent to which it was being complied with in order to give a measure of the control's actual effectiveness in a particular instance.
- The ICQ did not highlight the existence and effect of compensating controls (where one working control compensates for the failure of another) or redundant controls (where control procedures fulfil no purpose even though they may be complied with religiously).
- The ICQ did not allow for some objectives being inherently more important than others (or some exposures being inherently more potentially damaging than others).
- The completed ICQ gave no summary of its implications. Interpretation by the auditor of the significance of control weaknesses was difficult. It was a poor tool to use as a basis to draft the audit report.

USING SPREADSHEET SOFTWARE TO DESIGN CONTROL MATRICES

Spreadsheets provide an excellent opportunity to design control matrices so as to explore the relationships between exposures and controls in more precise and useful ways than ICQs permitted, although the first uses of control matrices predated the development of spreadsheet software.[1]

THE 'COMPLETENESS AND ACCURACY OF FINAL ACCOUNTS' EXAMPLE TO ILLUSTRATE THE MATRIX TECHNIQUE

The rest of this chapter provides an explanation of the control matrix technique using, for clarity of the illustration, a very small example of a matrix with only five *exposures* and six *controls*. The contract auditing topic selected for this illustration is the contracting sub-system 'Completeness and Accuracy of Final Accounts'. In practice the control matrix for this subject would probably be significantly larger – with more *exposures* and more *controls*. Chapter 28 gives a more realistic example of a control matrix for the audit of this contracting sub-system. The size of the matrix is dictated by the size of the system being analysed and by the level of detail to which the auditor wishes to take the subject. In general too much detail is counter-productive as it tends to conceal the major issues.

The orientation of the example in this chapter is *negative* in that it deals with *exposures* and *controls*. The technique described works just as well *positively* with management's *objectives* across the top axis and the *measures* which should be in place to improve management's opportunities to achieve their objectives being shown as the vertical axis. There are examples in this book which are designed positively. Some auditable units lend themselves to being dealt with in terms of exposures if management really have no objectives with regard to those activities other than to avoid unwanted consequences. Other auditable units can be oriented positively or negatively and to some extent different issues will be addressed by the matrix depending upon the orientation.

EXPOSURES AND CONTROLS

Table 32.1 shows just five illustrative *exposures* and six illustrative *controls*. The *exposures* and *controls* may not necessarily strike the reader as fitting his or her perception of managing the completeness and accuracy of final accounts within their enterprise – each user of this technique should tailor the matrix to their needs. Similarly, other entries in the matrix may not necessarily be appropriate to a particular enterprise.

Exposures are unwanted outcomes which management should endeavour to avoid. *Controls* are the procedures which should be in place to reduce or even to entirely eliminate the risk of the exposures. It is apparent from Table 32.1 that there are points of intersection between each exposure and each control which we shall use numerically later in this chapter to measure the effectiveness of each control over each exposure.

ALLOWING FOR DIFFERING DEGREES OF IMPORTANCE OF EXPOSURES

While this example has identified five potential exposures, some may be more important than others and it would be preferable that the amount of audit attention given to an exposure should be varied according to its importance. Before this can be achieved it is necessary to measure each exposure's importance. The degree of importance of an exposure is a function of its *inherent risk* to the enterprise adjusted by the extent to which it is under control (*control risk*). This parallels the approach we take to audit needs assessment in Chapter 33. We discuss control risk later in this chapter.

The way this technique allows for *inherent risk* is illustrated in Tables 32.2 and 32.3. Towards the top of Table 32.2 two dimensions of *inherent risk* are catered for. First what is called a *Scale* or *Type* score. To provide this score for each exposure, Table 32.3 is used as if it were a ladder. Keeping the nature of the exposure in mind the ladder is climbed from the bottom rung and the rung number is selected which applies to the highest category of risk that in all likelihood this exposure represents; it is that number which appears in the *Scale* or *Type* row of the matrix in Table 32.2. Once again, the reader may not necessarily concur with all of the judgements which have been made in designing this control matrix – to some extent they are dependent upon an assumed business environment which may differ from the reader's.

The second dimension of inherent risk is its *Size* ranking (Table 32.2). This is a simple three-point scale where the chosen value indicates the auditor's judgement of the likely size of the unwanted outcome which was selected in the *Scale* row for a particular exposure. So the *Scale* score needs to be selected before the *Size* ranking can be determined.

Several different categories on the ladder given in Table 32.3 may be applicable to a particular exposure. In general the one which represents the highest rung on the scale should be selected and recorded on the matrix. To be more precise, the *Scale* and *Size* scores should be considered to be linked and an applicable pair which together represents the highest number (when the chosen *Scale* and *Size* are multiplied together) should be chosen. Thus, for instance, if an exposure could be either the fourth or fifth rungs of the ladder and of large or medium probable size respectively, then the *Scale* score selected should be 4 as four multiplied by the relevant *Size* score of 3 results in a higher value than the alternative (5 multiplied by 2 for medium size).

CALCULATING INITIAL RISK

Now that we have determined the two dimensions of inherent risk we can calculate the initial overall *Risk* score for each of the exposures. This has been done towards the top of Table 32.4 where a score of 4 indicates the most important category of risk and a score of 1 would mean that the risk was insignificantly low. The formula used to produce this *Risk* score is given later in this chapter. For the moment this *Risk* score disregards control as no assumptions have yet been made as to whether or not the controls are effective or being complied with. So the *Risk* score on Table 32.4 is based on inherent risk only.

MEASURING CONTROL

Table 32.5 starts to develop the procedure for measuring *Control*. There are three measures of control where each control intersects with each exposure:

- *Best* The extent to which the control has the potential to reduce or entirely eliminate the exposure – assuming it was always being followed by management, staff (and perhaps others such as outside business partners including contractors) exactly as intended. A score of 5 would mean that this control would entirely eliminate the exposure if it was being followed by management, staff and others all the time exactly as intended. A score of 0 means it would have no effect even if it was being followed completely all the time.
- *Test* The extent to which this control *is* being complied with. A score of 5 means 100 per cent compliance. A score of 2 corresponds to 40 per cent compliance. A score of 0 means no compliance.
- *Both* A combination of the best (B) and the test (T) scores using the formula:

$$B - (5 - T) = \text{both score}$$

Table 32.6 gives illustrative *Best* control scores for the extent to which each control has the potential to reduce each exposure. The calculated risk scores remain unchanged from Tables 32.4 and 32.5 since Table 32.6 makes no assumptions that there is any compliance with any of these controls.

COMPLIANCE TESTING

Finally, Table 32.7 gives sample compliance (i.e. *Test*) scores. It is only these *Test* scores which have to be entered during the fieldwork of the audit. The control matrix designed before the outset of the audit fieldwork would contain the data shown in Table 32.6. If the spreadsheet is designed efficiently each compliance *Test* score need be entered once only and the spreadsheet will spread the score across the line and immediately calculate the *Both* scores. This has been done in Table 32.7. To arrive at the *Test* scores the auditors will probably continue with their established methods of compliance testing. The difference is that this control matrix technique requires them to conclude the results of their compliance tests on a numeric scale (0 through to 5) for each control tested. It is often preferable to use subjective judgement rather than scientific sampling techniques to arrive at the *Test* scores as this frees up more time for what follows in the audit after completion of the control matrix. What follows is often more constructive and beneficial to management.

RISK SCORES WHICH TAKE ACCOUNT OF CONTROL

The *Risk* scores at the top of each column have now been modified in Table 32.7 since each is now calculated on *all* the data in the column and some reliance can thus now be placed on certain controls which are now known to be complied with to some extent. The formula to compute each *Risk* score makes use of the *Type, Size* and all of the *Both* scores as follows where B is the sum of the cubes of the *Both* scores in the column:

$Type \times Size \times (125 - B)$ $=$ *Risk* of 4 if greater than 1,500

$=$ *Risk* of 3 if between 751 and 1,500

$=$ *Risk* of 2 if between 1 and 750

$=$ *Risk* of 1 if less than or equal to 0

Users of this technique may wish to develop their own formula for producing the *Risk* score from the data in the column. Alternatively, if they feel this formula is either too lax or excessively demanding, users may interpret the significance of the resultant *Risk* scores differently. A key feature of this formula is that by making use of cubes of the *Both* scores it places as much reliance upon two *Both* scores of 4 as on one *Both* score of 5.

MAKING USE OF THE RESULTS OF A CONTROL MATRIX

The *Risk* scores represent the main output of this matrix technique. It is intended that a *Risk* score of 4 indicates a critically important exposure due to its inherent nature and the relative absence of effective control over it. Having completed the control matrix early in the audit fieldwork, the auditors will divide the rest of their audit time so that they focus first upon exposures with *Risk* scores of 4 and proportionately less so on those with lower scores. There is no need to spend any further time on exposures with *Risk* scores of 1 as these exposures are either inherently marginal (based on their *Scale* and *Size* scores) or they have been eliminated by excellent controls which are functioning as intended.

The auditor's focus is likely to be partly upon further testing to determine whether the exposures have actually been exploited leading to real errors or losses. Auditors often call this type of testing *substantive* or *weakness* testing. Some internal auditors would argue that probing control weaknesses in this way may not be an appropriate part of their remit although different considerations would apply for external auditors.

Another part of the auditor's focus on the high risk exposures is likely to be (a) to devote time to work up recommendations to put to management which, if implemented. would have the effect of reducing the exposures in future, and (b) to persuade management to agree to and implement those recommendations. The matrix will be useful to illustrate to management the potential impact of these changes upon the levels of risk in the system.

The bottom of Table 32.7 gives overall inherent risk and control risk scores for the sub-system 'Completeness and Accuracy of Final Accounts'. These can be useful in audit contexts which require the auditors to give overall ratings for each audit. They can also be useful for future audit needs assessment purposes as explained in Chapter 33.

OBJECTIVES–ORIENTED MATRICES

Although our example has been *Exposures* oriented, we should not lose sight of the fact that the technique is as effective if the matrix shows '*Objectives*' across the horizontal axis and '*Measures*' as the vertical axis. We use the expression '*measures*' rather than '*controls*' for positively-oriented matrices as many would consider that management do not achieve their objectives merely by adhering to controls. The positive orientation can make the audit process much more acceptable to management. Management's mission is not just to avoid exposures; they are primarily in business to achieve objectives.

SUBJECTIVITY v. OBJECTIVITY

Once again, we must acknowledge that this matrix tool does not remove auditor subjectivity. The titles of the columns and rows are a matter of judgement as are the *Scale, Size* and *Best* scores, and indeed the design of the ladder *Scale* itself (Table 32.3). But it is valuable that the auditors are being required to record their judgement in numeric form as it forces the auditors to both make and record their judgements. The judgements which are behind a control matrix can be the combined, informed judgement of senior auditors and management. The matrix tool can then make good use of their experienced judgement when it is applied by more junior, less experienced auditors. In this sense this is an expert system. Over time a matrix can be improved in the light of experience. It is a valuable and concise part of audit 'documentation'. It is of course an example of automating the audit making use of the computer.

NOTE[1] *vide*, eg. Mair W.C., Davis K.W., and Wood D.M., 1972 *Computer Control & Audit*, (Institute of Internal Auditors Inc.).

Table 32.1 Exposures and controls (abbreviated example)

A – Mathematical inaccuracy and incompleteness in the final account
B – Inadequate control over variations and overspends
C – Discrepancies between financial and contract accounts figures
D – Failure to complete all the work
E – Failure to complete by specified dates

	Completeness & Accuracy of Final Accounts		EXPOSURES:				
			A	B	C	D	E
			=	=	=	=	=
	CONTROLS						
1	Item rates and contractor's bills of quantity are reconciled		?	?	?	?	?
			–	–	–	–	–
2	There is adequate documentation supporting variations		?	?	?	?	?
			–	–	–	–	–
3	All measurements are certified by the contract manager		?	?	?	?	?
			–	–	–	–	–
4	Payment certificates are properly authorised		?	?	?	?	?
			–	–	–	–	–
5	The completion certificate is signed		?	?	?	?	?
			–	–	–	–	–
6	There is appropriate comparison between actual and specified dates		?	?	?	?	?
			–	–	–	–	–

Table 32.2 Allowing for inherent risk of exposures

A – Mathematical inaccuracy and incompleteness in the final account
B – Inadequate control over variations and overspends
C – Discrepancies between financial and contract accounts figures
D – Failure to complete all the work
E – Failure to complete by specified dates

	Completeness & Accuracy of Final Accounts		EXPOSURES:					
				A	B	C	D	E
				=	=	=	=	=
	Calculated Risk Score:	Risk		2	2	2	4	2
				–	–	–	–	–
	Scale – see Table 32.3 (6 is most serious)	Type		4	2	4	5	3
	Size (3 is probable maximum)	Size		1	2	1	3	2
			–	–	–	–	–	–
	CONTROLS							
1	Item rates and contractor's bills of quantity are reconciled			?	?	?	?	?
			–	–	–	–	–	–
2	There is adequate documentation supporting variations			?	?	?	?	?
			–	–	–	–	–	–
3	All measurements are certified by the contract manager			?	?	?	?	?
			–	–	–	–	–	–
4	Payment certificates are properly authorised			?	?	?	?	?
			–	–	–	–	–	–
5	The completion certificate is signed			?	?	?	?	?
			–	–	–	–	–	–
6	There is appropriate comparison between actual and specified dates			?	?	?	?	?
			–	–	–	–	–	–

Table 32.3 Category scale for assessing the nature of the inherent risk

Contract auditing exposures-oriented scale

Point
of
Scale

6	Incorrect identification of original needs Should the business have embarked upon the project?
5	Need(s) unfulfilled
4	Unnecessary financial costs
3	Delay
2	Ineffective accountability
1	Inadequate information

(Start climbing this ladder from the bottom)

Table 32.4 Calculated risk scores

A – Mathematical inaccuracy and incompleteness in the final account
B – Inadequate control over variations and overspends
C – Discrepancies between financial and contract accounts figures
D – Failure to complete all the work
E – Failure to complete by specified dates

Completeness & Accuracy of Final Accounts		EXPOSURES:					
			A	B	C	D	E
			=	=	=	=	=
Calculated Risk Score:	Risk		2	2	2	4	2
			–	–	–	–	–
Scale – see Table 32.3 (6 is most serious)	Type		4	2	4	5	3
Size (3 is probable maximum)	Size		1	2	1	3	2
		–	–	–	–	–	–
CONTROLS							
1 Item rates and contractor's bills of quantity are reconciled			?	?	?	?	?
		–	–	–	–	–	–
2 There is adequate documentation supporting variations			?	?	?	?	?
		–	–	–	–	–	–
3 All measurements are certified by the contract manager			?	?	?	?	?
		–	–	–	–	–	–
4 Payment certificates are properly authorised			?	?	?	?	?
		–	–	–	–	–	–
5 The completion certificate is signed			?	?	?	?	?
		–	–	–	–	–	–
6 There is appropriate comparison between actual and specified dates			?	?	?	?	?
		–	–	–	–	–	–

Table 32.5 Control potential, compliance and actual

A – Mathematical inaccuracy and incompleteness in the final account
B – Inadequate control over variations and overspends
C – Discrepancies between financial and contract accounts figures
D – Failure to complete all the work
E – Failure to complete by specified dates

	Completeness & Accuracy of Final Accounts		EXPOSURES:				
			A	B	C	D	E
			=	=	=	=	=
	Calculated Risk Score:	Risk	2	2	2	4	2
			–	–	–	–	–
	Scale – see Table 32.3 (6 is most serious)	Type	4	2	4	5	3
	Size (3 is probable maximum)	Size	1	2	1	3	2
			–	–	–	–	–
	CONTROLS						
1	Item rates and contractor's bills of quantity are reconciled	Best	0	0	0	0	0
		Test ?	0	0	0	0	0
		Both	0	0	0	0	0
			–	–	–	–	–
2	There is adequate documentation supporting variations	Best	0	0	0	0	0
		Test ?	0	0	0	0	0
		Both	0	0	0	0	0
			–	–	–	–	–
3	All measurements are certified by the contract manager	Best	0	0	0	0	0
		Test ?	0	0	0	0	0
		Both	0	0	0	0	0
			–	–	–	–	–
4	Payment certificates are properly authorised	Best	0	0	0	0	0
		Test ?	0	0	0	0	0
		Both	0	0	0	0	0
			–	–	–	–	–
5	The completion certificate is signed	Best	0	0	0	0	0
		Test ?	0	0	0	0	0
		Both	0	0	0	0	0
			–	–	–	–	–
6	There is appropriate comparison between actual and specified dates	Best	0	0	0	0	0
		Test ?	0	0	0	0	0
		Both	0	0	0	0	0
			–	–	–	–	–

Table 32.6 Example control potential scores

A – Mathematical inaccuracy and incompleteness in the final account
B – Inadequate control over variations and overspends
C – Discrepancies between financial and contract accounts figures
D – Failure to complete all the work
E – Failure to complete by specified dates

Completeness & Accuracy of Final Accounts			EXPOSURES:				
			A	B	C	D	E
			=	=	=	=	=
Calculated Risk Score:	Risk		2	2	2	4	2
			–	–	–	–	–
Scale – see Table 32.3 (6 is most serious)	Type		4	2	4	5	3
Size (3 is probable maximum)	Size		1	2	1	3	2
		–	–	–	–	–	–
CONTROLS							
1 Item rates and contractor's bills of quantity are reconciled	Best		5	5	2	1	0
	Test	?	0	0	0	0	0
	Both		0	0	0	0	0
		–	–	–	–	–	–
2 There is adequate documentation supporting variations	Best		4	5	1	1	0
	Test	?	0	0	0	0	0
	Both		0	0	0	0	0
		–	–	–	–	–	–
3 All measurements are certified by the contract manager	Best		2	3	1	4	1
	Test	?	0	0	0	0	0
	Both		0	0	0	0	0
		–	–	–	–	–	–
4 Payment certificates are properly authorised	Best		2	2	5	5	4
	Test	?	0	0	0	0	0
	Both		0	0	0	0	0
		–	–	–	–	–	–
5 The completion certificate is signed	Best		1	1	1	5	1
	Test	?	0	0	0	0	0
	Both		0	0	0	0	0
		–	–	–	–	–	–
6 There is appropriate comparison between actual and specified dates	Best		0	0	0	0	5
	Test	?	0	0	0	0	0
	Both		0	0	0	0	0
		–	–	–	–	–	–

Table 32.7 Control matrix after inserting compliance scores

A – Mathematical inaccuracy and incompleteness in the final account
B – Inadequate control over variations and overspends
C – Discrepancies between financial and contract accounts figures
D – Failure to complete all the work
E – Failure to complete by specified dates

	Completeness & Accuracy of Final Accounts			EXPOSURES:				
				A	B	C	D	E
				=	=	=	=	=
	Calculated Risk Score:	Risk		1	1	2	4	1
				–	–	–	–	–
	Scale – see Table 32.3 (6 is most serious)	Type		4	2	4	5	3
	Size (3 is probable maximum)	Size		1	2	1	3	2
			–	–	–	–	–	–
	CONTROLS							
1	Item rates and contractor's bills of quantity are reconciled	Best		5	5	2	1	0
		Test	5	5	5	5	5	0
		Both		5	5	2	1	0
			–	–	–	–	–	–
2	There is adequate documentation supporting variations	Best		4	5	1	1	0
		Test	4	4	4	4	4	0
		Both		3	4	0	0	0
			–	–	–	–	–	–
3	All measurements are certified by the contract manager	Best		2	3	1	4	1
		Test	0	0	0	0	0	0
		Both		0	0	0	0	0
			–	–	–	–	–	–
4	Payment certificates are properly authorised	Best		2	2	5	5	4
		Test	2	2	2	2	2	2
		Both		0	0	2	2	1
			–	–	–	–	–	–
5	The completion certificate is signed	Best		1	1	1	5	1
		Test	2	2	2	2	2	2
		Both		0	0	0	2	0
			–	–	–	–	–	–
6	There is appropriate comparison between actual and specified dates	Best		0	0	0	0	5
		Test	5	0	0	0	0	5
		Both		0	0	0	0	5
			–	–	–	–	–	–

Inherent Risk (Size) score [5 is worst risk; 1 best]   2

Overall Control score [5 is worst risk; 1 best]   2

33

CONTRACT AUDIT NEEDS ASSESSMENT

Scope

This chapter explains a methodical way of determining which contracting activities should be audited and the audit resources which should be allocated to the audit of each of these activities. We use the expression auditable unit to refer to a contracting activity which may be the subject of an audit. Such an auditable unit may be, for instance, a contract sub-system or it may be a contract itself. Each of the contract sub-systems has been the subject of a chapter earlier in this book (Chapters 7 to 31) and they are listed in Table 33.10. Taken together, all auditable units comprise the audit universe.

An auditing function will invariably have an audit universe which includes many auditable units in addition to contracting activities and the method we describe in this chapter can be applied to determine relative audit need for all of the auditable units within such an audit universe which may be large and varied in nature. For the purpose of this chapter it is assumed that the audit universe of auditable units is limited to contracting activities. This may be the case where a team of specialist auditors focuses exclusively upon contract auditing, or where a more general audit function has already determined the quantum of audit resource to be allocated to auditing the contracting activity and then needs to allocate that quantum of audit resource between the audit sub-universe of different contracting activities.

The chapter starts with a detailed explanation of this method of audit needs assessment where the audit universe comprises these contracting activities. The chapter moves on to suggest ways of applying this approach where the audit universe is taken to be the contract sub-systems (Table 33.2 to 33.10) or the contracts themselves (Tables 33.11 and 33.12).

The method described entails the identification of the considerations which should underpin the determination of audit need and the representation of these considerations in an audit risk formula. The formula is then applied to each auditable unit within an audit universe so as to generate for each an audit risk score. The intention is that, in general, audit resources should be allocated over time to each auditable unit in proportion to the size of the audit risk score. The method also provides the opportunity to assess the total amount of audit resource, or the number of auditors, which is required to complete a programme of audits, and the impact upon the audit programme if audit resources are constrained.

Every audit and review function needs a way of determining its programme of future audits or reviews. The approach described in this chapter can be used by any group which has responsibility for conducting reviews of contracting activities – for instance, by a specialist contract audit group or by an internal audit function. In this chapter we are illustrating this approach with respect to audit universes of contract sub-systems and of contracts themselves. The general approach is equally applicable to determining audit need for other audit universes – such as accounting systems, IT systems, operational auditing – although different considerations and different audit risk formulae would be likely to be relevant in such cases. For other applications of this method readers may wish to refer to the companion volumes in this series *Effective Internal Audits – How to Plan and Implement* (Financial Times/Pitman Publishing, 1992) and *Auditing the IT Environment* (Financial Times/Pitman Publishing, 1994).

CHOOSING FACTORS FOR A 'CONTRACT AUDITING' AUDIT RISK FORMULA

Table 33.1 is our starting point. It is a list of considerations which contract auditors have identified as possibilities which they might bear in mind when they are making decisions about which contracting activities (*auditable units*) to include within their plan of audits to be conducted and the amount of audit resource which is justified for each included audit. It is offered as a check-list for others to use by marking the considerations which appear to them to be relevant in audit planning. Before being too influenced by the suggestions in Table 33.1 it is preferable for an audit planning team to jot down on a blank sheet of paper the considerations which seem to them at the outset of the planning exercise to be pertinent, based upon their past experience, and only then to use the list given in Table 33.1 to suggest further possible considerations they might have overlooked.

Table 33.1 has two further columns. The column entitled 'factor description' brackets together a number of 'consideration descriptions' so as to give them common labels. The rationale for this is that all of the considerations grouped together with a single factor label are being regarded as being related. The implicit guidance is that for the purposes of audit planning it is likely that it will be adequate to use the single given factor in cases where the audit planning team has marked more than one associated consideration. It is the factors themselves, rather than the marked considerations, which are carried forward to later tables and are ultimately used in the audit risk formula which is developed to perform the audit needs assessment. Users of this chapter are not obliged to agree with this guidance and can alter the factor descriptions as they desire.

There is a general requirement to minimise the number of factors selected so that the audit risk formula does not become unwieldy to use. The more factors in the audit risk formula, the greater the data collection and maintenance task. The factors in the formula should be minimised commensurate with the requirement that the audit risk formula should produce audit risk scores which reflect reasonably accurately the relative audit need for each auditable unit. The objective is to develop and use an audit risk formula which the audit planning team, and those to whom the team reports, are confident reflects the issues which ought to underpin their audit planning. A factor which would otherwise be included can be omitted if it always varies in proportion to another factor. As suggested, one consideration can be combined with another consideration, or a number of other considerations, to arrive at one factor only where all the considerations relate to a single issue.

Audit universes which are highly homogeneous make for the development of more reliable formulae. An example would be an audit universe which comprised only of shops or branches. It is much easier to arrive at an applicable set of factors each of which can be scored for every auditable unit within such a universe. This does not invalidate the technique for more heterogenous audit universes. In this chapter we suggest two different formulae for two different subsets of the contract auditing universe, and the audit department might have other formulae for other parts of their total audit universe. It follows that such an audit department will need a way to allocate total available audit resource between all the subsets of the audit universe – another formula may be used for that purpose or a more intuitive approach may be taken.

The challenge we are discussing here is the challenge faced by all audit managements of heterogenous audit universes. In allocating audit resources between auditable units they are having to weigh the factors which are relevant to one audit with the factors relevant to another audit, and so on, and the relevant factors will not be common to all audits. To simulate this planning approach in the audit risk formula method described in this chapter, our recommendation is that the audit risk formula should be designed so that not all factors have to be scored for each audit. The computation performed by the formula should be able to handle this variety, and it can do so readily using any spreadsheet package. The text at the bottom of Table 33.4 explains how the computation can be done to achieve this. At least one size, one control and one audit factor must be scored for each auditable unit being assessed. The scoring basis is discussed later in this chapter. A factor should be scored for an auditable unit if the auditor's judgement is that the factor is a relevant and necessary determinant of the quantum of audit resource justified for the particular audit and if the data is available to allow a reasonably reliable score to be given. This is analogous to the approach which audit management takes when using traditional, intuitive approaches to planning programmes of audits where the audit universe is highly variable.

THE CONTRACT AUDITING AUDIT 'SUB-UNIVERSES'

The sub-systems of the contracting process should each be candidates for inclusion within a future programme of audits. So should each of the contracts which is in progress. It would be possible to devise a single audit risk formula to allow audit need to be assessed for *both* these contract auditing sub-universes. In this chapter we take the alternative approach of developing two sample formulae – one for each contract auditing sub-universe. An audit review of each of the contracting sub-systems is appropriate as each contract in progress will rely upon the procedures of those sub-systems being effective. One audit approach would be to focus exclusively upon auditing the contracting sub-systems on the basis that if those systems are strong then all contracts are likely to be executed efficiently – in other words reliance can be placed on the effectiveness of internal control and compliance with controls need not be confirmed with respect to individual contracts in progress. Under this basis of auditing, individual contracts would only be reviewed as part of the auditor's testing to confirm the robustness of control within each of the contracting sub-systems.

A more comprehensive audit approach would be to regard both the contracting systems and the *contracts in progress* as auditable units to be audited. The audit approach when auditing the contracts themselves would in part be to confirm that the laid down procedures of the contracting sub-systems were being complied with. The auditor might go further and draw management's attention, with recommendations, to instances where, despite compliance, greater economy, efficiency, effectiveness and environmental responsibility could have been achieved. We recommend that both the contracting sub-systems and the contracts themselves should comprise the contract auditor's auditable units. It is most straightforward to develop a different formula for each of these two parts of the total contract auditing audit universe.

The audit risk formula for allocating audit resources between the contracts themselves is likely to be a more homogeneous formula than the formula for allocating audit resources between the contracting sub-systems as all contracts tend to have similar features though to varying degrees. However, this is less likely to be true if the audit universe of contracts includes a diversity of contracts ranging from construction contracts through to service contracts and even employment contracts.

At different times an enterprise is likely to find itself differently positioned with respect to contracts. Some businesses will find that contracts are cyclical with at one time many contracts being in their early stages of execution while at another time many may be nearing completion. If not cyclical, erratic availability of capital and spasmodic plans for expansion or retrenchment may mean that at any given time the majority of contracts are at a particular stage of completion. The implications of this are first that contract auditing may be more important for the business at certain times and that particular contracting sub-systems deserve more audit attention at certain times. If this unevenness of contracting applies within a business, the auditors should ensure that audit attention is given to those contracting sub-systems which are shortly to be relied upon by management to the greatest extent. The audit risk formula for contracting sub-systems can be designed to take account of this.

INHERENT, CONTROL AND AUDIT RISK

The final column in Table 33.1 categorises the contract auditing considerations and factors according to whether they address SIZE, CONTROL or AUDIT criteria. Size criteria are measures of inherent risk. By analogy, if someone leaves £1,000 on a desk unattended, the size (or inherent) risk is £1,000. The control criteria are measures of probability consequent upon the quality of internal control. Using the same analogy, if there is a 50 per cent probability of theft of the unattended £1,000 , we can say that *Risk = Size × Control* which in this case would be 1000 × 0.5 = 500.

In business we understand that risk is a function of *how much* (inherent risk, or size risk) × *how likely* (probability risk, or control risk). This is the natural way of assessing relative risk and it is therefore how we do it in this chapter. Later we shall see that an audit risk formula is structured as SIZE × CONTROL with one further refinement. Size adjusted by control gives us a measure of commercial risk. Our objective is to develop an *audit risk* formula which can compute an audit risk score for each auditable unit within our audit universe such that the computed score suggests the quantum of audit resource warranted for each auditable unit. We need to concede that audit time may not always be allocated in proportion to commercial risk (size adjusted by control). There may be special audit criteria which suggest further adjustments in order to turn *commercial risk* into *audit risk*. Care must be taken not to allow the AUDIT criteria to dominate in the audit risk formula: if we do so, we run the risk of allocating excessive amounts of audit time to relatively unimportant auditable units, and *vice versa*.

Good quality control reduces commercial risk associated with the inherent (size) risk. A complete absence of control cannot magnify the inherent risk but means that in all probability everything that is at risk will be lost. In the example we used above, the control risk was 0.5; the greatest it could have been would have been a score of 1.0. Later in this chapter we utilise this idea in the mathematical structure of the *control* part the example audit risk formulae. We also apply the same concept to the *audit* part of the formulae.

Table 33.2 shows the considerations and factors short-listed from Table 33.1 for development into a particular audit risk formula to be applied to the contracting sub-systems within an enterprise. Auditors planning in a different environment might have chosen different factors or have adjusted the wording. As it is the factors that are to be carried forward into the formula, the sequence of columns in Table 33.2 has been altered compared with Table 33.1. Note that six size factors have been short-listed in Table 33.2. Fourteen control factors have been short-listed as several of them are consolidations of two or more considerations. Similarly, twelve audit factors have been short-listed at this stage. The method described in this chapter requires that there should be at least one size factor, at least one control factor and at least one audit factor.

The *size* factor labelled 'overall [minplan] size score' and the *control* factor 'overall [minplan] control score' need some explanation. They are overall size and control scores computable for an auditable unit from the control matrices which are given as tables at the end of Chapters 7 to 31. Either an exposures-oriented control matrix or an objectives-oriented control matrix could be used for this purpose depending upon the emphasis required in drawing up the plan of audits. Chapter 32 explains this control matrix method and details of the **Control.IT MINPLAN** software are given in the Preface to this book.

These overall size and control scores are overall assessments of the auditable unit which are obtained as a result of detailed, well informed auditing work. They are therefore especially dependable and consequently have been given more weight in the formula as we shall see later in this chapter. Weighting factors is explained in the next section of this chapter. It is of course at the discretion of those who are developing the audit risk formula whether or not to include in the formula one or both of these overall **MINPLAN** measures and, if included, what weight to attribute to it. Doing so does provide an effective way of integrating audit assignment work (using the control matrix approach described in Chapter 32) with longer term audit planning (using the audit formula approach taken in this chapter). Conversely, the factor scores for an auditable unit and the audit risk score which they provide should be information which the audit team takes to the audit assignment of the auditable unit as it is useful intelligence, suggesting to the team where the main audit challenges are likely to be.

Having short-listed a selection of factors (Table 33.2), Table 33.3 supposes that audit management, in consultation with general management, has considered the matter in more depth and made certain adjustments to the shortlist to arrive at their final selection of factors – now four size factors, seven control factors and five audit factors.

WEIGHTING FACTORS USING A MATRIX TECHNIQUE

The formula for the contracting sub-systems audit sub-universe appears in Table 33.4; Table 33.5 is a summary of the factors within the formula. The factors have been differentially weighted so as to give more or less stress to individual factors in the determination of the resulting audit risk score for an auditable unit. The factor weights are shown above the factors in Table 33.4. This weighting has been a matter of judgement and, for a small number of factors, could have been done without any special aid. For a large number of factors it is unlikely that a reasonable weighting could be developed merely by casting one's eye along the list of factors as so many factors have to be compared against each other. For instance, to produce relative weights for the eleven control factors, fifty-five pairs of separate comparisons have to be made. Due to the structure of the formula, only factors appearing in the same part of the formula (the size, control or audit parts) have to be relatively weighted against each other. Tables 33.6, 33.7 and 33.8 show the application of a special matrix technique to develop the relative weights for the size, control and audit factors which have been used in the formula (Table 33.4).

The matrix technique for weighting factors requires the user to enter a value of the relative importance of one factor compared to another factor, and so on until every pair of factors has been compared in this way. Thus, if factor B is considered to be half as important as factor A, a value of 0.5 is entered in the appropriate cell. The user works in the cells *above* the diagonal line of 1's – the 1's being the cells which represent the comparison of each factor with itself – and the score entered in a cell is the user's assessment of the relative importance of the factor at the top of the column with the factor represented by the row. In determining the scores to be entered, the user should regard each comparison of a pair of factors as a new comparison and should not endeavour to make the score to be given consistent mathematically with earlier data entered within the matrix; this ensures that every factor is compared genuinely with every other factor. Below the diagonal line of 1's is another cell where the same two factors intersect, into which should be entered the reciprocal of the score entered in the associated cell above the diagonal line of 1's. The convention is that the matrix is always entered from the top; thus, if B is half as important as A, then A is twice as important as B.

When all the comparative data has been entered in this way a computation is conducted using all the data in the matrix so as to arrive at the relative factor weights which will be used in the formula. This computation is illustrated in Tables 33.6, 33.7 and 33.8. First, the columns and the rows are summed. Next, the totals of the columns are divided by the totals of the rows and a square root is taken of each of the results of these divisions. In this way, all the data in the matrix has been used, and the square roots have compensated accurately for the scaling impact of the divisions. The outcomes of the square roots indicate the relative weights which should be given to the factors in order to reflect the judgemental weights given to all the pairs of factors by the user. If several people are involved in developing this planning method, a higher degree of consensus reliability may be obtained by asking each to complete these matrices and then consolidating and averaging the results.

The computation illustrated in Tables 33.6, 33.7 and 33.8 takes account of all of the data in the matrix. This computation has the effect of averaging out any discrepancies within the data entered on the matrix which were caused by each comparison being made by the user as a fresh comparison with no intention of it being mathematically consistent with earlier comparisons made. This approach is preferable to completing the matrix so that every comparison is mathematically consistent with every other comparison; if the matrix were completed in this way the auditor's judgement would be restricted to the first few comparisons made.

As a proof that the matrix technique is mathematically sound the latter method of matrix completion can be experimented with. If the first row of the matrix were completed initially and then the remaining rows of the matrix were completed in a way which was mathematically consistent with the proportions expressed in the first row, then the final weights would be exactly the same as the data entered in the first row of the matrix. Of course it would be pointless to use the matrix technique in this way – except to prove that the technique is mathematically valid.

DESIGNING A SCORING SCALE FOR EACH FACTOR

Table 33.9 is illustrative of the type of scaling system which might be developed for the formula given in Table 33.4. A five-point scale has been used. Most size factors are usually hard and objective; for these, once the scoring scale has been set subjectively, the correct scores can often be determined by reference to the corporate database. The control and audit factors are more frequently soft and subjective but even here fairly hard guidance can often be given to assist in determining what score on the scale should be given for a particular auditable unit.

THE AUDIT RISK INDEX

The example developed in Tables 33.2 to 33.10 is for use with an audit universe of contracting sub-systems such as those covered in this book (Chapters 7 to 31). They are listed in the audit risk index given as Table 33.10 which allocates one line for each audit in the audit universe. Table 33.10 would naturally be a spreadsheet in which (a) descriptive data and (b) scores for formula factors would be entered for each audit. The spreadsheet would compute each audit's *audit risk score*.

The mathematics of the formula computation should be arranged so as to handle the absence of some of the factor scores for any auditable unit without unduly distorting the resulting audit risk scores. A factor should not be scored if the data is unavailable or undependable, or if a score would be misleading as the factor is not considered to be pertinent to the particular auditable unit being scored. The mathematics underpinning the formula is explained in Table 33.4, showing how this scoring flexibility can be achieved. The reader will also note from Table 33.4 that the maximum possible audit risk score which can be obtained is determined exclusively from the size part of the formula since this provides a measure of inherent risk. The size score is always adjusted downwards by the scores for the control part and then by the scores for the audit part of the formula unless there is no degree of control at all and there are no special reasons to suggest scaling down the amount of audit attention given to the auditable unit. Table 33.10 would also give the subsidiary scores for each of the three parts of the formula (size, control and audit) as it is helpful to audit management and to the audit team conducting the audit to know why a particular overall audit risk score for an auditable unit was obtained.

The theoretical maximum audit risk score that the formula can compute is 100 but in practice no auditable unit is likely to approximate this maximum. The spread of audit risk scores is likely to be between about 8 and 50 – which is sufficient to indicate the variations in audit resource which are justified to expend on each of these auditable units. The 'Audit Units Needed' column would specify the number of audit days (or alternative units) required in order to give the auditable unit the attention warranted by its audit risk score.

AUDIT RISK FORMULA FOR A UNIVERSE OF CONTRACTS

Up to now in this chapter we have worked with an audit universe of contract auditing sub-systems. There is no need to explain the methodology again in applying the methodology to preparing another audit risk formula where the audit universe is the population of contracts in progress. Tables 33.11 and 33.12 show in abbreviated form the development of a sample audit risk formula for this purpose. Of course, businesses should adapt this formula to fit their own requirements.

SUBJECTIVITY, OBJECTIVITY, RELIABILITY AND INDEPENDENCE

The technique discussed and applied in this chapter might be criticised for being too subjective and for attaching numbers to judgements with the risk that they are interpreted as being scientifically objective. There is considerable subjectivity associated with selecting the appropriate factors for the formula, weighting them, designing their scoring scales and, in the case of some of the soft, subjective factors, in scoring them using the scales. The resultant audit risk scores for each of the auditable units are data which must be interpreted, and the development of the audit plan of audits to be conducted as well as the determination of the number of auditors needed are also highly judgemental. Decisions such as the length of the audit cycle and the minimum duration of the fieldwork for an audit are also highly subjective.

So not too much must be claimed for this tool. Its merits are that it provides the opportunity to formalise the audit planning process which too often is conducted very informally, hastily and intuitively. There are many features within this method which improve the opportunity to exercise judgement in a methodical and more reliable way. The method can establish the basis to be used for determining audit attention to contracting and other activities and as such provides the opportunity to criticise it, to revisit it so as to improve it and to obtain approval of top management and the audit committee of the Board to its adoption. It provides an explanation for audit focus. It compels audit planners to commit themselves to their planning assumptions, to record them and then to express their judgement to all of the parameters (in numeric form); there can be no doubt as to what judgements they came to.

Internal audit independence is enhanced by providing senior management and the board with the opportunity to concur with the basis to be used for audit planning. It then becomes less necessary for the plan of audits itself, developed using this method, to be approved by senior management and the board. It becomes readily apparent when senior management is endeavouring to deflect internal audit away from work in certain areas or to work in other areas which are intrinsically less important. Primarily internal audit should be independent in the sense that the most senior point to which it reports should be confident that the scope of internal audit work has not been influenced inappropriately by pressure exerted by a more junior point within the enterprise.

CONSIDERATION DESCRIPTION	FACTOR DESCRIPTION	BRACKET
Extensions of time	DEGREE OF VARIATION FROM ORIGINAL SPECIFICATION	SIZE
Value of variations	DEGREE OF VARIATION FROM ORIGINAL SPECIFICATION	SIZE
Income generation potential (grants, rents, fees, charges)	INCOME POTENTIAL	SIZE
Relative importance of each sub-system in terms of risk	INHERENT RISK OF EACH SUB-SYSTEM	SIZE
Overall size score from the control matrix of this activity	OVERALL (MINPLAN) SIZE SCORE	SIZE
Financial implications of sub-systems failing	POTENTIAL FINANCIAL LOSS	SIZE
Revenue consequences	POTENTIAL REVENUE RISK	SIZE
Effect of system on overall effectiveness of the project	RELATIVE IMPORTANCE OF SUB-SYSTEM	SIZE
Extent and size of liquidated damages	SIZE OF FINANCIAL ADJUSTMENTS	SIZE
Extent and size of claims	SIZE OF FINANCIAL ADJUSTMENTS	SIZE
Values of contracts going through the sub-system	VALUE HANDLED BY SUB-SYSTEM	SIZE
Size of the contract	VALUE OF THE CONTRACT	SIZE
Value of the contract	VALUE OF THE CONTRACT	SIZE
Contract sum	VALUE OF THE CONTRACT	SIZE
Capital values	VALUE OF THE CONTRACT	SIZE
Number of contracts going through each sub-system	VOLUME OF CONTRACTS HANDLED BY SUB-SYSTEM	SIZE
Known previous problems	AUDIT 'INTELLIGENCE'	CONTROL
Known financial problems	AUDIT 'INTELLIGENCE'	CONTROL
Need to respond to rumours/whispers	AUDIT 'INTELLIGENCE'	CONTROL
Past experiences	AUDIT 'INTELLIGENCE'	CONTROL
Findings of last audit in this area	AUDIT 'INTELLIGENCE'	CONTROL
Previous weaknesses identified	AUDIT 'INTELLIGENCE'	CONTROL
Extent of compensating controls	COMPENSATING CONTROLS	CONTROL
Degree of mutual independence of relevant sub-systems	COMPENSATING CONTROLS	CONTROL
Complexity of the contract	CONTRACT COMPLEXITY	CONTROL
Whether contract is subject to EEC regulations	CONTRACT CONDITIONS (STANDARDISATION ETC.)	CONTROL
Conditions of contract (standard or not)	CONTRACT CONDITIONS (STANDARDISATION ETC.)	CONTROL
Existence of standing orders and their compliance	DEFINITION OF INTERNAL PROCEDURES	CONTROL
Degree of control by standing orders	DEFINITION OF INTERNAL PROCEDURES	CONTROL
Standard of documentation of sub systems	DEFINITION OF INTERNAL PROCEDURES	CONTROL
Contract duration	DURATION OF THE CONTRACT	CONTROL

Table 33.1 Contract auditing 'bale' of factors

Contract period	DURATION OF THE CONTRACT	CONTROL
Direct requests from management departments	EXPRESSED CONCERN OF MANAGEMENT	CONTROL
Extent of changes of systems in relevant departments	EXTENT OF CHANGES TO RELEVANT SYSTEMS	CONTROL
Professional disciplines involved	EXTENT OF PROFESSIONALISATION	CONTROL
Extent that involved staff are professional	EXTENT OF PROFESSIONALISATION	CONTROL
Frequency of use of the relevant sub-systems	FAMILIARITY WITH WELL-USED SYSTEMS	CONTROL
Financial status of consultants	FINANCIAL STATUS OF THE CONSULTANT(S)	CONTROL
Financial status of contractor	FINANCIAL STATUS OF THE CONTRACTOR(S)	CONTROL
Quality of the consultant employed	GENERAL QUALITY OF THE CONSULTANT(S)	CONTROL
Quality assurance of contractor (eg. BS 5750 registered)	GENERAL QUALITY OF THE CONTRACTOR(S)	CONTROL
Quality of the contractor involved	GENERAL QUALITY OF THE CONTRACTOR(S)	CONTROL
Reputation of the contractor	GENERAL QUALITY OF THE CONTRACTOR(S)	CONTROL
Current developments within the construction industry	INDUSTRY CONDITIONS	CONTROL
Extent of changes of staff in relevant departments	LEVEL OF STAFF AND MANAGEMENT CHANGES	CONTROL
Modus operandi (in-house/private consultants/contractors)	MODUS OPERANDI	CONTROL
Consultants or not	MODUS OPERANDI	CONTROL
Method of pay and of operation of consultants employed	MODUS OPERANDI	CONTROL
Type of contract (eg. 'design and build')	NATURE OF THE CONTRACT	CONTROL
Nature of contract	NATURE OF THE CONTRACT	CONTROL
Form of contract	NATURE OF THE CONTRACT	CONTROL
Type of contract (eg. one-off; 'CLASP' etc)	NATURE OF THE CONTRACT	CONTROL
Overall control score from the control matrix of the activity	OVERALL (MINPLAN) CONTROL SCORE	CONTROL
Previous experience with this contractor	PAST EXPERIENCE WITH THE CONTRACTOR(S)	CONTROL
Previous experience with this type of contract	PAST EXPERIENCE WITH THIS CONTRACT TYPE	CONTROL
History of contractors	PAST EXPERIENCE WITH THIS CONTRACTOR	CONTROL
Extent of separation of duties	QUALITY OF INTERNAL CONTROL	CONTROL
Known problems/weaknesses	QUALITY OF INTERNAL CONTROL	CONTROL
Soundness of sub-systems operated by relevant departments	QUALITY OF INTERNAL CONTROL & CO-ORDINATION	CONTROL
Quality of interdepartmental communication	QUALITY OF INTERNAL CONTROL & CO-ORDINATION	CONTROL
Quality of supervision	QUALITY OF MANAGEMENT	CONTROL
Scale of fluctuations	QUALITY OF PROJECT CONTROL	CONTROL
Existence and quality of 'programme of works'	QUALITY OF PROJECT DOCUMENTATION	CONTROL
Scope for deviation from procedures of the sub-systems	SCOPE FOR DEVIATION FROM STANDARD PROCEDURES	CONTROL
Complexity of the relevant sub-systems	SYSTEMS COMPLEXITY	CONTROL

Table 33.1 continued

CONSIDERATION DESCRIPTION	FACTOR DESCRIPTION	BRACKET
Technical status of consultants	TECHNICAL REPUTATION OF THE CONSULTANT(S)	CONTROL
Technical status of contractor	TECHNICAL REPUTATION OF THE CONTRACTOR(S)	CONTROL
Client requests	CLIENT CONCERN	AUDIT
Special client constraints (eg. need for security/safety)	CLIENT CONCERN	AUDIT
Overlap of contract audit scope with related systems audits	EXTENT OF COVERAGE WITHIN SCOPE OF OTHER AUDITS	AUDIT
Previous audit coverage	EXTENT OF COVERAGE WITHIN SCOPE OF OTHER AUDITS	AUDIT
Degree of previous audit coverage of relevant sub-systems	EXTENT OF PREVIOUS AUDIT COVERAGE	AUDIT
External audit activity	EX rENT OF RELIANCE UPON EXTERNAL AUDIT	AUDIT
Activity by other review agencies	EXTENT OF RELIANCE UPON OTHER REVIEW AGENCIES	AUDIT
Geographical implications for audit coverage	GEOGRAPHICAL CONSTRAINTS	AUDIT
External influences - professional bodies	INFLUENCE OF PROFESSIONAL BODIES	AUDIT
Availability of audit resources	INTERNAL AUDIT CAPACITY	AUDIT
Level of audit resources - time	INTERNAL AUDIT CAPACITY	AUDIT
Current developments in audit techniques	INTERNAL AUDIT COMPETENCE	AUDIT
Level of audit resources - experience	INTERNAL AUDIT COMPETENCE	AUDIT
Technical resources available to audit	INTERNAL AUDIT COMPETENCE	AUDIT
Level of audit resources - training	NEED TO DEVELOP AUDIT EXPERIENCE	AUDIT
Phase (early or late) in multicontract project	OPPORTUNITY TO AFFECT OUTCOME	AUDIT
Whether capital programme is growing or declining	OPPORTUNITY TO BENEFIT FROM THE AUDIT	AUDIT
Need to move to current contract auditing	OPPORTUNITY TO BENEFIT FROM THE AUDIT	AUDIT
Management policy constraints to conduct an audit	REQUESTS FROM MANAGEMENT	AUDIT
Special requirements of legislation and regulations	SPECIAL LEGAL OR REGULATIVE AUDIT NEED	AUDIT
Government legislation (eg. CCT)	SPECIAL LEGAL OR REGULATIVE AUDIT NEED	AUDIT
External influences - political	THIRD PARTY SENSITIVITY	AUDIT
External influences - pressure groups	THIRD PARTY SENSITIVITY	AUDIT
Political considerations	THIRD PARTY SENSITIVITY	AUDIT
Political sensitivity	THIRD PARTY SENSITIVITY	AUDIT
Timing of last audit in this area	TIME SINCE LAST AUDIT	AUDIT

Table 33.1 continued

BRACKET	FACTOR DESCRIPTION	CONSIDERATION DESCRIPTION
SIZE	INHERENT RISK OF EACH SUB-SYSTEM	Relative importance of each sub-system in terms of risk
SIZE	OVERALL (MINPLAN) SIZE SCORE	Overall size score from the control matrix of this activity
SIZE	POTENTIAL FINANCIAL LOSS	Financial implications of sub-systems failing
SIZE	RELATIVE IMPORTANCE OF SUB-SYSTEM	Effect of system on overall effectiveness of the project
SIZE	VALUE HANDLED BY SUB-SYSTEM	Values of contracts going through the sub-system
SIZE	VOLUME OF CONTRACTS HANDLED BY SUB-SYSTEM	Number of contracts going through each sub-system
CONTROL	AUDIT ''INTELLIGENCE'	Findings of last audit in this area
CONTROL	AUDIT 'INTELLIGENCE'	Past experiences
CONTROL	AUDIT 'INTELLIGENCE'	Known previous problems
CONTROL	AUDIT 'INTELLIGENCE'	Previous weaknesses identified
CONTROL	COMPENSATING CONTROLS	Extent of compensating controls
CONTROL	DEFINITION OF INTERNAL PROCEDURES	Standard of documentation of sub-systems
CONTROL	EXPRESSED CONCERN OF MANAGEMENT	Direct requests from management/departments
CONTROL	EXTENT OF CHANGES TO RELEVANT SYSTEMS	Extent of changes of systems in relevant departments
CONTROL	EXTENT OF PROFESSIONALISATION	Professional disciplines involved
CONTROL	EXTENT OF PROFESSIONALISATION	Extent that involved staff are professional
CONTROL	FAMILIARITY WITH WELL-USED SYSTEMS	Frequency of use of the relevant sub-systems
CONTROL	LEVEL OF STAFF AND MANAGEMENT CHANGES	Extent of changes of staff in relevant departments
CONTROL	OVERALL (MINPLAN) CONTROL SCORE	Overall control score from the control matrix of the activity
CONTROL	QUALITY OF INTERNAL CONTROL	Known problems/weaknesses
CONTROL	QUALITY OF INTERNAL CONTROL	Extent of separation of duties
CONTROL	QUALITY OF INTERNAL CONTROL & CO-ORDINATION	Soundness of sub-systems operated by relevant departments
CONTROL	QUALITY OF INTERNAL CONTROL & CO-ORDINATION	Quality of interdepartmental communication
CONTROL	QUALITY OF MANAGEMENT	Quality of supervision
CONTROL	SCOPE FOR DEVIATION FROM STANDARD PROCEDURES	Scope for deviation from procedures of the sub-systems
CONTROL	SYSTEMS COMPLEXITY	Complexity of the relevant sub-systems

Table 33.2 Initial selection of possible factors for a contract sub-systems audit risk formula

BRACKET	FACTOR DESCRIPTION	CONSIDERATION DESCRIPTION
AUDIT	CLIENT CONCERN	Client requests
AUDIT	EXTENT OF COVERAGE WITHIN SCOPE OF OTHER AUDITS	Previous audit coverage
AUDIT	EXTENT OF PREVIOUS AUDIT COVERAGE	Degree of previous audit coverage of relevant sub-systems
AUDIT	EXTENT OF RELIANCE UPON EXTERNAL AUDIT	External audit activity
AUDIT	EXTENT OF RELIANCE UPON OTHER REVIEW AGENCIES	Activity by other review agencies
AUDIT	INFLUENCE OF PROFESSIONAL BODIES	External influences - professional bodies
AUDIT	INTERNAL AUDIT CAPACITY	Level of audit resources - time
AUDIT	INTERNAL AUDIT CAPACITY	Availability of audit resources
AUDIT	INTERNAL AUDIT COMPETENCE	Level of audit resources - experience
AUDIT	INTERNAL AUDIT COMPETENCE	Current developments in audit techniques
AUDIT	INTERNAL AUDIT COMPETENCE	Technical resources available to audit
AUDIT	OPPORTUNITY TO AFFECT OUTCOME	Phase (early or late) in multi-contract project
AUDIT	OPPORTUNITY TO BENEFIT FROM THE AUDIT	Whether capital programme is growing or declining
AUDIT	SPECIAL LEGAL OR REGULATIVE AUDIT NEED	Special requirements of legislation and regulations
AUDIT	SPECIAL LEGAL OR REGULATIVE AUDIT NEED	Government legislation (eg CCT)
AUDIT	TIME SINCE LAST AUDIT	Timing of last audit in this area

Table 33.2 continued

BRACKET	FACTOR DESCRIPTION	CONSIDERATION DESCRIPTION
SIZE	OVERALL(MINPLAN) SIZE SCORE	Overall size score from the control matrix of this activity
SIZE	RELATIVE IMPORTANCE OF SUB-SYSTEM	Effect of system on overall effectiveness of the project
SIZE	VALUE HANDLED BY SUB-SYSTEM	Values of contracts going through the sub-system
SIZE	VALUE HANDLED BY SUB-SYSTEM	Financial implications of sub-system failing
SIZE	VOLUME OF CONTRACTS HANDLED BY SUB-SYSTEM	Number of contracts going through the sub-system
CONTROL	COMPENSATING CONTROLS	Degree of mutual dependence of relevant sub-systems
CONTROL	COMPENSATING CONTROLS	Extent of compensating controls
CONTROL	EXPRESSED CONCERN OF MANAGEMENT	Direct requests from management/departments
CONTROL	EXTENT OF PROFESSIONALISATION & QUALITY OF MANAGEMENT	Quality of supervision
CONTROL	EXTENT OF PROFESSIONALISATION & QUALITY OF MANAGEMENT	Extent that involved staff are professional
CONTROL	EXTENT OF PROFESSIONALISATION & QUALITY OF MANAGEMENT	Professional disciplines involved
CONTROL	FAMILIARITY WITH SUB-SYSTEM	Frequency of use of the relevant sub-system
CONTROL	FAMILIARITY WITH SUB-SYSTEM	Extent of changes of systems in relevant departments
CONTROL	FAMILIARITY WITH SUB-SYSTEM	Extent of changes of staff in relevant departments
CONTROL	OVERALL (MINPLAN) CONTROL SCORE	Overall control score from the control matrix of the activity
CONTROL	QUALITY OF INTERNAL CONTROL	Standard of documentation of sub-system
CONTROL	QUALITY OF INTERNAL CONTROL	Findings of last audit in this area
CONTROL	QUALITY OF INTERNAL CONTROL	Known previous problems
CONTROL	QUALITY OF INTERNAL CONTROL	Past experiences
CONTROL	QUALITY OF INTERNAL CONTROL	Previous weaknesses identified
CONTROL	QUALITY OF INTERNAL CONTROL	Quality of interdepartmental communication
CONTROL	QUALITY OF INTERNAL CONTROL	Known problems/weaknesses
CONTROL	QUALITY OF INTERNAL CONTROL	Extent of separation of duties
CONTROL	QUALITY OF INTERNAL CONTROL	Scope for deviation from procedures of the sub-system
CONTROL	QUALITY OF INTERNAL CONTROL	Soundness of sub-system operated by relevant departments
CONTROL	SYSTEMS COMPLEXITY	Complexity of the relevant sub-system

Table 33.3 Final selection of factors for a contract sub-systems audit risk formula

BRACKET	FACTOR DESCRIPTION	CONSIDERATION DESCRIPTION
AUDIT	EXTENT OF COVERAGE WITHIN SCOPE OF OTHER AUDITS	Previous audit coverage
AUDIT	EXTENT OF RELIANCE UPON OTHER REVIEW AGENCIES	Activity by other review agencies
AUDIT	INTERNAL AUDIT COMPETENCE	Level of audit resources - experience
AUDIT	INTERNAL AUDIT COMPETENCE	Technical resources available to audit
AUDIT	INTERNAL AUDIT COMPETENCE	Current developments in audit techniques
AUDIT	OPPORTUNITY TO BENEFIT FROM THE AUDIT	Phase (early or late) in multi-contract project
AUDIT	OPPORTUNITY TO BENEFIT FROM THE AUDIT	Whether capital programme is growing or declining
AUDIT	SPECIAL LEGAL OR REGULATIVE AUDIT NEED	Government legislation (e.g. CCT)
AUDIT	SPECIAL LEGAL OR REGULATIVE AUDIT NEED	Special requirements of legislation and regulations

Table 33.3 continued

SIZE:

$$20 \frac{(\overset{3}{A} + \overset{1}{B} + \overset{2}{C} + \overset{2}{D})}{n1}$$

CONTROL:

$$\frac{(\overset{1}{A} + \overset{3}{B} + \overset{2}{C} + \overset{2}{D} + \overset{5}{E} + \overset{2}{F} + \overset{2}{G})}{n2}$$

AUDIT:

$$\frac{(\overset{1}{A} + \overset{1}{B} + \overset{1}{C} + \overset{3}{D} + \overset{2}{E})}{n3}$$

At least one factor must be scored within each of the three sets of brackets.
Each factor scored is scored on a scale 1 through 5.
The score given to a factor is weighted by the weight shown above the factor letter.
Within a set of brackets the weighted factor scores are summed.
The sum of the contents of the SIZE brackets only is multiplied by 20.
The sum of each of the brackets is divided by n1, n2 or n3 respectively.
 – n1 is the sum of the weights of the SIZE factors scored.
 – n2 is 5 x the sum of the weights of the CONTROL factors scored.
 – n3 is 5 x the sum of the weights of the AUDIT factors scored.

Table 33.4 Contract sub-systems: sample audit risk formula

Table 33.5 Contract sub-systems: factors in audit risk formula

SIZE FACTORS:

A   OVERALL (MINPLAN) SIZE SCORE
B   RELATIVE IMPORTANCE OF SUB-SYSTEM ~
C   VALUE HANDLED BY SUB-SYSTEM
D   VOLUME OF CONTRACTS HANDLED BY SUB-SYSTEM

CONTROL FACTORS:

A   COMPENSATING CONTROLS
B   EXPRESSED CONCERN OF MANAGEMENT
C   EXTENT OF PROFESSIONALISATION & QUALITY OF MANAGEMENT
D   FAMILIARITY WITH SUB-SYSTEM
E   OVERALL (MINPLAN) CONTROL SCORE
F   QUALITY OF INTERNAL CONTROL
G   SYSTEMS COMPLEXITY

AUDIT FACTORS:

A   EXTENT OF COVERAGE WITHIN SCOPE OF OTHER AUDITS
B   EXTENT OF RELIANCE UPON OTHER REVIEW AGENCIES
C   INTERNAL AUDIT COMPETENCE
D   OPPORTUNITY TO BENEFIT FROM THE AUDIT
E   SPECIAL LEGAL OR REGULATIVE AUDIT NEED

Table 33.6 Contract sub-systems: weighting matrix for size factors

WEIGHTING MATRIX (7 FACTORS, A to G)			A	B	C	D	
Chosen SIZE factors							
OVERALL (MINPLAN) SIZE SCORE	A		1	0.5	0.4	0.5	2.4
RELATIVE IMPORTANCE OF SUB-SYSTEM	B		2	1	0.8	1.5	5.3
VALUE HANDLED BY SUB-SYSTEM	C		2.5	1.25	1	2	6.75
VOLUME OF CONTRACTS HANDLED BY SUB-SYSTEM	D		2	0.67	0.5	1	4.17
Sum of columns			7.5	3.42	2.7	5	
Sum of columns divided by adjusted sum of rows			3.13	0.64	0.4	1.2	
Square root of above row figures (X)			1.77	0.8	0.63	1.1	
Minimum value in above row (Y)			0.63	0.63	0.63	0.63	
Factor weighting (X/Y, rounded)			3	1	1	2	
			(A	+B	+C	+D)	

Table 33.7 Contract sub-systems : weighting matrix for control factors

WEIGHTING MATRIX (7 FACTORS, A to G)		A	B	C	D	E	F	G		
Chosen CONTROL factors										
COMPENSATING CONTROLS	A	1	3	2	2	4	2	2		16
EXPRESSED CONCERN OF MANAGEMENT	B	0.33	1	0.9	0.6	2	1	0.75		6.58
EXTENT OF PROFESSIONALISATION & QUALITY OF MANAGEMENT	C	0.5	1.11	1	0.9	3	1.5	1		9.01
FAMILIARITY WITH SUB-SYSTEM	D	0.5	1.67	1.11	1	3	1.5	0.8		9.58
OVERALL (MINIPLAN) CONTROL SCORE	E	0.25	0.5	0.33	0.33	1	0.5	0.3		3.22
QUALITY OF INTERNAL CONTROL	F	0.5	1	0.67	0.67	2	1	1		6.83
SYSTEMS COMPLEXITY	G	0.5	1.33	1	1.25	3.33	1	1		9.42
Sum of columns		3.58	9.61	7.01	6.75	18.33	8.5	6.85		
Sum of columns divided by adjusted sum of rows		0.22	1.46	0.78	0.7	5.7	1.24	0.73		
Square root of above row figures (X)		0.47	1.21	0.88	0.84	2.39	1.12	0.85		
Minimum value in above row (Y)		0.47	0.47	0.47	0.47	0.47	0.47	0.47		
Factor weighting (X/Y, rounded)		1	3	2	2	5	2	2		
		(A	+B	+C	+D	+E	+F	+G)		

Table 33.8 Contract sub-systems: weighting matrix for audit factors

WEIGHTING MATRIX (5 FACTORS, A to E)		A	B	C	D	E	
Chosen AUDIT factors							
EXTENT OF COVERAGE WITHIN SCOPE OF OTHER AUDITS	A	1	1	0.67	3	1	6.67
EXTENT OF RELIANCE UPON OTHER REVIEW AGENCIES	B	1	1	1	3	1	7
INTERNAL AUDIT COMPETENCE	C	1.49	1	1	3	2	8.49
OPPORTUNITY TO BENEFIT FROM THE AUDIT	D	0.33	0.33	0.33	1	2	4
SPECIAL LEGAL OR REGULATIVE AUDIT NEED	E	1	1	0.5	0.5	1	4
Sum of columns		4.83	4.33	3.5	10.5	7	
Sum of columns divided by adjusted sum of rows		0.72	0.62	0.41	2.63	1.75	
Square root of above row figures (X)		0.85	0.79	0.64	1.62	1.32	
Minimum value in above row (Y)		0.64	0.64	0.64	0.64	0.64	
Factor weighting (X/Y, rounded)		1	1	1	3	2	
		(A	+B	+C	+D	+E)	

Table 33.9 Scoring scale for contract sub-systems audit risk formula

SCORING SCALE:

****

SIZE FACTORS

- -

A OVERALL (MINPLAN) SIZE SCORE

(Largest size)

5=
4=
3=Use score obtained from the MINPLAN control matrix of this sub-system
2=
1=

(Smallest size)

- -

B RELATIVE IMPORTANCE OF SUB-SYSTEM

(Largest size)

5= Proper functioning of this sub-system is vital for the success of most contracts
4= Proper functioning of this sub-system is important for the success of most contracts
3= Improper functioning of this sub-system may have a material impact on most contracts
2= Improper functioning of this sub-system is likely to have a small impact on most contracts
1= Improper functioning of this sub-system is unlikely to have an impact on most contracts

(Smallest size)

- -

C VALUE HANDLED BY SUB-SYSTEM

(Largest size)

5=Over £80 million, or more than £8 million at risk to this sub-system
4=Over £60 million, or more than £6 million at risk to this sub-system
3=Over £40 million, or more than £4 million at risk to this sub-system
2=Over £20 million, or more than £2 million at risk to this sub-system
1=Less than £20 million, or less than £2 million at risk to this sub-system

(Smallest size)

- -

D VOLUME OF CONTRACTS HANDLED BY SUB-SYSTEM

(Largest size)

5= More than 20 per year at present
4=16 – 20 per year at present
3=11–15 per year at present
2=6 –10 per year at present
1 = Fewer than 5 per year at present

(Smallest size)

Table 33.9 continued

CONTROL FACTORS

- -

A COMPENSATING CONTROLS

(Largest control risk)

5=Insignificant overlap with controls in other sub-systems
4=Minor overlap with controls in other sub-systems
3=Some significant overlap with controls in other sub-systems
2=Strong overlap with controls in other sub-systems
1=Very strong overlap with controls in other sub-systems

(Smallest control risk)

- -

B EXPRESSED CONCERN OF MANAGEMENT

(Largest control risk)

5=Priority concern being expressed by senior management and/or the Board
4=Strong pressure from senior management and/or the Board to audit this sub-system
3=Some concern being expressed by senior management and the Board
2=Management and the Board are known to have few concerns in this area
1=Management and the Board have indicated they have no concerns in this area

(Smallest control risk)

- -

C EXTENT OF PROFESSIONALISATION & QUALITY OF MANAGEMENT

(Largest control risk)

5=Staff are unqualified for the task and/or management is weak
4=Staff are largely unqualified for the task and/or management is rather weak
3=There is a reasonable level of competence technically and managerially
2=All key staff are excellently and appropriately qualified technically and managerially
1=All staff are excellently and appropriately qualified technically and managerially

(Smallest control risk)

- -

D FAMILIARITY WITH SUB-SYSTEM

(Largest control risk)

5=Sub-system rarely used in this form by present staff
4=Significant changes to staff and/or to procedures have occurred recently
3=Sub-system materially unchanged but staff and management inexperienced
2=Sub-system has been used before without material change by same staff
1=Existing procedures of sub-system in frequent use by same, experienced staff

(Smallest control risk)

Table 33.9 continued

```
------------------------------------------------------------------------
```

E OVERALL (MINPLAN) CONTROL SCORE

(Largest control risk)

5=
4=
3=Use score obtained from the MINPLAN control matrix of this sub-system
2=
1=

(Smallest control risk)

```
------------------------------------------------------------------------
```

F QUALITY OF INTERNAL CONTROL

(Largest control risk)

5=Known or suspected to be very unsound
4=No past audit experience; OR known or suspected to be weak
3=Sound (and confirmed as such during last audit visit)
2=Above average (and confirmed as such during the last audit visit), with standard
   corporation systems in use generally
1=Excellent; no significant reorganisations; little scope for intentional manipulation

(Smallest control risk)

```
------------------------------------------------------------------------
```

G SYSTEMS COMPLEXITY

(Largest control risk)
5=Extremely complex
4=Quite complex
3=Average complexity
2=A few complexities
1=Straightforward

(Smallest control risk)

```
************************************************************************
```

AUDIT FACTORS

```
------------------------------------------------------------------------
```

A EXTENT OF COVERAGE WITHIN SCOPE OF OTHER AUDITS

(Maximum justification for allocation of internal audit resource)

5=Sub-system not covered at all in any other audit work
4=Only minor overlap with other audit work
3=Some material, but not major overlap with other audit work
2=Major element of the sub-system addressed in the context of other audits completed
1=Sub-system fully addressed in the context of other audits completed

(Minimum justification for allocation of internal audit resource)

```
------------------------------------------------------------------------
```

Table 33.9 continued

B EXTENT OF RELIANCE UPON OTHER REVIEW AGENCIES

(Maximum justification for allocation of internal audit resource)

5=
4=Score on a range 1 to 5 where 1 indicates that the scope
  of other non-internal audit reviews comprehensively
3=covers accounting, financial AND operational aspects;
  and complete reliance may be placed upon this work. A
2=further factor to be considered is the adequacy of the
  reporting lines of these other reviews.
1=

(Minimum justification for allocation of internal audit resource)

C INTERNAL AUDIT COMPETENCE

(Maximum justification for allocation of internal audit resource)

5=Audit staff are expert in this area
4=Audit staff have some experience in this area
3=Audit staff will be able to grasp the operational, control and audit aspects
2=Audit staff will find it difficult to address this area effectively
1=Audit staff will be incapable of conducting an audit of this sub-system

(Minimum justification for allocation of internal audit resource)

D OPPORTUNITY TO BENEFIT FROM THE AUDIT

(Maximum justification for allocation of internal audit resource)

5=All the major risks can be addressed and significantly reduced by management
4=Many of the risks are amenable to management control
3=Some major risk areas are within the control of management
2=Management can be effective only marginally to reduce risks
1=There is nothing that management will be able to do to reduce the risks

(Minimum justification for allocation of internal audit resource)

E SPECIAL LEGAL OR REGULATIVE AUDIT NEED

(Maximum justification for allocation of internal audit resource)

5=It is imperative that this area is audited for legal/regulatory reasons
4=(not used)
3=It is desirable that this area is audited for legal/regulatory reasons
2=(not used)
1=There is no legal/regulatory reason for internal audit involvement .

(Minimum justification for allocation of internal audit resource.)

AUDIT RISK INDEX:

SIZE: 3 1 1 2 (A+B+C+D)

CONTROL: 1 3 2 2 5 2 (A+B+C+D+E+F+G)

AUDIT: 2 1 1 3 2 (A+B+C+D+E)

Chapter No.	Audit Title	Audit Group	Principal Audit Location for Fieldwork	Date of Last Audit	Date of Planned Audit	Audit Code Number	Audit Units Needed	Audit Risk Score	Size Score	Control Score	Audit Score
7	Contract management environment										
8	Project management framework										
9	Project assessment and approval										
10	Engaging monitoring and paying consultants										
11	Design										
12	Assessing the viability and competence of contractors										
13	Maintaining an approved list of contractors										
14	Tendering procedures										
15	Contract and tender documentation										
16	Insurance and bonding										
17	The selection and letting of contracts										
18	Management information and reporting										
19	Performance monitoring										
20	Arrangements for sub contractors and suppliers										
21	Materials plant and project assets										
22	Valuing work for interim payments										
23	Controlling price fluctuations										
24	Monitoring and controlling variations										
25	Extensions of time										
26	Controlling contractual claims										
27	Liquidations and bankruptcies										
28	Contractor's final account										
29	Recovery of damages										
30	Review of project out-turn and performance										
31	Maintenance obligations										

Table 33.10 Contract sub-systems audit risk index

BRACKET	FACTOR DESCRIPTION	CONSIDERATION DESCRIPTION
SIZE	DEGREE OF VARIATION FROM ORIGINAL SPECIFICATION	Extensions of time
SIZE	DEGREE OF VARIATION FROM ORIGINAL SPECIFICATION	Value of variations
SIZE	INCOME POTENTIAL	Income generation potential (grants, rents, fees, charges)
SIZE	SIZE OF FINANCIAL ADJUSTMENTS	Extent and size of claims
SIZE	VALUE OF THE CONTRACT	Value of the contract
SIZE	VALUE OF THE CONTRACT	Capital values
SIZE	VALUE OF THE CONTRACT	Size of the contract
SIZE	VALUE OF THE CONTRACT	Contract sum
CONTROL	CONTRACT COMPLEXITY	Complexity of the contract
CONTROL	DURATION OF THE CONTRACT	Contract duration
CONTROL	DURATION OF THE CONTRACT	Contract period
CONTROL	EXPRESSED CONCERN OF MANAGEMENT	Direct requests from management/departments
CONTROL	FINANCIAL STATUS OF THE CONSULTANT(S)	Financial status of consultants
CONTROL	FINANCIAL STATUS OF THE CONTRACTOR(S)	Financial status of contractor
CONTROL	GENERAL QUALITY OF THE CONSULTANT(S)	Quality of the consultant employed
CONTROL	GENERAL QUALITY OF THE CONTRACTOR(S)	Quality assurance of contractor (e.g.BS 5750 registered)
CONTROL	GENERAL QUALITY OF THE CONTRACTOR(S)	Quality of the contractor involved
CONTROL	GENERAL QUALITY OF THE CONTRACTOR(S)	Reputation of the contractor
CONTROL	QUALITY OF MANAGEMENT	Quality of supervision
CONTROL	QUALITY OF PROJECT CONTROL	Scale of fluctuations
AUDIT	EXTENT OF RELIANCE UPON OTHER REVIEW AGENCIES	Activity by other review agencies
AUDIT	OPPORTUNITY TO AFFECT OUTCOME	Phase (early or late) in multi-contract project
AUDIT	OPPORTUNITY TO BENEFIT FROM THE AUDIT	Need to move to current contract auditing
AUDIT	THIRD PARTY SENSITIVITY	Political sensitivity
AUDIT	THIRD PARTY SENSITIVITY	External influences - pressure groups
AUDIT	THIRD PARTY SENSITIVITY	External influences - political
AUDIT	THIRD PARTY SENSITIVITY	Political considerations

Table 33.11 Final selection of factors for general contracts audit risk formula

Table 33.12 Sample general contracts audit risk formula

$$\text{AUDIT RISK} = \frac{\overset{1\ \ 2\ \ 1\ \ 3}{20\,(A+B+C+D)}}{n1} \quad \frac{\overset{2\ \ 2\ \ 3\ \ 1\ \ 2\ \ 2\ \ 3\ \ 2\ \ 2}{(A+B+C+D+E+F+G+H+I)}}{n2} \quad \frac{\overset{1\ \ 3\ \ 2\ \ 2}{(A+B+C+D)}}{n3}$$

SIZE: CONTROL: AUDIT:

SIZE FACTORS –
A DEGREE OF VARIATION FROM ORIGINAL SPECIFICATION
B INCOME POTENTIAL
C SIZE OF FINANCIAL ADJUSTMENTS
D VALUE OF THE CONTRACT

CONTROL FACTORS –
A CONTRACT COMPLEXITY
B DURATION OF THE CONTRACT
C EXPRESSED CONCERN OF MANAGEMENT
D FINANCIAL STATUS OF THE CONSULTANT(S)
E FINANCIAL STATUS OF THE CONTRACTOR(S)
F GENERAL QUALITY OF THE CONSULTANT(S)
G GENERAL QUALITY OF THE CONTRACTOR(S)
H QUALITY OF MANAGEMENT
I QUALITY OF PROJECT CONTROL

AUDIT FACTORS –
A EXTENT OF RELIANCE UPON OTHER REVIEW AGENCIES
B OPPORTUNITY TO AFFECT OUTCOME
C OPPORTUNITY TO BENEFIT FROM THE AUDIT
D THIRD PARTY SENSITIVITY

APPENDICES

APPENDIX 1

Glossary

ACA	Association of Consultant Architects
ACE	The Association of Consulting Engineers
BEAMA	British Electrical and Allied Manufacturers Association
BEC	Building Employers Confederation
BPF	British Property Federation
BPIC	Building Project Information Committee
CASEC	Committee of Associations of Specialist Engineering Contractors
CCTA	Central Computer & Telecommunications Agency
CESMM	Civil Engineering Standard Method of Measurement (issued by the Institution of Civil Engineers)
CSD	Chartered Society of Designers
CD81	Standard Form of Building Contract With Contractor's Design
CIPFA	The Chartered Institute of Public Finance and Accountancy
DLO	Direct Labour Organisation
EC	European Commission
ECU	European Currency Unit
EEC	European Economic Community
FCEC	The Federation of Civil Engineering Contractors
FEIC	The European International Federation of Construction
FF76	Fixed Fee Form of Prime Cost Contract
FIDIC	Federation Internationale des Ingenieurs Conseils
HMSO	Her Majesty's Stationery Office
IAD	Internal Audit Department
ICE	Institution of Civil Engineers
IEE	Institution of Electrical Engineers
IFC84	Intermediate Form of Building Contract (1984 Edition)
IMechE	Institution of Mechanical Engineers
ISO	International Standards Organisation
JA/C	Jobbing Agreement Conditions
JA/T	Jobbing Agreement Tender
JCLI	Joint Council for Landscape Industries
JCT	Joint Contracts Tribunal
MC87	Management Contract (1987 Edition)
MF/1	Model Form of General Conditions of Contract
MIS	Management Information System
MTC89	Measured Term Contract (1989 Edition)
MW80	Agreement for Minor Works
NEC	New Engineering Contract
NJCC	National Joint Consultative Committee for Building
NSC	Nominated Sub-Contracts

PC	Prime Cost
PCC	Standard Form of Prime Cost Contract
RG75	Agreement for Renovation Grant Works where an architect/superintending officer is appointed
RIBA	The Royal Institute of British Architects
RICS	The Royal Institution of Chartered Surveyors
SBCC	Scottish Building Contract Committee
SCALA	The Society of Chief Architects of Local Authorities
SCQSLG	The Society of Chief Quantity Surveyors in Local Government
SFA/92	Standard Form of Agreement for the Appointment of an Architect
SFBC	Standard Form of Building Contract
SMM	Standard Method of Measurement of building works (issued by RICS)
XG75	Agreement for Renovation Grant Works where no architect/superintending officer is appointed

APPENDIX 2

Forms of Contract

Noted in this section are brief details of the more common standard forms of contract for the building, civil engineering, mechanical and electrical engineering industries. Where possible we have noted amendments current at the time of writing. Please note that this list is not intended to be either definitive or comprehensive, but aims to provide general guidance to the reader. It should also be stressed that amendments and updates are progressively applied to all forms of contract, therefore readers are advised to obtain clarification as to the prevailing versions from the appropriate issuing or drafting authority.

The contracts are listed in alphabetical sequence. However, the various forms issued by the Joint Contracts Tribunal, are prefixed with JCT. In some cases (such as for the JCT forms), there are supplementary documents covering nominated sub-contractors, etc. Not all these additional documents and their variations may be listed below.

The contracts listed primarily relate to England and Wales, unless international relevance is specifically noted. In some cases, versions are available to meet the needs of the Scottish legal system. For example, the Edinburgh office of RICS Books is able to supply Scottish editions of the JCT range of contracts supported by the SBCC (Scottish Building Contracts Committee).

The 'obtainable from' references relate to the following key:

1 Royal Institute of British Architects (RIBA)
2 The Institution of Civil Engineers (ICE)
3 The Association of Consulting Engineers (ACE)
4 The Institution of Mechanical Engineers (IMechE)
5 The Institution of Electrical Engineers (IEE)
6 The Federation of Civil Engineering Contractors (FCEC)
7 The Royal Institution of Chartered Surveyors (RICS)

Ref.	*Description*
ACA2	The ACA Form of Building Contract – Developed by the Association of Consulting Architects and published as a second edition in 1984, partly to counter criticisms of the JCT80 conditions. There is also a ACA Form of Sub-contract. Both these documents are obtainable from sources 1 and 7.
FCEC	FCEC Form of Sub-Contract – To be used with the sixth edition of the ICE Conditions of Contract as described below. This contract, which was published in 1991, is available from sources 2, 3 and 6.
FIDIC	These are international forms of contract, based upon the ICE Conditions described elsewhere. Their creation has been a collaborative

effort between FIDIC (The International Federation of Consulting Engineers) and FEIC (The European International Federation of Construction). There are a number of forms, including the following examples:

- FIDIC Conditions of Contract (International) for Works of Civil Engineering Construction, with Forms of Tender and Agreement (Also known as the Red Book).
- FIDIC Conditions of Contract (International) for Electrical & Mechanical Works (including Erection on Site) with Forms of Tender and Agreement (or the Yellow Book).
- FIDIC International Model Forms of Agreement between Client and Consulting Engineer (3 × version).

Copies of all FIDIC forms of contract are available from sources 2 and 3.

GC   The General Conditions of Contract – These are contracts, published via the HMSO, which are used for Government works involving the Property Holdings organisation, and do not lend themselves to other general uses. As one would expect the conditions tend to favour the employing organisation. The following classifications are currently available:

- GC/Works/1 General Conditions of Contract for Building and Civil Engineering – Mechanical and Electrical Works and Services Standard Form of Contract. Published in 1990.
- GC/Works/2 General Conditions of Contract for Building and Civil Engineering – Minor Works Lump Sum and Prime Cost Standard Forms of Contract. Published in 1990.
- General Conditions of Contract for Building and Civil Engineering – Minor Works Measured Terms and Call-Off Standard Forms of Contract. Published in 1993
- General Conditions of Contract for Building and Civil Engineering – Standard Form of Contract, Lump Sum With Quantities. Published in 1990.
- General Conditions of Contract for Building and Civil Engineering – Standard Form of Contract, Lump Sum Without Quantities. Published in 1991.

Within each grouping there may be a number of specific contract forms, for example within the first group noted above the following variations are apparent:

- Ref. C910 – Operation, repair and maintenance of mechanical plant. The price being based upon on a fixed annual sum paid at monthly intervals.
- Ref. C1020 – Lump Sum contract for minor (up to £150,000 estimated value) mechanical and electrical services and plant.
- Ref. C1030 – as for C1020 but for above £150,000. Also includes a liquidated damages clause.
- Ref. 1301 – For specified work and costed per task.
- Ref. 1804 – Repair of plant. A two-stage contract where normal competitive tendering is not appropriate.

The complete range of contracts is available from HMSO, and source 7.

ICE   ICE Conditions of Contract – The sixth edition was published in 1991 as the result of consultation between the Institution of Civil Engineers, the Association of Consulting Engineers, and the Federation of Civil Engineering Contractors. The contract is suited for use in association with major civil engineering schemes or projects, and can be applied to both the private and public sectors. Although the contract specifies that the necessary work has to be carried out, by the contractor, to the satisfaction of the engineer, there is a separate contract formed between the employer and the engineer. This contract, and all the others noted under the ICE grouping, are available from sources 2, 3 and 6.

As noted elsewhere, the FCEC Form of Sub-Contract is specifically designed to be used with the 6th Edition of the ICE Conditions of Contract. A Form of Sub-Contract is also available for the previous (i.e. 5th edition) of the Conditions of Contract.

ICE   ICE Design and Construct Conditions of Contract – This contract, also a development, was published in 1992. Although born out of the creation of the 6th edition of the conditions detailed above, it is specifically targeted at the design and construct requirements.

ICE   ICE Conditions of Works for Minor Works (1988) – This is a simplified version of the ICE Conditions of Contract noted above, and it is aimed at schemes valued at below £100,000 and less than six months in duration. Nominated sub-contractors are not catered for in the conditions.

ICE   ICE Conditions of Contract for Ground Investigation (1983) – As the title suggests, this is a very specific form of contract, which is available from sources 2, 3 and 6.

JCT   Various forms of contract are listed under this group, all with the prefix JCT to differentiate those issued by the Joint Contracts Tribunal.

JCT80   The Standard Form of Building Contract – Published in 1980 and based upon the 1963 form, this contract is available in six versions:

- Private with Quantities
- Private with Approximate Quantities
- Private without Quantities
- Local Authorities with Quantities
- Local Authorities with Approximate Quantities
- Local Authorities without Quantities.

The JCT80 contract includes the definition of responsibilities allocated to both the architect and the quantity surveyor.

Amendments: There are currently twelve amendments which apply to JCT80, of which numbers 1 to 9 are incorporated, when applicable to the contract variant, into the latest printing (1991). The remaining three, as noted below, are available separately:

- Amendment 10 (issued March 1991 and corrected March 1993)
- Amendment 11 (issued July 1992 and corrected September 1992)
- Amendment 12 (issued July 1993).

In addition to the above main forms of JCT80 contract, there are a number of supplements available:
- Fluctuation Supplement (Local Authorities) – Revised September 1987
- Fluctuation Supplement (Private) – Revised May 1988
- Formula Rules Supplement (*see* * following JCT PCC 92)
- Sectional Completion Supplement (SCS) – Last printed April 1992
- Contractor's Designed Portion Supplement (CDPS) – Last printed September 1991 (See comment under JCT CD81 contract notes)
- Scottish Supplement – Last Revised January 1992. This supplement adapts JCT80 for use under Scottish Law.

Nominated Sub-contractor arrangements are catered for in the following forms, which are to used in association with the JCT80 contracts noted above:

- NSC/1 Nominated sub-contract tender and agreement
- NSC/1a Tender document only, per NSC/1
- NSC/2 Employer/nominated sub-contractor agreement
- NSC/2a As for NSC/2 but when NSC/1 tender is not used
- NSC/3 Nomination of a sub-contractor. Used when NSC/1 has been used
- NSC/3a As for NSC/3, but when NSC/1 has not been used
- NSC/4 Nominated sub-contract. Used when NSC/1 tender has been used
- NSC/4a As for NSC/4 but when NSC/1 tender is not used
- TNS1 Tender for Nominated Suppliers
- TNS2 Warranty for Nominated Suppliers.

Where amendments have been applied to the various NSC docments noted above, they have been incorporated into subsequent reprints. However, the amendment texts are still available from RIBA.

JCT CD81 Standard Form of Building Contract with Contractor's Design – This form is used in isolation when the contractor is to both design and construct the building per the employer's requirements, and where he is responsible for the design of the whole of the works. This type of contract is known generically as Design and Build.

The Contractor's Designed Portion Supplement is not a CD81 document, but a supplement to the JCT80 contracts. It is applied in relation to modifying the JCT80 conditions, where the contractor's design responsibility is for only part of the works. (*See* under JCT80.) The Formula Rules for the CD80 form are available in a separate document, *see* * following JCT PCC 92.

JCT FF76 Fixed Fee Form of Prime Cost Contract – First published in 1967 this form owes its origins to the JCT63 contract which was superseded by the JCT80. FF76, which is to be reviewed and updated, may be used where firm indications of the price cannot be accurately assessed in advance.

JCT IFC84   Intermediate Form of Building Contract – Published in September 1984 by JCT as an intermediate form between the complexity of the JCT80 and the restricted form of the MW80 Minor Works Form, detailed below. The contents allow use by either private or local authority employers, with or without quantities. The current printing incorporates amendments 1 to 6.

The following Supplementary forms can also apply to IFC84:

- NAM/T Tender and Agreement for named sub-contractors
- NAM/SC Sub-contract conditions for named sub-contractors
- NAM/SC/FR Sub-contract formula rules for named sub-contractors (*see* * following JCT PCC92)
- IFC/SCS Sectional Completion Supplement
- ESA/1 RIBA/CASEC Employer/Specialist Agreement
- Fluctuation Supplement (IFC/FS)
- Formula Rules for IFC84 (*see* * following JCT PCC92).

Where the supplementary forms have been subject to amendments, these have been incorporated into the current versions.

JCT MC87   Management Contract – Published in 1987, this contract will be used when the contractor is to manage the total project including sub-contracting arrangements. This form of contract can also be referred to as the Head Contract.

The following documents can be used with MC87, all were published in December 1987:

- WKS1/1 Section 1 Invitation to Tender
- WKS1/2 Section 2 Tender by Works Contractor
- WKS1/3 Section 3 Agreement
- WKS2 Works Contract 2 – Conditions of Contract
- WKS3 Works Contract 3 – Employer/Works Contractor Agreement
- Phased Implementation Supplement. Two versions are available for Management Contracts and Works Contracts.
- Formula Rules for the Works Contract (*see* * following JCT PCC92).

JCT MTC89 Measured Term Contract – This form, which was introduced in November 1989, can be used where there is a need for regular maintenance or minor works, and where the employer wishes to engage one contractor on one contract for a number of separate jobs for a specified period.

JCT MW80   Agreement for Minor Works – As the name implies, this contract is intended for minor and simple building works with values up to £70,000 at 1987 prices. The absence of relevant clauses and the unbalanced allocation of risk, make this form of contract totally unsuitable for large projects. The Minor Works Supplement includes references to tax charges and deductions.

JCT PCC92 Standard Form of Prime Cost Contract 1992 – This form provides for a fee to the contractor which is determined, at the employer's choice, either as a fixed or a percentage fee. The following documents are also associated with this form of contract:

- NSC/T(PCC) Tender
- NSC/W(PCC) Agreement
- NSC/N(PCC) Nomination
- NSC/A(PCC) Agreement.

* Formula rules for all JCT contracts are available in consolidated form in two volumes, the first relating to Main Contract Formula Rules, and the second affecting Sub-contractors and Works Contracts.

Please note that copies of all JCT forms of contract are available from sources 1 and 7.

MF The following two model forms of contract for Electrical and Mechanical engineering operations, are jointly published by The Institution of Electrical Engineers, The Institution of Mechanical Engineers, and The Association of Consulting Engineers:

- MF/1 Model Form of General Conditions of Contract, including Forms of Tender, Agreement, Sub-Contract and Performance Bond for use in connection with Home or Overseas Contracts – with erection.
- MF/2 Model Form of General Conditions of Contract, including Forms of Tender, Agreement, Sub-Contract and Performance Bond for use in connection with Home or Overseas Contracts for the supply of Electrical or Mechanical Plant.

MF/1 and MF/2 contracts are available from sources 3, 4 and 5.

NEC The New Engineering Contract – This contract, published in 1993 by the Institution of Civil Engineers (ICE), is a form for engineering and construction projects. It aims to be more flexible and internationally acceptable than the ICE Conditions of Contract described elsewhere in this appendix, which is based on the requirements of the British legal framework. The contract comprises of ten documents including the main contract and sub-contract.

APPENDIX 3

Useful Addresses

The Association of Consulting Engineers, Alliance House, 12 Caxton Street, London SW1H 0QL. Telephone 071-222-6557.

The Central Computer & Telecommunications Agency, CCTA Library, Riverwalk House, 157–161 Millbank, London SW1P 4RT. Telephone 071-217-3331.

The Chartered Institute of Building, Bookshop, Englemere, Kings Ride, Ascot, Berkshire SL5 8BJ. Telephone 0344-874640.

The Chartered Institute of Public Finance and Accountancy, 3 Robert Street, London WC2N 6BH. Telephone 071-895-8823. Publications department Telephone 071-895-8825.

The Chartered Institute of Purchasing and Supply, Easton House, Easton on the Hill, Stamford, PE9 3NZ. Telephone 0780-56777.

The Federation of Civil Engineering Contractors, Cowdray House, 6 Portugal Street, London WC2A 2HH.

The Institution of Civil Engineers, 1–7 Great George Street, London SW1P 3AA. (For publications see entry for Thomas Telford Services Limited below.)

The Institution of Electrical Engineers, Publication Sales Department, P.O. Box 96, Stevenage, Hertfordshire SG1 2SD.

The Institution of Mechanical Engineers, Publication Sales Department, P.O. Box 24, Northgate Avenue, Bury St Edmunds, Suffolk IP32 6BW. Telephone 0284-763277.

Thomas Telford Services Limited, Thomas Telford House, 1 Heron Quay, London E14 4JD. Telephone 071-987-6999. (NB: Wholly owned subsidiary of the Institution of Civil Engineers.)

Royal Institute of British Architects, 66 Portland Place, London W1. (RIBA Publications Ltd., Finsbury Mission, 39 Moreland Street, London EC1V 8BB. Telephone 071-251-0791)

Royal Institution of Chartered Surveyors, 11 Great George Street,London. Telephone 071-222-7000. (RICS Books, Surveyor Court, Westwood Way, Coventry CV4 8JE. Telephone 0203-694757. Scottish Book Shop, 9 Manor Place, Edinburgh EH3 7DN. Telephone 031-225-7078).

APPENDIX 4

Bibliography

The following list of publications and material is provided as the basis for further reference by readers. It is deliberately broad in nature and aims to reflect the interests of both the private and public sectors from the viewpoints of employer, auditor, contractor and professional alike. The entries have been grouped relative to professional bodies and other sources. However, in practice the jointly produced publications may be obtainable from additional sources which are excluded from this list.

See also Appendix 2 for details of available Forms of Contract and sources of copies.

General

Jones, G. P., *A New Approach to the Standard Form of Building Contract*, (Construction Press, London, 1983).

Lewis, A., *Principles of Contract and European Commercial Law*, (Tudor Business Publications, 1992).

Robinson, T. H., *Establishing the Validity of Contractual Claims*, (The Chartered Institute of Building, out of print).

ACE (The Association of Consulting Engineers)

ACE Conditions of Engagement 1981(amended) Model Conditions of Engagement with suggested Fee Scales. Various forms available.

Commentary on Model Form MF/1 – a Practical Guide.

Commentary on Model Form MF/2 – a Practical Guide.

Construction, Insurance and Law, (FIDIC Publication).

Guidance on the Preparation, Submission, and Consideration of Tenders for Civil Engineering Contracts Recommended for Use in the United Kingdom, (1983).

Guidelines for the Evaluation of Consultants' Performance, (FIDIC Publication).

Central Computer & Telecommunications Agency (CCTA)

A Guide to Procurement within the Total Acquisition Process, (CCTA, 1991).

Chartered Institute of Management Accountants

Gee, K. P., *Contract Cost Escalation Clauses*, (1981).

CIOB (The Chartered Institute of Building)

Armstrong, W. E. I., *Contractual Claims Under the 6th Edition of the ICE Conditions of Contract*, (Chartered Institute of Building, 1991).

Bright, K. and Dunstan, M., *The Secure Site – An Impossible Dream*, (1991).

Burnett, R. G., *Insolvency and the Sub-Contractor*, (Chartered Institute of Building, 1991).

Clark, K. A., *Measured Term Contracts and Introduction to Their Use for Building Maintenance and Minor Works*, (1991).

Cook, A. E., *Construction Tendering: Theory and Practice*, (Batsford, in association with the Chartered Instutute of Building, London, 1991).

Dickason, I. J., *JCT80 and the Builder – an Introduction*, (Chartered Institute of Building, 1982, revised 1985).

Dickason, I. J., *JCT80 and the Builder – Supplement*, (Chartered Institute of Building, 1992).

Franks, J., *Building Contract Administration and Practice*, (1991).

McGowan, P. H., *Allocation and Evaluation of Risk in Construction Contracts*, (1992).

Wilkie, M. and Howells R., *Practical Building Law*, (1987).

Wood, R. D., *Builders Claims under the JCT (1963) Form of Contract* (2nd revised edition, 1978).

Wood, R. D., *Contractors Claims Under the GC/Works/1 – Edition 2 Form of Contract* (2nd revised edition, Institute of Building, 1986).

Wood, R. D., *Contractors Claims Under the JCT Intermediate Form of Contract*, (1991).

CIPFA (The Chartered Institute of Public Finance and Accountancy)

A Guide to the Financial Management and Audit of Contracts, (London, 1989).

Audit Occasional Paper 6 – Audit of Major Construction and Improvement Work Undertaken by DLO's, (1987).

Contract Audit Guidance Notes – (ICE Conditions – Fifth Edition, 1983).

Contract Audit – JCT Guidance Notes, (1992).

Contract Audit (Site Visits) Guidance Notes, (1984).

Control of Building Projects – The Role of Professional Officers in Local Government, (1982).

Value for Money Auditing – The Investigation of Economy, Efficiency and Effectiveness, (1991).

HMSO

EC Directives affecting contracts and tendering, include the following:

Official Journal of the European Communities – Legislation

L13 Volume 20 Directives 77/62/EEC (21 December 1976) co-ordinating procedures for the award of public supply contracts, and *77/63/EEC* (21 December 1976) amending *Directive 71/306/EEC* setting up an Advisory Committee for Public Contracts.

L127 Volume 31 Directive 88/295/EEC (22 March 1988) amending Directive 77/62/EEC relating to the co-ordination of procedures on the award of public supply contracts and repealing certain provisions of *Directive 80/767/EEC*.

L209 Volume 35 Directive 92/50/EEC (18 June 1992) relating to the co-ordination of procedures for the award of public service contracts.

L210 Volume 32 Directive 89/440/EEC (18 July 1989) concerning co-ordination of procedures for the award of public works contracts.

L215 Volume 23 Directive 80/767/EEC (22 July 1980) adapting and supplementing in respect of certain contracting authorities *Directive 77/62/EEC* co-ordinating procedures for the award of public supply contracts.

L297 Volume 33 Directive 90/531/EEC (17 September 1990) on the procurement procedures of entities operating in the water, energy, transport and telecommunications sectors.

ICE (The Institution of Civil Engineers)

Barnes, M. (Ed.), *Financial Control*, (1990).
Boyce, T., *Successful Contract Administration*, (1992).
CESMM3 – *Civil Engineering Standard Method of Measurement*, (3rd Edition, 1991).
Construction Industry Council, *The Procurement of Professional Services – Guidelines for the Application of Competitive Tendering*, (1992).
Cottam, G. and Hawker, G., *ICE Conditions of Contract for Minor Works: a User's Guide and Commentary*, (1991).
Engineers and Auditors, A joint statement by ICE and CIPFA, (1992).
Fisher, N. and Shen Li Yin, *Information Management in a Contractor – A Model for the Flow of Data*, (Thomas Telford, London, 1992).
ICE Arbitration Procedure 1983, (Separate versions for England and Scotland), (Institute of Civil Engineers).
ICE Conditions of Contract – 5th & 6th Editions Compared, (1991).
ICE Design and Construct Conditions of Contract, (ICE, ACE and FCEC, 1992).

RIBA (Royal Institute of British Architects)

Arbitration Rules (for JCT contracts), (1988).
Ashworth, A., *Contractual Procedures in the Construction Industry*, (Longman Scientific and Technical, Harlow, 2nd Edition, 1991).
Clamp, H. and Cox, S., *Which Contract? – Choosing the Appropriate Building Contract*, (RIBA Publications, London, 1989).
Code of Procedure for Single-Stage Selective Tendering, (National Joint Consultative Committee for Building, 1989).
Code of Procedure for Two-Stage Selective Tendering, (National Joint Consultative Committee for Building, 1983).
Consolidated Main Contract Formula Rules, (for use with JCT80, IFC84 and CD81 contracts), (1987).
Fellows, R. F., *1980 JCT Standard Form of Building Contract: a Commentary for Students and Practitioners,* (Macmillan Education, Basingstoke, 1988).
Guidance Note 2: Performance Bonds, (National Joint Consultative Committee for Building, 1986).
JCT Minor Works Form of Contract: a Practical Guide, (1991).
Madge, P., *A Concise Guide to the JCT 1986 Insurance Clauses*, (1987).
Madge, P., *A Guide to the Indemnity and Insurance Aspects of Building Contracts,* (RIBA Publications, London, 1985).
Powell-Smith, V. and Sims, J., *The JCT Management Contract: a Practical Guide,* (1988).
Practice Notes on JCT Contracts – Note 9 to 13: Sub-Contracting under JCT80, (1982).
Practice Notes on JCT Contracts – Note 20: Deciding on the Appropriate Form of JCT Main Contract, (1988).
Practice Notes on JCT Contracts – Note IN/1: Intermediate Form of Building Contract, (1984, Revised 1990).

Project Specification: A Code of Procedure for Building Works, (BPIC (Building Project Information Committee), 1987).
Standard Method of Measurement of Building Works (SMM7), (RICS and BEC, 1987).
The Use of Standard Forms of Building Contract, (1990).

RICS (The Royal Institution of Chartered Surveyors)

Abrahamson, M. W., *Engineering Law and the I.C.E. Contracts*, (Applied Science Publishers, London 4th Edition, 1979).

Aqua Group: *Contract Administration for the Building Team*, (BSP Professional Books, Oxford, 7th Edition, 1990).

Aqua Group: *Tenders and Contracts for Building*, (BSP Professional Books, Oxford, 2nd Edition, 1990).

Barrie, D. S. and Paulson, B. C. Jr, *Professional Construction Management*, (McGraw-Hill, London, 3rd Edition, 1992).

Boyce, T., *Successful Contract Administration*, (1992).

Bunni, N. G., *The FIDIC Form of Contract – the fourth edition of the Red Book,* (BSP Professional Books, Oxford, 4th Edition, 1991).

Chappell, D. M., *Which Form of Building Contract?* (Architecture Design and Technology Press, London, 1991).

Clamp, H., *The Shorter Forms of Building Contract*, (3rd Edition, 1993).

Eggleston, B., *ICE Conditions of Contract – A Users Guide*, (Blackwell Scientific Publications, Oxford, 6th Edition, 1993).

HMSO, *General Conditions of Contract for Building and Civil Engineering – Mechanical and Electrical Works and Services Standard Forms of Contract*, (1990).

Hughes, G. A. and Barber, J. N., *Building and Civil Engineering Claims in Perspective,* (Longman Scientific and Technical, Harlow, 3rd Edition, 1992).

Introductory Guidance to Insurance Under JCT Contracts, (RICS Books, 1991).

Jones, N. F., *A Commentary on the JCT Intermediate Form of Building Contract*, (BSP Professional Books, London, 2nd Edition,1990).

Kliem, L., *People Side of Project Management,* (1993).

Lock, D. L., *Project Management, 5th Edition*, (1992).

Murdoch, J. and Hughes, W., *Building Contract Law*, (1992).

Murdoch, J. and Hughes, W., *Construction Contracts Law and Management*, (1992).

NJCC, *Code of Practice for Selective Tendering for Design and Build*, (1985).

NJCC, *Guidance Note No. 2 – Performance Bonds*, (1986).

Pilcher, R., *Principles of Construction Management*, (McGraw-Hill, 3rd Edition, 1992).

Powell-Smith, V. and Sims, J., *Building Contract Claims*, (2nd Edition, 1988).

Powell-Smith, V. and Chappell, D.M., *A Building Contract Dictionary*, (2nd Edition, 1990).

Raftery, J., *Models for Construction Costs and Price Forecasting*, (RICS Research Technical Paper Number 6, 1991).

Stephenson, D. A., *Arbitration Practice in Construction Contracts*, (E. & F. N. Spon, London; 3rd Edition, 1993).

Thomas, R., *Construction Contract Claims*, (Basingstoke: Macmillan; Macmillan Building and Surveying Series, 1993).

Turner, D. F., *Building Contracts: A Practical Guide*, (Longman Scientific and Technical, Harlow, 1987, 4th edition, 2nd impression).

APPENDIX 5

CIPFA Statement on Contract Auditing

The Institute Council has considered the section of the Chief Inspector of Audit's report for the year ended 31 March 1979 on contract auditing (paragraphs 108–120). It is the Council's view that all the Chief Financial Officers should review their organisation's approach to this aspect of audit work. It is felt that it is timely to emphasise the relevance of the Institute's publication *Financial Examination and Audit of Capital Contracts* to the development of a modern, professional approach to contract auditing and in order to assist in this task the Council offers the following guidelines.

Audit objectives

Although the audit approach to building and engineering contracts in organisations will vary, the overall audit objectives should be universal and should include:

1 assessing and reporting on the adequacy of the organisation's standing orders relating to contracts and associated financial regulations;
2 reviewing and reporting on the extent to which procedures comply with the policies and procedural rules of the organisation;
3 reviewing the adequacy of systems for controlling the operation of contract works from initial planning stage to post completion assessment;
4 reviewing and reporting on the extent to which management information is prompt, adequate, accurate and designed for the needs of all the users;
5 appraisal of the system for controlling and recording the utilisation of resources, including staff;
6 reviewing the use of consultants and agency services provided by other organisations;
7 monitoring the arrangements for the security of the organisation's assets and for recovering the cost of rechargeable works;
8 prevention and detection of fraud, error and impropriety; and
9 identification of losses due to waste, inefficiency, etc., and recovery where appropriate.

Methods to be used in attaining these objectives

To attain the objectives stated above it will be necessary for the auditor to be concerned with all stages of capital works and the check list given below, whilst not necessarily exhaustive, gives some indication of the areas which should be included in the audit plan for examination:

A. Pre-contract stage

a the system for and effectiveness of project appraisal within the organisation;

b the systems for admitting contractors to the approved list (where one is maintained) and for reviewing their performance and current viability

c the methods for the selection of contractors invited to tender

d the system for regulating the tendering procedures and the letting of contracts

e the system for reviewing the suitability of conditions of contract and tender documents; and

f insurance, liquidated damages, and bonding procedures.

B. Currency of contract

a the system and documentation for providing financial information to enable costs to be adequately controlled including reporting procedures

b the system of on-site control regulating valuations of work for interim payments

c the system for the examination and control of price fluctuations

d the system for the control and issue of variations; and

e the system for the receipt and evaluation of contractual claims.

To satisfy himself on the above matters it will be necessary for the auditor to visit site/divisional offices.

C. Post-contract stage

a the system for ensuring that when the final account is produced it is complete and accurate

b the system to ensure that liquidated damages have been recovered where appropriate

c the system for post-contract reporting; and

d the system for post-completion assessment.

D. Other matters

a the system for the examination and evaluation of any request for an ex-gratia payment; and

b the system for dealing with liquidation and bankruptcy.

The Institute Council wish to draw attention to the provisions of the Local Government Finance Act 1982 and the Accounts and Audit Regulations 1983 which define the duties and responsibilities of the responsible financial officer and in particular, to the provisions regarding internal audit. Quite clearly the arithmetical check of the final account advocated by the Manpower Commission in 1952 can no longer be accepted and the requirement to maintain a current internal audit of the accounts of the body must clearly be extended to contract accounts. The current-contract audit approach is endorsed by the Chief Inspector of Audit in his report.

Training

The Institute Council recognises that there is a need to provide adequate training for contract auditors with particular reference to current contract auditing. The Institute proposes, therefore, to promote courses at national and regional level.

Relationship with other professions

The Institute Council recognises there is a need to ensure that all professions engaged in contract work have a clear appreciation of the respective roles their members play at all stages of the contract. The Council therefore welcomes the fact that the Contract Audit Working Party are in the process of developing statements with the Royal Institution of Chartered Surveyors and other professional bodies, on the roles of the technical officer and the internal auditor. When finalised and approved by the appropriate institutes, these should go some way to ensuring that misunderstandings regarding their relationship in the field of capital account auditing need not arise.

Standing orders and financial regulations

The Institute Council recognises there is a need to ensure that standing orders and financial regulations relating to contract procedures are clear and contain all the necessary safeguards relating to financial control.

APPENDIX 6

Summary of Contract Clauses

The contents of this summary are intended to provide readers with a key into the significant contents of four commonly used standard forms of contract. The noted subject areas are related to primary clause or condition references. Not every contract clause is included on the summary. Where the clause has been modified by the issue of a subsequent amendment, the reference number of the amendment is noted in brackets after the clause number.

The precise versions of the contracts used as the basis for this analysis are described below, and it should be stressed that other variants may exist where the applicability and context of the relevant clauses are possibly subject to different usage and interpretation. Where separate documents have a bearing these are also referred to, for example the Fluctuation Clauses applicable to the JCT80 contract. Appendix 2 describes the range of variants available for the four forms of contract noted here and many other available contracts.

1   *The Standard Form of Building Contract 1980 Edition* – generally known as JCT80. The version used in our analysis relates to Local Authorities with Quantities and incorporates amendments up to number 12 issued in July 1993.
2   *The ICE Conditions of Contract 6th Edition*
3   *GC/Works/1 – General Condition of Contract for Building & Civil Engineering – Mechanical & Electrical Works and Services Standard Forms of Contract – Form C1030* The selected version (C1030) relates to lump-sum mechanical and electrical services and plant contracts with an estimated value in excess of £150,000.
4   *MF/1 – Model Form of General Conditions of Contract – Home or Overseas Contracts – with Erection – 1988 Edition* This version includes Forms of Tender, Agreement, Sub-Contract and Performance Bond.

Description	JCT80	ICE6th	C1030	MF/1
Roles and Responsibilities (Chapter 7)				
– Contractor	1.4, 2, 10	8, 14, 15 & 16	6, 7, 11, 16.1 & 25	5 & 13
– Architect or Contract Administrator	11			
– Instructions issued by	4			
– Engineer		2		2
– Superintending Officer (Engineer)			6	
– Clerk of Works	12			
Insurance and Performance Bonds (Chapter 16)				47
– Injury to Persons and Property – Indemnity to Employer	20	22	20 & 36	43
– Insurance against injury to persons or property	21 (Amend. 12)	22, 23, & 24	20 & 36	43
– Insurance of the Works	22, 22A to 22K	21	36	47.1 & 47.2
– Performance Security / Bond / Guarantee		10		8
– Evidence of Insurance	21.1.2 & 21.1.3	25		
– Limitation of Liability				44
Nominated Subcontractors (Chapter 20)	35 (Amend. 10/11)	59	24	3.2, 33.3 & 53.1
Nominated Suppliers (Chapter 20)	36			
Performance Monitoring (Chapter 19)				
– Workmanship and Standards (Quality)	8	13, 36 & 38	6.1, 11, 13 & 14	13 & 23
– Suspension of Works		40		25
– Progress		45 & 46	5	27.6 & 34
– Tests (on completion)			12	23, 28 & 35

Summary of key contract clauses

Description	JCT80	ICE6th	C1030	MF/1
Materials and Goods (Chapter 21)	8.2, 8.3 & 16		2 & 30	
– Transport of equipment and materials		30.1 & 30.2		21 & 24
– Materials & goods unfixed or off-site	16	54		
– Certificates - Off-site materials or Goods	30.03			
– Quality of Material (and removal)		36 & (39)	14	23
– Plant and Contractor's Equipment		53	34.4	23, 37 & 38
Certificates and Payments (Chapters 22 & 28)	30 (Amend. 12)			
– Interim Valuations and Payments	30.1	60.1 & 60.2	30	39 & 40
– Amounts on Interim Certificates	30.2	60	30.3 & 32	39
– Off-site materials and Goods	30.3		30.2	
– Retention	30.4 & 30.5	60.5 & 60.6	30.1	39.5
– Final Adjustments of Contract Sum	30.6	60	33 & 34.3	
– Interim Certificates - Nominated Sub-contractors	30.7			
– Final Certificate (Issue and Effects)	30.8 & 30.9	60	31 & 32	39
– Provisional Sums	13.3	58.1	29	5.4
– Prime Cost Items		58.2	28	5.5 & 5.6
Price Fluctuations (Chapter 23)	37, 38, 39 & 40			
– Contributions, levy and tax fluctuations	38*			
– Labour and materials cost and tax fluctuations	39*	69	9	6.2
– Use of price fluctuation formulae	40*			
* Separate documents				
Variations (Chapter 24)	13 (Amend. 12)			27
– Definitions	13.1	51	8	27.1
– Instructions	13.2	51	8.1	27.2 & 27.5
– Valuation	13.4 & 13.5	52	8.2	27.3

Summary of key contract clauses continued

Description	JCT80	ICE6th	C1030	MF/1
Extensions of Time (Chapter 25)	25 (Amend. 12)	44	22	33
Contractual Claims (Chapter 19, 26 & 29)	26 (Amend. 12)	12		41
– Determination by Employer	27 & 28A	63	7 & 35	49
– Determination by Contractor	28 & 28A		8.3, 34.5 & 47	25, 27.4, 33 & 51
– Liquidated Damages / damages for non-completion (Chapter 19)	24	47	23	35.8
Liquidations & Bankruptcies (Chapter 27)	27.2		35.1b	50
Completion (Chapters 28, 29 & 31)	17 (Amend. 12)			
– Certificate of Practical Completion	17.1		32	
– Certificate of Completion of making good defects	17.4		32	36
– Clearance of Site		33	34.2	18.3
– Certificate of Substantial Completion		48	32	
– Outstanding Work and Defects (Defects Liability)	17	49, 50 & 61	32 & 34.2	26, 28 & 36
– Taking Over (including by Section)				29 & 30
– Certificate of non-completion	24			
Settlement of Disputes / Recovery of Damages (Chapter 29)			33	52 & 53
– Arbitration	41 (Amend.10/11)	66.6 & 66.8	44	52
– Frustration		64		

Summary of key contract clauses continued

Description	JCT80	ICE6th	C1030	MF/1
General Matters				
– Interpretations and Definitions	1	1	1	1
– Contract Documents	5 (Amend. 12)	5, 6 & 7	3 & 4	4.1, 15 & 16
– Contract Sum	3 & 14			5
– Statutory Obligations, Notices, Fees & Charges	6 (Amend. 12)	26, 27, & 68	16.2	6.1, 11.2/3 & 12
– Levels and setting out Works	7	17 & 18	10	22
– Royalties & Patent Rights	9	28	17	42
– Value Added Tax	15 + Supplement	70		
– Partial Possession by Employer	18			
– Assignments, Sub-contract & Sub-letting	19	3 & 4	21	3
– Date of Possession	23	42		
– Works by Employer or person employed by employer	29	31	38	11.6 & 18.4
– Statutory Tax Deduction Scheme - Finance (No2) Act 1975	31			
– Outbreak of Hostilities	32 (Amend.11)	65		46
– War Damage	33 (Amend.11)			46
– Antiquities	34	32		
– Performance of Specified Work	42 (Amend.12)		6	
– Works Commencement Date		41		
– Access to Site		37	15, 40 & 41	11.1
– Provision and Interpretation of Information		11.1		
– Adverse Physical Conditions and Artificial Obstructions		12		5.7
– Programme of Works		14		14
– Safety and Security (including confidentiality & secrecy)		8.3 & 19	18, 19 & 40 to 43	9.1, 18 & 20
– Care of the Works		20	18	43.1
– Interference with traffic and adjoining properties		29		21
– Avoidance of damage to highways, etc.		30		21
– Returns of labour and Contractor's Equipment (i.e. Information)		35	46	17.3
– Time of Completion	23, 24 & 25	43	22	32.1

Summary of key contract clauses continued

Description	JCT80	ICE6th	C1030	MF/1
General Matters (Continued)				
– Urgent Repairs / Emergency Powers	6.1.3 & 6.1.4	62	37	
– Application to Scotland (i.e. Scottish Law)		67		
– Special Conditions (to be defined by the parties)		71		
– Measurement				
– Quantities		55		
– Measurement and Valuation		56	27	
– Method of Measurement		57	27	
– Corrupt Gifts to Persons in the Crown's service			39	
– Racial Discrimination			45	
– Dayworks			46	19.2
– Purchaser's Risks				45

Summary of key contract clauses continued

APPENDIX 7

Category Scales Used in Control Matrices

The control matrix technique used in this book, and explained in detail in Chapter 32, measures the inherent and control risks of each objective or of each exposure. The measurement of inherent risk has two dimensions – first, the category of the inherent risk and secondly its likely size. The category of the inherent risk is shown in the 'scale' (or 'type') row near the top of the control matrix as a number in the range 1 to 6 for each objective or exposure. The scale used is also given a number immediately after the word 'scale' – such as *Scale* 30. Example control matrices are provided at the end of Chapters 5 and 7 to 31, and they make use of either *Scale* 30 or 31, details of which are provided in this appendix. *Scale* 30 is oriented to *Objectives*, and *Scale* 31 is oriented to *Exposures*. When using the technique, users can either modify the existing Scales or develop their own versions tailored to the particular needs of their operating environment.

Category scale 30 (objectives)

Point of scale

6 (Most serious) Strategically vital to the business or organisation. Strategically significant targets must be attained. Apply appropriate and quality solutions.

5 Significant contribution to business operations and planning activities. Business or project to be effectively and efficiently managed. Projects must be completed on time and within budget. Operational and quality targets must be achieved.

4 Overall budget, cost and profit targets must be achieved. Contributes significantly to reliability and accuracy of data, records and management information. Maintain organisation reputation and image.

3 Minimise disruption and contract administration costs. Must comply with regulatory requirements. Maintain good relationships with contractors. Actively demonstrate accountability. Maintain staff morale and commitment.

2 Contributes significantly to administrative and operational economies and efficiencies.

1 (Least serious) Generate administrative economies.

Category scale 31 (exposures)

Point of scale

6 (Most serious) Failure to achieve either business objectives, performance targets, quality targets, or service provision obligations. Incorrect identification of requirements.

5 Substantial costs, loss of business or erosion of competitive edge. Requirements partially unfulfilled. Serious breach of sector regulations.

4 Significant delay or disruption to project or business. Notable adverse effects on reputation or image. Breach of regulations.

3 Significant costs or losses. Limited business disruption. Adverse effects on contract relationships. Inadequate accountability.

2 Administrative or accounting errors with limited operational impact.

1 (Least serious) Detectable but minimal impact upon the business or service.

INDEX